A History of Character

A History of Character
the story of midland, texas

by Jimmy Patterson

Published by
The Abell-Hanger Foundation
and
The Permian Basin Petroleum Museum

A History of Character: The Story of Midland, Texas
Text copyright © 2014 by Jimmy Patterson
Photographs copyright © 2014 by Karen Patterson

Historical photographs courtesy of the Midland County Historical Museum,
the Scharbauer family archives, and the Meadows family. Used by permission.

Published in the United States of America by
The Abell-Hanger Foundation, Midland, Texas, and
The Permian Basin Petroleum Museum, Midland, Texas.

The author gratefully acknowledges the support of the
project underwriters listed on p. xi.

All rights reserved. Printed in the United States of America.
No part of this book may be used or reproduced in any manner or form,
electronic, mechanical, photocopying, recording, or otherwise, including storage
and retrieval systems, without the written permission of the publisher.
For information visit www.historyofcharacter.com.

Editor and project manager: Janet Frick
Designed by Stephanie Bart-Horvath
Jacket design: Stephanie Bart-Horvath and Darrell Dunton

Library of Congress Control Number: 2014912241
ISBN: 978-0-578-14426-9 (trade hardcover)
ISBN: 978-0-578-14427-6 (ebook)
First Edition

To the memory of the Honorable John Hyde

A History of Character: The Story of Midland, Texas would not have been possible if not for the encouragement provided me at the outset of this process by the Honorable John Hyde. Judge Hyde was one of our city's preeminent historians, but more, he was one of our longest-standing persons of character and the finest of gentlemen. His heartfelt enthusiasm for Midland's story easily rubbed off on anyone who had the privilege of witnessing his presentations. Before his death in January 2012, Judge Hyde was a driving force behind this book and provided the emotional and intellectual support necessary for me to pursue a project that started simply enough but quickly evolved into a passion. Thank you, Judge Hyde, for your guidance and friendship.

Midland is the kind of place where you can show up with nothing, work hard, have a dream, and end up making something out of yourself.
—President George W. Bush,
in correspondence with the author, February 2012

contents

Project Underwriters   xi

Foreword   xiii

Preface   xv

Acknowledgments   xvii

Prologue   "The Response of This Community Was Remarkable"   1

Part One: A Place with Character . . . and Colorful Characters
Midland's historical highlights from the 1840s till today

1   What the First White Settlers Found   11

2   A Young Town Pulls on Its Cowboy Boots   22

3   A Town of Faith and Morals   30

4   Land of Droughts and Sandstorms, Blizzards and Floods   39

5   How Midland Became the Oil Capital of West Texas   47

6   The Scharbauer Legacy   63

7   Wassail, Gingerbread and Generosity   72

8   Aviation in the Land of the High Sky   83

9   "This Sprawling, New, Oil-Rich Town"   91

Contents

10	Theatre, Music, and a Mickey Mouse Rumor	109
11	Race Relations in Midland	120
12	Midland Debates Key Issues in High Courts	136
13	An Infamous Murder	147
14	Midland's Shift From Democrat to Republican	158
15	The Longest Love Affair in the History of Midland	173
16	"We'll Never See a Bank Like That Again"	183
17	Toddler's Rescue Brings Much-Needed Optimism	192
18	Midlanders on the National Political Scene	203
19	The City's Bold Progress Continues	213
20	How the Wolfberry Changed Midland	224
21	Water Precious as Oil	233
22	Midland: A City of Character	243

Part Two: People of Integrity, Past and Present
A few of the Midlanders who have helped make us who we are

George and Gladys Abell   256
Ernest Angelo   258
Joan Baskin   260
Dr. George Bell   262
Irma Bueno   264
Bobby Burns   266

Contents

Laura Bush   268
President George H.W. Bush   270
President George W. Bush   272
Jno. P. Butler   274
Frank Cahoon   276
Art Cole   278
Dr. Viola Coleman   280
Bill Collyns   282
Michael Conaway   284
The Cowden Family   286
Tom Craddick   288
Barbara Culver-Clack   290
Dr. David Daniel   292
Ed Darnell   294
Newnie Ellis   296
Donald L. Evans   298
Murray Fasken   300
Herman Garrett   302
Susan Graham   304
Barney and Helen Greathouse   306
Rosalind Redfern Grover   308
Frank Haag   310
Henry Halff   312
Jim Henry   313
Harvey and Harriet Herd   315
T.S. Hogan   317
Judge John Hyde   319
C.J. Kelly   321
W.W. Lackey   323
Dr. Al G. Langford   324
Ed Magruder   328
Randolph Marcy   330
Len 'Tuffy' McCormick   332
Nancy McKinley   333
Henry Meadows   335
James Mims   337

contents

The Morales Family   339
Joan Nobles   341
Gary Painter   343
Jess Parish   345
Wes Perry   347
Frank Pickrell   349
Eileen Piwetz   351
Foy Proctor   352
Judy Rankin   354
John and Rosalind Redfern   356
The Scharbauer Family   359
David L. Smith   361
Charles Spence   363
Dr. Jno. B. Thomas   365
Ed Todd   367
Marvin Ulmer   369
Addison Wadley   371
Cyril "Cy" Wagner and Jack E. Brown   373
Clayton Williams   375
Michael Williams   377
Dr. Dorothy Wyvell   379
John and Charlene Younger   381
The People of Midland   383

Afterword   "That Is Midland": City's Character Shines After Tragedy   385

Appendix: Key Events That Shaped Midland's Character   389

Endnotes   399

Bibliography   419

Index   425

About the Author   444

project underwriters

Through the years, Midland's story has often consisted of people selflessly helping others. This book is a continuation of that heritage of generosity we have built for more than a century. Without the support of all the men and women listed below, *A History of Character: The Story of Midland, Texas* could not have been written or published.

To all who played a role in financially supporting this project, my humblest gratitude for your trust, support, and encouragement:

Scott and Sherry Atkinson
Jim and Paula Henry
Patty and Tevis Herd
Craig and Katie Hubbard
Mike and Madolyn LaMonica
Jon Morgan
Wes and Roni Perry
Clarence Scharbauer III and Kerry Scharbauer
Todd and Karen Sparks

The Abell-Hanger Foundation
The Permian Basin Petroleum Museum

foreword

In *A History of Character: The Story of Midland, Texas*, Jimmy Patterson has done a wonderful job of capturing the uniqueness of a special community by examining the defining characteristics of the people who have lived here, their stories, and the watershed moments that have defined Midland as a whole.

It is a story of perseverance in a harsh, geographically isolated country. Early cattle ranchers settling this area were required to be courageous risk takers and become self-sufficient. Yet here is the paradox of Midland: those who sought to be self-sufficient learned to both help and lean on their neighbors in times of need.

The economic opportunities afforded by the oil business created the perfect venue for entrepreneurs to find incredible financial success through hard work, determination, technical knowledge, risk assumption—and often, pure luck. Newfound wealth has enabled many Midlanders to give freely to others around them, on a scale they could only have dreamed of before. Whether Midland needed a financial institution, better schools, or a better hospital, time and again these self-reliant individuals came together for the greater good of their community, and generosity became a hallmark of the character of Midlanders.

In meeting the people of Midland in this book, you will see the common threads weaving through their stories and personalities: perseverance through difficult times; generosity; hard work; fervent patriotism; deep, abiding faith in God; love of adventure; an offbeat sense of humor; and a firm belief in the American Dream—all attributes that, when combined, speak of what we value so greatly here: character. We've made a history of it.

To outsiders looking at Midland, this city's uniqueness can't be easily understood or explained. Still, Jimmy's book brings the intangible flavor of Midland and her character to life.

—David L. Smith
Executive Director, Abell-Hanger Foundation

preface

Fort Worth may be where the West begins, but Midland is where the West is at.

—Native Midlander James Mims,
recalling a popular saying from the 1930s

MIDLAND IS A SPECIAL PLACE. Many of its residents say there is no other place like it. The same can be said of thousands of other towns and cities in this remarkable land of ours, but when people say, "There's no place like Midland," you know they mean it.

Stephen Ives and Ken Burns, co-producers of the PBS documentary *The West*, wrote, "No book can ever encompass the whole story of the West. There are as many valid approaches to telling it as there are able historians willing to try."[1]

This is equally true of Midland—which, as James Mims pointed out, is very much a part of the American West. Midland is fortunate to have its share of notable historians, record keepers, and lifelong residents who carry with them long and cherished memories of what this place means to them and to all of us. In this sense, Midland has nearly as many historians as people. Everyone has his own story to tell or her own definition of what's important in our history. This book represents a sharing of many of those histories. If you've ever lived in Midland, or if you're interested in visiting or moving here, I hope I have included many of the stories important to you.

In writing this book, I have tried to follow the advice of former Midlander Smith Ray, a descendent of the town's first sheriff, Theo Ray. In 1970 Smith Ray warned that local history should be more than "just a collection of anecdotes or the background of a few people to celebrate the centennial of their ancestors being run out of the East."[2] Thus I have done my best to view Midland from multiple angles and portray it as a composite whole.

By trade, I am not a historian; I am a writer. I brought my family here in 1988, thinking I might stay for two years. Then, as my imagination had it, I would take my wife and children to Connecticut. Something about New England and its natural beauty had always appealed to us. One month led to another, the kids settled and became comfortable in school, acquaintances became long-term friends, and we found a church family. By then we had forgotten where Connecticut was on a map.

preface

My family began making its own history here. Midland had gone from career stopover to home.

Raising a family in West Texas will do that. As I like to tell people from bigger cities and places perhaps more beautiful, ugly can grow on you if you give it long enough. You settle in, you adapt, and before you know it, no one gives much thought to the harsh desert land that lies beyond our city-limit signs.

The decision to write this book did not come easily. At first I was intimidated by the prospect of leaving a good job with the *Midland Reporter-Telegram* to set out alone and accomplish a task of this complexity. In fact, it has taken more than four years. But, after I discussed this project with Judge John Hyde, we both saw it as something that needed to be done.

I conducted almost one hundred interviews with more than seventy-five people en route to putting this book together. One of the most helpful Midlanders was Judge Hyde himself, whose devotion to his adopted hometown was commendable. During one of our many conversations, he uttered a phrase that would work its way into the title of the book. "Of all the stories I've either read, heard, or told," he said, "the one common thread that runs through them all is the high quality of character of Midland's people."

That statement helped bring this project into focus for me. Because of the sheer number of people I interviewed who told me, "There's no place like Midland," much of this book focuses on the inherent integrity and goodness that seem so commonplace here. Certainly, like anywhere else, we have had our share of dark times. We have wrestled with tragedies, oil busts, social and class struggles, and droughts. But we have endured, and it has been largely because of our respect for one another, our love of life, our hard work, and our giving spirit. We are where we are today because of all the good people—men and women, transients and lifers, movers and shakers, athletes and artists, moms and dads, clergy and laity, professionals and laborers—who have helped forge a place we can be proud to call home.

By the time you finish this book, I hope you will understand why so many Midlanders love this unique city and cherish its history.

—*Jimmy Patterson*

acknowledgments

Several people and organizations have been closely involved in the success of this project, and I'd like to thank each of them for the unique roles they have played:

President George W. Bush
Darrell Dunton
Dennis and Ellen Hopkins
Andy Iverson
Clarence Scharbauer Jr.
Kathy Shannon

David L. Smith
Jack Swallow
The *Midland Reporter-Telegram*
The Midland County Historical Museum
The Midland County Library

Thanks also to the many people who gave the gift of their time and knowledge, many of whom have spent hours sharing their insights in interviews:

Jim Alsup
Ernest Angelo
Bill Bain
Tom Barnett
Stephanie Bart-Horvath
Joan Baskin
James Beauchamp
Pastor George Bell
Mark Bell
Rebecca Bell
Grant Billingsley
Mike Bradford
Diane Brenner
Lou Brown
Bobby Burns
President George W. Bush
Lalo Camarillo
Joe Ed Canon
Mike Canon
Mary Lou Cassidy
Joe Chavez
Art Cole

Conrad Coleman
K. Michael Conaway
June Cowden
Linda Cowden
Nadine Craddick
Tom Craddick
Craft Office Systems
Jose Cuevas
Barbara Culver-Clack
Dr. David Daniel
Jean Denton
Joe Dominey
Stewart Doreen
Monsignor Larry Droll
Arlen Edgar
Donald Evans
J. D. Faircloth
Ike Fitzgerald
Janet Frick
Rosalind Grover
Merle Haag
Betsy Haney

acknowledgments

Stacie Hanna
Bill Heck
Katie Heck
Jim Henry
Doug Henson
Tevis Herd
Dr. Diana Davids Hinton
Craig Hubbard
Bill Hunt
Judge John Hyde
Tim Jebsen
Bill Kleine
Nicole Lancto
David Lindemood
Joan Love-Davis
Joe Mabee
Ed Magruder
Jane McAbee
Len "Tuffy" McCormick
Guy McCrary
Pat McDaniel
Lloyd McDonald
Mike McGregor
Henry Meadows
John Meadows
T. O. Midkiff
Mrs. T. O. Midkiff
David Mims
James Mims
Celia Morales
Felipe Morales
Jerry Morales
Gerald Nobles
Joan Nobles
Joe O'Neill
On the Same Page Book Club
Gary Painter
Andrew Park

Jess Parrish
Wes Perry
Eileen Piwetz
Fred Poe
Abigail Powers
Judy Rankin
Dr. Debbie Reese
Col. Joe Richards
James Roberts
Juandelle Lacy Roberts
Roger Robles
The Honorable Dean Rucker
Jim Salners
Chris Scharbauer
Clarence Scharbauer Jr.
Clarence Scharbauer III
Berry Simpson
Buddy Sipes
David L. Smith
Charles Spence
Katie Spriggs
Paul St. Hilaire
Jack Swallow
Carroll Thomas
Dr. Steve Thomas
Ed Todd
Sid Trevino
James Upham
Jack Van Berg
Ralph Way
Carole Wayland
David Wayland
Dave Wedel
Clayton Williams Jr.
Margaret Williams
Barbara Yarbrough
Dr. Charles Younger
Michael Williams

acknowledgments

Quite a number of people also devoted time and energy to this project by writing biographical profiles of friends, relatives, or associates, for Part Two. I am very grateful for their contributions. Those writers are:

Ernest Angelo
Joan Baskin
Grant Billingsley
Herb Cartwright
Mary Lou Cassidy
Conrad Coleman
June Cowden
Linda Cowden
Arlen Edgar
Rosalind Grover
Tevis Herd
Ellen Hopkins
Stan Jacobs
Bob Jones
Ed Magruder
Pat McDaniel
Henry Meadows

John Meadows
Russell Meyers
Wes Perry
Eileen Piwetz
Delnor Poss
Dr. Debbie Reese
Juandelle Lacy Roberts
The Honorable Dean Rucker
John Rutherford
David L. Smith
Charles Spence
Katie Spriggs
Jack Swallow
Dr. Steve Thomas
Ed Todd
Dr. Charles Younger

My heartfelt thanks go to all the people listed above, who immeasurably widened the scope of this book.

On a more personal note, I'd like to give special thanks to my wife, Karen, who has stood by me not just through thirty years of marriage but for the last four years as this project came together. She was there when the occasional discouragement came and when the many successes were celebrated. Karen's contributions, through her unyielding support and her beautiful photographs, are immeasurable. The love and support of our children, too, has been a huge boost to me during this project. I'm a lucky, lucky man.

All three of our children—Jennifer Park, Kelsey Patterson, and James Patterson—were raised in Midland. Karen and I wish to extend a sincere thank-you to Midland, its public school system, and the many teachers who helped form our children into the adults they have become.

A History of Character

prologue

"The Response of This Community Was Remarkable"

It was something you just don't have the words for, to feel the honor and patriotism of Midland. One of the women said to me, "It's not a real attractive place, but it's the people that make it special." I was only there for three days or so, but that was evident.
—Colonel Joseph P. Richards,
U.S. Marine Corps Commanding Officer

EARLY IN THE EVENING of August 1, 2011, David Wayland was in the checkout line at the Albertson's on Andrews Highway in Midland, buying dog food, when he felt the buzzing of his cell phone in his pocket.

He didn't recognize the voice. The call was from Quantico, Virginia, site of the military installation where his son, Patrick, had been stationed until his transfer to Florida several months earlier. David asked himself why the call was coming from Quantico. What would anyone there know about his son, who was no longer in Virginia? "I just couldn't make the connection," he recalled.[1]

David's sense of confusion gave way to the dread realization that something was not right at all.

"We Regret to Inform You . . ."

Next came the words no parent ever wants to hear, and they quickly snapped David into focus.

Prologue

"We regret to inform you that your son has been seriously injured in a training accident at the United States Marine Corps training facility in Pensacola, Florida. You and your wife need to get to his bedside," the Marine spokesperson said. The call had come from Quantico because that's where all calls about seriously injured service members originate.

David's emotions began to seep in as he told the story six months later. "When the caller mentioned a training accident," he said, "I thought maybe Patrick had been flying. That's what he was in training to do."

David immediately called his wife, Carole, and rushed home. Both were overwhelmed with anxiety and felt an immediate need to get to Patrick as soon as possible, but doing so would be difficult. Florida was more than a day away by car, and they had no access to a chartered jet. A Southwest flight would take hours, maybe even the better part of a day once ticket acquisition, security, transfers, and layovers were factored into the equation. David and Carole felt helpless.

But what began to unfold defies adequate description to this day.

An Overwhelming Show of Support

David called a friend who worked for a man who owned a plane. Then he called Steve Schorr, the family's pastor at First Presbyterian Church.

Schorr knew of a church member who was generous and willing to help whenever and however called upon. Ben and Roxane Strickling took Schorr's call and listened to the pastor's story about Patrick and the family's efforts to get to their son. The Stricklings had belonged to First Presbyterian for many years, and their son, Kelly, had grown up with Patrick.

"Let's Go. The Plane Is Ready."

David still remembers what happened next. "While Carole and I were sitting at the kitchen table, trying to figure out what to do, a truck pulled up outside. Steve walked up to our front door, rang the bell, and said, 'Let's go. The plane is ready.'" Only two hours had passed since David had answered the call from Quantico.

"We were taxiing down the runway at eight o'clock," David said. "It was three hours from wheels up to wheels down. We went straight to the hospital. We were at Patrick's bedside by 11:15 p.m."

"The Response of This Community Was Remarkable"

Prayer Vigils, Anonymous Help of All Kinds

As David and Carole walked out of their home with Patrick's two younger sisters, Meagan and Lisa, people began putting money in David's pockets and in Carole's purse, wishing them well and assuring them prayers would be with the four of them, and with Patrick. "We left Midland at eight," David said, "and there was immediately a prayer gathering at our church that night."

First Presbyterian workers encouraged the family to start a Caring Bridge Internet page in hopes that the steady stream of phone callers would instead be able to find information on Patrick by way of the well-known website where families and friends visit during a loved one's illness or following a serious injury. Carole said First Presbyterian was "bombarded" with calls from people wanting to help. A second prayer vigil was held Tuesday, four days after word of Patrick's accident had first arrived. More than three hundred people attended.

"Midland was there in full force," Carole said. "People wanted to do something, anything, to help themselves feel better and to help us feel better. People put out flowers, mowed our yard. We don't know who it was to this day. My friend Charlene ironed my clothes, put up my shirts. People were offering to have our house cleaned for us before we returned to Midland. This town did amazing things for us."

The Mysterious Death of a Promising Young Marine

U.S. Marine Second Lieutenant Patrick Trevor Wayland died August 5, 2011, at the age of twenty-four, after an agility test in his Marine Corps training. The preliminary ruling by the medical examiner was natural causes. Before the medical team in Pensacola pronounced his passing, six of Patrick's organs were harvested and donated to five people, including a fellow Marine who received a kidney.

It took medical professionals seventeen weeks to report back to the Waylands and the Marines on the cause of death. Even then, exactly what happened remains something of a mystery. He did not have a heart attack; his heart was donated. Something led to a cardiac arrest, though, and David is convinced he knows what it was.

"Patrick was as stubborn and strong and bullheaded as anyone you will ever meet," David said out of fondness and love for his son. "I think he told himself he was going to pass that agility test or die trying."

Regardless of the precise cause of Patrick's death, his love for his hometown—as well as his hometown's love for him—remains clear. In addition to detailing his career as a Marine in training, Patrick's obituary in the *Midland Reporter-Telegram* described his childhood and youth in Midland:

Prologue

He was active in Little League baseball, youth soccer, church league basketball and church activities. He attended Midland High School, where he played both varsity football and basketball. During high school, he was an academic letterman and was in the National Honor Society. Patrick was reared in the First Presbyterian Church, where he was an active member of their youth program. In 2006, Patrick received a Congressional nomination and accepted an appointment to the United States Naval Academy in Annapolis, Maryland.[2]

When Patrick was returned to Midland and laid to rest on August 12, 2011, he and his family and friends were accompanied by seventy-five Marines from around the country, and another Marine from Shanghai, China. Carole said as impressive as the support and prayers were for her and her family in the days leading up to her son's death, what happened when Patrick was returned to Midland was even more inspiring.

Midlanders' Warm Hospitality for Seventy-Five Marines

"To me, the thing that best showed the character of Midland is when the Marines came here the next week, the people from Midland embraced them," David said. "All of them. Their transportation from the airport was taken care of. They stayed in the homes of people here. They were taken care of by Midlanders the entire weekend. Midland made such an impression on them that they will never forget it here."

A local restaurant fed all military people who had come to town for the funeral. Residents lined the streets of Midland as Patrick's casket was transferred from the airport to the church. The Midland High School football team, which dedicated its entire 2011 season to Patrick's memory, was street side in that funeral procession as Patrick passed by. At the first Midland High game of the season, David and Carole were honored at the fifty-yard line at halftime, accepting a signed football from the team as a photo of Patrick was displayed on the Jumbotron. Each member of the football team held a small American flag during the tribute.

Among those in attendance at the funeral was Col. Joseph P. Richards, Patrick's commanding officer in Pensacola. So impressed was Col. Richards with the hospitality shown him during his visit to Midland, he wrote a letter to the editor of the *Midland Reporter-Telegram* upon his return home to Florida. Headlined, "A Colonel Says Thank You to Midland," it was addressed, "To All the Great Americans in Midland, Texas,"[3] and read in part:

"The Response of This Community Was Remarkable"

Your tremendous respect for Patrick and the Wayland family was a beautiful sight to see. The return home of Patrick, from the military honors on the Southwest Airlines ramp through Midland, what an impressive police escort and motorcade past Midland High and First Presbyterian Church. All of you standing along the way, American flags waving . . . it was inspiring. Thank you so much for that special tribute to Patrick and the Wayland family.

The future of our nation is in great shape because of great Americans like you all. 2nd Lt. Patrick Wayland was a great Marine. He understood it wasn't all about him; it's about others, helping all those around him. We had the pleasure to serve with Patrick, but we know he was raised in a great family, in a great community instilling those values of honor, courage and commitment.

Very respectfully, and Semper Fidelis,
Col. Joe Richards, USMC
Commanding Officer
MATSG-21

Col. Richards's first inkling that Midland might be different from other places in the nation happened while he was still in Florida. "A woman from Midland who was in Pensacola turned to me," he said, "knowing that I was Patrick's boss, and told me, 'You know, Colonel, we want anyone who wants to be with Patrick in Midland to be there. We don't want money to stop whoever wants to be there. You just get us the names and we'll get them there.'"[4] It is not known how many of the seventy-five Marines attended solely because of the woman's generosity.

Col. Richards said what was particularly striking was that as the visiting Marines were trying to honor Patrick by their presence in Midland, the people of Midland were trying to honor him and those visiting Marines.

"When I landed in Midland," said Richards, "I was introduced to a gentleman who I have to think was behind a lot of the generosity. Everyone [was] thanking me, and he said, 'Y'know, we love our country in Midland, and we really love our military.' That comment stuck with me," Richards said. "From the time we arrived until the time we left I couldn't even buy a cup of coffee. Everyone opened their homes, their businesses. It was a very moving experience. They didn't have to do that. But they wanted to."

Prologue

An Easy Place to Connect with People

David and Carole Wayland moved to Midland in 1982. Carole grew up in Plainview, Texas, and considered herself a West Texan. David is a native of Washington, D.C., and had taken a job at an architectural firm before ultimately finding employment in the planning department at the City of Midland, where he worked for almost twenty-five years. Since 2000, as executive director of Safe Place, Carole has helped women battling the emotional and physical scars left as the result of physical abuse and sexual assault.

Neither of the Waylands knew quite what to expect when they started their lives in Midland. They met and married, and after it was apparent that they would stay for longer than the two years they had initially set as their objective, they settled down and began to raise a family. After everything their family has been through in Midland, both good and bad, it is no surprise to hear them both say they'll never leave.

"What I loved about Midland was just the energy here, at that time particularly," Carole said. "People were coming together from all over the place, and you immediately got connected with other people. I lived and worked in Dallas immediately before coming here, and it was kind of difficult to make connections outside of your work, and I just loved it when I moved here. When I decided to come and start working in Midland, I ended up having to have emergency surgery, and I thought to myself I would have died in Dallas. But people just took care of me here. I remember thinking that I wanted to move to West Texas because it is a great place to be when you have an adverse situation."

To have the same sort of kindnesses offered by fellow Midlanders thirty years later, during the family's most trying time as they dealt with the injury and death of their son, is hard to imagine, David said.

"It makes me wonder how a family would survive this type of thing if they didn't have this kind of support," he said. "I don't think it can be done without all the support and cards of love and encouragement. I can't imagine not having a church and faith, and the people in this community."

A Birthday Party for a Grieving Younger Sister

Parents appreciate it when others do something caring for their children, especially during difficult times. Two days after Patrick was buried, Meagan Wayland, one of Patrick's two younger sisters, had a birthday.

"All of her friends wanted Meagan to feel like it was her day, and so they planned a huge birthday party for her and just absolutely showered her with wonderful gifts and time," Carole said. "It's been that way, really, at every holiday since Patrick's death: people calling, worried about how we are getting through the situation."

Character Binds Together Much About Midland

People in bandanas, suits and ties, blue jeans and dresses attended the funeral. The reception given to Patrick and his Marine brothers who were visitors to Midland was reminiscent of a quarter century earlier, when people from all corners of town came together to help rescuers attempting to save eighteen-month-old Jessica McClure, the young girl who had fallen down an abandoned water well in southwest Midland. And it was similar to the community spirit displayed four years before that, when Midlanders—and many from Odessa—attempted to rally together to shore up First National Bank before it eventually failed and fell into the hands of federal regulators.

In the case of Jessica McClure, the job itself could only have been handled by the professionals: the first responders, doctors, engineers, and drillers who worked together to get Jessica out safely. It was the people helping the helpers—those hundreds, maybe thousands of anonymous Midlanders behind the scenes—who exemplified the town's character, just as it was for the people helping Patrick Wayland's family and friends as they flew in, one after another, to say farewell: people who wanted no credit, but only to see that visitors who were in their city in memory of a deceased friend were well cared for.

All those Midlanders—and those who have and have not been recognized since—collectively represent the spirit of Midland and the purpose of this book. In the twenty-four years between Jessica's and Patrick's stories, and in the century before Jessica, there have been hundreds of untold stories similar in nature, stories that say much about us and our high character. Some of those stories are told in this book.

A History of Character: The Story of Midland, Texas reveals a great deal about Midland's past, its present, and its promising future. Midland is not perfect; no city could claim to be. We have had our struggles and triumphs, our booms and our busts. Often our generous nature has shone clear and inspiring; other times we have regretted our actions and tried to make good on mistakes. But on the whole, Midland is a city of character.

I hope its story will inspire native Midlanders, new Midlanders, and those who've never had the opportunity to call this town home.

part one

A Place with Character . . . and Colorful Characters

Midland's historical highlights from the 1840s till today

chapter 1

WHAT THE FIRST WHITE SETTLERS FOUND

It is important to know and to appreciate your heritage. If you don't remember the past and the tender moments of our heritage there will be nothing left of ourselves to be remembered proudly.
—Nancy McKinley, Midland historian

IF YOU TRAVEL FIVE MILES EAST OF MIDLAND on westbound Interstate 20, between mile markers 141 and 142, you'll find a rest area. Pull off there and look for the historical marker titled MARCY TRAIL.

Stop and listen.

Close out the sounds of the cars and trucks roaring by on the highway and listen instead for the sound of the wind—the blowing grass, the trees. Focus on the look and feel of the arid landscape. Do this, and you will feel and hear and sense what those who came first felt and heard and sensed.

The area is, of course, now void of another aspect of those early days that made travel difficult and survival precarious: the Comanche, also called the Great Horsemen of the Plains.[1] These Native Americans depended on the plains' plentiful herds of buffalo as a primary source of food and other basics essential to their way of life.

Captain Randolph Marcy and the Marcy Trail

No one who ventured across these plains we now call home dared challenge the indigenous tribal people until a man named Randolph Marcy set out from Santa Fe in 1849, charged with finding the most level land he could for the purpose of mapping a route for the railroad.[2]

The route he found would one day be called the Marcy Trail. From Fort Smith, Arkansas, to Santa Fe, New Mexico, it was the most easily traversable, and a portion of it the most level.[3] A religious man, Marcy once wrote, "The Great Creator of the universe has made this the perfect place for the railroad. We will not have to build a single tunnel."[4]

It was reported that Captain Marcy, later a colonel and inspector general of General George McClellan's Army of the Potomac,[5] had been killed by the Comanche in 1852 while making his way across the plains. But it wasn't true. Marcy would live until 1887, when he died peacefully at his New Jersey home, the same year John Scharbauer settled in Midland, and windmills and barbed-wire fences—two early signs of progress—began popping up in town.[6]

Marcy's nineteenth-century journey through our region was accomplished with the help of his Comanche guide, Manuel, whom Marcy considered "of much more than ordinary judgment and character . . . the best guide that can be found in New Mexico."[7] Manuel "knew every water hole and stream on the Staked Plain and assured Marcy he could guide the party across."[8]

Marcy's notable achievements numbered many, but as Thomas W. Cutrer pointed out, "the one perhaps most important to our area's roughly quarter of a million inhabitants today is that he simply forged a path through these parts. He proved it could be done, and it was safe and feasible. The path he cleared would later make it possible for the Butterfield Stage line, the Texas and Pacific Railroad, and even the Bankhead Highway—the Broadway of America—to chart courses through what later became Midland. Marcy's expeditions and mapping, and his insistence the area was safe, were an invaluable part of Midland's prehistory."[9] Decades later, the Broadway of America would roughly follow Marcy's trail through the heart of Texas: Texarkana, Dallas, Abilene, Midland, Odessa, and El Paso.

The Slaughter of the Buffalo

The Comanche were driven away during the late nineteenth century, largely because they lost their food supply when white men decimated the plains buffalo. According to Paul H. Carlson and Bruce A. Glasrud in their book *West Texas*, "Between 1873 and 1880, hunters slaughtered hundreds of thousands, if not millions, of bison on

What the First White Settlers Found

the plains of West Texas."[10] Officials believe that more than five thousand buffalo were killed in what is now Howard County in 1878 alone.[11]

How the T&P Railroad Gave Midland Its Name

In 1881 the Texas and Pacific Railroad was built through Midland, and the town received its first official designation: Midway. It was not original; in fact, eight other Texas communities claimed the same name at the same time. The "Midway" settlement that ultimately became Midland was so named because the stop on the T&P was exactly halfway between Fort Worth and El Paso.[12] Three years later, in 1884, when it was deemed that Midway could not be used as the new community's name, a vote was held among residents. Midland was offered as the new suggestion, and the majority of townspeople who voted approved the new name.

The stop on the T&P was also known for something other than being the halfway mark between Fort Worth and El Paso. For railroad workers, Midway Station brought apprehension as it marked the advance into the wild, unexplored area known as the Llano Estacado, sometimes called the Staked Plains, and the beginning of the most rigorous effort to lay tracks.[13]

The laying of the railroad marked the unofficial beginning of the community, two years after what would be the last Comanche raid on the territory in 1879. During that attack, Texas Ranger W. B. Anglin, a twenty-five-year-old member of one of Virginia's first families who landed in Texas following the Civil War, was the last known person killed by Native Americans in West Texas.[14] Soon after, the Comanche would be all but gone from the region. With the Comanche no longer a threat, and the railroad facilitating transportation, West Texas was open for sheepmen, cattlemen, and, years later, oilmen.

Midland's Early Pioneers

In 1882 the human population of Midway was two.[15] Herman Garrett, a sheepman, pitched camp on land that would one day be the site of First National Bank. The other resident was Lum Medlin, a famed buffalo herder.

"Lum Medlin and Herman Garrett were the first real residents of Midland," said Judge Hyde. "In fact, I used to think ['Medlin' was] how Midland got its name.

Lum was a buffalo skinner who collected hides and sold them for profit." Hyde said buffalo skinning was likely the first true industry in West Texas before the railroad came through.[16]

"There were no cattle in the early days," said Pat McDaniel, director of the Haley Memorial Library and History Center. "John Scharbauer came here from Fort Worth, and he made a ton of money after raising and selling ten thousand head of sheep. It was a market created and a market that endured because of the grass, more or less. When those early settlers came here, we had belly-high grass."

The region grew rapidly between its founding and the appearance of oil; the Cowdens settled on land west of Midway near the New Mexico line in 1883. The Wadley family came in 1884 and established Midway's first lumberyard, which would evolve into the Burton-Lingo Lumber Company, the longest continuously running lumber company in the community.[17]

A Wide Expanse of Ranchland: First Sheep, Then Cattle

Like much of West Texas, Midland County was ranchland in the days when it was founded and settled. The sheepmen came first, attracted by the abundance of grass and sources of water, features that were, believe it or not, common to West Texas more than 130 years ago.[18] According to Judge Hyde, there were five sizable lakes in and around Midland County in those pre-twentieth-century years.

Herman Garrett started the ranching tradition in Midland County when he brought sheep from California to El Paso.[19] Disembarking from the Southern Pacific there, Garrett proceeded to drive his herd 300 miles through the wilds of Far West Texas, across the desert and the Pecos River, and finally into Midland County.[20]

The railroad brought ranchers to the area because cattle were transportable in freight cars. By 1890 twenty-nine ranches had been established in the county, and the agricultural census reported 14,867 cattle and 13,364 sheep in the area. Both sheep and cattle far outnumbered people; according to the U.S. Census, the human population numbered 1,033 in 1890.

By the turn of the twentieth century, cattle located on seventy-three ranches dominated the local economy. Almost 45,000 head were reported in the area, while the number of sheep had declined to only 2,257. In contrast, only one acre of cropland—used to farm oats—was reported in the county that year.[21] Ranching remained the dominant economy in Midland until about 1923.[22]

What the First White Settlers Found

A Few Notable Pioneer Families

As director of the Haley Memorial Library and History Center, Pat McDaniel has studied the pioneer history of Midland for years. Volumes of information remain stored in the library, and few people are more knowledgeable about Midland's early years than McDaniel. He has provided much of the information for this section.

No history book on Midland would be complete without mention of some of the more prominent ranching families who helped settle the land in the nineteenth and early twentieth centuries. These families came from many points around the globe and all shared two things in common: a spirit of settling on the new frontier and the sense of independence that paved the way for others who would come later.

The Scharbauers, Holts, Cowdens, Midkiffs, Halffs, Haleys, Barrons, and Jowells were among the pioneer ranching families who would help set in motion the direction of the town in its early days.

The Scharbauers

The Scharbauer family first migrated to New York when Ferdinand Scharbauer disembarked from a German sailing ship on which he was a passenger in 1846. He and his wife, Rosa, became naturalized citizens and raised seven children, including four sons. Joseph remained in New York, where he and his father maintained the family's leatherworks shop. The remaining sons—John, Christian, and Phil—went their separate ways but would all, in their own time, find their way to West Texas.[23]

Christian, born in 1850, married Jennie McCarty. Together they had three children—two daughters, and a son born in 1879. The boy's name was Clarence.

Clarence's uncle John, and John's wife, the former Kate Tompkins, were prime movers in landing the family in West Texas. In 1880, when they had saved $2,400, John and Kate moved from their home in New York to Eastland, Texas. Two years later, they moved to Abilene. John took on a partner in the sheep-raising business, and his herd quickly grew to 1,100 head. After grazing them in Taylor and Nolan Counties for three years, Scharbauer bought out his partner and drove his herd to Mitchell County in 1884. Three years later he landed in Midland, and the Scharbauer name quickly become a fixture here.

In 1890 Clarence Scharbauer, his father, Christian, and his uncle John brought the first registered Hereford cattle, more than 3,000 of them, to John Scharbauer's ranch. Already the area's largest sheep ranchers, they would quickly become one of the most successful cattle-ranching families in West Texas, and in 1913 they would form the Scharbauer Cattle Company. From that moment on, it seems that whatever the Scharbauer family touched turned to gold—and not just for the family, but for Midland itself.

The Holts

One of the first ranchers to settle in Midland was O. B. Holt, a Central Texas son of a cotton farmer who was schooled briefly at Southwestern University in Georgetown before heading west and landing in Midland in 1886.

"I got together 230 head of [milk cows] and drove from Waco to Midland," Holt said.[24] The drive from Waco to Midland took Holt two months because of what was at the time the worst drought the state had ever experienced.[25] "I had to water the cattle several times with a ten-pound lard bucket, dipping the water out of a tank and pouring it into a sheep trough," Holt said.[26]

The Holts bought their first well from Jim and Barney Whalen, close to where the Whalens had a buffalo camp. For $60, Holt bought and built a windmill and wooden troughs, and turned his cattle loose. Rangeland was free in those days, and ranches were typically twenty miles apart.[27] "There was no trouble over anyone coming in," Holt said. "There was no opposition."[28]

"O. B. Holt was one of the first presidents of First National Bank," said Pat McDaniel. "He was a very astute cowman, and he earned and held a lot of respect from all the other cow people in the area."[29] McDaniel said of Holt and his contemporaries, "The first generation of cow people who settled here prior to oil and gas really built and gave the community an undergirding."[30]

The Cowdens

The Cowden family tree is as multi-branched as the mesquite that seems only slightly more plentiful to West Texas than the family itself. The family has abundantly populated the region since first arriving here in 1883, and its pioneer members and their descendants have contributed generously to Midland.

The Cowdens' Texas experience began when brothers William Hamby Cowden and George Franklin Cowden, both born in Georgia, came to Texas as young boys. Thrust into early roles of responsibility following the death of their father, the two young men had a spirit of adventure and patriotism and signed up to soldier in the Mexican War. George would advance to the rank of captain, and together the two would march from Alabama to New Orleans and sail with Winfield Scott to Veracruz, Mexico.

What the First White Settlers Found

In 1856, when William and George began the trek back from Mexico to Georgia after the war, they were taken by the beauty and expanse of the wide-open lands of Texas. At that point in history, pioneers had settled only as far west as Palo Pinto County. When the Cowdens originally came westward, Midland had not yet been tramped on by anyone but the Comanche and Captain Marcy, as he and his U.S. troops searched for a suitable route for the railroad.[31]

The Cowden brothers made three different moves of one hundred miles each before finally ending up in Palo Pinto County. The frontier's western leading edge at that time, Pat McDaniel said, was likely in the area of Fort Griffin, northeast of Abilene, between Albany and Throckmorton.

According to the Cowden family's published history, when the two brothers were in Palo Pinto County, the Civil War broke out. Though too old for active service, they became members of the Home Guard. Later, "When the Texas and Pacific Railroad was finished to Fort Worth in 1880 and gave promise of being extended through the great plains of the West, the two Cowden families began to make their plans for moving farther west," according to the Cowden Family History.

The Cowden family tree grew more detailed when George married Elizabeth Whiteside. Nine children soon followed. The fifth child was William Frederick Cowden, known as Fred. "He married Martha Courtney," McDaniel said. "She passed away and he then married Emma Long. Martha gave William nine children. The Cowdens were spread out pretty quickly with those two generations."

Fred Cowden was the first person in Midland to own an automobile. Tragically, he was also the first person to be involved in an automobile accident, which resulted in Martha's death.[32]

Among later generations of Cowdens was Frank Cowden, Fred and Martha's grandson. He married June Wilkinson, and Linda Cowden is their daughter. June Cowden said Frank often talked of how Fred and Martha Cowden arrived in Midland and stepped off the train. "They came out in the summertime from Fort Worth, and Frank's grandmother put her foot down and said, 'My feet; there are ants all over them! They're burning!' Fred Cowden told her, 'You don't have ants. You have stepped in sand.'

"The first Cowdens came here because of grass and open country and an opportunity to acquire land," June continued. "Fred used to say that when he would go to the barn in the morning, he had to pull arrows out of the cows before he could milk them."

Today the Cowdens are seventh-generation West Texans.[33] Ever since the first members of the family settled here in 1883, four years before even John Scharbauer arrived, the family name has been as notable and as enduring as those of most other pioneer families.

The Cowden descendants who remain in West Texas are mostly of the lineage of William Frederick and Martha Cowden, but adding further to the early mix was William Hamby Cowden, who married Caroline Mary Liddon. They had eleven children together. After Caroline's death, William married her sister, Catherine. They had no children.[34]

Pat McDaniel said the Cowdens were actively involved in the community, especially during the 1930s, 1940s, and 1950s. "They all served on school boards, church boards, and bank boards. Anything it took to build a community they were involved in."

As is recorded in the family's history, "Wherever the Cowdens stopped for any length of time, they became property owners and influential citizens. The heroic struggles and adventures through wilderness and over plain to reach their new far-flung homes are largely records of the past, sealed with the sweat of their brows and the tears of their eyes."[35]

Several decades after the earliest Cowdens came here and the town continued to grow, Linda Cowden remembered a favorite story about her father, Frank.

"We moved into town in the early 1950s to a house at 1700 West Storey, right down from Memorial Stadium, and back then we were on the outskirts of Midland. You could look way to the north and see they were building San Jacinto Junior High," Linda Cowden said. "I remember one day my father saying, 'Why would they put a junior high school out in the country, away from town?' First Baptist Church was out in the country, too. We used to go to a seamstress who was way out in the country, and her business was located where Furr's Cafeteria is now."

The Midkiffs

Historian Pat McDaniel explained that the Midkiffs frequently lived farther out in the county than some of the other families but through the years were considered to be important community builders in their own right.[36]

John Rufus Midkiff, great-grandfather of T. O. Midkiff, brought the family to West Texas in 1896 in a covered wagon. A Confederate soldier during the Civil War, Midkiff was a private in Hardeman's Regiment, Texas Cavalry, and a stockman and farmer by profession. In 1902 Midkiff moved into southeast Midland County, where his descendants still own property. Shortly after the turn of the century, Midkiff turned part of his home into the area's first post office, which would also later contain the rural area's first telephone. As postmaster and owner of the first verbal communications device, Midkiff continued to expand and became somewhat of a noted entrepreneur when he began stocking groceries on consignment from a Midland grocer. Items such as flour, sugar, coffee, beans, salt, and canned peaches and tomatoes were popular with cowboys passing through the rugged land.[37]

John R.'s son, Thomas Oscar Midkiff, grandfather of T. O. Midkiff, came to West Texas with a friend, Scott McCaskill, in 1895, when Midkiff was just twenty-two years old. Midkiff and McCaskill's way of landing in Midland was somewhat like the flip of a coin. While stopped in Fort Worth on horseback after riding in from Indian Territory (modern-day Oklahoma), the two decided they wanted to live in a place that was genuine cattle country. They arrived at the T&P train station in Fort Worth and told the conductor they would travel as far as their remaining money would take them. The friends' funds were exhausted by the time the train reached Midland, so both began their new life in West Texas.[38]

After a year working as a cowboy, Midkiff returned to Indian Territory and married Lillie Davenport, on whom he had been sweet for two years. The two had planned to start life anew by moving to Midland but were slowed when Thomas's father, Oscar, lost his second wife to illness. Eventually the father would make the move to Midland with his son and Lillie, but he was far from happy about the arrangements his son had planned: John R. told his boy he would not make the trip to Midland in a covered wagon with "a dang woman." Lillie decided to stay behind until her new husband and father-in-law arrived and sent for her. At that point, Lillie boarded a train and headed west. Years later, she would tell her grandchildren that the train was even worse than the covered wagon. The train, she said, was dirty, damp, and smelly, and what was worse, she feared for her safety when all the men on board began to cuss and stare at her during the trip.[39]

The Halffs

The Halff family patriarch who eventually settled in Midland, Mayer Halff, was born in France and migrated to Texas in 1850 with his father, Adolph. After Adolph's death aboard the steamship *Nautilus*, which sailed out of Galveston and ultimately sank during a hurricane, Mayer and his son, Henry, established the Quien Sabe Ranch in 1884, one of the most legendary spreads in Midland County. Located in the south and east portions of the county, it was made up of between five hundred and six hundred sections of land and was so big that the northern borders of the ranch stretched all the way to the south part of the city of Midland itself.

PART ONE: A PLACE WITH CHARACTER

Henry was educated at Stanton Military Academy in Virginia and the Eastman Business College in Poughkeepsie, New York. After Mayer's death, Henry inherited the family's vast estate. By then it took up parts of not only Midland County, but Upton, Crockett, and Pecos Counties as well. Despite his wealth, Henry Halff was considered a gentleman, respected by working cowboys and cattlemen alike, and his integrity was widely known in West Texas. The Halff legacy, spurred mainly by Henry, was that of land development, cattle breeding, and the general welfare of West Texas.[40]

The Haleys, Barrons, and Jowells

The Haley Family, for whom the Haley Library is named, came to Midland in 1904. J. Alva Haley, father of J. Evetts Haley, was one of the town's early mayors, serving the unexpired term of the town's first mayor before winning election as Midland's second mayor. The Barron family, also instrumental in the formation of Midland National Bank, were key pioneers as well.

Spencer Jowell made the trip west with his two Cowden cousins. William Cowden ended up settling in southeast New Mexico and eventually founded the Jal Ranch, and also established a homestead in Midland County to provide a better education for his children. Jowell would make a name for himself as a working cowboy and rodeo performer.

The Grit to Survive

More than 125 years after Midland's first settlers arrived, historian Pat McDaniel still marvels at the tenacity it must have taken for all those who came first to keep from picking up and moving down the trail, given the lack of the simple things in life:

> Not a lot of people will talk about it, but the Cowden family was selling a lot of eggs and butter, trying to make a living in those drought years when they couldn't feed their cattle. They were as susceptible to the ups and downs of the economy as anyone else until the oil boom came along. John Scharbauer and Clarence Sr. had exceptional business acumen. They were first-rate entrepreneurs. So was O. B. Holt.
>
> No one had a reason to survive, economical or cultural, other than the fact that the people here just made this town survive. They created banks

and schools and churches, and the wives who moved out here with their husbands had a huge impact.[41]

The steadfast drive to simply endure, regardless of the hardships, was a trait found not just in the families whose names are still common today in Midland, but in anyone who chose to stay here.

A 1965 study by the University of Texas showed that there were three primary reasons for the prosperity that eventually came to Midland: "a simple accident of history, a railroad placed in what would become an oil center, and city and county leaders with resources and great vision."[42]

chapter 2

A Young Town Pulls On Its Cowboy Boots

You can't have a cow camp on the side of a railroad track turn into what [Midland] is today without visionary thinking. In some cases it was luck and not visionary thinking, but there were most certainly people here in those early years willing to spend their time and treasure to make something happen.

—Pat McDaniel, Midland historian

Every town exists not just by itself, but within a broader social context. This is true even for towns settled by self-sufficient pioneers.

Midland Becomes a Force to Reckon With

As far back as the mid-1880s, Midland was starting to carve out its own unique identity in relation to the surrounding towns and the state of Texas. One of the town's first political battles was to establish Midland County. It was a cause picked up with much vigor by Charles Rathbun, then editor of one of Midland's first newspapers.

A Skirmish of Editorials in 1885

In 1874 the Texas Legislature voted to honor Tom Green, leader of one of Texas's Civil War regiments and one of that war's most able cavalry commanders, by naming a county after him. At that time it was the largest county in the entire country.[1]

That one supersized county (originally 60,000 square miles) would later be divided into several smaller ones.²

Midland's first newspaper, the *Enterprise*, began publication in 1884. Only a year later, Rathbun, the editor, declared that the state must act to carve Midland County out of Tom Green County.

Though Midland was a sleepy, dusty burg in the middle of a land still largely unsettled, Rathbun wrote with confidence of how he saw his town, and provided yet another example for us today of the progressive nature of the people who have always lived here: "Midland must be a county seat, as every prosperous railroad town should be. *The Enterprise* would prefer the organization of a new county in this large one ... but if that is not accorded by the legislature we will have to vote [to move] the Tom Green County Courthouse here and inconvenience our San Angelo neighbors, as much as we would regret it," Rathbun wrote.³

The editor of the *San Angelo Standard* took exception to Rathbun's outrageous suggestion, firing back in an editorial of his own, "Don't you think, Charlie, it is a little too previous to talk about moving the county seat before you have a single voter or even a saloon with which to influence him? Go a little slow and fill up the country surrounding your imaginary village or the results will be disastrous to you...."⁴

Creative Marketing Makes Midland a County Seat

According to Bert Rawlins, the former editor of the *Midland Gazette*, a newspaper that followed the *Enterprise*, "It was discovered that there were not enough regular inhabitants in the proposed county and city to justify organization. That was remedied by announcing a town lot sale in Midland and setting special excursion rates on the T&P Railroad from as far east as Colorado City. On the day of the sale, visitors let us have their support by signing the petition and the matter was adjusted."⁵

Author John Howard Griffin described the situation further: "The transporting of people to Midland via rail was an early creative form of marketing the town, a Chamber of Commerce–like effort that offered people a mini vacation if only they would debark the train and sign the petition until enough names existed to make a legitimate request to 'legally' become a county seat in the eyes of Austin lawmakers."⁶

Despite the acrimony of the *San Angelo Standard* editor, on February 28, 1885, a special act of the Texas Legislature granted Rathbun's wish: Midland County was created, and the town became the county seat.⁷

Part One: A Place with Character

Midland Incorporates as a City and Elects Its First Leaders

Five months after Midland County grew out of Tom Green County, the first government leaders were elected: E. B. Lancaster was named county judge, and Theo Ray, sheriff; T. B. Wadley was the county's first treasurer, and A. B. Rountree was named clerk.[8]

Midlanders attempted to incorporate as a city in November of 1903, but their efforts failed by a vote of 60–36. A second vote passed on July 16, 1906, and S. J. Isaacks, who later became the first judge of the Seventieth District court, was elected first mayor. The young town continued to struggle.

Midland Independent School District formed in 1907, and on December 1, 1908, Clarence Scharbauer and Ruth Cowden married in what the newspapers called the social event of the decade.[9]

By 1910 the population of Midland County had grown to 3,464. Within the city limits, the number was 2,192. Midland was still more than a decade away from its first real boom.

A year after the county refused to renew the city's charter in 1910, citizens voted a second time to incorporate, 154–53, on January 24, 1911. J. M. Caldwell was elected mayor, and the city operated under an aldermanic government until the first council was formed in 1940.[10]

Early Midland Landmarks

Midland has had a number of nicknames over the years. "Queen City of the Prairie" is maybe most eloquent and romantic among them. "The Windmill City" and "the Tall City" reflect the town's physical appearance during different periods.

Drift Fences and Windmills

Midlanders had early and ample opportunities to prove their resourcefulness through the construction of drift fences and windmills.

Drift fences were built to keep cattle contained and to prevent the free roaming of livestock in search of warmer climes. Some settlers adamantly opposed the fences—some even fought over them bitterly—because the fences were seen as a restriction to freedom and a barrier to the open rangeland that made the West appealing.[11] Still, drift fences were inevitable to progress as ranchers saw the need for complete enclosure to keep others' herds out and their own herds in.

A Young Town Pulls On Its Cowboy Boots

Closer to town, Midlanders battled the Great Die-Off of 1886–87. When they discovered that water could be found only a short distance below the surface, they set out to build a series of windmills. So many of the contraptions were constructed, in fact, that pioneers began calling their home the Windmill City.[12]

Some people dug wells by hand. The water found at shallow levels was enough to meet personal needs of family members, but not nearly enough to irrigate large crop areas. Those first wells were located at what are now the intersections of Wall and Weatherford, Main and Texas, and Main and Wall Streets. Residents were welcome to come to town with their buckets and obtain an adequate supply for themselves.

Midland's First Two Banks and Original Courthouse

First National Bank, an institution that played a critical role in much of Midland's history, was first chartered in 1890 after having been open for two years as a privately held bank. Clarence Scharbauer Jr. said that his father "helped start First National Bank in 1899 and 1900, and he ended up running the whole thing."[13] (For more about the history of this remarkable bank and all it did for Midland, see Chapters 7 and 16.)

In 1902 Odessa National Bank moved to Midland and retained its original name for a year before settling on Midland National Bank.[14]

In 1905, bolstered by a sizable population increase, residents voted to build a new three-story courthouse made of Pecos red sandstone. Construction costs totaled $26,000. The surrounding square featured a bandstand, a town windmill, and a watering pond.[15]

Devastating Fires

Several major fires were fought in the early 1900s. A 1909 blaze rampaged through much of the downtown business district, burning the Llano Hotel, Midland National Bank, and First National Bank to the ground. Several other businesses burned in the same fire.[16]

By 1910, city officials were finally able to pump in water.

Fairview Cemetery

At the intersection of two streets bearing the names of two of Midland's most prominent families—Cowden and Nobles—sits Fairview Cemetery, Midland's oldest and most historic final resting place. The burial ground is filled with people who made important contributions to the town; Proctor, Cowden, Scharbauer, and

Thomas are just four of the prominent families with ancestors buried there.

Fairview is a significant part of the community. At the time of his death in 2012, Judge Hyde was working on a paper that would have shown as many as twenty-five Civil War veterans—from both the North and South—are buried there. "Union soldiers came to Midland, so even back then there was something about this place," he said.[17]

The archives of Fairview Cemetery itself give more detailed information about this. "The military stones of veterans alone give one the picture of the settling of Midland County. It shows Midland to be a melting pot . . . of people from so many other places, including Texas, Georgia, Indiana, Mississippi, Arkansas, California, New York, Illinois, Virginia, Missouri, Louisiana, Montana, West Virginia, Kansas, Oklahoma and Tennessee."[18]

Commissioners agreed to donate ten acres for the purpose of establishing a cemetery in 1885. The Ladies Cemetery Association, headed by Mrs. O. B. Holt, president, set about to hire a caretaker at a rate of $30 a month. The LCA took out an advertisement in the *Midland Livestock Reporter*, which read, "Someone is wanted to work and look after our cemetery. If you want the place, call Mrs. O. B. Holt."[19] A caretaker was eventually found and hired. He moved into a house on-site.

According to historian Nancy McKinley, editor of *The Pioneer History of Midland County, Texas, 1880–1926*, a pair of bank robbers who were on the run rode up and buried stolen cash under the caretaker's house with a posse hot on their trail. Though McKinley claims in her book to have spoken with more than a handful of old-time Midlanders who corroborated the story, no buried treasure has ever been found at or near the cemetery.

"I add this story just for color," McKinley wrote. "There is no verification for it that we can find."[20]

The Thomas Building: Site of Medical Care in Early Midland

The Thomas Building may have stood in the shadow of the Hogan Building and the huge Scharbauer Hotel across the street, but it can boast something that the other two cannot: it came first, opening on January 1, 1928. The other two historically prominent buildings would not open for several months. Also, unlike the Scharbauer Hotel, the Thomas Building still stands and remains in use. Its builder, Dr. John B. Thomas, played a vital role in the medical history of Midland.

Dr. Felix P. Millar, who practiced in Midland at the turn of the twentieth century, gave a sobering description of what medicine was like in some of those early years before Thomas arrived in town. "All physicians were obstetricians and surgeons. There were no hospitals, laboratories or X-rays available. The kitchen table, the folding top of a sewing machine, were ideal for operating tables. Electric lights were not available. Ether was not available or safe to use near a flame, so chloroform was more suitable and safe. Any cowboy, housewife or patient could use it under directions from the doctor."[21]

Under these conditions, the town dealt with the diseases of the time—typhoid, smallpox, and diphtheria—as the new century was ushered in.[22]

When Dr. John B. Thomas came to Midland in 1905, bringing with him a hand-cranked X-ray machine, he immediately saw that there were an inadequate number of beds for the sick and infirm. Partnering with Clarence Scharbauer in 1919, Thomas bought the rebuilt Llano Hotel and located a hospital wing on the second floor, complete with an operating table. In 1922, with the assistance of Josephine Guly, Midland's first trained nurse, Thomas cared for patients in a facility at Marienfeld Street and Kansas Avenue, and in 1928, he would build the Thomas Building, which still stands occupied today at Loraine Street and Missouri Avenue.

On the top floor of the Thomas Building was a twenty-five-bed hospital. Thomas said in 1928 that every other floor had been leased, "every square inch," by oil companies. The building was fully occupied again after World War II ended and Midland's population exploded. Several years after a NO VACANCY sign was posted in the 1950s, an additional floor was completed, providing even more space. The sixth-floor medical facilities were finally no longer needed after Thomas spearheaded a successful fund drive to establish what is now Midland Memorial Hospital.[23] (The founding and expansion of Midland Memorial Hospital are described further in Chapters 9 and 19.)

According to his two surviving grandsons, brothers John and Henry Meadows, Dr. Thomas was always dressed to the nines, in a suit and a tie with a diamond stud, and he was rarely seen without a cigar dangling from his mouth.[24]

John Meadows added, "Dr. Thomas would pull me aside and open up the cigar box, and would always have three horny toads in there he'd named Hoover, Truman, and Eisenhower. He had a really dry sense of humor."

Thomas had a curious aversion to people who were left-handed, according to the Meadows brothers, but he was much better known for his friendliness and generosity, and for his devotion to improving health care for Midland.[25] A medical student at Texas A&M–Galveston, he was among the survivors of the 1900 hurricane that killed between 6,000 and 12,000 people and destroyed much of the island.[26]

Part One: A Place with Character

Thomas's best friend was Jno. P. Butler,* and it was because of the well-known banker that Thomas stumbled onto what would become a family fortune in the oil and gas business. When he first came to Midland and established his medical practice, Thomas bought a house on a city block bordered the present-day Big Spring, Wall, Missouri, and Colorado Streets. Henry and John Meadows shared the following story:

> Mr. Butler was after my grandfather to sell him that city block across from the courthouse so they could build a new First National Bank building. But my grandfather never wanted to sell it.
>
> Butler came to his friend and made his best and final offer. "What's it going to take?" Butler asked Thomas.
>
> Dr. Thomas thought for a minute and finally told Butler, "Well, I've always wanted to be in the oil business."
>
> Mr. Butler told our grandfather, "We've just foreclosed on a bunch of minerals, and I'd be willing to swap you those minerals for that city block."
>
> That's how Mr. Butler and First National Bank ended up with that block. And that's how Dr. Thomas ended up in the oil business.[27]

Henry Meadows said the rights traded to his grandfather are still in the family and still paying royalties to this day.

Two Other Buildings That Changed Midland's Fate in the 1920s

Two buildings that forever changed the face and future of Midland were the Scharbauer Hotel, built by Clarence Scharbauer, and the sturdy new Hogan Building, built by T. S. Hogan.

It would be difficult to overstate the importance of the two structures. According to John Paul Pitts, longtime oil editor of the *Midland Reporter-Telegram*, "Historians tell us that two buildings, the Scharbauer Hotel and the Hogan Building, both built in 1928 and both class acts for this part of the state, were major factors in making Midland the administrative and exploration center of the

---

*Jno. P. Butler's formal first name was pronounced "John," but he always wrote and signed it "Jno."

Permian Basin oil industry. The two structures came at a time when oilmen flocking to the area needed both office space and a home away from home."²⁸

Clarence Scharbauer Jr. conceded that had it not been for those two buildings, Odessa might very well have eventually wrested the "Oil Capital of West Texas" title from Midland. (Chapter 5 will show in more detail how these two early Midland landmarks played such a critical role in determining the city's future.)

"The hotel and the Hogan Building . . . that's why Midland is like it is," said Scharbauer Jr. "Oil was in Ector County then, and Odessa could have been another Tulsa, and Midland would have been a wide spot in the road, but the oilmen had a place to stay and office here."²⁹

chapter 3

A Town of Faith and Morals

Religion, widely practiced and dynamic, influenced every phase of life. It left its imprint on the land, the people and the institutions. If one can scarcely imagine the typical West Texas town without its Saturday night dances, its gaming and saloons, neither can one imagine it without its Sunday morning strains of "My Faith Looks Up to Thee," and "Amazing Grace," followed by the fiery words of the Gospel sung and preached to the distant bawling of a cow somewhere out on the prairie.
—John Howard Griffin, *Land of the High Sky*

Aside from oil, there are two things that have long been in plentiful supply in Midland: churches and Mexican restaurants.

Four years after Herman Garrett brought his herd of sheep here from California, two years after the town changed its name, and just nine months after the first governmental officials were elected, Midlanders began organizing houses of worship. One could only imagine that the two-burrito plate and honey-covered sopapilla special must have followed soon after.

Faith Abounding: Midland's First Churches

The Methodists, Presbyterians, and Baptists were the earliest faiths to form in Midland, with the Methodists actually being the first to assemble as a congregation.[1] Those pioneer Midlanders were not wealthy, but they wanted a good community to live in—a fact clearly reflected in the number of churches that developed so quickly.[2]

A Town of Faith and Morals

Methodist

The Methodists opened their first house of worship with just one male and five female members, on August 22, 1885.[3] J. H. Barron, a well-known merchant in Midland's early days, wrote in a letter dated August 23, 1885, to his future wife, Annie Aycock, stating that he and Brother J. A. Scoggins, the church's first pastor, had organized a church. That church would become First United Methodist.

Interestingly, Barron is also credited with being a founding member of the first Baptist congregation a short time later and was even named clerk of that church by the congregation.[4]

The initial First United Methodist Church was built in the 100 block of North Main in 1889, and five years later would move to the corner of Main and Illinois, its home for well over a century now. During the five years between the time its original structure was razed and its new home was built, the congregation met in the Ritz Theater and other locations downtown.[5]

Presbyterian

In 1885 the Presbytery of Dallas sent representatives to West Texas, seeking to establish roots in Midland, Big Spring, and any other area that was deemed to be in need of the faith. The Presbyterians organized four months after the Methodists, on December 22, 1885.[6]

In 1896, following the drought years that would play a part in diminishing the town's overall population, the membership at the Presbyterian church dropped to two, and in 1897 the church was ordered dissolved by the Presbytery of Fort Worth.[7]

Yet Presbyterianism did not die in Midland. At the turn of the century, W. D. Watts, a local rancher, headed an effort to reorganize. His plan to regroup was fortified when he formed a building committee with C. P. Fuller, the town postmaster, and F. H. Burney, a local teacher. After selecting a site at Big Spring and Wall Streets, they awarded a contract for construction. In November 1899 sixteen people signed a charter establishing what is still known today as First Presbyterian Church. In May 1900 the building was dedicated, and a series of pastorates would follow.[8]

The Presbyterians, a generous and friendly body, were not without controversy in early Midland. As the *Midland Reporter-Telegram* reported in 1985, "The Rev. Ted Holifield was called by the church in Midland in 1923. While church records indicated he preached excellent sermons, the board of elders discovered that Holifield had married a divorced woman. Holifield sensed the elders' disapproval and resigned."[9]

Part One: A Place with Character

Old-timers called Holyfield's marriage to a divorced woman "the straw that broke the camel's back," according to the *Midland Reporter-Telegram*. "The congregation made no attempt to find a replacement. Sunday school classes at the discouraged church were dismissed and some members suggested dissolution of the congregation. The church rolls shrank."[10]

A visit in 1925 by the widow of a Presbyterian minister who was also a sister to a member of the congregation would change the church's fate yet again. The congregant, a Mrs. Muirhead, expressed her dismay that no religious education was being conducted and was able to persuade her sister to help remedy that situation.[11] As the church school classes grew, so, too, did life at the church, and the congregation resumed its place in the still-young town.

Baptist

Visiting Sweetwater pastor J. A. Moore is credited with being the first person to preach a Baptist sermon in Midland.[12] Baptists were the third congregation to form, but they were the first to actually build a house of worship. The charter members voted on an annual salary of $125 for their new pastor, Rev. S. B. Callaway. The Baptists' first home was at the corner of Marienfeld and Illinois, but since Rev. Callaway was able to appear only once a month to preach, the church voted to loan the building out to other congregations on the Sundays that the preacher was elsewhere.[13]

Callaway's salary grew to $500 annually and the service schedule increased to twice monthly, but the preacher would soon leave Midland, and his successor, Rev. Leander Millican, oversaw the relocation of the church to North Main and Illinois Streets. At the time, the intersection was called Baptist Corner. The church remained in that location for fifty years before moving to its present location, at Garfield and Louisiana Streets.[14]

It didn't take long for First Baptist to establish itself as the largest church body in Midland. By 1900 its rolls had grown to 363, which represented a larger congregation than all other churches in Midland combined.

Catholic

The historical records of St. Ann's Church indicate that the first Catholic Mass in Midland was celebrated in a tent on August 15, 1881, four years before the Protestants opened their doors in the town.[15] That celebration of the first Holy Eucharist was void of even the simplest accoutrements that Catholics now take for granted.

Amenities like flooring (let alone air-conditioning!) were absent, and conditions were likely dusty and hot. It was not until seventeen years later that the first Catholic church was built, which would later come to be known as St. Ann's.[16]

Rev. Edward Harrison, one of St. Ann's first pastors, wrote that the origin of the Catholic Church in Midland could be summarized in the words of one of the town's pioneers:

> We settled in Midland some 50 years ago, the year 1884; at that time it was a very small place. Our nearest church was at Marienfeld [now Stanton], at the time cared for by the Carmelite fathers. We used to go there once or twice a year. Then, after four or five years, one of the Carmelite fathers by the name of H. A. Boniface came once a month to say Mass in a Mexican dug-out in East Midland. I have heard my mother say many times that she and my younger sister would be the only Americans in the congregation. There were no other Catholics in Midland at the time. Shortly afterward, Mass was said at a Mexican's house east of what is now downtown Midland. The congregation was still comprised of all Mexicans and we felt that having Mass above ground was quite an improvement.[17]

In the spring of 1886 a Catholic school was built, the first between Fort Worth and El Paso. Church records also reflected that the summers of 1886 and 1887 in Midland were "particularly harsh with very hot, dry weather that caused crops to dry up, forcing many settlers to move."[18]

First Christian Church

In 1890 First Christian Church (which adopted the name "First Christian Church: Disciples of Christ" beginning in 1968) established the fifth denomination in the young town. According to the history of the church, "Sixteen persons desiring to be called simply 'Christians' began the organization of what was to become First Christian Church, under the guidance of A. J. Bush. Not having a building of their own and often without a preacher, they met in the homes of members on Sunday afternoons for the observance of the Lord's Supper, singing and prayer."

Then, in 1892, the growing congregation purchased two lots on the corner of Loraine and Illinois, erecting upon the site a small white frame building. Evangelist Dr. James B. Sweeney, Dean of AddRan College, the forerunner of Texas Christian University in Fort Worth, dedicated the building and conducted the church's first revival. Mr. Kuby Ferguson was called to be the church's first resident pastor, and by 1907 the congregation had outgrown the small white church it had built only fifteen years earlier. In 1908, a larger building known as the Old Red Brick Church was dedicated on the same patch of land downtown as the smaller, preceding church. During construction, services at First Christian were held in the Midland County Courthouse. When Midland National Bank burned in 1909, it took with it all of First Christian's membership and administrative records, which had been stored in the bank during construction of the new building.[19]

First Christian Church again fell victim to fire on January 20, 1957, when the main church building was totally destroyed in a blaze that began at four a.m. The *Midland Reporter-Telegram* referred to it as "one of Midland's costliest fires in history." Firefighters tried for twelve hours to extinguish the flames, and firemen were given a temporary respite from the aggressive blaze before it reignited and claimed the entire structure. Perhaps most impressive was the story of how the church went on—while the building's ruins were still smoking.

"Although the fire had not yet been completely extinguished," church records reported, "Clarence Saint, the minister, held worship services in the Youth Center at 8:30 the morning after, and again at 10:50 a.m., as usual. Hymnals were borrowed from First Baptist Church, communion ware and a pulpit from First Presbyterian Church and chairs were delivered by National Guardsmen, and came from Midland Community Theatre, Pioneer Natural Gas and the American Legion."[20]

Sunday Afternoons and Community Sings

In his book *Land of the High Sky*, John Howard Griffin described the crucial importance of the church to social life in Midland's early decades. "Since no other forms of diversion existed, social life centered around the church. Church suppers, ice cream socials, Sunday School picnics and bazaars were given not only as a means of getting together but also to raise money."[21]

Singing was one of the best-loved traditions in early Midland, often used as a diversion from the realities of the hard-luck existence of the day. Community sings were often held on Sunday afternoons in churches during the time of growing congregations.

Another favorite pastime was simply visiting, or "fellowshipping." In Griffin's words, "It was not considered an imposition for 10 to 20 persons to go home with a friend after church to spend the day. Cooking for the additional crowd was no problem. The women helped the hostess and the men helped the host. Additional food was available merely by going into the yard and killing a few more chickens. If the company chose to spend the night, which they frequently did, they put down pallets."[22]

When families would return home after church, if there were no visitors that day, conversation turned to the Bible. Griffin wrote that favorite reading matter in family homes, in addition to the Bible, included Longfellow, Dickens, the *Atlanta Constitution*, and the *Baptist Herald*. "The mother knitting or mending on one side of the fireplace, the father reading on the other while the children quietly attended their studies or games, was the usual sitting room picture."[23] The description brings to mind a Norman Rockwell painting.

A Town of Clean Morals and Mostly Clean Living

Like its reputation for surviving repeated droughts, heat, and wind, Midland's long-standing trademark of being a town of high character, clean morals, and mostly clean living dates back almost to day one.

The Rivalry Between Midland and Odessa

It's hard to pinpoint exactly why the rivalry between Midland and Odessa began. It seems unlikely that the time-honored adage—you raise your family in Midland and hell in Odessa—was the seed for the squabble now more than a century old. Some question the existence of such a rift and insist it is talk heightened by media so tensions can conveniently be added to books like *Friday Night Lights*.

Midland is Midland, and Odessa is Odessa. Differences exist and are acknowledged. The oldest story hinting at any friction between the two towns dates back to the turn of the twentieth century.

Swapping a Bank for a Brothel

"Midland National Bank was chartered out of the Odessa National Bank, which failed," said historian Pat McDaniel. "The running joke was that everybody was happy because Midland traded Odessa a whorehouse for a bank by sending our prostitutes over there and getting a bank in return."

That joke would reappear years later when Sheriff Ed Darnell tweaked the punch line. "Big Ed always said there was an unspoken agreement between the sheriffs' departments in the two counties," McDaniel said. "He said he wouldn't have any running of prostitutes in Midland unless they were high class. All the low-class prostitutes, he said, had to stay in Odessa."

Y'Best Watch Your Manners, Cowboy

In its centennial edition published July 4, 1985, the *Midland Reporter-Telegram* wrote that while most offenses in early Midland were for card playing and other gaming sins, there were scattered stories of rude behavior in the presence of women.

The first arrest in Midland was for the use of loud and abusive language. "Although not controversial for cowboys of those times, if a profane vocabulary was exercised in the presence of women . . . he'd better leave the county," the paper quoted author John Howard Griffin.

Another early arrest accused a man of "bursting in on a service" at First Presbyterian Church. The man, according to the newspaper, "demanded the congregation break up the meeting and go home. The offender received the maximum punishment of the day: He was severely reprimanded and told to go home himself."[24]

Several years later, in March 1908, a Mr. B. Hutchinson, uncle of Foy and Leonard Proctor, was arrested and charged with "running or driving an automobile faster than eight miles per hour in the city." The case was later dismissed after authorities learned that the main damage incurred by Mr. Hutchinson was that he scared a couple of horses, which broke free of their hitching posts and ran for the country.

Some of the legal infractions in early Midland were more serious, however.

Law and Order: The Story of Lorenzo Porez

Sometime after nightfall on July 20, 1890, a band of thieves stole saddles from a ranch in what is now Reagan County, near Centralia Draw. The next morning, Sam Murray, a rancher in the area, climbed atop his horse and set out on a search for the crook. After learning from an eyewitness that four horsemen had been in the area the night before and were seen heading west, Murray stopped by the neighboring Bartlee Ranch and signed on another cowboy, Will Landrum, to take part in the search. Together, Murray and Landrum tracked the four riders twenty-five miles, into Upton County. When they caught up to them, Murray and Landrum saw the stolen saddles in the bandits' possession. One of the riders was Lorenzo Porez.

Outnumbered two to one, the members of the posse were surprised by the four outlaws, who had circled behind them and were now galloping toward them and firing their weapons. Murray and Landrum returned fire but quickly became separated as they fled across the prairie. The bandits divided, two in pursuit of each cowboy. In his last sighting of Landrum, Murray saw Lorenzo Porez and another rider about two hundred yards behind the cowboy.

After securing additional backup, Murray returned to where he had last seen Landrum. What he found was the cowboy's riderless horse and hat, lying near a pool of blood. A few yards into a stand of furrowed brush, the search team found Landrum's body. Murray and the others would report later that it appeared the horseman had been lassoed off his mount, dragged into the bushes, and fatally stabbed in the chest.

Murray and others in his posse saw four horsemen escaping in the distance. Three of the four were ultimately apprehended and were locked in the Midland County jail by September 1890. The indictment formally charged Porez with the crime.

A Midland County jury found Porez guilty of first-degree murder. A punishment of death by hanging was assessed.[25]

Texas governor James Hogg later issued a stay of execution as he considered a plea for clemency filed by Porez's counsel, but in November 1891 the governor telegraphed Judge William Kennedy, of the Thirty-Second District, rescinding the stay of execution, making Porez's date with the rope imminent. In the telegram, Governor Hogg wrote, "I have reviewed the file. Let the law take its course."

A death warrant was issued, and Sheriff Allison was instructed to hang Porez on Friday, November 27, 1891, between eleven a.m. and sunset. A scaffold was constructed on the east side of the courthouse, and a crowd gathered to view what would be the first execution in that part of the state.

Porez stood atop that platform, a scratchy rope around his neck. The late-autumn air was probably cool. A crowd assembled. The men of the town were joined by the women—and even children. Standing alongside Sheriff W. D. Allison was Father Albert Wagner, a priest from nearby Marienfeld who had arrived to administer last rites to the condemned man.

Despite the presence of the law and the clergy, the assembled had in fact come to see the man with the noose around his neck. There was a chance, the crowd surely thought, that Porez, a simple thief-turned-murderer, might do or say something that would make this day even more memorable. And he did.

Sheriff Allison asked Porez if he had any last words. The condemned man said he was sorry for killing Will Landrum. He asked the dead man's family for forgiveness and, filled with contrition, exonerated one of the men he had been known to ride with. He also told the sheriff where he could find the other man involved.

Part One: A Place with Character

His final words trailing off, Porez had said what he had come to say, and took another breath, his last. The sheriff pulled the lever. Porez dropped. And he dangled above the grounds of the Midland County Courthouse, swinging lifeless for the gathered men—and women and children—to see.

It would be the only hanging the people of Midland County would ever witness: in the more than 120 years since, only three other men have been condemned to die by Midland County juries and have had their sentences carried out, two by electrocution and one by lethal injection. As of 2014, a fifth man sat on death row awaiting his final day.[26] Only four men in 122 years is the equivalent of one execution every 30.5 years.

When Porez hanged, his case was Indictment No. 87, making him one of the first criminals Midland law enforcement ever arrested. By 2011 that number had reached more than 39,000.

Judge Hyde told Porez's story to many gatherings, always finishing with how Porez's body was buried in a secret place. Hyde believed the horse thief was laid to rest in a sort of boot hill in what is now the west central portion of Fairview Cemetery on A Street.

Mrs. J. H. Frame wrote years after Porez's execution that her teacher had "marched us all out to see the hanging as an admonition." Apparently the teacher's tactics worked. "Not one of us kids ever hung," Mrs. Frame said.[27]

chapter 4

LAND OF DROUGHTS AND SANDSTORMS, BLIZZARDS AND FLOODS

The land of promise quickly became a land of despair because rainfall was nonexistent, with no more than 12–16 inches in normal years and five inches or less in others. And then there were times when Mother Nature added insult to injury, pouring down so much rain at one time that crops were washed away by floodwaters.
—John Howard Griffin, *Land of the High Sky*

MAYBE THE ONLY THINGS THAT COME ALONG in West Texas with as much regularity as oil booms and busts are droughts. Midland has withstood many of them, most notably in 1886–87, 1909–10, 1916–18, 1933–34, and 1949–56, and in the early years of the 2000s and 2010s.[1] (The most recent droughts are discussed further in Chapter 21.)

While ranchers and cattlemen in the area seemed to survive the dry times more easily than others, the lack of rain hit oilmen hard. With prices hovering at 10 cents a barrel, residents of the Permian Basin were paying $1 per gallon of water, outlandish in those times.[2] Dry spells were often accompanied by blinding sandstorms that would leave deposits of West Texas's most plentiful natural resource ankle-high in some doorways. Judge John Hyde told this story: "Several years ago when I was doing a program at Midland College, a man came up to me and said his grandfather had come to Midland as a Methodist preacher. When he got off the train, one of our famous sandstorms was blowing through. The preacher was greeted by a local, who saw the incredulous look on the preacher's face. The local man, welcoming him off the train, looked at the preacher and said, 'It's a right smart blow, ain't it, Reverend?'"[3]

Part One: A Place with Character

The Great Die-Off of 1886

It wouldn't take long to test the mettle of early Midlanders. Barely a year after the town's first churches had been established, those who filled the pews would need all the faith they could muster as a severe and protracted drought began in earnest.[4] In 1886 a dry spell that would one day be called the Great Die-Off cost many West Texans their livelihood. "Without rain, the water catches quickly dry up, grasses wither and dust casts a pall over everything. Such was the case in Midland in 1886 and 1887," wrote John Howard Griffin.[5]

True to form and exercising a spirit of independence that has been a part of the people of West Texas since day one, early Midland officials never requested emergency government aid that had been provided to surrounding counties and communities.

The Staked Plains became the Scorched Plains, but Midland's citizens downplayed the drought in hopes of focusing instead on what they all hoped was a bright future. An early example of the town's renowned spirit showed itself during the dry spell. As Griffin wrote, "While disheartened settlers streamed eastward from other West Texas towns [to escape the drought], they continued to come to Midland."[6]

Mrs. W. F. Fahrenkamp, who survived the great drought of 1886, remembered how the grass turned from plentiful and knee high to a parched and barren land in only a year. "What before had been green fields of wheat was now burned and withered stubble, and sandstorms reigned supreme," she said.[7]

A Pioneer Saved by His Horse

Paradoxically, droughts in West Texas were often paired with an extreme form of precipitation: blizzards. One of the area's first pioneers, O. B. Holt, ended up moving north of Midland, where he lived in a dugout and cooked on a skillet over an open fire. Despite the dry conditions, Holt remembered times when intense blizzards would so disorient him that he would finally give up trying to find his way out.[8]

"I had one horse that saved my life," said Holt. "I'd started out in the early morning and rode fence line all day. By night the snow was a foot deep. I figured I was about ten miles from the ranch. I tried to pull in one direction but the horse kept wanting to go another. I finally gave him his head. I could hardly get off him when we reached camp."[9]

Holt dismounted, staggered through the door of his two-room dugout, and led his mount inside out of the intense blizzard. After throwing a blanket over the horse, he kept the animal in the kitchen all night.

Land of Droughts and Sandstorms, Blizzards and Floods

When he sold his land to the C. C. Slaughter family several years later, Holt did not include in the transaction the horse that saved his life.[10]

The Time It Never Rained: The Drought of the 1950s

The drought of the 1950s was the costliest natural disaster in the state's history. Midland was in the middle of the driest of conditions. The financial losses exceeded those of the Dust Bowl years, and the drought was blamed on everything from an angry God to sunspots. It was so monumental that it prompted the "modern era of water planning in Texas."[11] (This is discussed more fully in Chapter 21.)

The drought began in late spring of 1949 in the lower Rio Grande Valley, affected the western portions of Texas by the fall, and had covered nearly all of the state by the summer of 1951. By the end of 1952, the water shortage was critical. In the Trans-Pecos area of the state, west of Midland, only eight inches of rain fell the entire year of 1953. Conditions only grew worse from 1954 through 1955 and early 1956. Then, in the spring of 1956, the drought ended abruptly with slow, soaking rains throughout Texas.[12]

Dark Storms of Sand and Dust

Rosalind Grover remembers the 1950s drought vividly. "There were terrible dust storms. My word, it was awful. You would hear the sand hitting the car, it sounded like glass hitting the cars. And this business of no water … it is kind of the norm out here. We worried about it in the 1950s, but nobody wrung their hands like they do now. The Paul Davis Field, that was a discovery that made a huge difference in the water for Midland. But you just knew there wasn't a lot of water. Drought was normal."[13]

Judge John Hyde said about this era, "Since people began the effort to tame this parched prairieland, the scarcity of water has been a perennial challenge and drought a frequent companion. During the Dust Bowl era of the 1930s, dark clouds of eroded topsoil limited visibility to a few feet. That pattern was repeated, though not to the same magnitude, during the 1950s, when automobile headlights were needed during the daytime as drivers maneuvered through dust storms."[14]

Ranchers' Struggles to Save Their Livestock

W. D. Dunn Reiger, secretary-treasurer for the Scharbauer Cattle Company, recalled the drought of the 1950s as far worse than the rainless spells of 1909–10,

PART ONE: A PLACE WITH CHARACTER

1916–18, and 1933–34. "During the first three droughts, cattlemen could, somewhat successfully, shift their cattle around to spreads over West Texas," Reiger said. "But the drought of the 1950s was too widespread [for cattlemen] to do this with much success." Reiger often remembered telling people that in the drought of the 1950s, a cow's hide would bring more than the cow."[15]

Clarence Scharbauer Jr. said the 1950s drought was why he and fellow Midland pioneer Foy Proctor teamed up to buy the Matador Ranch, west of Amarillo, where the drought was less severe. "It was so bad, but we didn't want to sell our cattle," said Scharbauer. "We looked at several ranches and they were selling the Matador. I took ninety head of cattle and steer calves in trucks to the Matador, and another 100 two-year-old heifers and unloaded them up at the South Mill."[16]

Joan Nobles is a lifelong resident of West Texas who worked as a cowhand on her family's ranch at age nine and later taught Gregory Peck to ride a horse. She hasn't forgotten helping drive two hundred head of cattle to the family's ranch in New Mexico to save its herd.

"It was heartbreaking," Nobles said. "When the drought hit, we had built a really good family business. We had a ranch in New Mexico at the time that still had grazing grass on it, and we took a couple hundred head to that ranch to pasture. Back at the ranch house in Midland when we added onto it, we had a big picture window and there was a big patch of grass outside the window. But when the drought hit, it was just a big clump of sand. There was not one blade of grass showing. That's how bad it was."[17]

Because of the lack of grass in Midland, Nobles said the family had to repeatedly sell down the herd just to buy feed for the cattle that remained. "We sold our yearlings down until we had a hundred head of heifers that were positively perfect, every one of them. All that was left was the best. Finally, the day came when we had very little remaining in the bank and Gerald, my husband, said, 'Joan, we can't do it anymore.' We sold those hundred head, and four days later we had a four-inch rain."[18]

The Paul Davis Field

It was in the summer of 1952 when the Midland City Council finalized the first phase of a contract that would bring sufficient amounts of water to a community of 60,000. The source of the water in the council's landmark deal would one day come to be known as the Paul Davis Field.

The water didn't come off of Paul Davis's field, though he was a landowner and was in the oil business. Instead, it was referred to as the Paul Davis Field because

Davis served as chairman of the committee looking for a new supply of water for Midland, and his group helped secure that supply, according to longtime city manager Fred Poe. The field was an aquifer north of town where engineers drilled for accessible groundwater and transported it by pipeline to the city water plant, where it was redistributed to users in the city.

Comparing the 1950s with Today

It is easily understandable that today's farmers and ranchers compare and contrast the current dry spell with the record one in the 1950s if they've lived through both—but experts still insist that what Texans are enduring in the 2010s is far from how bleak conditions were in the 1950s. Robert Mace, the Texas Water Development Board's executive director, said losses from the drought in 1949 into 1956 were $22 billion in today's dollars.[19]

T. O. Midkiff, whose family has ranched south of town for generations, still lives on a ranch near the Upton-Midland county line. He saw both the current drought and the one in the 1950s. "It's hard to compare them," Midkiff said. "In the early 1950s, my uncle went eleven months and recorded just a half inch of rain. Today, it's hard to compare because the oilfield traffic is stirring up the dust and the roads are all tore up."[20]

The Cloudburst of 1968

Once in a while, Midland gets too much rain, not too little.

The days before May 9, 1968, were normal enough. No measurable rainfall had been recorded in Midland that month, and the weather forecast in the Midland newspaper that morning called simply for cloudy skies with a 30 percent chance of rain. Certainly words like "epic" and "biblical" had not been introduced into the weather conversation for the day. But then the sky opened.

Talk to people almost a half century later who experienced the deluge, and their memories are still vivid. The intensity of rainfall that day, they say, is impossible to exaggerate. The storm killed one man and resulted in millions of dollars in damages to homes, businesses, and infrastructure. Almost five inches of rain fell in a two-hour period, which brought flooding that paralyzed the city. According to the *Midland Reporter-Telegram*, "Traffic was brought to a standstill in many sections of the city as streets were turned into torrential rivers, running floorboard high on parked cars. The Scharbauer Hotel lobby was ankle deep in water, and the basement of the County Courthouse, where several offices are located, was flooded and the water was still rising about 1:30 p.m."[21]

So great was the downpour that the Midland unit of the Texas State Guard was dispatched. Odessa was largely spared, and city officials there sent many emergency vehicles to assist Midland in its cleanup and rescue operations. The Texas Highway Patrol even prevented people from driving into Midland by closing the entrances into town on Highway 80 and Interstate 20.

A woman went into labor in the lobby of Parkview Hospital on the city's east side as medical personnel attempted to find a way to transport her to Midland Memorial. Parkview had no obstetrics facilities.

Water rose five feet in the basement of the U.S. Post Office downtown, and the phone company reported receiving almost 300 calls of disrupted service, most of which amounted to slow dial tones and busy signals that sounded before callers finished dialing.

H. D. Neighbors, a forty-six-year-old salesman from Lubbock, was the only fatality in the storm. A chilling account of his last moments was published in the *Midland Reporter-Telegram* the following day:

> [Neighbors] was killed when his auto was washed off West U.S. 80 and into a draw running along the side of the highway at Midland Drive. Two Dallas men had a narrow escape on West U.S. 80 at the same time Neighbors was killed. Dave Stewart and Quinn Porterfield said they were driving east on the highway alongside Neighbors's car. Both cars stopped when the water became too deep to drive through.
>
> The Dallas men carried on a conversation with Neighbors and both drivers decided to back up until the swiftly running water subsided. The Dallas car backed up about ten feet when a torrent of water came rushing across the highway. Both autos were swept into the draw. Neighbors's car was thrown into a railroad trestle and he became trapped inside.[22]

Several days later, when the waters had receded and the damages began to be assessed, the *Midland Reporter-Telegram* reported that total rainfall in some areas had topped seven inches, although the official amount recorded by the National Weather Service was 4.75 inches. "Soaked carpets were strung across fences and some were even spread on rooftops to dry. Furniture was stacked outside or hauled to storage places until water and silt could be removed from residence interiors. Fences were crumpled and lawns covered with debris. All available units were pressed into service to pump water from areas where homes still were underwater, particularly in the Wadley-Barron Park section on North A Street."[23]

Midland rancher Joe Mabee was on his ranchland north of town but drove into town sometime after the heavier rainfall had begun to let up. He remembers clearly helping kids at Hillander School "get out of cars that were floating." Craig Hubbard, a Midland landman, was in junior high at the time and clearly remembers sitting in class and watching the football field at the school become slowly immersed by the floodwaters. One of Hubbard's friends, longtime Midlander Jack Swallow, had his own unique recollection of that wet day. "I remember they were planting trees in front of Midland High School. Even though it was raining like crazy, at the Youth Center, across Illinois, they were serving lunch that day. I remember we were all standing in the trophy room at the front of the school watching the rain come down. We were dumbfounded. We watched two guys take off running toward the Youth Center. They had dug the holes for those trees but hadn't put the trees in them yet, and all of a sudden you saw these two guys who were running just disappear. Both of them hit the holes and went down and the water was over their heads."[24]

Swallow said another classmate who drove a fancy pinkish-purple Oldsmobile hardtop forgot to roll up his windows before class that morning. When he returned to his car after school, water was "flush up to the windows," Swallow said.

The flood of 1968 also brought a biblical invasion of frogs. As Hubbard recalled: "The parks in Midland are recessed for drainage purposes, and there are frogs that live in those parks. When it dries up, the frogs go into the mud and hibernate. When it rains, particularly that rain, they come out. We used to sleep with our windows open at night, and we lived half a block from Hill Park. I had to shut my windows because the frogs were so loud."[25]

"It was deafening," added Swallow, a neighbor of Hubbard's in 1968.

Lloyd McDonald remembers being in his office at Fitzgerald & Kerr, in the basement of the Midland Tower building. "It just rained and rained and rained. I had a VW and I had parked it at a meter on Missouri Street downtown. After it let up and I thought we could get to our cars, I saw that it had floated out into the center of Missouri Street. When I finally made my way home, as best I could, I had to find the highest ground to 1600 Harvard. I had to drive past Wadley-Barron Park on A Street, and it was of course impassable."[26]

Part One: A Place with Character

The floodwaters had risen to the second level of a house across from Wadley-Barron Park, which at the time belonged to the director of the Midland-Odessa Symphony and Chorale. The two-story house often floods in heavy rains, even today, and on that May day in 1968, the high waters lifted the home's grand piano off the floor and turned it over.[27]

"On the south end of Wadley-Barron Park at the same time, a woman drove her car off Cuthbert Street into a low area." McDonald said a man rescued the woman and brought her to safer, higher ground, but when she got there, she turned around and walked back toward her waterlogged car.

"Where are you going?" the man pleaded with the woman.

"My husband told me if I ever left my headlights on again I was in big trouble," she was reported to have said.

Ike Fitzgerald ran a golf driving range across from Ranchland Hills Country Club and had seen enough storms to know it was time to head home the day it hit. " I was at the golf course and I could see the clouds building. I knew what was coming," Fitzgerald said. "It came in from the north as I remember, and I got in the car and came home. It still took a good time to get home because it had already started."

Although Judge John Hyde had not yet moved to Midland when the heavy rains fell, his research turned up a couple of significant anecdotes, which he often shared during his history presentations. "The [*Midland Reporter-Telegram*] had a rain gauge on its roof, and it had close to ten inches in it. All areas within the city recorded rain of significant proportions, and later the City of Midland hired engineers to do a study on the intensity of the storm. It was determined that the event was a 300-year rain."[28]

chapter 5

How Midland Became the Oil Capital of West Texas

Oil has caused a transformation and has remade part of West Texas, where landowners have increased their bank accounts, and towns and cities have sprung up where there were formerly only bald prairies. The Santa Rita well gave new hope to the whole West Texas territory and with its discovery a new era was born.
—Texas State Historical Commission

Exactly what is the Permian Basin, and why does it have so much oil and gas? Who was Santa Rita, and why would anyone name an oil well after a saint? Finally, how did one oil well, two buildings, and a San Angelo rainstorm interact in the 1920s to make Midland the (perhaps improbable) oil capital of West Texas?

Hidden Underground Riches in the Permian Basin

The Permian Basin is a vast area of West Texas and southeastern New Mexico, rich in oil and gas deposits. It covers about 75,000 square miles, an area roughly one-quarter of the size of the entire state of Texas, and is named for the geologic time period during which many of its rocks formed.

Earth scientists believe that during the Permian period, between about 299 million and 251 million years ago, the area that became the Permian Basin was low in elevation and was covered by the Permian Sea for millions of years. Microscopic organisms that lived and died in that sea settled to the bottom in layers,

Part One: A Place with Character

where they mingled with minerals. Some of these minerals were washed into the basin from the surrounding land, while others were precipitated from the high mineral content of the sea's water.

As more layers accumulated, earlier layers were buried deeper. Gradually, over millions of years, the pressure from the weight of the rock layers and sea above combined with the heat of Earth's interior below to cause a chemical change in the remains of the microscopic organisms. They became hydrocarbons: compounds of hydrogen and carbon, including the natural gas and oil that we rely on as important sources of energy today.

An Oil Gusher Named for a Saint

Frank T. Pickrell, who drilled the Santa Rita oil well, might have been almost as surprised as Saint Rita herself by the impact of his discovery during the coming century—not only for Midland, but for many other West Texas communities as well.

Who Was Santa Rita?

Rita lived in a small village called Cascia in fifteenth-century Italy. She begged her parents to allow her to enter a convent, but instead they arranged for her to be wed. Finding herself in an eighteen-year marriage to a tempestuous husband, Rita prayed and received the sacraments of the Catholic Church faithfully and frequently, and tried desperately to fulfill her wifely duties to a man who constantly mistreated her.[1] He even taught the couple's two sons to treat her badly too. Still, Rita prayed for them all.

One day her husband was mortally wounded in a fight. Before he died, he was able to repent. Rita had never stopped praying for that repentance, and she continued to pray for the repentance of her two sons. Both of them also died before their mother.[2]

After their deaths she prayed that she might suffer like Christ. She entered an Augustinian convent and lived out her days in prayer, fasting, and penance. For never giving up her faith despite the most difficult of circumstances, she came to be regarded by Roman Catholics as the patron saint of impossible causes.[3]

Catholics celebrate her feast day every year on May 22, the anniversary of her death in 1457.

How Midland Became the Oil Capital of West Texas

Why Santa Rita Had an Oil Well Named for Her

On May 28, 1923, six days and 466 years after Saint Rita's passing, the oil gusher that opened the door to West Texas petroleum prosperity came in at a camp town named Texon, built at a wide spot in the road about an hour's drive south of Midland by today's standards. Camp towns were temporary settlements built by oil companies at a particular drilling site for employees and their families. Houses, schools, entertainment venues, sports facilities, a movie theater, a grocery store, a dry goods store, and even a swimming pool were built just for employees of Texon Oil. When the oil supply was exhausted, people relocated to other areas, and the town site was largely abandoned. All that remains today is a very small field office for another oil company not affiliated with Texon Oil.

Pickrell, president of Texon Oil Company, directed the activities at the Texon camp town that led to the spudding and drilling of the Santa Rita.[4]

Since it was far too early to speculate on whether oil was possible or not in West Texas, some may wonder why invoke the patron saint of the impossible? According to the Texas State Historical Commission's book entitled *Santa Rita*, "During the early days of financing, Pickrell interested a group of Catholics in his Texas project. Either cautious by nature or saddened by the ways of oil in previous speculations, they sought the advice of a priest, who, apparently no less skeptical, admonished them to invoke the aid of Rita, Saint of the Impossible."[5] When the well was actually discovered, Pickrell named it after her.

The Santa Rita's Lasting Impact on West Texas

"No other event has had [such a] lasting effect on the economy of Midland as the discovery of the rich oil and gas deposits throughout the Permian Basin," said Judge John Hyde. "When the Santa Rita well blew in, in Reagan County, the economy of the Permian Basin changed forever. [All these] years later, the ancient seabed on which Midland sits continues to sustain the economy. The hydrocarbons trapped beneath the surface throughout the basin have brought population, prosperity, and technological advances to many of us. Today, new techniques to coax petroleum to the surface have revitalized leases that were once thought depleted. Rightly so, because the quest to supply petroleum for America's insatiable appetite for gasoline-powered vehicles is unending."[6]

Other discoveries vital to oil in West Texas—including fields in McCamey and Scurry Counties and the Yates Field near Iraan—would play important roles in the early days, but none would have quite the lasting impact of Santa Rita. For it was after

PART ONE: A PLACE WITH CHARACTER

that first big discovery that bold investors like T. S. Hogan, Clarence Scharbauer, and Dr. John B. Thomas would commit resources to buildings in downtown Midland that bore their own names to attract oil professionals here. As Roger M. Olien and Diana Davids Hinton phrased it in their book *Wildcatters: Texas Independent Oilmen*, "Overnight, what had been foolhardy became visionary."[7]

The winning combination of the Santa Rita, the Scharbauer Hotel, and the Hogan Building revolutionized Midland simply by attracting oilmen. When they and their children and grandchildren stayed here and drilled for future petroleum reserves (Spraberry in the 1940s and 1950s and the Wolfberry, Wolfbone, and Cline Shale today being just four examples), the independent spirit that came with the early movers and shakers in the industry was forged. That spirit has grown and weathered storms and clearly shaped who we have become since those earliest years.

The Scharbauer Hotel: Gracious Hospitality and Countless Deals

The Scharbauer was not just any hotel; it was one of the finest hotels in Texas. It was also—and remains in its absence—an important piece of Midland history. An overnight resting place for oil-industry professionals and businessmen, the Scharbauer was a significant community landmark where deals were made, and where clients, prospects, and friends shared meals and determined futures. Thirty-four years after its doors opened, F. W. Barnett, the manager of the hotel in 1962, said the Scharbauer was "a complete city under one roof."[8]

A Hotel Built on Profits from Whiteface Cattle
Clarence Scharbauer built the hotel on profits made from whiteface cattle, according to Scharbauer Jr. Perhaps one of the most remarkable aspects of the hotel was that Scharbauer paid the construction bills as they were incurred, using money from his cattle operation in a "pay as you go" venture. The family didn't have income from oil until 1938, almost ten years after the hotel had opened its doors. It featured 150 rooms at its opening, and by 1931 another 100 rooms were added, largely due to the increase in oil-field activity in the Permian Basin.

The Scharbauer Lobby: *The* Place to Make Deals
"Every club that met, every convention and event in town was held at the Scharbauer. It was the place in Midland for many years," Scharbauer Jr. said in 1985. "Every major

deal that was ever made in Midland was probably made in the Scharbauer Hotel. It was the place to make deals."[9]

The Scharbauer's lobby was ranchlike with a flagstone fireplace and continual activity; the legendary room bested anyplace else in the country for livestock sold and oil deals made. *Life* magazine, which would make a Midland Army Airfield bombardier the subject of one of its covers in 1942, returned in 1948 and wrote that oil deals totaling over $50 million a month were made in the hotel's lobby.

Clarence Scharbauer Jr. said his father loved making money in cattle and oil, but just as much he loved seeing other people make money. It didn't bother the elder Scharbauer if other people made more than he did, according to his son.

"Much was made about oilmen having their own chair in the lobby," said Scharbauer Jr., "but that was never really the case. Many did have their favorite spot in which to sit and hold court but it was a public lobby. There were a lot of truckers that hung out in that lobby."[10]

Visitors often remarked that the Scharbauer was the busiest hotel lobby in the country, with constant conversation and people coming in and out all day, most of them wearing Stetsons and boots. The Scharbauer's decorations and furnishings were comparable to those of other well-known, big city hotels, but the atmosphere was certainly different. A lobby painting of Scharbauer Jr. depicted the businessman and empire heir as a simple, hard-working cowboy on horseback, waving his hat.[11]

Judge Hyde said it would be impossible to [discuss Midland's history] without including the role of the Scharbauer Hotel and [the] family responsible for it. "When it was built, they had bellhops who helped people in and out of the hotel," Hyde said. "One day, soon after its opening, the bell stand was particularly busy with guests. So a man who happened to be in the lobby saw a couple and helped them take their luggage to the room. The guest tried to tip the man but had no luck. 'But don't you work here?' the guest asked. That helpful man was Clarence Scharbauer himself, who reportedly said, 'No, I don't. I own this hotel.'"[12]

An Inviting Place to Woo Job Prospects

Midland and the Permian Basin have long had their detractors just as they have had their supporters. Some people come for a visit, see the lack of beauty in the land (forgetting, perhaps, that they are in the desert. According to *Santa Rita*, published by the Texas State Historical Commission, oilmen "did not look kindly on the Permian Basin after having explored much and found little."[13]

Part One: A Place with Character

John Bartlett, the head of the U.S.–Mexican Border Commission, once said of the Permian Basin, "It can never be rendered useful for man or beast save for a public highway."[14] According to Judge John Hyde, even Randolph Marcy, the first white man to set foot in the area in 1849, believed the area was not then and never would be "anything but uninhabitable."[15]

And of course, through the decades, there has been one frequently told story about Midland and its need for an exterior facelift. Oil companies have supposedly flown prospects into town after dark and put them up in the finest hotel downtown so that when they wake in the morning, they see the physical attractiveness of the downtown area itself. Once hands shake and prospect becomes employee, the family takes its tour and begins to get a glimpse of the flat, brown desert that lies beyond the city-limit signs. But by then it is too late.

Though oil-company prospects were not flown in during the 1920s, they were provided overnight accommodations at what was for decades one of the finest hotels in the state.

A Penthouse with a Dog, and Sometimes a Pony

As plush and famous as the lobby was for deal making, the penthouse may even have one-upped it. "It was as fine a penthouse as you would find anywhere in Texas," said Scharbauer Jr., who lived on the uppermost floor from the time he was three years old until he was married. "We had eighteen to twenty rooms with big patios. I had a large playroom on the north end and had my own Boston bulldog, Billy Bob, up there, and on occasion I even slipped my pony up the back elevator to the penthouse. I never thought it strange, living in a penthouse on the top of a hotel. It was just home."[16]

The Hogan Building and Its Colorful Builder, "Mr. Midland"

Thomas S. Hogan was born in Chippewa Falls, Wisconsin, in 1869. He was a state senator and secretary of state from Montana,[17] who declared Lubbock his official residence for many years, spent much of his life on the West Coast, died in Los Angeles, and was buried in El Paso. Why, then, would someone so well traveled come to be known as "Mr. Midland" and "Midland's Living Legend," as he was hailed in his September 27, 1957, obituary in the *Dallas Morning News?*

Simple. Hogan was one of the first men to visualize Midland as something more than a one-horse ranching town. Somehow, from his Montana home, he was

How Midland Became the Oil Capital of West Texas

able to see that Midland was perfectly positioned to be the center of the growing oil industry.[18]

By funding the construction of the Hogan Building in 1929, T. S. Hogan and his son Fred gave Midland a giant boost toward becoming the oil capital of the Permian Basin. The Hogan Building would play a pivotal role in the town's future—so much so that eighty-five years later Midlanders should still be thanking T. S. Hogan for his foresight.

Though Hogan spent only a short time here, by electing him to the Hall of Fame, the Permian Basin Petroleum Museum honored him for his important contribution and all it has brought to Midland and the Permian Basin. The Hogan Building (later also called the Shell Building and the Petroleum Building) is now considered Midland's primary historical landmark.

A Visionary in a Leather Coat and Tall Leather Boots

Judge John Hyde said in 2011, "T. S. Hogan was quite the visionary. He came out here in his riders' pants, knee-length leather boots, and a leather coat; he looked almost like Indiana Jones. If there was ever a rugged individual, he was, but he also saw something about Midland. People always wondered why not San Angelo or Odessa? But . . . [it was his vision of Midland] that helped capitalize on the oil industry."[19]

T. S. Hogan himself once said, "Everybody thought Big Spring would be the center of the oil business, or maybe San Angelo. But we were convinced that it would be further west, largely because of our study of geological information, which defined what now is the Permian Basin."[20]

Construction, Grand Opening, and the "Human Fly"

Hogan came to Midland in 1925, and his first big oil deal was the sale of the 74,000-acre John T. McElroy Ranch in Crane and Upton counties for $3 million.[21] Four years later the Hogans funded the construction of the twelve-story Hogan Building and the adjoining Yucca Theatre. Both still stand at the intersection of Colorado and Texas Avenues and are in use today. (The history of the Yucca Theatre is described more fully in Chapter 10.)

Construction took 284 working days, an average of nine hours a day with a crew of seventy-five men per day. Hogan's weekly payroll on the project was $6,000. When the building opened, it was 87 percent leased by thirty-four major and independent oil companies. Thousands of invitations were sent out throughout the

Southwest when the Hogan Building staged its formal opening.[22]

Midlanders admired the new structure, and it gave them hope for their town's future. "Build it, and they will come" was the overriding thought. Hogan capped off his accomplishment by hosting a lavish grand opening.

James Mims, now in his nineties, was at the opening of the building. "When they dedicated it, they had a fellow climb up all twelve stories on the outside. On the top floor he had a 4x4 clamped over the corner, above the street, and an inner tube around him. He was up there cavorting on that thing for the longest time. It was spooky. They called him the Human Fly."[23]

Many West Texas historians agree: were it not for the vision and subsequent contribution of T. S. Hogan, early oil-industry professionals very well might have established their base of operations in San Angelo or Colorado City or Odessa. They chose Midland because the Hogan Building offered ample office space, and because the Scharbauer Hotel offered a place for them to rest for the night.

For Once, Midland Has a *Lucky* Dry Spell

One other factor that led Midland to becoming the center for the petroleum industry in the Permian Basin was, ironically, the weather.

In 1928, Honolulu Oil's president visited his company's San Angelo headquarters. A prime objective of his trip was to make site visits to Honolulu's drilling operations in the oil fields that surrounded San Angelo. Instead, company officials were stuck in a hotel for three days in Angelo, unable to travel to the wells. Heavy rain for three days had made the unpaved routes to the wells impassable.[24]

Much as Midland's ranchers and cattle might have envied and welcomed that amount of rain either then or now, it may have proved one of the only times in Midland history when a dearth of rainfall was actually beneficial for the Tall City.

A company geologist explained what happened next. "The president came in with a map and told us, 'There's a little town up here by the name of Midland,' he said. 'It's in the geographical center of this oil play. They have a nice hotel there and a fellow by the name of Senator Hogan, whom I personally knew in Montana, is building an office building. Whether you like it or not, you are moving to Midland.'"[25]

Midland's population had risen to 5,484 by 1930, a figure that represented an increase of 67 percent from a decade earlier. The city's future looked bright.

The Great Depression: Oil Prices Fall Sharply

Unfortunately, Midland was not immune to the effects of the Great Depression, even though the economic trickle-down was somewhat delayed. A mere four months after the Hogan Building's lavish opening came the infamous crash of Wall Street, and within weeks the building was nearly vacant. Tenants moved out—often in the middle of the night—and broke long-term leases they had only recently signed. Such an exodus of rental income forced Hogan to turn over the building to Mercantile National Bank of Baltimore, which carried a $600,000 mortgage. (Shell Oil would later purchase the building, and even today some refer to it as the Shell Building.[26]) Some Midlanders started calling the structure Hogan's Folly because it sat empty after being so highly anticipated and promoted a few months earlier.

Old-timers alive today still argue about whether Hogan's Folly was in fact used to store hay. Judge Hyde would often state in his presentations that the building was used for this purpose, citing records, photos, and several conversations with longtime Midlanders.

"It never happened," said James Mims. "It makes a good story, but it never happened."

Even though only 25 percent occupied, the building remained open. Lawsuits never materialized for unpaid rent because Depression-era hard times swept the country and affected virtually everyone.[27]

By the early 1930s, with the stock market in the tank, the Permian Basin was faced with sharply dwindling oil prices that at their lowest reached 10 cents a barrel. Production also tailed off during the skid, and almost a third of Midland's workforce was unemployed. With prices at historically low levels, "operators had no incentive to expand their production," wrote Samuel D. Myres. "In fact, the prices that prevailed for some four years were hardly sufficient to maintain production already established."[28]

Oilmen used the Depression to conduct geological surveys in hopes of finding oil-rich areas where they could raise the money to drill whenever the country finally pulled itself out of its doldrums. Smaller towns in the area, such as McCamey, Wink, and Hobbs, faced the exodus of hundreds of families that suddenly found themselves on the brink of financial collapse because of the downturn in drilling brought by the low prices. Many left for the suddenly oil-rich fields of East Texas, according to Myres, who wrote that during the Depression, "an eerie silence fell over

Part One: A Place with Character

the fields and oil towns of West Texas and Southeast New Mexico. The Depression closed in and held the region in its relentless grasp."[29]

Positive Thinking from Midland's Chamber of Commerce

As any Chamber of Commerce president worth his salt would do, Paul Vickers talked up Midland as the economy languished in those difficult years of the early 1930s. He did not have an easy job, promoting a town that was suffering like many others during the Depression. Vickers, though, did yeoman's work in selling Midland not only as the oil capital of West Texas, but its cattle capital too, and the potash capital of America. He praised Midland's merits as an airport town, a farm town, a school town, and "one of the very greatest hotel cities," while making absolutely certain that people knew there was plenty of water:

> Midland has 40,000 acres in cultivation and 360,000 acres of fertile but cheap land waiting for the cotton and grain sorghums farmer. Poultry, stock raising and dairying are growing industries. Two ice cream factories take all milk....
>
> Midland has every modern city convenience. Midland has two long-distance phone systems, two telegraph systems, in short Midland is a thoroughly modern city....
>
> Midland's present available water supply is five times more than is needed. Move to Midland where you can have all the water you want to drink, swim in, use on your trees and flowers and water your lawn. Midland has an unlimited supply of good water.[30]

Gradual Recovery Begins

By the winter of 1934, the nation and the Permian Basin had started to dig out, and the tall structures built in downtown Midland began to fill, finally allowing the city to take advantage of its reputation as the oil capital of West Texas. Oil companies resumed exploration and production efforts again. Twenty-five new fields were discovered in 1934 and 1935, including the Goldsmith Field in Ector County, second in production only to the Yates Field.[31] Government regulations on production, and a new tariff placed on foreign oil to cut back on the dumping of cheap oil on the American market, helped pave the road to recovery.[32] By 1935 the worst was over. When oil companies began to return to Midland in 1936, Hogan's Folly had returned to the fame and glory it had promised seven years earlier. [33]

How Midland Became the Oil Capital of West Texas

Humble Oil Helps Lead Midland Out of the Depression

As the effects of the Depression continued to ease in the mid-1930s, Humble Oil Company's decision to move seventy houses and many of its employees to Midland from McCamey in 1935 helped establish Midland as the oil center.[34]

Humble gave Midland its largest single-event population increase with the relocation not only of employees but their living quarters as well. "Not until the second boom [in the 1930s] did the Hogan Building justify the man and his vision. Oil companies needed space. Big Spring and San Angelo competed to become the center, but the oil companies along with associated drilling contractors and well-servicing companies came to Midland where an almost empty office building was ready and waiting," John Howard Griffin wrote.[35] Thanks in part to Humble's move, Midland's population exploded to 9,352 at the dawn of 1940, an increase of more than 70 percent in just one decade.[36]

As market conditions improved and area drilling activity increased in the latter half of the 1930s, the Permian Basin oil and gas community in Midland also grew because scientists and landmen employed by major oil companies were tempted to go independent.[37]

Frank Haag: Versatile Public Servant During the 1930s

Benjamin Franklin Haag was a Midland County attorney, school board member, Methodist church steward, Mason, Rotarian, Midland mayor, and state representative. According to surviving daughter-in-law Merle Haag, he was being groomed by Governor Coke Stevenson to become a future Texas governor himself. Yet surprisingly little is known about one of Midland's earliest persons of influence.

Building Good Roads

Haag had the foresight to understand the crucial importance of good roads and highways. He was primarily responsible for the paving of highways that led into and out of Midland. As his son Merwyn wrote in a short biography after his father's death:

> He expressed his concerns to forward-looking people about the need for better roads between Midland and other West Texas towns.... He realized that it did not matter how great a town you had: if it was not accessible by a good system of roads, growth would be minimal [and] he set out to

make his concerns known not only to the people of Midland but to the citizens of neighboring towns. Therefore, the first order of business for the new Midland Chamber of Commerce was to formulate a good plan for a system of roads leading into and out of Midland to the areas where oil and gas were being drilled and discoveries were being made.[38]

Frank Haag's influence helped establish State Highway 349, north to Lamesa and south to Rankin; State Highway 158, east to Sterling City and west to Andrews; Farm Roads 1379, 3059, 259; Farm Road 1555 to Texon; and Farm to Market 1788 to Andrews.[39]

Former Midland Chamber of Commerce communications manager Bruce Partain wrote in July 2001, "As our area developed, Mr. Haag worked to ensure safe, speedy access to the oilfields. State Highways 158 and 349 probably would have not developed at the speed required by the fast-moving oil industry without Mr. Haag's assistance and promotion."[40]

Ensuring Adequate Water Supply

Haag was also one of the first early residents to realize that soon enough, Midland would face a challenge with its water supply. "He knew that in order to make the city attractive for oil companies, their employees and families, the town must have a water supply of sufficient quantity and storage capacity," according to daughter-in-law Merle Haag, ninety-two.

As mayor at the time of the dawn of the oil era in the 1920s, Haag seized upon the opportunity to develop an adequate water supply. When he took office it was impossible to produce more than 240,000 gallons of water every twenty-four hours. The city's average storage capacity maxed out at only 125,000 gallons. With the city water supply used primarily in those days by businesses, schools, and fire protection (most residents had their own windmills for private use), Haag launched a project to develop a supply that would meet the needs of a town not of 3,000, but of 30,000.

Under his direction, the city of Midland negotiated a deal in which the city purchased Cloverdale Farms, a settlement with an adequate water supply. By the end of his term in 1929, Haag had ensured that the citizens of Midland had a water system that could produce 500,000 gallons of water per day, and a potential of supplying as much as 1 million gallons a day. Haag's forward thinking also provided the city with a storage capacity for 1.1 million gallons.[41] (For more about Midland's more recent efforts to obtain adequate water, see Chapter 21.)

Developing Commerce, Schools, and Public Relations

Frank Haag was also concerned about commerce in the region. He saw West Texas as a place with much potential. He was the first president of the Midland Chamber of Commerce and also played a vital role in developing chambers of commerce in several other small West Texas towns.

Haag is also credited with helping establish a new high school in Midland. He served for six years on the Midland school board and believed providing children with a quality education was not only one of a community's greatest responsibilities, but one of its greatest duties.

Frank Haag was the mayor of Midland when Senator T. S. Hogan and his son, Fred, visited several West Texas communities. These entrepreneurs were investigating the Permian Basin, determining which town would be progressive enough to support the construction of a twelve-story office building for the incoming oil companies. Mayor Haag and his colleagues must have made a positive impression, because the Petroleum Building and Yucca Theatre were built in Midland.

Haag's Ironic, Untimely Death

Fellow legislators described Frank Haag as a man who showed rare promise. Sadly, that promise was cut short by his death at the age of only forty-seven.

It was Haag's work securing better roads and highways around Midland that ultimately led to his death in an automobile accident, a tragic irony. He and three others—Clarence Scharbauer, County Judge Elliott H. Barron, and Paul Vickers—were returning to Midland after a meeting with the state highway commission in Austin, where Haag had been to lobby for better highways in the area. The vehicle he was driving crested a hill northwest of Sterling City. An oncoming pipe truck crossed the center stripe. Haag swerved out of the way and overcorrected, rolled the truck three times, and he was ejected. According to the *Midland Reporter-Telegram*:

> Scharbauer said the machine was being driven at about 45 mph when the truck was struck, and when the car overturned Haag was thrown about 40 feet away, through the top. All were rendered unconscious and when consciousness returned, Scharbauer and Judge Barron were tightly wedged in the back seat and Vickers, in front, had one leg through the top. Those in the back seat assisted Vickers out and when it was determined he was not seriously injured, began a search for Haag.[42]

PART ONE: A PLACE WITH CHARACTER

He died on July 13, 1933, of a skull fracture as a result of the car accident.[43]

"Representative Haag was my friend and a friend to everyone," said Clarence Scharbauer. "He was progressive and fought for the common good as few men have done. His death is a blow to us all."[44]

Midland attorney Frank Stubbeman wrote that when his colleague and friend died, every business establishment in Midland closed, certainly a testament to Haag's character and contributions.[45]

The Petroleum Club of Midland

The roots of the Petroleum Club of Midland stretch back to the 1930s, when oilmen would meet in the Scharbauer Hotel's coffee shop. Before long there were more men than chairs, and the powers that guided the gathering of geologists, engineers, wildcatters, and executives decided they needed a permanent place to call home and hold court. On December 1, 1947, the Petroleum Club was officially chartered, and its membership was instantly 200. The group bought the Wolcott Home, built in 1917 for the Wolcott family and located at the corner of Big Spring Street and Illinois Avenue. They continued to meet there until 1980, when the club's current marbled-exterior downtown location, at Marienfeld and Wall Streets, was built.

The Honest John Table

The club was described by Tom Sealy, one of its original members, as a luncheon group focused on the petroleum industry. One of its earliest traditions was something called the Honest John Table.

"The waitress brings the check and hands it to Reese Cleveland," recalled Sealy in a 1985 article in the *Midland Reporter-Telegram*. "Reese writes a letter of the alphabet on the envelope. Then he calls on someone at the table and they say a letter of the alphabet and the entire table [continues saying the alphabet, going around in] sequence. Whoever says the [correct] letter has to buy lunch."[46] It could be [a costly] hour for the lucky soul on whom lunch fell, but these were oilmen, after all.

The Honest John tradition stretches back even to the days when the club met at the Scharbauer's coffee shop. Most of the men who frequented the group were bachelors, and the game was begun to help some of the more meagerly incomed oilmen. The men who sat at the Honest John Table at the Scharbauer Hotel are still considered the Petroleum Club's charter members.

The Club's Years at the Wolcott Home

The Petroleum Club thrived during its thirty-two years in the Wolcott Home.

According to a 2009 article in the *Midland Reporter-Telegram* by historian Bill Modisett, the Wolcott Home was named for George Wolcott, who was raised in the Dallas area but moved to West Texas as a young adult. A rancher for several years, he married and moved to Martin County in 1895. The home built for the family on its move to Midland in 1917 was modern to the point of having a vacuum cleaner, a household item virtually unheard of at the time.

Falling membership and a revitalization of downtown Midland prompted the club to relocate into its present facility in 1980, and the Wolcott Home was soon destroyed. However, the current Petroleum Club has experienced a resurgence of members because of a wave of petroleum-related prosperity brought on by the recent increase in hydraulic fracturing and horizontal drilling. Today the club plays host not only to oilmen but to lavish, exclusive dinner parties. Nonprofit organizations frequently host luncheons, dinners, annual meetings, and other special events there as well.

A Grand Old Hotel Goes Down Fighting

After Midland's most famous hotel had accommodated countless guests and hosted countless wheeler-dealers for forty-five years, Clarence Scharbauer Jr. made the decision to close and level the building because its upkeep had become uneconomical. In calling for its implosion, Scharbauer Jr. acknowledged that the building was a Midland landmark. A "Last Roundup at the Hotel Scharbauer," sponsored by the Midland County Historical Society, was celebrated on July 15, 1973, with an estimated 1,200 to 1,400 in attendance.[47.]

A favorite story of many longtime Midlanders is how stubbornly the old building resisted the idea that it was no longer needed.

An estimated 15,000 people gathered in downtown Midland on Sunday morning, October 28, 1973, to watch the hotel come down. At 9:02 a.m., dust from the first dynamite blast began to clear. Behind the wall of smoke emerged the hotel's south wing—virtually intact. The north wing, too, was damaged but still standing. "The shocked crowd and puzzled demolition crew that had cheered the explosion looked with awe and respect," the *Midland Reporter-Telegram* stated. "All realized the classy building that had been so much a part of Midland for forty-five years was

Part One: A Place with Character

not going to take her leave easily. Help from oil field rigging trucks, bulldozers and a second blast at 5:12 p.m. proved futile. By this time the crowd had begun to cheer for the hotel."[48]

The blasting foreman finally called off any additional attempts at dynamiting the structure. "No more blasting," he said. "We'll have to pull her down."[49]

Scharbauer Jr. remembered, "The south part of the hotel, which my mother and I had built, was a little stronger than the front part. The front part of the hotel daddy built was across the alley from First National Bank. He added another hundred rooms. Then my mother and I, in 1950, during the Spraberry boom, we added another 200 rooms down Loraine to Missouri. That hotel was a moneymaker for a while there. It stayed full."

When the demolition crew returned the next day, Monday, October 29, the building still refused to give way. Equipment breakdowns and numerous snaps of thick, 1½-inch steel cables were common. Little progress was made, even using a wrecking ball. Tuesday the same lack of progress was recorded.

On Wednesday, October 31, 1973, Halloween Day, the hotel finally gave way. "The foreman was heard saying, 'She's weaving now—about six inches to a foot every time we pull.'" At noon that day, the Scharbauer Hotel was finally reduced to a pile of rubble four days in the making.[50]

Clarence Scharbauer III was in his teens when the building was demolished and has his own memories of the establishment's final days and what it meant to the town. "People were very upset when they tore it down," Scharbauer III said. "But it was taking a quarter of a million dollars just to keep it open every quarter. It had 350 rooms, and only ten or eleven were being used at any one time."

Scharbauer III said in its final days, the hotel had become a "nooner," frequented by oilmen with their female guests during the workday, and although attempts were made to refurbish it, when the price tag came in at $8 million, the family decided instead to have it torn down.

In its stead a few years later, Hilton came to Midland, constructing a two-winged tower on the same ground where the Scharbauer had stood. Although a quality hotel still stands at the location, it is not the Scharbauer. Even so, "to have a Hilton hotel in your community in the 1970s was huge," Scharbauer III said.

chapter 6

THE SCHARBAUER LEGACY

I liken that family to the current that has carried this community. You don't see it, but it is carrying everything along. The Scharbauer family has been and is our current. They have done remarkable things.
—Rosalind Grover

THE SHARBAUERS HAVE BEEN one of the most important families in Midland since the town's earliest days. Clarence Scharbauer III says his grandfather was the most influential Scharbauer of all. While Christian Scharbauer had "the guts and foresight to come here and stick it out and get this thing going," Scharbauer III said, it was Christian's son, Clarence, who brought it all together in the early 1900s, not only for his own family but for many.

Clarence Scharbauer (1879–1942)

The first Clarence Scharbauer was involved in all aspects of the family business and most every aspect of the early community of Midland. He helped found a bank (First National), started the town's first radio station (KCRS), built a historic hotel, and was the founding member of Midland Country Club. "There wasn't anything he didn't start or do or go to," Scharbauer III said.[1]

Early Life
In 1889, when he was just ten years old, Scharbauer went to work for his uncle John on the family sheep farm and was put in charge of a herd near Stanton. He picked

63

PART ONE: A PLACE WITH CHARACTER

up sheepherding as if he had been born to it, and at age sixteen, he had a herd of cattle running under his own brand—the VXL. According to Griffin's book, "the older cowboys who worked with him said he commanded respect by being the first up in the morning, the hardest working and the last to retire at night. They soon forgot his youth."[2]

Scharbauer graduated from high school in Midland in 1898, briefly attended business school in Waco, and took a course at Baylor before returning home to help his father and uncle form the Scharbauer Cattle Company,[3] one of the longest-operated and most respected businesses in Midland since its founding.

Scharbauer married Ruth Cowden on December 1, 1908, joining together two families whose names remain among the most recognizable in Midland. They had two sons: John Christian, born in 1911, and Clarence Jr., born in 1925.

The elder Clarence Scharbauer became a noted leader among cattle ranchers, but life would change forever for the family when oil was discovered on its ranchland in 1935, bringing a level of wealth beyond what the family's ancestors could have ever imagined.

Rancher, Banker, Hotelier, Philanthropist

"Scharbauer took a scientific interest in improving Texas," Griffin wrote in *Land of the High Sky*. "The first to bring in registered Herefords, he established a ranch of more than 3,000 acres south of Midland."[4] By the time he died, Scharbauer owned ranchland in Gaines, Dawson, Martin, Midland, and Ector counties in Texas, and Lea and Chaves counties in New Mexico. Until his final illness confined him to his bed, he would visit at least one of his ranches every day.[5]

Bill Collyns, longtime editor of the *Midland Reporter-Telegram*, was one of Scharbauer's contemporaries and friends. "Mr. Scharbauer loved this place," he once said. "He really wanted to see Midland do well, and if people made money that was great. That's why he started the bank and the radio station [KCRS]. He wanted to see Midland thrive. He knew if Midland was going to do well, he was going to do well."[6]

Scharbauer was a significant provider for Midland. In addition to his cattle, he was involved in the hotel business even before financing the inn that would bear his name. He was a principal investor in the Llano Hotel downtown, and a leader in a number of civic organizations, including the Midland Chamber of Commerce. As a banker, and as a leader of First Baptist Church, Scharbauer assisted in the construction of virtually every bank and church in Midland.[7] He was also instrumental in improving roadways into and out of Midland during the early years of the oil industry.

The Scharbauer Legacy

Clarence Scharbauer Jr. remembered the story of how his father put bank depositors at ease with a simple yet grand gesture during the Great Depression. It was during a time of widespread economic uncertainty, when the people of Midland had begun to squirm about their financial security. "One day during the Depression," said Scharbauer Jr., "when people had started making runs on the bank and wanted to get their money, my daddy went in to work and put a lot of the bank's cash on tables in the First National Bank lobby, which was in that old white building that still stands at the corner of Wall and Main. When he put the money out on the table, a lot of people came down to the bank. And he would tell them, 'Now, any of you who feel like you want your money, here it is, we'll give it to you.' Of course when they saw they could access it, they didn't want it anymore. They were just afraid they couldn't get to it."[8]

Retellings of the story through history have suggested that armed guards stood alongside large Plexiglas containers, which securely held the cash. The total amount Scharbauer put out for the people to view also differs. Most versions say it was $250,000. Even Scharbauer Jr. himself was uncertain as to the exact amount but agreed it was likely $250,000.

One of Scharbauer's most generous gestures was the leasing of 450 acres of his land to the United States Army on July 1, 1941, so the country could establish an Air Force bombardier school.[9] "Scharbauer said he had no desire to sell a foot of his land but if the Army wanted it, it could have it," the *Midland Reporter-Telegram* said. "Scharbauer worked closely with Army officials and Midland civic leaders to aid the Army in every way and establish the big training school as quickly as possible."[10]

Illness and Death

After falling ill in 1941, Scharbauer visited the Mayo Clinic in Minnesota, where it was determined he had stomach cancer. Surgery was performed and doctors were optimistic he would recover, but a year later, he was sick again and returned to the clinic. This time, the prognosis was dire. Scharbauer was told he had no more than two months to live. So sick was he, in fact, that on the trip back to Midland, he developed yellow jaundice while on a stop in Fort Worth. Hopes for a recovery faded as his condition was, by now, quite serious.[11] Scharbauer died on October 2, 1942, in the penthouse apartment at the Scharbauer Hotel, surrounded by family, friends, and business associates. It was easy to see how widely admired the elder Scharbauer was just by reading his front-page obituary in the *Midland Reporter-Telegram*.[12] It opened in a manner befitting the pioneer leader:

Part One: A Place with Character

Clarence Scharbauer has gone down the trail. He would want no eulogies.... To him, supper at the chuckwagon after a hard day in the saddle meant more than a banquet. Roping, riding and branding held more allure for him than conducting his many successful businesses from a plush swivel chair.... Always actively interested in everything that would make Midland a better place in which to live, Scharbauer gave freely of his time and wealth for the betterment of the community.... Into scores of businesses he put his fortune and efforts, but he preferred to be known as a rancher, and the cowmen were always his friends. Many a friend of the range had damp eyes Friday when news of Scharbauer's death spread through the city he loved and helped build.[13]

Years before his death, Scharbauer had asked his friend Percy Mims to sing "When They Ring the Golden Bells" at his funeral. And it was done just as he had requested. His pallbearers read like a who's who of Midland: Roy Parks, Leonard Proctor, Jno. P. Butler, Marvin Ulmer, Ed Whitaker, Foy Proctor, E. P. Cowden, and Ralph Barron. Addison Wadley served as an attendant with the body as it lay in state before his funeral.[14]

The church was said to have assembled the most beautiful floral offering in the history of Midland, and mourners traveled hundreds of miles to pay their last respects.[15] Midland had lost its most prominent citizen to date, who had guided the town through so many of its community efforts.

Clarence Scharbauer Jr. (1925–2014)

The death of Clarence Scharbauer Sr. in 1942 hastened his teenage son Clarence Scharbauer Jr. into adulthood, perhaps before he was fully ready.

Early Adulthood

"I had gone down to Texas A&M, and when I left home, I knew he was going to die," Scharbauer Jr. said. "He was unconscious when I got home from A&M. I was just seventeen."[16]

Scharbauer Jr. said the last thing his father told him was, "Always be a gentleman."[17]

After his father's death, Scharbauer Jr. left college and moved in with his mother. Two years later, he was ready to sign up for a stint in the U.S. Navy, but the draft board told him he had no business going to war because of his father's death and because he was the sole male child remaining to carry on the family name. Still, he insisted on enlisting. "I went in for a couple of years; everyone wanted to go. I came home when I was twenty-one. We had ten ranches in the family and there was a lot to do, and they turned the whole business over to me. But Daddy left me in pretty good shape. I took it and ran with it," Scharbauer Jr. said.[18]

Rancher, Horse Breeder, Philanthropist
Scharbauer Jr. married Dorothy Turner on August 27, 1949, and together they raised four children: Clarence III, Douglas, Chris, and Pam.

Scharbauer Jr. continued the family's traditions of ranching and philanthropy. He loved horses and became a well-known breeder and championship horseman, collecting numerous honors, including membership in the American Quarter Horse Hall of Fame (1992) and the Texas Horse Racing Hall of Fame (2001). He received the Golden Spur Award for National Rancher of the Year (1991) and the lifetime achievement award from the Texas Thoroughbred Association (2007). In fact, the Texas Thoroughbred Association memorialized the famed horseman by renaming its Texas Stallion Series after Scharbauer Jr. in 2014.[19]

Midland philanthropist Rosalind Grover still remembers meeting Scharbauer Jr. for the first time. "My first recollection of Clarence Scharbauer Jr. was one evening when my mother took us to the Midland rodeo at the old fairgrounds," she said. "We were horse crazy, so she took us to the back to pet the horses. Clarence came up to us, doffed his hat, and said, 'Good evening, Mrs. Redfern.' I was so impressed with his manners and style. Now, sixty years later, of all the people from whom I have ever raised money, no one has ever given more generously and more graciously and with more style than Dorothy and Clarence Scharbauer." [20]

The Man Who Might Not Have Been
For all of his contributions to the city of Midland in the latter half of the twentieth century and into the twenty-first, Clarence Scharbauer, Jr. might never have been born, if not for a family tragedy in 1924.

Clarence and Ruth Scharbauer had a son before Clarence Jr. John Christian "J. C." Scharbauer was born in 1911. While the adolescent boy was working horseback at the family's Five Wells Ranch, J. C.'s horse fell on him and killed him. He was just thirteen. The horse reportedly stepped in a large hole on the ranchland, threw J. C., tumbled over, and landed on top of the young boy.

Part One: A Place with Character

"My mother always told me that Daddy nearly lost his mind," Scharbauer Jr. said. "They decided to have another baby. Daddy didn't care if it is was a boy or a girl."

Scharbauer Jr. said if not for the death of his brother, his parents would not have tried for more children.[21]

A Horseman's Last Hurrah

Scharbauer Jr. died from complications following emergency surgery in Midland on February 21, 2014. Fittingly, he had one final triumphant moment. Just a week before his death, he watched on the Internet as Fiftyshadesofgold, the final promising racehorse he owned, won the Texas Stallion Stakes at Sam Houston Park, in Houston.[22]

Horse breeder Ken Carson, manager of the Scharbauer-owned Valor Farms breeding facility in Pilot Point, Texas, said, "He got to see his filly win before he died, and that really pleased him. He was a great man, loved horses and loved horse racing. He loved horses like kids."[23]

Upon his father's passing, Clarence Scharbauer III said, "He loved Midland. This town will not likely soon forget the generosity and the mark that both he and my mother left on it in their years working together for Midland."[24]

A Champion Racehorse Named Alysheba

The Scharbauer family is most noted in horse-racing circles for having owned Alysheba, a former Horse of the Year, Breeder's Cup winner (1988), and winner of both the Kentucky Derby and the Preakness in 1987. Scharbauer Jr. was not the actual owner of Alysheba. Instead, the horse was co-owned by his wife, Dorothy, and their daughter, Pam.

In 1959, when she was twenty-eight years old, Dorothy Turner Scharbauer watched as her father's racehorse Tomy Lee won the Kentucky Derby by a nose. Tomy Lee, an American Thoroughbred sired by the famed Tulyar, had given his all in what was a controversial race. But after seventeen minutes of deliberations, track officials finally declared Tomy Lee the victor.

The horse's trainer, Frank Childs, said he did not like races that were held too close together, so he recommended that Tomy Lee not compete in the Preakness and Belmont. The horse was shut down until he finished sixth at the Cinema Handicap at Hollywood Park in Florida six weeks later.[25]

The Scharbauer Legacy

But the thrill of the race was in Dorothy Turner's blood by then. She had long expressed a desire to keep alive the Thoroughbred ownership started by her father. Her husband, Clarence Scharbauer Jr., was especially partial to quarter horses, but together he and Dorothy would leave a lasting imprint on riding sports and the horse-racing world.

A Yearling from Keeneland Park, Kentucky

Alysheba was perhaps the most significant living being in Midland history to have never set foot (or hoof) in West Texas.

To date, the home of Clarence Scharbauer Jr. is the only home—and Midland the only town—that has hosted two Kentucky Derby trophies: Tomy Lee's from 1959 and Alysheba's from 1987. The Scharbauer trophy cabinet and a nearby room devoted to the family's love of equine sports and big game is impressive in the sheer number of awards, mounted game, and other merits and distinctions.[26] But it was Alysheba that put Midland on the map simply by doubling the number of Derby championships that locally owned horses brought home in the most prestigious event of the sport of kings.

Alysheba was sired by Alydar out of the mare Bel Sheba. Described in racing circles as the best horse to have never won a major championship, Alydar is remembered as the only competitor in the history of Thoroughbred racing that placed in all three legs of the Triple Crown, finishing second to Affirmed in all three races in 1978.[27] The Scharbauer family, with Dorothy and daughter Pam listed as the horse's official owners, bought Alysheba for $500,000 when he was a yearling at Keeneland Park in Kentucky.

"A Great, Great Horse"

As good as Alysheba was in 1987, he was even better as a four-year-old in 1988, winning seven majors and six Grade I stakes that year, including the Santa Anita Handicap, the Meadowlands Cup, the Woodward Stakes, and the Breeder's Cup Classic. He was the U.S. Champion three-year-old in 1987, and Older Male Horse of the Year and U.S. Horse of the Year in 1988.

At the track, the horse won Pam and her mother $7 million. When he was finally retired, Alysheba would stand stud and produce eleven stakes winners. After breeding fees, he earned Pam and Dorothy Scharbauer close to $20 million.[28]

His trainer, the famed Jack Van Berg, said, "He was just a great, great horse. We never got to see the best of him. He'd do things you couldn't believe."[29]

PART ONE: A PLACE WITH CHARACTER

"The best horse that ever lived was Secretariat," Scharbauer Jr. said. "But without a doubt, Alysheba was the second-best horse we've ever seen. He was what you call free. He carried more weight. He went in carrying 126 [or] 128 pounds, and the other horses in the pack would be carrying 114 [or] 112 pounds."[30]

Alysheba was euthanized on Friday, March 27, 2009, due to what equine doctors referred to as "a chronic degenerative spinal condition that led to ataxia and instability. A fall by the famed horse the day before resulted in a break in his right hind femur, an injury it would not have been able to withstand due to severe pain and advancing years. He is buried at the Kentucky Horse Park's Hall of Champions across from the grave of John Henry, whom many enthusiasts of the sport hold to be the greatest horse of all time.[31]

"Michael Jordan in Horseshoes"

"You can't have an argument about the best horses in the last twenty-five years of the twentieth century and not include Alysheba. I always describe him as Michael Jordan in horseshoes," said Churchill Downs official Jack Asher.[32]

"I remember he was a heavy favorite in the Preakness, in front of a huge crowd," Scharbauer III said, "and when they led him out, here comes [Chris] McCarron on Alysheba by himself, and Alysheba got right in front of the stands and just stopped. Chris McCarron never messed with him, he just let him do what he wanted. Alysheba stopped and he turned and he stared at the crowd for, like, a minute, as if he was saying, 'That's right, I'm here. How you guys doing?' McCarron just sat on him, and four or five horses went around him. The crowd just went ballistic. It was the damnedest thing I ever saw."[33]

Clarence Scharbauer III (born 1951) and the Family's Continuing Legacy

The third Clarence Scharbauer is involved in numerous aspects of Midland life, including real estate development. He and his wife, Kerry (Wallace) Scharbauer, are also committed to the generations-old tradition of philanthropy, ensuring that the legacy set forth by the first Clarence Scharbauer will continue.

"When my grandfather died," Scharbauer III said, "he left half of everything he owned to his wife Ruth, my grandmother, and the other half to my dad. When Ruth died, she left that inheritance to me, Doug, Chris, and Pam—my brothers and sister—which meant that for all of our lives, we've been partners."³⁴ Of the four siblings, Clarence III and Doug still live in Midland.

Scharbauer III cites Luke 12:48 when speaking of his family: "From everyone to whom much is given, much shall be required." Scharbauer III said it has been by those words that his family has tried to live for more than three generations, quietly helping Midland in innumerable ways. Though too extensive to include in its entirety, the list of the family's philanthropic contributions includes:

★ The Scharbauer Sports Complex, built on land donated by the family.

★ Midland Memorial Hospital's new eight-floor tower, which opened in 2012, is named the Dorothy and Clarence Scharbauer Jr. Patient Tower after the family's $25 million contribution toward its construction. (For more about this, see Chapter 19.)

★ In 2012, the family established the Scharbauer Foundation. Bolstered by a substantial inheritance left by Ruth Scharbauer and Clarence Scharbauer Jr., nonprofit organizations and causes in Midland and West Texas will benefit from the family's generosity for literally generations.

But for all the money they have given and despite the roads, parks, streets, and structures that bear their name, a limited amount of the family legacy has been publicly preserved for historical purposes. A historical video was commissioned in the 1990s, voiced by noted Western narrator Red Stegall, but aside from that and assorted newspaper and magazine articles, there is very little else, which is how the family desires to be remembered, Scharbauer III said.

chapter 7

WASSAIL, GINGERBREAD, AND GENEROSITY

You could depend on [Jno. P. Butler, chairman of First National Bank]. He had a purpose. . . . No matter how tough the economy got, he never changed his methods: you always helped local people.
—Judge Mike Bradford

As with countless other cities across the United States, the Tall City's development and continued progress have often relied on its philanthropists and financial institutions. Midlanders tell stories of both First National Bank, on which this chapter will focus, and Midland National Bank, and how much the people who ran those lending establishments helped not only businesses and nonprofits in the city, but thousands of individuals who had a dream.

A Legendary Bank with Remarkable Leaders

First National Bank opened in 1890. The historical marker still visible today at the bank site says its first officers were A. W. Hilliard, president; W. H. Cowden, vice president; and W. E. Connell, cashier. It was chartered in 1900.

The success of an organization often trickles down from the top. First National Bank remains legendary in Midland, largely because its policies and culture were shaped by some of Midland's greatest leaders—particularly Jno. P. Butler, whose name was synonymous with First National Bank's for years.

Midland County Judge Mike Bradford was an employee at First National Bank in the 1970s. He said when talk arises of the most important people ever to serve

Midland, Butler is certainly among the top five or ten. And while some may see C. J. Kelly and not Butler as the mover and shaker at First National—"Mr. Kelly was diminutive in size but big in actions"—it was Butler who was, as Bradford put it, "the quiet ray of sunshine."[1]

Clarence Scharbauer

"My daddy was to Midland what Amon Carter was to Fort Worth," said Clarence Scharbauer Jr., invoking the name of a man well known for his civic involvement and philanthropy in that city. Scharbauer Jr. described how his father played a critical role at First National Bank since 1899 and made some key personnel decisions. "He hired Mr. [Marvin] Ulmer as his president. And he brought Mr. and Mrs. Jno. P. Butler to Midland."[2]

Marvin Ulmer

In January 1952, three days before the annual stockholders' meeting at First National Bank, one of Midland's most prominent citizens died. Marvin Ulmer had served as a banker, Midland mayor, and community leader.

"In his 45 years as a banker and civic leader, Ulmer helped guide the economic and cultural growth of the region," author Howard Griffin wrote. "During his presidency at the bank, he acknowledged that oil loans, once considered suspect, were desirable banking business. His shrewd liberality brought oil depositors to the bank, oil men to his board of directors and established oil loans as valid banking."[3]

Hailed as a "number one civic leader," Ulmer was among the great contributors to the progress of Midland in the early and middle part of the twentieth century. He also had the distinction of being sandwiched between Clarence Scharbauer and Jno. P. Butler, two of Midland's greatest leaders, while serving as president of First National Bank.

C. J. Kelly

Another of First National Bank's giant figures through the years was C. J. Kelly. David L. Smith recalled that Kelly was nearly as revered as Butler. Illness, though, cut his career short.

Ike Fitzgerald was a recipient of First National Bank's generosity and still remembers when Kelly loaned him money. "C. J. was the first person I ever borrowed money from," Fitzgerald said. "I went to him because I wanted to put in a skating rink. He didn't know too much about skating rinks. He asked me what I needed, and I said a 10,000-square-foot building."[4] Fitzgerald found the land, west of downtown, and paid $6,000 for a half block, money he obtained in the loan from Kelly.

Judge Dean Rucker, 318th District Court judge in Midland, still recalls C. J. Kelly from an incident when he was a teenager. "I remember when I was about sixteen or seventeen, I overdrew my checking account," Judge Rucker said. "Like a lot of other kids my age at that time, I thought as long as I had checks, I had money. My dad didn't think that was so funny. He told me to contact C. J. Kelly, and Mr. Kelly asked me to come down and visit with him. I was scared to death. But when I walked into his office, he sat me down and spent thirty minutes teaching me how to balance a checkbook. I never forgot that. That's just the kind of man he was."[5]

First National Bank was a community builder, fence mender, and peace bringer, yet it still might be surprising to know it was even capable of bringing those of opposing political parties together.

"The bank gave a whole lot of people the opportunity to do something," Ernest Angelo said. "I didn't fully appreciate that until I got away from it. C. J. Kelly was a pretty active Democrat, and Republican-party politics was my deal. I pretty much ate, drank, and slept politics. I owed money to the bank, too, but that's the thing I always appreciated: despite the huge political differences we had, I never had any problems on any loans. They never pressured me, and I came to really like C. J. and appreciate what he had done for the town."[6]

Jno. P. Butler: Banker, Friend, and Hero

Virtually no one else in Midland has garnered as much universal respect as Jno. P. Butler. When he died on October 20, 1997, Butler was hailed by longtime friend Bill Collyns, former editor of the *Midland Reporter-Telegram*, as one of Midland's top citizens. "It is hard to say how many lives he touched as a civic and banking industry leader," Collyns said.[7]

When Butler replaced Ulmer as president of First National Bank in 1952, he was already a known entity. Born to Hardin Richard Butler and Sophoronia Jane Butler in Mount Calm, Texas, in 1901, Butler married Alva Wallace and moved his family from Littlefield to Midland in 1927, when he started work as a teller at First National. He was promoted to cashier in 1942 and vice president/cashier in 1947.

"Father had been banking since he was about sixteen years old," said Butler's daughter, Jane McAbee. "He got his start at a little bank in Bosque County, near Waco. He graduated from high school but that was it. When he moved to Littlefield, he didn't like the job there because he said the president of the bank was involved in some practices he didn't like. Mr. Ulmer and Mr. Scharbauer gave him his job when he came here."[8]

By the time he was named chairman of the bank in 1963, Butler had served Midland as a city councilman, president of the Midland Chamber of Commerce, chair of the chamber's highway committee, director of the Texas Good Roads Association, president of the Midland Lions Club, chairman of the Vestry at Trinity Episcopal Church, director of Midland Country Club and vice president of the South Plains Bankers Association.[9] He was also a Shriner and a 32nd Degree Mason, and later he served on the board of directors of the Permian Basin Petroleum Museum, where he was named a Top Pioneer in 1975.[10] "It would be difficult to find anything in Midland that Jno. P. Butler was not involved in," said Bill Collyns. "Many organizations would not have made it if not for his help, and many businesses would not have made it without his financial support."[11]

The Bank That Never Said No

Butler knew exactly what he wanted to do with First National Bank, the kind of relationships he wanted to forge, and the future he wanted to set in motion in Midland. For the next three decades he did just that. He became one of the most respected figures in Midland's history by virtue of his leadership, strong character, and willingness to make Midland a better place simply through helping people achieve dreams.

"[Butler] had one philosophy: If the customer was local, the answer was never no," said Judge Mike Bradford, who moved to Midland in the 1970s after being offered a job by Butler. When Butler conveyed that philosophy to him, Bradford had to ask for clarification. "You mean say yes to *everyone?*" Bradford asked.

"He said again, 'The answer is never no.' He never told me to ask the customer how much they made or how little they made. The bank had ways to evaluate that. But he said, 'If it's the ladies' knitting club in Greenwood or the local association of grocery sackers in north Midland, we support them.'"

Bradford said he could remember only one time when the answer was no. It happened when a local group turned out to be more of a front for something else than a true business, someone just trying to get a little extra money in their pocket, Bradford recalled. "I told Mr. Butler, 'You said never say no, but here are the facts,'"

Bradford said. "So he came out of his office and *he* told them no."

According to Midlanders familiar with the earlier days, First National Bank required the signatures of two directors in order for a loan to be turned down—as opposed to two signatures needed for an approval.

Butler's Genius for Friendliness to Everyone

The late David Mims said Butler was a true gentleman in every sense of the word: compassionate, kind, and someone who would hear a person's name once and remember it forever.

"That was his genius," Mims said of Butler's ability to connect on a friendly level with everyone. "People may not have known what kind of a banker he was, but they knew he was a good, good person."[12]

What made Butler even more special to people was that he was, in fact, as good a banker as he was a person. He also surrounded himself with other community and business giants during his long career with the bank. Katie Spriggs, one of Butler's four grandchildren, said her grandfather and First National Bank were inextricably linked.

> The First National Bank lobby had a marble interior, and when you walked in the front doors, there was an enclosed glass office on the left. My grandfather was in the office just through the front doors of the lobby. When he was promoted to chairman, they proudly announced, "Mr. Butler, we have a better office for you." So they put him in the new office, off the main lobby. They moved his large wooden desk and rehung the large painting he had been given by my grandmother on the occasion of his last promotion, when he had been named president.
>
> He was there about a week and he went to the facilities people and said, "Can we have a little talk about my new office?" When he nicely asked to have his old office back, the facilities manager asked him why. My grandfather looked at him and said, "Because where you've put me, I can't see who's coming in and out the front door of the bank every day."[13]

Mr. Butler was quickly returned to his old office at the front of the bank and remained there for the rest of his tenure at First National.

David L. Smith, executive director of the Abell-Hanger Foundation, once worked for Butler. Smith said Butler, a former Marine, was a man of his word. If he said something, you could bet it would happen. "If he told you he was going to do something, you knew he was going to do it," Smith said. "And that was the kind of people that were attracted to Mr. Butler, too."[14]

Smith's story about the way Butler treated Smith's father helped set the younger Smith on a course and planted in him a seed of how honor, character, and integrity in all things—particularly, family, business, and community—should be practiced:

> Dad was a natural gas consultant who did a lot of work with the Turpin-Smith law firm. At Christmastime, one year during a boom, Turpin threw a party and I was invited because I worked at the bank, and I went up to the Christmas party. I was talking to my dad, and I guess Mr. Butler was in eyesight of the two of us, and I looked at my dad and I asked him if he had ever met Mr. Butler, and he said no. So I turned and said, "Mr. Butler, I'd like you to meet my dad, Monroe Smith."
>
> They shook hands and my dad said, "Mr. Butler, I've been a customer of the bank ever since I've been in Midland, and everything I have today is because First National Bank believed in me. I want you to know I'm very grateful for it."
>
> Mr. Butler said, "Well, Mr. Smith, you don't owe us a thing. We had a contract, and you did your part and we did our part, and we're very glad it worked out for you."
>
> I always thought that encounter captured the true character of Jno. P. Butler because a lot of people would take that compliment personally and they would say, "Yes, you're welcome." Not Jno. Butler. What was good for the customer was good for the bank, and it ended right there.
>
> He was so loved by this community, and when you live in a town the size of ours, and you are in the business of banking, it is hard to have the kind of admiration Jno. Butler had. I have never, ever, ever heard anybody say anything disparaging about Jno. P. Butler.[15]

Free Refreshments for Everyone, Customer or Not

Longtime Midlanders say the corner of Texas Avenue and Colorado Street was always abuzz with people, particularly during the Christmas holidays.

"There were few things like Christmastime at that bank, going into the lobby and seeing that huge Christmas tree and being served wassail and gingerbread cookies," Judge John Hyde remembered. "It was magical."[16] Those wassail and gingerbread days were yet another aspect that made First National Bank unique to the community.

But the bank's special hospitality wasn't reserved for Christmastime. "On the mezzanine level there was a coffee bar—a huge one that seated over 100 people—year-round," said Judge Hyde. "It didn't make any difference to anyone at that bank if you banked there. They'd serve you anyway."[17]

In his frequent lectures on Midland history, Hyde would often tell the story of how one bank director walked up to another and asked, "How long are we going to give away coffee and wassail?" And he was told, likely by Jno. P. Butler, "As long as this bank is here."[18]

Judge Mike Bradford also remembered the free coffee days, before the advent of Mr. Coffee machines, which drove people to their offices for an instant pot of fresh-ground brew. "We didn't care if you were a client or not," Bradford said. "We wanted you there. We wanted you to feel comfortable there. Because what would happen? You'd come to the bank and have a cup of coffee, and then you'd start talking to someone, and ultimately, you would become a bank customer. And we did that all on a non-cost-analysis basis. We didn't care what it cost; we did it."[19]

Butler's Compassion for Customers in Trouble

Numerous stories are still told of how when Butler had to foreclose on someone or repossess a car, he would pay them a personal visit simply to see how they were holding up. "[Butler] was always of the mind-set that if a person couldn't pay him back, it was because that person couldn't pay him back. It wasn't because they didn't want to," said David L. Smith.[20]

Midland attorney David Lindemood, who once worked for Butler, still considers his former boss to be his hero. "Always has been, always will be," Lindemood said. "Everyone, even men his age, called him Mr. Butler. I've never heard anyone say anything bad about him. Even the people who were foreclosed on by Mr. Butler loved him. He would go by and take them food he had purchased with money from his own pocket. And he would say to them, 'This is what I have to do. I'm sorry.' But he'd always make sure they had a place to stay and enough food to feed their family."[21]

"He had a very interesting way of teaching people valuable lessons," said Butler's granddaughter Katie Spriggs.

One time he told me he had to go visit one of his customers, and I told him I would like to go with him. We got in his Lincoln, and we drove out and saw a woman. She had evidently called my grandfather and said, "Mr. Butler, I know I'm overdrawn at the bank $500."

He told her he wanted to come and talk to her about it to see what they could do about it together. "I'm sure we can sort this out," he told her. So we got there, it was a very modest house, and the woman told my grandfather she didn't have any money, and she didn't know how she was going to get the money to pay the overdraft.

Spriggs recalled that her grandfather asked the woman if there was something she could part with.

The woman pointed to some old crystal in her kitchen, admitted she never used it and had no relatives to whom she could give the crystal. I was only about fifteen years old when my grandfather looked at me and asked, "What do you think?" I said I thought the crystal was beautiful.

Butler took the items from the woman and considered the debt settled. Spriggs is still the proud owner of the crystal, a gift from her grandfather.

We drove home in silence that day, but I knew he had taught me a very important lesson about people and life with that one generous gesture. I still have that crystal pattern today. We've often served guests using it. It's one of my most cherished possessions.[22]

Butler's Instinct for Helping Midland Grow

Butler's longtime friend Bill Collyns said Butler accomplished and worked for all he did not out of a sense of duty to his job, but out of his love for Midland. Hundreds of Midlanders who lived when Butler did have stories about its most honored citizen.

"Mr. Butler was a fine, fine man, and he was a fine, fine banker and community builder," David L. Smith said. "He did that without any regard for personal gain. He was altruistic in his own way, and he wanted what was best for the bank and what was best for the community. Jno P. Butler's personal needs were way down the list. He didn't worry about getting rich; he was a man of admirable character in the way he dealt with people. He tried to be honest, a man of integrity in everything that he did, and that came through."[23]

Part One: A Place with Character

"People loved Father," said Butler's daughter, Jane McAbee. "He just liked people, and he liked helping people get their start and pushing the town along to help it get its start."[24]

Midland County judge Mike Bradford moved to Midland from Fort Worth after Butler gave him a job as a recruiter for the bank. Butler called on Bradford to help Midland increase its stature by recruiting more high-profile professionals: doctors and lawyers who would provide the kind of services any decent-size town needs to sustain itself and progress toward a better future.

> He told me our community needs things to survive. "We have water, food, the oil industry. What we need to survive is good transportation, shopping, a vibrant medical community and a dental community. And we have to have entertainment," he said.
>
> I started thinking about all the items on his list, and the first thing I thought was that it was the oddest thing anybody had ever told me, but then I thought what he described is what all makes up the social fabric of the community. It was interesting to learn from Mr. Butler that what we needed in Midland for the families that were coming here with the oil companies in order for them to want to stay here and help build this community. If they couldn't shop and they had no medical services, they weren't going to stay. And as a result, the good management of those oil companies wouldn't stay either. They'd go someplace else, too.[25]

Guy McCrary and Doug Henson were part of the bank's economic-development division. First National Bank, McCrary said, was on the cutting edge of economic-development efforts and diversifying the local economy long before the days of the Midland Development Corporation. One of the reasons the bank was so strong in that area, McCrary said, was "there was nobody else in town big enough to push that effort."[26]

"Because you worked for that bank, you kind of had credibility—just being employed with the bank," McCrary said. "It gave employees, I daresay, almost a 'swagger' simply because the bank had its hands in so many different enterprises. I quite literally can think of almost nothing of any community value that the bank wasn't involved in."[27]

Clarence Scharbauer III says Butler and Kelly did more for Midland than most people could ever imagine:

Wassail, Gingerbread, and Generosity

There have been four or five men I've had the pleasure of knowing in this community that are good men from the heart. Jno. P. Butler is one. C. J. Kelly is one. Moose Trobaugh, Joe Pevehouse [both community leaders and philanthropists]. They put their money where their mouth is, and if they didn't have it, they'd go get someone else to put it there. Kelly was unbelievable. I always heard that he would sit down and say, "OK, Christensen Stadium? We've got to do something about it. YMCA? We've gotta fix it." And then he'd go around the table: "Can you do twenty grand? Can you do thirty? Can you do fifty?" And he'd raise the money to get all those things done in twenty or thirty minutes.

Mr. Butler was a kinder, nicer, sweeter gentleman. C. J. was, "Charge, let's go!" They raised more money around that board table. Dad would always say, "Oh man, we've got another board meeting, and it's probably gonna cost me twenty grand." But that's just how it worked.[28]

Butler as a Father and Baseball Fan

Jane McAbee remembers her father and his affectionate nature with great fondness. She said, "We used to live on Big Spring Street, and he would take me to the bank on Saturday mornings and check his mail to see what had gone on in the last week. I was alone with him on those Saturday mornings. The machines were all quiet." McAbee said her father often showed interest in hearing her stories about her friends and her classmates. She treasured the regular walks to the bank she made with him on those mornings.[29]

McAbee remembered that her father often read Westerns—and only Westerns. He was especially fond of Louis L'Amour novels, and the last movie he ever watched starred Clark Gable. He smoked and watched the nightly news on television. He was also an avid golfer. Longtime friend Lloyd McDonald said the only bad thing he ever heard anyone say about Butler was that he always hit it to the left off the tee.

Like many in that day and time, Butler was an avid fan of baseball. He watched it, traveled to parks to see it, attended a World Series in New York with his family, and even played it. It was his respite.

"I remember driving to Royalty one year on a dirt road so Father could play in a bush-league game," said McAbee. "There were several little towns that had teams and played together."[30] McAbee said her father would never wash his uniform after his team won, and her mother would make him change out of the uniform in the garage as a result. "He would streak across the house in his underwear, because he definitely considered it bad luck to wash his uniform during a winning streak."[31]

"Most of All, Our Friend"

When Jno. P. Butler died in 1997, the *Midland Reporter-Telegram* editorial board said his "impact on Midland was much broader—and more diverse—than just his role in the business world, impressive though that was. Now he is gone. But not forgotten."[32]

A full-page advertisement in the same paper a few days later had another touching tribute to the man who had done so much for so many Midlanders: "For over 70 years, our community was richly blessed by the presence and personality of John Butler. He was our business associate, our leader, our advisor and most of all, our friend. We will miss him dearly."[33]

chapter 8

AVIATION IN THE LAND OF THE HIGH SKY

The airport is our lifeline to the rest of the world.
—Bobby Burns, former mayor of Midland

PAUL VICKERS, PRESIDENT of the Midland Chamber of Commerce during the Depression, was not exaggerating when he called Midland an airport town. Midland's history with airplanes is almost as long as the history of airplanes themselves.

The Pliska Plane: 1912

John Pliska, a blacksmith described as being years ahead of his time, built his own airplane—and then flew it over Midland in 1912.[1] Born in Austria, Pliska came with his parents to Texas, and after 1903 followed his trade to West Texas. He was a master blacksmith, and even shod U.S. Army horses that were sent to Midland by Gen. John J. Pershing prior to World War I.

Aided by local auto mechanic Gray Coggin, Pliska completed construction and test-flew his plane after first witnessing the stopover of the Wright Brothers' Model B aircraft in Midland in 1911. Though he spent $1,500 on the engine, Pliska's aircraft was greatly underpowered. Still, the accomplishment was noteworthy. The plane he built and flew could stay aloft for intervals of up to fifteen minutes. "The open-cockpit craft, made mostly from buggy and windmill parts, had a 33-foot wingspan, a 27.5-foot fuselage and was 7.5 feet high."[2]

Pliska tried to improve his biplane by replacing the cheap canvas on the wings with more expensive balloon silk, but this effort actually made the plane less

Part One: A Place with Character

airworthy. It was not until after his repeated tinkering with the craft that it was finally able to fly one to two miles between rests.³

According to a 1985 article in the *Midland Reporter-Telegram*, the plane was scheduled for an exhibition flight in Odessa on July 4, 1912, but failed to remain airborne for any great lengths of time. "Several of the cowboys who had arrived to see the flight demanded their money back."⁴

The Pliska Plane hangs today over the baggage claim area at Midland International Airport.

The Midland Army Airfield: 1942–1946

In his 2001 book *The Stars Were Big and Bright: The United States Armed Forces and Texas During World War II* (Vol. 2), author George E. Alexander quoted Thomas Bellingham, a cadet at the Midland Army Airfield: "There was just absolutely nothing to look at out there. One old timer I knew called that whole Midland-Odessa part of Texas the 'Flat Brown,' and I think he was being overly generous."⁵

First impressions can be important and long lasting. Yet for the thousands of men who came to train at the U.S. Army Air Forces bombardier school at the Midland Army Airfield in 1942 and throughout a good portion of World War II, first impressions were often followed by impressions that ran much deeper. When those displaced cadets met the people of West Texas, many made the decision to stay here after they returned from the war.

In a *Midland Reporter-Telegram* article headlined "Science of War Taught," written for the publication's centennial edition, the bombardier school was called "Uncle Sam's most potent weapon. Not only was the school one of just 14 across the country that taught bombardiering, it was also the largest. The government believed that at the type of bombardier schools found in Midland and elsewhere, the men learning and working with bombsights would actually shorten the length of the war."⁶

"The value their training had in the overall war effort defies calculation," Judge Hyde told the *Midland Reporter-Telegram* in 2011. "Within a few months of the Japanese attack on Pearl Harbor and America's entry into the war, the old Midland Sloan Field became Midland Army Airfield. In a span of just three years, the school graduated more bombardiers than any other training base in the United States, and in the first seventeen months of its operation, more than 800,000 practice bombs were dropped."⁷

Midland quickly offered up land for the training facility when the government put out the word that it was looking to build more training facilities in the early 1940s.

Aviation in the Land of the High Sky

Midland also offered its municipal airport and even spent $590,000 in improvements on the facility in anticipation of being named a government training post. "On Friday, June 13, 1941, Texas Congressman R. E. Thomason, a member of the Armed Services Committee, announced that an advanced bombardment and twin-engine flying school would be located eight miles west of Midland on an 800-acre site.[8]

At first, $4.5 million was appropriated for the construction of over 100 buildings at the base, including classrooms, barracks, officers' quarters, an officers' club, a bomb storage building, and a 175-bed hospital. A second appropriation in May 1942, totaling $2.25 million, expanded the base, enlarged the flying field, and extended the runways.[9]

Training 6,627 Bombardiers During World War II

Cadets were trained on the Norden bombsight, dropping sand-filled bombs onto makeshift targets built to resemble battleships to scale on the ground. The targets were painted in white to show gun turrets and specific details of ships at 10,000 feet.

The joke of the day was that properly trained cadets could accurately hit a pickle barrel at 20,000 feet, but the training on the bombsights was far from fun and games, often making cadets nauseous or worse as they sat in a seat that slid along a track made to resemble the conditions a nose gunner or tail gunner would face in combat operations.[10]

"Ultimately," Judge Hyde wrote in November 2011, "the training and reliance on American airpower proved to be a valid decision: On April 7, 1945, torpedo planes and dive bombers from the USS *Yorktown* located the Japanese battleship *Yamato* in the China Sea near Okinawa. In an air attack that took less than two hours, the American planes struck the *Yamato* with 11 torpedoes and eight bombs, sending it to the bottom of the South China Sea. America's commitment to develop and train bombardiers proved to be a critical decision in the victory over aggression, and Midland was an integral part of that victory."[11]

Sloan Field was named after Stewart Sloan, who had leased 240 acres to begin his own private airport and flying school. Sloan was killed in a plane crash on January 1, 1929, less than two years after acquiring the land for the airport. The field, which would be designated Army Airways Station in May 1930, was kept operational by his brother and sister and eventually sold to the City of Midland in 1939. After repairs, including improved runways and landing light installations, local officials, including Clarence Scharbauer and Marvin Ulmer, another prominent banker who was also Midland's mayor at the time, began what would be a successful campaign to have the field designated a training base for the army's flight-training program. Interestingly, it was Clarence Scharbauer's lease of an additional 450 acres of his ranchland that ultimately convinced military officials to locate in Midland. With the war in Europe heating up in the early 1940s, the airport—complete with the additional acreage from Scharbauer—was leased to the federal government for one dollar a year, and construction began that would transform the municipal airport into a military installation.[12]

The base had been named the Midland Army Flying School. On September 6, 1942, it received its formal dedication as Midland Army Airfield, and the school was renamed the Army Air Force Bombardier School.[13]

Cadet Robert L. Walker, son of Mr. and Mrs. J. T. Walker, became the first native Midlander to graduate from the bombardier school. Known to his friends and family as Bobby, Walker graduated from Midland High School in 1939 and attended North Texas Agricultural College at Arlington and the University of Texas.[14]

In the nearly three years it educated bombardiers, from April 1942 until January 1945, a total of 6,627 officers were graduated after having flown 861,510 hours and dropping 1,245,107 practice bombs. During one particularly busy time, between 1942 and 1944, bombing runs were conducted twenty-four hours a day, and bomb-bay doors opened and unleashed their payloads every forty seconds.[15]

The Airfield's Return Gifts to Midland after the War

The airfield has regifted itself in three primary ways since it was decommissioned as a military installation on June 15, 1946:

The airport itself. The former Army training site became Midland Regional Airport and is known today as Midland International Airport, a modern and increasingly busy terminal that serves not only Midland, but Odessa and residents of smaller towns throughout West Texas.

Individual buildings relocated elsewhere. Many of the buildings utilized during the war and training efforts were parceled off and sent to other parts of the city. The clubhouse at Ranchland Hills Country Club was at one time the officers' club at the airfield. A Quonset hut used at the installation was later moved and reopened as one of the early structures that housed Midland Community Theatre. That early theatre site sat near what is currently the downtown County Library. Another building parceled off by the bombardier school upon its decommissioning housed the first classroom at St. Ann's School in Midland. "Over 100 buildings were given back to the community, turned over by the Army after the airfield was closed," Judge John Hyde said.

Cadets who returned after the war. By far the most valuable by-product to emerge from the Midland Army Airfield following the war was people. Educated, upstanding men and women had been sent to West Texas, thinking it represented the remotest outpost of the free world, only to eventually become endeared to it and, in some cases, fall in love with it. Those who came back here to establish new lives after the war brought with them strong moral values, a determined work ethic, and a sense of community and giving back that would invigorate a town already well known for its civic-mindedness.

"The generation that came after World War II, that's probably what made this town. People like Kenny Jastrow who came back here and were always volunteering their time," said local historian and attorney David Lindemood. "They were strong Army people who were making this a better place."[16]

One of the many people who came to West Texas and decided to stay after the war was Arden Grover, who married Rosalind Redfern and became a well-respected West Texas oilman. In Grover's case, though, he came to Midland after the Korean War, not World War II, and long after the Army Airfield had been decommissioned and closed.

"Arden was in Korea with Malcolm McCurdy," remembered Rosalind Grover, "and Malcolm told Arden after the war he was going to go visit his sister in Midland and asked him to come by for a visit. Arden came to Midland to stay for a week and ended up staying his entire life. When people like Arden started coming to Midland, the economy heated up."[17]

A Horrifying Overhead Collision: 1956

What began as a peaceful autumn afternoon quickly descended into chaos and carnage on October 24, 1956. High above a southwest Midland neighborhood, a T-33 fighter jet on a practice run from Big Spring's Webb Air Base collided in midair with a Cessna 170. Two Air Force captains from Illinois were killed, as well as five members of a family on the private plane.

Many witnessed the collision and the mortally wounded victims plummeting to earth. In one case, according to published reports, a female victim fell through the roof of a home and landed in a bathtub at the residence.

Miraculously, no one on the ground was injured, and property damage was limited to four homes. The collision occurred over the subdivision known as

Part One: A Place with Character

Permian Estates, the pinwheel-shaped neighborhood west of Midkiff Road and north of Business 20. Debris and bodies rained down over the 3500 block of Apache Drive. The site of the tragedy was only a few blocks away from where eighteen-month-old Jessica McClure would fall down a well thirty-one years later.

According to a report filed with United Press International, "The jet wreckage crashed into the home of Mr. and Mrs. R. A. Saunders, who weren't home at the time. 'If it hadn't been for my sister I probably would have been in that house and been killed myself,'" Mrs. Saunders said, adding that her sister had insisted they go shopping.

An artical in the *Midland Reporter-Telegram* read, "The engine of the civilian plane crashed into the kitchen of Mrs. Billy Crowe. Only minutes earlier she had taken her children—Janice, 1, and Debra, 3—into the living room. Wreckage and bodies were strewn all over the middle-class residential area. A child was found crumbled in a flowerbed. Webb Air Force Base said one of the airmen in the T-33 had ejected himself, but his chute failed to open. The body of the other airman was found in the burned Saunders home."[18]

Midland mayor Ernest Sidwell issued his sympathies for the families of those killed. "A miracle has happened in our city in that a major airplane accident has occurred in a thickly populated residential section and yet not a resident was killed," Sidwell said. "The heartfelt sympathy of all Midlanders goes out to the relatives and friends of all those who lost their lives in the crash."[19]

More than 700 children had just been released from class for the day at Jane Long Elementary, eight blocks to the west, at the time of the collision. None were injured.[20]

Midland International Airport

By the 1980s, Midland International Airport suffered from multiple, sizable leaks in water and sewage systems. Carroll Thomas, mayor of Midland from 1986 to 1992, said the preexisting facility was built on a concrete slab foundation, which had led to its most serious issues.

"It leaked like a sieve," Thomas recalled. "It needed a lot of work, and we added it all up and that number got to be pretty sizable. It just wasn't a quality building, and it wasn't something you wanted to dump a whole lot of money into."[21]

Assessing the Options

"The vision for the new airport came from Carroll Thomas," said Bobby Burns, mayor of Midland from 1994 to 2001. "It was when Carroll was mayor that he and the council talked about what to do with it. Do they update, improve?" Thomas began to see that a new airport was the way to go, but at the time there was no push to do so. Before he reached that conclusion, though, Thomas found himself in many conversations about what to do with the facility.[22]

Thomas said after several meetings with then airport director Ken Day, he asked him one day, "'How would you just like to have a whole new building?' I brought it up. We were having a lot of meetings about remodeling, trying to take a package to the public, but we finally began to see that wasn't the right approach."[23] The airport, Thomas said, was going to be here for many years, and the only way to start, or restart, was to do so fresh.

Council members and airport committee members began to visit facilities in cities that were similar in size to Midland, which drew the ire of some citizens. Some felt the taxpayer-funded trips were more junket than research.

"We chartered a plane, and people never understood that," Thomas said. "We were taking six or eight guys, and by the time we had scheduled flights and hotels, it was the same amount as if we took a commercial flight," Thomas said.[24]

After visiting eight sites, the committee finally decided it would try to model any new airport building after Anaheim's John Wayne Airport. "It was the last airport we looked at," Thomas said. "We walked in and saw it and said, 'This is fabulous—this is just what we need. We want this look at half the price.'"[25]

Thomas said airport architects smiled and told him that the committee's dream airport and dreamier cost would be a challenge. "They told us the final price would be something like $432 million," he said. "I was a little suspicious of that."[26]

Eventually Thomas's run as mayor ended, and J. D. Faircloth served one term. Bobby Burns said that when he became mayor, the airport project was "still sitting there with the same challenges. . . . Carroll and J. D. both began to see that a new airport terminal was the right thing to do, but by the time I got into office, it was a very unpopular thing to tackle. People were worried about ongoing costs and tax increases."[27]

Burns cited a privately sponsored poll that showed only 20 percent of respondents would be in favor of fixing the airport. He still remembers the airport project as being unfavorably received by voters even as council members "busted themselves" working on it for two to three years. Using much of the committee's legwork and construction findings, Burns's next big task was turning 20/80 into 80/20. And he did.

The Midland City Council had the authority to issue bonds and proceed with building a new airport. Instead, the council went to the citizens and asked for their approval. Burns knew that every time he went on television or was quoted in the newspaper, he was the lead salesman for the new airport.

"Our job as leaders was to paint a picture and show them exactly what we were talking about and how it was going to work," Burns said. "There was a need, and we could do it with no new taxes."[28]

"There were a lot of opponents of the project, because it caused a financial burden if it couldn't pay its own way. In retrospect it is paying its own way, and there have been no second thoughts about it whatsoever.... For a city our size to have the kind of airport we have, when you talk about economic development, oil and gas, it puts that lifeline out to the rest of the world."[29] Burns said the airport issue was one of the main reasons he decided to run for mayor, and he never shied away from putting his name on the line to fight for it.

The New Airport, Completed in 2000

At 160,000 square feet, the new terminal is almost double the size of the previous facility. After Gates 3–5 opened in January 1999, the old terminal was demolished, and ramp construction was completed. Gates 1 and 2 then opened in 2000. The staggered opening meant airport visitors did not face delays or detours during work.

The total cost of the building was $35 million, with the cost of the ramps coming in at $45 million. The $80 million total was less than 20 percent of the $432 million cost quoted earlier to Mayor Carroll Thomas.

chapter 9

"This Sprawling, New, Oil-Rich Town"

Midland has an arrogance and a confidence. Midland is unafraid of the world, and it comes from the oil and gas business. . . . We had an asset the rest of the world didn't have.

—Bobby Burns, former mayor of Midland

The Spraberry Trend, discovered in the 1940s, brought what Midland County had been promising since the 1920s: people in big numbers, all in search of hydrocarbons pulled from the earth that would provide tens of thousands of residents with a sustainable economic base and personal income.

The Discovery of the Spraberry Trend

Oil was first recovered in Midland County in November 1945, when a Humble Oil and Refining Co. discovery well, the No. 1 Mrs. O. P. Buchanan, yielded 4,540 barrels in 1945 and another 11,700 in 1946 before trailing off considerably. Three years later, while the Canyon Reef development in Scurry, Kent, and Borden Counties proved to be a significant find, particularly toward the end of 1948, it was the discovery of the Spraberry Trend in the Midland Basin in 1949 that changed life for many people in Midland County.

"The Spraberry came to be known as a promoter's paradise because you weren't going to drill dry holes," said pioneer Midland oilman Arlen Edgar. "Promoters could go out and raise money and promise there would be some kind of production, and that would be the truth."[1]

PART ONE: A PLACE WITH CHARACTER

But, Edgar continued, it wouldn't necessarily be the whole truth because despite how rich the Spraberry was, wells didn't hold up long. "At $3 [per barrel of] oil, which is what it was in those days, if not less, the economics weren't that outstanding. It was safe drilling, though."[2]

Edgar is a self-admitted lover of wells that last forever, one reason he said he likes the Permian Basin so much. "The Spraberry is why we're all still here. I remember five or ten years ago, I was hoping for another really big play. The [Permian] Basin was mature," Edgar said, "and I wasn't sure how long we were all going to last other than just as a harvest operation. Then Jim Henry came along with his techniques, and the Wolfberry evolved. Now we've got the Wolfberry, the Wolfbone out in the Delaware Basin, the Wolffork and all its variations, the Cline Shale Play east of us. Put it all together and it's really exciting, and it portends for a long and exciting future for our area."[3]

Samuel D. Myres's book *The Permian Basin: Era of Advancement* details just how quickly discoveries in the Spraberry began to unfold in 1949. "The original discovery occurred in a small field in Dawson County during January. Within a week, similar production was found in the Benedum Field of Reagan County. Toward the end of February, Spraberry oil was encountered in the Tex-Harvey Field in Midland County and thirty days later, in the North Gail Field in Borden County." The exploitation of the enormous area to be included in the trend, Myres wrote, would become a challenge of the first magnitude.[4]

The discoveries of fifty-two new fields were completed in West Texas in 1949 alone, with Scurry and Lea Counties the most active. But it was the Spraberry that would ultimately prove to be the linchpin for what would, decades later, come in with the Wolfberry Play, discovered in the early part of the twenty-first century.

Standing alone, the Spraberry in and of itself, is a singularly significant event in the history of West Texas, particularly for Midland.

"There is no doubt that the discovery of the Spraberry was one of the ten most important things to have happened in Midland, maybe top five," said Dr. Diana Davids Hinton, a professor of petroleum history at the University of Texas of the Permian Basin, and coauthor of the book *Wildcatters: Texas Independent Oilmen* and other works related to the industry and its history.[5]

Before the full development of the Spraberry had showed good promise, Hinton said the Canyon Reef find in Scurry County was so monumental that it actually delayed the discovery of the Spraberry.

"If you had to choose between [Canyon Reef] and looking for oil in Midland

County, it was no contest; you would go to Scurry County," Hinton said. "Jim Henry, as well as many other oilmen, refers to the Spraberry as the largest inaccessible single source of oil. It may have been in an area the size of Connecticut, but the problem was how do you get it out and make money? If you go in and have enough producing wells, even thirty barrels a day, it can make you money, but if you don't have enough of them, you can take a real financial bath on it."[6]

It wasn't until January 1949, six years after the first discovery in the Spraberry, that commercial production was established in the zone. After receiving a shot of nitroglycerin, Seaboard Oil Company's Lee No. 2-D began to produce as many as 319 barrels per day.[7]

Hinton said the Spraberry teased the oil industry with a small showing in 1943, but it wasn't until after the end of World War II when the trend would be fully exploited. "By the time the Spraberry came in," Hinton explained, "there had been discoveries [in all the counties] around Midland County, but not in Midland County. The first discovery came in 1943, but that was during the war, and it was terribly hard to do projects during the war because of the incredible amount of red tape you had to contend with."[8]

Respected longtime West Texas oilman Buddy Sipes, a young boy at the dawn of the Spraberry, remembers that the conclusion of World War II brought with it a great amount of agonizing because of a lack of jobs. Adding insult to injury was one of the region's more formidable droughts, from 1949 to 1956. The Spraberry, Sipes said, was a godsend: "If it hadn't been for the discovery of the Spraberry Trend, this would have been a really desolate place."[9]

At the end of the war, the price of a barrel of oil was hovering around the $2 mark and rose to $3 in the early 1950s. When the Spraberry came along and the economy started picking up, it was a marriage made in heaven because the Spraberry was proving economical on a widespread basis.[10]

"Operators were just beginning to get into the juicy part of the trend," Sipes said. "You had the big companies in here developing everywhere. Even though you had the development going on before World War II, it accelerated down in Crane and Ector Counties and other sites, and that just ignited things, and people really started ramping up, and the money started flowing into West Texas again. There were a lot of oilmen in Midland. People like Bob Wood and Eddie Chiles and those people, they made a lot of money. They lost a lot of money, too."[11]

Hinton's glimpse into the early days of the Spraberry also told the story of how Los Angeles promoters used questionable methods to build interest in the oilfield.

Part One: A Place with Character

"A whole bunch of models came out to the rig," said independent operator E. E. Reigle. "They had them working the tongs and the brake and all that, and every one of them was naked."[12]

The Spraberry was named after Dawson County farmer Abner Spraberry, who owned the land upon which the original discovery was made in 1943. After its initial yields, oil in the Spraberry has been historically known for its difficult recovery. Olien and Hinton wrote that by 1952, a solution to extraction problems had not been found and, "in three brief years the whole trend went from 'America's giant oil field' to its local designation as the world's largest unrecoverable oil reserve."[13]

By then, though, Midland's population had boomed, jumping one thousand residents from 1945 to 1950. The 1950s would see another enormous boost in population, most of which could be attributable to oil. In 1950 Midland's estimated permanent population was 21,700. By 1960 it had grown to 62,625, nearly tripling in only ten years.[14]

Young couples accounted for the majority of people moving to Midland in the 1950s, resulting in over 14,000 births during the decade. From 1949 to 1959, enrollment at Midland schools jumped from 3,686 to 14,647. Twelve new elementary schools, three junior highs, a new high school, and fourteen other school buildings were built during this period of intense growth.[15]

Though Midland schools experienced dramatic expansion, it was not as much as consultants expected. The district had predicted a doubling of school enrollment from 10,000 to 21,700, a rate for which the district would have to compensate by building four new schools a year. "The experts were wrong," Hinton and Olien wrote. "[Student] growth was overestimated by more than half."[16]

Midland was alive with the hopes and dreams of economic prosperity during those years. "After the war, the red tape was gone," Hinton said. "You could actually do projects in the oil field, and geologists and engineers were no longer being drafted, and the roughnecks and roustabouts and drillers were back, so companies again had the personnel to carry out their projects. There was also a lot of pent-up consumer demand. During the war there was rationing, and it wasn't easy—if it was even possible—to get a new car, so after the war America had a huge boom."[17]

Hinton said the postwar high times were experienced in every industry sector in the late 1940s and 1950s, not just in the Permian Basin, even though the oil patch in West Texas especially benefited because of the period's prosperity. "Oil prices rose to levels that were way beyond what they had been before the war,"

Hinton said, "and during the war, prices had been frozen, which was another thing that held back progress."[18]

Sipes agreed with Hinton that the Spraberry is probably among the top two or three most significant pieces of Midland history. "The timing and the extent of it and the fact that it has been growing all these years are what have made the Spraberry significant," Sipes said. "People don't realize that if you have something that you can continue to build on, that makes a big difference."[19]

In contrast, Sipes said, some thought SACROC to be a significant find, but after three or four years, when it was over, it was over. And remains over. As technology has continued to improve, though, the Spraberry has continued to expand.

While not as economically significant as the oil itself, a secondary by-product of the Spraberry has, without question, been one of a legacy of leadership left behind for future generations. Jim Henry, president and cofounder of Henry Petroleum, put it this way: "We have had managers at Texaco and Exxon and Pure Resources and Conoco Phillips who have created in Midland a lot of leadership. Leadership that has gone on after them. To a person, everyone I have talked to over the past fifty years has told me Midland is a unique place. It must have something to do with that pioneering cowboy spirit that was here so long ago. There's always been that idea that we're going to tackle it and we're not going to get help from the federal government. And while we're at it, we're going to help our fellow man, too."[20]

Midland's "Snowballing Popularity"

Midland's transformation from pioneering cow town to major petroleum center was in full swing by the 1950s and 1960s. What had once been a quiet little burg was rapidly becoming a bustling city, looking more and more like it does today.

By 1950 some 215 oil companies had established offices in Midland. While an economic plus, the influx of workers created problems in downtown Midland, including inadequate office space and downtown parking shortages, a problem that Midland has experienced almost since cars began to take up space in our workaday lives. But inadequate parking can be a good problem to have.

Jack Wilkinson, once called the Tall Man of the Tall City, oversaw the construction of a number of business developments in downtown in the 1950s: the Wilkinson-Foster and Permian buildings, the fourteen-story V&J Tower, and the Wilco Building, which towers twenty-two stories. "Pretty soon, Midland was

Part One: A Place with Character

the headquarters of the independent oil man in Texas," Wilkinson said. "During the 1950s, almost every square foot of space was rented, so we built more offices. People said we were over-building, but that wasn't the case. Almost every building made money for its investors. It was hard to go wrong in Midland."[21]

By the end of the 1950s, Wilkinson's projects accounted for over one-third of the office buildings in Midland. Nearly every major oil company in the nation at that time contributed to the building frenzy, as did the major banks—including Midland National and First National.

The 1950s were not without challenges, especially with such a surge in population. Water needs and transportation were both great concerns, and Midlanders approved the issuance of bonds totaling $15.4 million to incorporate wells in the Paul Davis Field. The field held a supply of water adequate for 150,000 people for fifty years.

And then there was the petroleum industry, which continued its remarkable progress. A video produced for the town's centennial celebration in 1985 stated, "By 1950, the Permian Basin was the most active drilling area in the world—producing a million barrels a day. Right here, we were producing almost as much oil daily as Venezuela—the second-largest oil-producing country in the world. Young men and women from all parts of America came to make their fortunes in Texas and to contribute to the growth and improvement of Midland."

In 1952 Midland was more than sixty years old, and a reporter from the *Baltimore Sun* came to town to write about the boom conditions: "New cars, expensive homes, several impressively tall buildings, a very social country club, more than $4 million in building last year. All testify to the snowballing popularity of this sprawling, new, oil-rich town."

"Sprawling was right," the video continued. "The sewer system, streets, even parks and playgrounds for children couldn't match the growth rate."

Centennial documents told another interesting story, which seemed to indicate that turning to the citizenry for financial assistance in order to fund projects to improve living conditions and infrastructure is something we have done with much success for many years, despite occasional organized efforts to defeat municipal initiatives. "Bond issues were the financial order of the '50s," the centennial archives said. "Even as far back as 1947, Midlanders were going to the polls, passing bond issues in the millions for education, city improvements and practically everything else that needed to be done. What the citizens wouldn't take from the federal government they provided for themselves."[22]

Midland's first growth spurt during the phenomenal expansion period was in the southwest part of town.[23] "[Growth] shifted to the west and southwest in the course of the fifties; minority neighborhoods in south and east Midland grew rapidly as well," Olien and Olien wrote in *Oil Booms*.[24]

Increased oil production also brought about an increase in flares: intentionally ignited, controlled fires burning off excess combustible vapors at the top of a tall pipe near an oil-producing well. Drilling for oil often releases natural gas also, and during the 1950s there was an overabundance of natural gas without adequate space to store it. The many flares often brought a significant brightness to the night sky—a light so bright, in fact, that for many Midlanders it often appeared to be sunrise for those looking eastward.[25]

One challenge facing those who came to Midland because of the area's phenomenal new oil finds occurred in 1953 when the Texas Railroad Commission, in order to minimize the waste of natural gas brought on by the flares, limited oil production to ten days per month.

"All operators [in the Spraberry] lost money during the shutdown. By the end of 1953, small independents in the trend were barely afloat; their income was diminished by natural production declines and the shutdown had interrupted it for months. After production resumed, many operators found that their wells could not be revived to more than a fraction of pre-shutdown output," Olien and Hinton wrote in *Wildcatters*.[26]

A Safe Town, but Not Completely

Many longtime residents fondly recall Midland in the 1950s and 1960s as a safe place where there was little fear of crime. "I would tell my parents that I was going out to ride my bike, and as long as I was home by dark, we never had any worries," said longtime Midlander Jack Swallow.

The late Bill Kleine said Midland in the 1950s was a young person's town. "A wonderful place to be young in," Kleine said. "There was a lot of optimism, a lot of things happening."

Little League and Outdoor Sports

When Rosalind Redfern (later Rosalind Grover) was twelve years old, she was a huge fan of baseball, which was in its heyday in the 1940s and 1950s. She likes to tell of the time her father brought Carl Stotz, the founder of the national Little League program, to Midland, to help establish the sport in the growing West Texas city. It was, she said, a turning point in her life:

> My father was instrumental in the founding of Little League in Midland. One time, he brought Carl Stotz, the man who was director and founder of the National Little league in Pennsylvania to Midland. At that age I loved baseball. My father went to pick him up at the hotel, and I was in the back seat while my father was driving.
>
> You know how sometimes you have a seismic shift in your world? We were driving down Missouri Street—I still remember right where we were, we were right behind the parking garage at the bank—and I announced that I was going to play baseball. I was so excited. But this man turned around and said to me, "Oh, young lady, wouldn't you rather be at home playing with your dolls?"
>
> I said to him, "No, I would not!" I never understood why he said that. It never dawned on me that I wasn't going to be allowed to play baseball. I didn't realize it was a boys-only deal, and it broke my heart not to be able to play baseball. And after that moment, I refused to listen to games for years.
>
> Time marched on, and I marched on and it didn't bother me nearly as much not to be involved. My daughter didn't play, they didn't have Little League for girls then, but when my niece came along, girls could finally play Little League ball. It was back in the 1970s, and I marched over to her one day and said, "Look! Girls can play baseball! This is fabulous—you have to go over there and try out!"
>
> And do you know what she told me? She said, "Oh, Aunt Roz, I'd rather just stay at home and play with my dolls." [27]

Joe O'Neill, a mutual friend of Bill Kleine and George W. Bush, came to Midland in 1948 when he was three years old. Though most of his memories of the Bush family would come during George W. Bush's second extended stay in town in the 1970s and 1980s, O'Neill still has a few recollections of their childhood together.

"George and I played on the same Little League teams from the time we were six years old on," O'Neill said. "Charlie Younger grew up across the street from the [future] president. We played baseball together in the summer and the president's dad was an assistant coach. He went to San Jacinto, I went to St. Ann's. We didn't really see each other anywhere else except for when our folks went to the country club. The Bush family moved to Houston when George W. was in the ninth grade, and then he went to Andover, Yale, and the Air Force, and then got into politics."[28]

Younger, a Midland orthopedic surgeon, also has pleasant memories of Midland during that same time, and President Bush himself recalled with fondness the town from a much younger vantage point.

"We originally lived over on Brunson Street near West Elementary," Younger said, "and later moved over to Ohio Street, catty-cornered to the Bush house, in about 1953. I grew up in that house. If you were to ask within a one-mile radius of that house which family is going to one day be the first family of the country, you might not have picked the Bushes. There might have been fifty others you would have picked. They were just like everyone else."

Younger said the Bush family first came to Midland with nothing more than a willingness to work and a desire to succeed. "They probably had something they could have fallen back on if necessary, but they didn't fall back. They lived in a humble little house that economically was probably in the bottom ten percent in the neighborhood," Younger said.

People didn't keep track of how much your house cost in those days, Younger said, adding that the Midland existence was idyllic and there were any number of reasons why it fit that definition:

> There were no drugs. Everyone kind of monitored each other's kids, and if you got out of line, you were pretty easily recognized and dealt with. It was just the perfect community. There were a lot of risk takers, a lot of optimism, a lot of characters. It was truly a wonderful place. I can't imagine a better place to grow up in the 1950s.
>
> We got caught smoking one time when we were little. . . . It was Bob Zonne and me, and we grew up together, went to school and to West Point together. He became a captain in the Army and was killed in Vietnam. But when we were in the fourth grade, we got hold of a pack of his mother's cigarettes, Sir Walter Raleighs, so we all thought we would go out to the alley and smoke a cigarette.
>
> We hadn't been there ten minutes when driving down the alley came Tugboat Jones, the head football coach at Midland High. He stopped the car, got out, looked at us, and said, "Boys, I want you in my office at four o'clock."

Part One: A Place with Character

I went home and locked myself in the bathroom, I was so scared. My mother knew what had happened, and she coerced me out of the bathroom.

We went over to the coach's office and he read us the riot act. And I will always remember that on the edge of his desk, there was a full ashtray of smoked cigarette butts. He told us we would never play sports for him if he caught us again. And it was the last time a tobacco product ever touched my lips.[29]

Aside from the isolated smoking-in-the-alley story, the most adventurous, envelope-pushing behavior for many youths in the 1950s, Younger said, was throwing water balloons at passing cars. Even President George W. Bush recalled similar antics:

Charlie [Younger] talks a lot about water-gun fights, and I'm sure I engaged in all kinds of activities like water-gun fights. I remember we used to go to vacant lots and build forts and throw clods at each other.

My memories of Midland were outdoors and playing outdoors with friends. I remember well riding my bicycle from our house on Ohio Street to Sam Houston Elementary School. I also remember our little dog chasing me to school, and me having to tell the teacher I'd be right back after I took the dog back home. And even though I'd miss the opening bell, the teacher was very sympathetic of a young lad having to return the dog.

I remember a lot of outdoor activities in Midland, particularly baseball. I was a baseball fan growing up, and I loved to play with my pals. When I got older, older being eleven or twelve years old, we moved to the outskirts of town on Sentinel Drive. We had a buffalo wallow in the back of the house that became a Little League park. I used to spend hours playing baseball with my pals as well as Little League baseball.[30]

Millionaires' Kids: Tempting Targets for Kidnappers

Even with as many stories of how Midland was a safe town in the 1950s and 1960s, it was not entirely so. Sid Trevino, the first Hispanic police lieutenant to work at the Midland Police Department, remembers that shortly after he started on the force, there was talk of kidnapping plots targeting Midland because of the wealth of some of its citizens.

"When I came to work in Midland, there were seventy millionaire families in town," he said, adding that plots born in Dallas and Fort Worth to take children for ransom were very real in Midland in those days.[31]

One of those youngsters who faced the threat of kidnapping was the daughter of a respected businessman, John Redfern, who had moved his family from New Jersey to make his living in oil. His daughter, Rosalind (later Rosalind Grover), eventually became one of Midland's hardest-working philanthropists and a supporter of numerous causes.

"My father always kept a low profile," Grover explained. "He didn't even want Redfern to be the first name of his company." One of the reasons for this was his family's safety and privacy, both of which were threatened in 1952. More than sixty years after the incident, Grover's recounting of what happened is a cautionary tale for anyone with small children.

"A man was stopped by police on Lamesa Highway, north of Midland," Grover said. "He had a list in his pocket and a stash of weapons. The list he had contained the names and addresses of three families in Midland. He was on his way to Midland to kidnap the children. My family's name was on that list. When that happened, my father said he wanted to have the lowest profile possible."

Flag-Redfern Oil Company had just discovered the Denton Pool, a field that would make everyone involved wealthy. But Redfern remained steadfast. "I never want to have that kind of notoriety," he once said. And from the time he first received the news about his children being on the receiving end of a kidnapper's plot, he remained as low-key as a man of his means could be.

"He drove normal cars, he never did anything flashy, we had a low-profile house," Grover remembered. "He later told me, 'It scared the life out of me when the police called and told me they had picked that man up.'"[32]

The Need for Expanded Medical Care

With the dramatic increase in Midland's population, it became more and more obvious that sufficient medical care was the only way to assure Midland of continued growth. Gone were the days of private practitioners making house calls in buggies that served as makeshift ambulances. A new multilevel medical-care facility that opened its doors on July 11, 1950, was a far cry from what Midlanders had depended on for treatment just a few years earlier.

Dr. John B. Thomas opened a hospital facility on a second-floor wing of

Part One: A Place with Character

Midland's Llano Hotel in 1919. In 1922 the town's first nurse, Josephine Guly, arrived. Dr. Thomas opened the Thomas Building in 1928, and on its sixth floor was the town's hospital. (For more about medicine in early Midland, see Chapter 2.)

A small hospital in the 200 block of Big Spring Street was opened in the early 1930s, but its chief physician, Dr. W. E. Ryan, enlisted in the Army at the beginning of World War II and was killed in action. An active community member and president of the Chamber of Commerce, Dr. Ryan closed his hospital prior to enlisting.[33]

After Ryan's death, Dr. Lloyd W. Leggett opened Western Clinic-Hospital during the 1940s, but the town's population growth in the postwar years made additional health-care choices essential.

Midland Memorial Hospital

"As Midland's population grew during the post–World War II oil boom, it became apparent that a larger, community-supported hospital was needed," former teacher and hospital auxiliary member Edna Brown Hibbitts wrote. "The Midland Memorial Foundation was chartered in 1947 in response to the need."[34] Land was donated by E. P. Cowden and Clint Dunagan at the corner of Illinois Avenue and Andrews Highway for the purpose of building the new facility.[35]

When Midland Memorial Hospital opened in 1950, it had seventy-five beds, twenty-six physicians, and seventy-eight additional employees. Board members viewed the facility as capable of serving the town's population of nearly 22,000. The nearly 59,000-square-foot state-of-the-art medical facility came at a cost of $1.372 million.[36]

The hospital was erected as a memorial to the pioneer settlers of Midland, to the men and women who died in defense of their country, and to the loved ones who will be memorialized by gifts to the hospital. The list of the hospital board's charter members contained a number of notable Midlanders: George T. Abell, James N. Allison, Ralph M. Barron, H. G. Bedford, Jno. P. Butler, Frank Cowden, Clint Dunagan, George W. Glass, Lester Grant, O. C. Harper, A. N. Hendrickson, Mrs. J. Howard Hodge, John W. House, Ralph Lowe, J. E. Mabee, R. L. Miller, J. S. Noland, Foy Proctor, Mrs. Ruth Scharbauer, Frank Stubbeman, Dr. John B. Thomas, Fred Turner, M. C. Ulmer, Fred Wemple, and Fred S. Wright.[37]

Dr. Thomas was one of the hospital's most ardent supporters long before vision became reality. The July 9, 1950, *Midland Reporter-Telegram* described the new medical facility's huge importance to the man who had already practiced medicine in Midland for forty-five years when the hospital opened.

"It will be a dream come true for Dr. Thomas, who has labored long and hard for a large, modern hospital to care for the needs of ever-growing Midland and vicinity. It was Dr. Thomas who lifted the first shovel of soil from the site of the new hospital as ground was broken for the institution in 1948, and it was Dr. Thomas who has devoted practically all of his time to the new hospital since his retirement from private practice. Associates praised him for his diligent efforts and excellent leadership in the planning, financing, building, equipping and furnishing of Midland's fine new hospital. He has also been one of the largest individual contributors to the institution."[38]

Praise from civic leaders was overwhelming at the hospital's opening. "Midland Memorial Hospital is the very finest I have ever had the pleasure of seeing, providing Midland with the best and most modern hospital facilities in the Permian Basin Empire," said Robert L. Wood, president of the Midland Chamber of Commerce in 1950. "Seeing this new hospital will make one proud to be a resident of a community whose citizens have made such an institution possible."

Jack Wicker, then vice president of Midland National Bank, echoed Wood's sentiments, saying, "Certainly the new hospital represents a great accomplishment for its sponsors and is an achievement of which they can be proud. Midland will achieve greater stature in the community of West Texas cities, becoming the medical center of the vast Permian Basin Empire."[39]

Delbert Downing called the hospital's completion "no doubt the most significant achievement of an imposing list of outstanding accomplishments by the citizens of Midland."[40]

In 1977 the hospital district was formed, and a $10 million expansion program began. Financed by the only general obligation bond issue in the hospital's history, the expansion included a maternity wing, critical care unit, and post-critical care unit. Total beds numbered 195 after the expansion was completed.

On the occasion of the hospital's thirty-fifth anniversary, then president Ray W. Branson announced that the "Hospital on the Plains" would jump from its original seventy-five beds to 272 by the end of the summer of 1986. He noted the significance of Midlanders' willingness to help fund indigent care through the establishment of the Midland County Hospital District in 1977.[41]

In 1994 the hospital expanded again, adding almost 100,000 square feet on the north side. This changed the face as well as the main entrance of the hospital, relocating the front doors to the north part of the building facing Garfield Street. The expansion also brought a new emergency department, laboratory, and a testing and diagnostic center. The hospital also welcomed a medical office building in 2007, an 88,000-square-foot building on the north side of the campus.[42]

The most recent addition to Midland Memorial Hospital is the Dorothy and Clarence Scharbauer Jr. Patient Tower, completed in 2012. (For more about the funding and completion of this eight-floor tower, see Chapter 19.)

The Permian Basin Petroleum Museum

There had long been talk in coffee shops, oil fields, and boardrooms in West Texas of the need for a museum to commemorate the work accomplished and history created in the oil fields. The discussions reached a more formal stage in 1964 at a joint meeting of the chambers of commerce of Midland, Odessa, and Monahans. While representatives from all three towns agreed that a museum was badly needed, it wasn't until two years later that a solid plan was put in place—and another sixteen months after that before a target date for groundbreaking was set. Even with all the preplanning, initial work, and hope, the beginning of construction would not come until 1973.

With the help of donor dollars totaling $830,000, construction finally began in 1973, when George T. Abell, noted for his accomplishments in the patch and his love of history, gave $100,000 for the project through the Abell-Hanger Foundation, named after him and his wife, Gladys. Abell also donated most of the land for the museum: thirty-four of the forty-one acres. A community campaign, "A Call to Greatness," was led in Midland to raise the remainder of the $370,000.

In the nearly forty years since its opening, the Permian Basin Petroleum Museum has inducted more than 135 members into its Hall of Fame and has become a crucial resource for any student of the industry's history.

In a statement that still holds true today, the late John Paul Pitts, former oil editor of the *Midland Reporter-Telegram*, said the museum is "unquestionably the largest and most elaborate in the world." Samuel Myres, author of *Permian Basin: Era of Advancement*, noted that the museum, years in the coming, was at one point to have been called the World Petroleum Museum and Hall of Fame, a name certainly in keeping with the larger dreams of many oil professionals and West Texans.

The Permian Basin Petroleum Museum and Hall of Fame opened September 13, 1975, keynoted by no less than President Gerald Ford. During his presentation,

President Ford spoke of the United States Constitution's guarantee of the oilman's drive for the pursuit of happiness.

"Americans," Ford said, "have dreamed big dreams, taken great risks, sometimes failed miserably and sometimes succeeded magnificently—but always with courage and determination. That freedom to dare is the secret of our greatest national achievements."

In a mere thirty-three words, Ford captured the oilfield worker, from roughneck to operator. He could not have delivered his words at a more appropriate venue.

"The men and women to whom this museum is dedicated lived and enjoyed freedom to the fullest," he continued. "The spirit of enterprise and the daring this museum records in the petroleum industry must be kept alive all across America."[43]

The greatest names in the history of the oil industry in Texas are forever enshrined in the museum's hall of fame.

George and Gladys Abell's Lasting Gift to Midland

One of the independents who made a name for himself during the town's second boom would become one of Midland's leading citizens and have his name, George T. Abell, forever etched into the walls of the Permian Basin Petroleum Hall of Fame. His wife, who grew up as Gladys Hanger, came from a well-to-do Fort Worth family. Both of them would become Midland's longtime champions, a couple whose contributions would extend well past their time on earth.

Born in tiny Wakeeney, Kansas, George Thomas Abell graduated from Colorado A&M (now Colorado State University) with degrees in civil and mechanical engineering. With education in hand, he went to work for Midwest Exploration Company, a Denver-based organization. When the company failed to find oil in the Rockies, it expanded its search to West Texas in 1923.[44] In 1927 Abell moved to Midland, where he entered the petroleum business as an independent operator. Discovering and developing in the Abell, Gomez, Pecos Valley, South Ward, Shipley, and other Permian Basin fields in the 1930s, he earned a reputation as a successful wildcatter and producer.[45]

David L. Smith, executive director of the Abell-Hanger Foundation, called George Abell a self-made man who experienced most of his successes in oil and gas, drilling around the Pecos River and near Fort Stockton. As oilmen go, Smith said Abell was fairly successful, but not as wildly successful as others. Abell's fortune was built over a long period of time. He found his riches more in gas than in oil. Politically, he was known to be very conservative. Low key and a lover of history, Abell would even help underwrite a book about the history of the petroleum industry.[46] "He was active in many aspects of the community," Smith said. "He was on the school board and was instrumental in getting the hospital built in the 1950s. For a long time he was involved in everything that mattered in this community."[47] Smith described Gladys as the quintessential oilman's wife.

Joe Mabee, a Midland rancher and philanthropist, called Abell a "high-class gentleman" who was quiet, unassuming, and congenial to all and who gave to Midland because he loved Midland and for no personal gain.[48]

The late John Younger was a close friend of both the Abells, and painted them as down-home people with a love of community and friendship. "George was always interested in having little groups of friends over to eat barbeque in the backyard," Younger said. "Very often those groups got into singing, and someone would start out with a song and others would join in. George was a bright man, a Christian man; he was a patriotic man and knew how to get things done. Mrs. Abell was a strong supporter of nursing students and would often fund nursing scholarships. Anything that had to do with nursing, Gladys was happy to contribute to."[49]

The Abells were inseparable, Younger said. After her husband's death, Mrs. Abell was frequently found gardening in her backyard, wearing her late husband's shirts and trousers, digging in the dirt.

The Abell-Hanger Foundation, Established in 1954

George and Gladys Abell would make their most significant contribution to Midland with the establishment in 1954 of the Abell-Hanger Foundation. "What was unique about their foundation is instead of naming it the Abell Foundation, they named it Abell-Hanger, which, in 1954, was a very progressive thing to do to honor both families in the name," Smith said.

Legacy Scholarships and Support for Numerous Nonprofits

The Abell-Hanger Foundation is one of four Midland family foundations that have helped thousands of students pursue their dream of a college education through the Legacy Scholarship program. Along with foundations started by Helen and Barney Greathouse, Harriet and J. Harvey Herd, and the Clarence Scharbauer family, the Abell-Hanger Foundation has awarded scholarships to 11,387 Midland County high school students to attend Midland College through the 2013 academic year.[50]

From 1986 until today, Smith said, the foundations have "created an environment where people want to go to college in Midland County, and if they can do two years here, they can go anywhere. It's hard for some people to imagine that $1,500 or $2,000 would keep some people from going to college, but there are people like that without question. The Legacy Scholarships have helped those people and many more."

But the Abells' generous role in the scholarship program is only the beginning. Many charitable organizations in Midland have been helped because of George and Gladys Abell.

Managing the Foundation's Finances

Mrs. Abell was not a businessperson. Born in 1900, she was not yet thirty when the Great Depression began. She had a different appreciation for money than others in similar positions, even than her late husband.

"I remember going to visit her and taking with me a book of grant requests and I would sit down with her and explain it to her the best I could so I could truly get a feel from her what she wanted me to do," Smith said. "When I went to the board, if I could tell them what she wanted to do, they would immediately approve it. In a group of men, she would be reluctant to speak up, so I would help facilitate that for her and spent many hours at her home talking to her. She was always extremely kind."[51]

Smith said both Mr. and Mrs. Abell "would be astonished at what the foundation has become. They just thought they knew what they were worth." George Abell, Smith said, was successful over many years and "might have thought he was worth $10 million in the 1950s and 1960s. Abell took ill with Alzheimer's disease in the 1970s. Almost simultaneously, oil and gas values went through the roof and Mr. Abell died. Everything that he owned was working interest. Smith explained:

> [George Abell] owned his properties, and the tax laws required that we sell that working interest upon his death. The tax laws became problematic because his estate owned half the working interest, and Mrs. Abell, who survived her husband, owned the other half.
>
> Through the careful stewardship of Jim Trott, a petroleum engineer who worked for Abell, and Maurice Bullock, an estate attorney, the Abell-Hanger Foundation was able to sell off Abell's holdings for $43.5 million, which substantially grew the worth of the foundation posthumously. The

brilliance of that decision was that even though the money was made, once they sold their working interest (which was the bulk of the value), they decoupled themselves from the oil and gas business, so when the oil business goes south, it doesn't affect the foundation. That puts us in a position where we can do things when times are tough. There's not a better example of that than the Legacy Scholarships."[52]

With a contribution of $35 million from Mr. Abell's estate and $45 million from Mrs. Abell's estate, the couple invested $80 million in the foundation. As of 2014, trustees have grown the value of the Abell-Hanger Foundation to about $175 million, more than double the total original contributions from George and Gladys Abell, and the foundation has dispersed nearly $200 million in grants.[53] "I think those numbers would be terribly difficult for both of them to get their arms around," Smith said. "Particularly Mrs. Abell. To her, $10,000 was a lot of money. A million would, to her, be like a trillion. It was just beyond her comprehension."

In 2004, fifty years after the Abell-Hanger Foundation was established, a Midland Center filled with community members paid a special tribute to the two benevolent citizens at a banquet. Many guest speakers from charitable organizations described the work they had been able to do because of the foundation's support, and expressed their heartfelt gratitude. The program's emcee was Dr. David Daniel, then president of Midland College—one of the principal beneficiaries of Abell's generosity.

Several years after the fifty-year tribute, longtime Midlander June Cowden summed up the feelings of the whole community, noting the Abells' enormous financial contribution to Midland. "Imagine Midland if you took that away," she said. "They started that foundation in 1954, when they had $5,600 in the bank. They've done so much for Midland."[54]

chapter 10

THEATRE, MUSIC, AND A MICKEY MOUSE RUMOR

When I came back to Midland after the war, here were all these young guys, bankers' sons mostly, also coming to Midland. Bankers would say "Send that young Harvard grad son of yours to Midland, Texas. There's oil there." And that's how a good many of those young fellas ended up there. And those young guys wanted everything, and why not? Life was good. Everybody was having fun. Out of that came a couple of very good museums, a hospital, and a theatre.
—Art Cole, founder of Midland Community Theatre

LONG BEFORE ART COLE OPENED the Midland Community Theatre in 1946, and decades before U.S. Senator John Tower (R-Texas) swooped in to save a damsel in distress as a Summer Mummers guest actor in the 1960s, the arts have had a strong presence in Midland. The Yucca Theatre was the town's first venue for the dramatic arts.

The Yucca Theatre

Credit for the Yucca Theatre can be laid directly at the feet of Montana senator T. S. Hogan, in his knee-length leather boots. Responsible for many important Midland developments during the 1920s—including the Hogan Building, which played such a vital role in Midland's development—Hogan saw a need not only for a large office building, but also for funding of the arts in the still-young town. So he built the Yucca right next door.

Part One: A Place with Character

Hogan informed Midlanders he would build the theatre in 1927. Two years later, on December 5, 1929—six months after the opening of the adjoining building that bears his name—the first curtain call came to the Yucca. The original production was *Rio Rita*, a musical comedy revue, and Hogan and the local theatre community spared no expense to ensure the grandest opening night: The premiere featured the Jubilee Players of New York City.[1]

Architecture and Versatile Design

Hogan commissioned Fort Worth architect Wyatt C. Hedrick to design the theatre, which to this day features "an elaborate façade with intricate Gothic Revival detailing."[2] The interior was the work of New Yorker H. B. Layman and features Egyptian Revival–style architecture. A historical marker at the entrance of the Yucca, 208 North Colorado Street, says the theatre's versatility of design made it "suitable for a variety of activities." The Yucca gained a reputation for that beauty and versatility; even in the midst of the Great Depression of the 1930s, it drew traveling vaudeville companies.[3] In the years since, it has also been used as a cinema and as a venue for concerts, improvisational comedy, melodrama by the Summer Mummers, and special nonprofit events.

A Theatre Saves a Theatre

The Yucca Theatre closed as a movie venue in 1974, and the sandwich shop in its lobby closed later in the 1970s.[4] The old landmark building was empty and had fallen into disrepair. As Judge John Hyde recalled, the structure was saved from demolition by a peculiar circumstance:

> During the boom, when they quit using the old Yucca, it went vacant for quite some time. There was some talk of tearing it down so they'd have more space. The last boom, they built buildings; now it seems like they're tearing them all down during this one. I remember, though, when talk came of tearing it down, no one could find the architectural plans and they didn't know if the steel that supported the Yucca went into the Petroleum Building. And [they] were concerned that if they destroyed it, it might damage the structural integrity of the bigger building....
>
> I remember walking into it in the 1970s, after they quit showing movies there, and it was vacant, and I thought how sad that they are going to tear it down. It is so majestic-looking in all its design.

And about that time, along comes [Midland Community Theatre]. They get it, they preserve it, and it looks again like it did in 1929."[5]

Art Cole and the Midland Community Theatre

The theatre company that saved the Yucca Theatre in 1999 was founded by a man who came to Midland during World War II. Midland theatre lovers still thank the U.S. Army Air Forces for drafting a young man named Art Cole and sending him from the security of his home in Fostoria, Ohio, to dusty West Texas.

An Army Engineering Clerk Who Decided to Stay

Cole liked what he saw when he was stationed at Midland Army Airfield. Trained in theatrical arts, he was working for a traveling production company when he was sent to Midland, and on arrival he found there was no theatre here, even though the changing makeup of the population desired a strong fine-arts presence in their town.

When he was taken into the combat zone aboard a ship bound for destinations in the South Pacific, the U.S. Army Air Corps didn't stock the ship with many reading options. Fortunately, Cole had picked up a few theatre-arts magazines before leaving home, and in those magazines was a series of articles on how to establish a community theatre in a town that didn't have one. The articles served as the spark Cole would need to develop a desire to return to Midland and give his all to establishing that theatre.[6] Cole's story of reading theatre-arts articles isn't the only stroke of luck that would help keep him in West Texas.

"I was drafted and shipped to Midland on Easter Sunday, April 5, 1942, about four months after the attack on Pearl Harbor," Cole said from his Santa Fe home in July 2011. "It was a brand-new base and bombardier school in Midland. They hadn't even graduated their first class of bombardiers yet. The day we arrived, the new guys in all the barracks said, 'It looks like rain,' and all the veterans said, 'Oh hell, it's not going to rain, we've been here since February and it hasn't rained a drop.' Well, on Wednesday, April 8, 1942, three days later, it rained, there was a little hail, it snowed, and there was one hell of a dust storm; a blue norther."[7]

Cole convinced his superiors at the airfield that he was a typist and that was the only talent he had. He was made an engineering clerk in the bomber's squadron, keeping aircraft records for a year.

Part One: A Place with Character

A Lucky Break for Art Cole and for Midland

"I had no idea where I was going when I came to Midland, but you talk about luck," Cole said. When he returned from combat duty, he remained here, but he tended to hang out with friends in Odessa until one day he had a revelation.

"Me and a couple of buddies used to go to Odessa and get drunk," Cole admitted. "I woke up one Sunday on the courthouse lawn in Odessa, and on Monday one of my friends who worked in public relations came to me and said, 'Art, there's a theatre group in Midland.' My friend got word somewhere that they were casting for *Arsenic and Old Lace* and convinced me that we should both go over and audition."[8]

Cole credited his friend, a former editor of *The New York Times Magazine* before the war, with introducing him to public relations, for which Cole would develop quite a knack in the coming years.

When he returned to Midland after World War II, he met with a group of theatre devotees one Sunday afternoon. The group was headed by Naomi Lancaster, herself a significant figure in the community at the time. Cole offered to go to work for three months to establish a theatre, feeling certain that ninety days would be all he would need to effectively gauge whether it would be a success. He asked for just $200 a month for living expenses.

When he finished his presentation that Sunday afternoon, a supporter in the back of the room stood up and said he didn't feel Cole could survive on such a small income. "Heck," the man said, "we'll give you $250 a month."[9]

Midland Community Theatre's first production, *George Washington Slept Here*, opened in 1946.

Getting the Best Out of Theatre Volunteers

Cole and his wife, Ruth, were so instrumental in forming Midland Community Theatre and developing it in its early years that their names now adorn the state-of-the-art complex in north Midland.

"He got things out of people that they didn't even know they had," said former Midlander Jim Salners:

> By the time I got to Midland in the 1970s, there was still just the two of them, Art and Ruth, running the theatre, with one person in the box office. They were doing a full set of shows. Art designed them all. He would make a working model of every single set and then turn it over to volunteers who

Theatre, Music, and a Mickey Mouse Rumor

would take a ruler and multiply or expand it, and build it. The volunteers flocked to Art and Ruth because of their personalities. Ruth did the books; we always said she was such a penny pincher she would pick up a penny out of the latrine.

When I was told to come from Odessa to Midland, I walked into the Midland Community Theatre just to look at it. There was a man up on the stage painting a picket fence for *To Kill a Mockingbird*, and I thought, "Here's my chance to be a worker bee and get the real skinny on the theatre."

I walked up and said to the man, "Can you tell me about this theatre?" and he said, "Yeah, I'll give you a little tour," and he showed me everything. That man turned out to be Art. He not only directed the plays, but he built the sets, designed the sets—and he even gave tours. He directed the plays; he didn't bring in outside help and he didn't bring in outside directors. What he gave Midland was quality theatre out of the person next door. Everybody was a volunteer. [10]

Salners gave an example of how the theatre's volunteer spirit all came together when one day during rehearsals for *Horse Feathers*, a fire broke out. Midland Community Theatre had hired an intern that summer named Kathy Turner, who would go on one day to be known to theatre audiences and moviegoers as Kathleen Turner (*Romancing the Stone, War of the Roses, Who Framed Roger Rabbit?*).

"Kathy was working with Art, learning the craft," Salners said. "When the fire started in the predawn hours, the water system came on, and all the sets and seats were ruined. Soaked. And it looked like there would be no chance we were going to open that night. All 550 seats were soaked. Ruth made a few phone calls at four or five that morning, and by nine that morning, there were more than 150 people—Kathleen Turner included—crawling all over that theatre. Twenty or thirty people built a new set. All the volunteers brought their hair dryers and were trying to dry out the seats."[11]

Sure enough, *Horse Feathers* opened that night as scheduled.

Summer Mummers: Melodrama Still Thrives

In 1949 Art Cole started the Summer Mummers, which performs melodramas every June through September as the main annual fund-raiser of Midland Community Theatre, its parent organization. The Mummers opened its sixty-sixth season on June 6, 2014, and has been running at the Yucca Theatre since 1981.

Part One: A Place with Character

In the 1960s, U.S. senator John Tower (R-Texas) swooped in to save a damsel in distress as a Summer Mummers guest actor. As longtime Midlander Katie Heck remembers it: "The plot, as most anyone in Midland can tell you, is always exactly the same, [and it was] even then. The villain has the heroine in his grips, and she says, 'You wouldn't take advantage of a poor, defenseless maiden, would you?' John Tower comes out onstage and dispatches the villain, the crowd goes nuts, and of course John is pleased as Punch that he got to grab the villain and free the maiden."[12]

Training Volunteers for Other Nonprofits All Over Town
Longtime community fund-raiser Rosalind Grover has come to the aid of Midland Community Theatre many times and remembers the days when Art and Ruth ran the show at Midland Community Theatre:

> Art trained all the nonprofit volunteers in our community back then on how to run a successful organization, including Junior League volunteers, symphony volunteers, and museum volunteers—not just theatre volunteers. I give him a lot of credit for laying the groundwork for so many nonprofits. He was a true genius and knew how to make things happen, and I don't know that many people recognize all the contributions he made to Midland. You have to have someone with the vision, and we were lucky to have had a man of vision like Art. Several people can have good vision at the same time, but if you have that one person who can put it all together, that's where you're better off for it . . . and Art was that person.[13]

Cole liked to tell the story of how both the theatre and the hospital ran concurrent fund-raisers in the late 1940s. That hospital was Midland Memorial, an important addition to the city, and one that was on its first capital campaign. "The hospital was raising money and we were, too. And do you know what?" Cole said. "They got what they needed and we got what we needed. It's an amazing thing, Midland. There's always been some money there."[14]

A Man with Quiet Charisma
Cole was a good first-impression man. At ninety-one, he could still quietly take control of a room and remained one of Midland's most cherished treasures, a rare person who possessed equal doses of character, vision, leadership, and ability. His legacy revealed itself slowly through his measured words and memories. He carried himself

in the dignified manner of many of the hundreds of thousands of members of his generation, people who served and fought bravely, and when the last shot had been fired, returned stateside to make their country an even better place than they had left.

Despite his charisma and magnetic personality, Cole still liked to think of himself and his role in the success of the theatre as "just a part of a long series of very lucky events." To hear him tell it, he was nothing but surprised to have ended up in Midland, much less to have had the impact he did.

Art Cole died on January 22, 2012, only twenty-one days after Ruth, who had worked beside him in Midland Community Theatre for so many years.

Roy Orbison Writes Three Hit Songs in Midland

West Texas may be desolate in its landscape, but it is rife with musical legends who hail from several of the area's smaller towns.

A Crop of Famous Musicians from West Texas

Buddy Holly was from Lubbock and recorded his major hits at a studio just across the Texas border in Clovis, New Mexico.

Woody Guthrie spent some of his most creative writing years while surviving the Dust Bowl years in the Panhandle town of Pampa; country swing founder Bob Wills hailed from Turkey, southeast of Amarillo. Waylon Jennings, one of the pioneers of country music's outlaw movement, was from Littlefield, northwest of Lubbock. All are now gone but remain hugely influential, genre-changing artists in their fields.

Orbison's Streak of *Billboard* Hits

Add to that impressive list of West Texas music legends the name Roy Orbison. The future songwriter was born in Vernon, and later his father settled the family in the oil town of Wink while looking for a job there. Roy went on to become one of the most revered artists in the Rock and Roll Hall of Fame. His and Buddy Holly's music were said to have directly influenced the Beatles, who held both men in the highest artistic regard. At one point early in their career, the Beatles even opened a show for Orbison.

"Only the Lonely," Orbison's breakthrough song, was written in Midland. It peaked at No. 2 on *Billboard*'s Hot 100 in 1960.

Part One: A Place with Character

Orbison and his songwriting partner Joe Melson lived briefly on the town's east side in 1959, where they wrote not just "Only the Lonely" but "Uptown" (No. 72, *Billboard*'s Hot 100, 1959) and "Blue Angel" (No. 9, *Billboard*'s Hot 100, 1960) as well. The duplex at 1217 East Nobles Street where the two lived and wrote is gone now, and all that remains is a vacant field.

"Joe wrote 'Blue Angel' on the way home from Midland Memorial Hospital after his wife had given birth to a baby girl," said Linda Melson, daughter-in-law of the songwriting legend. "He was pulled over by a police officer for speeding. Joe explained to him that his wife had just had a baby and he was excited and was writing a song about it (while speeding home). Joe got to the house where Roy was and said, 'I've just written another hit.'"[15]

Melson worked in ARCO's accounting department during his time in Midland. The penning of the song that has influenced the careers of musicians from the Beatles to Bruce Springsteen stands as one of the most notable artistic achievements to have ever occurred in Midland.

Had fate taken another turn, it might have even been bigger for the partners— not that a No. 2 *Billboard* hit isn't significant enough. Orbison and Melson once drove from Midland to Nashville, where they had an appointment at Roy Acuff's publishing company. On a whim, the two men stopped in Memphis. They planned to pitch "Only the Lonely" to Elvis Presley, hoping he might one day record it. When the two arrived at the doors of Graceland, they were told by the guard that Presley was asleep. The guard refused to wake the superstar, so Orbison and Melson drove on to Nashville, where they did pretty well for themselves without any assistance from Presley. In addition to the three songs written in Midland, Melson also cowrote "Runnin' Scared" and "Blue Bayou" with Orbison.[16]

The Wink Westerners and the Teen Kings

As culturally important as these early Orbison songs were in the annals of popular music, and as compelling as it is that they were written in Midland, another piece of history is perhaps even more remarkable: Orbison's entire career may have been launched in Midland, thanks to a chance meeting between the Wink resident, Johnny Cash, and Elvis Presley following a concert by the latter two at Midland High School on October 12, 1955.

Bear Mills, a freelance writer and former Midland schoolteacher, wrote in the *Midland Reporter-Telegram* how Orbison and his band, the Wink Westerners, would frequently play high school dances in the Midland-Odessa area. They were also regularly featured on TV stations KMID and KOSA.

"Roy later formed the Teen Kings and began seeking as much media attention as he could find," Mills wrote. "One of the performances he arranged was a Wednesday afternoon appearance on KMID. Also scheduled to appear on the show was up-and-coming superstar Johnny Cash, who was in town for a show that also included Elvis." The article in the *Midland Reporter-Telegram* stated:

> Cecil Holifield Jr., a student at [Midland High School], whose father owned the Record Shop stores in Midland and Odessa, said his dad not only promoted the Presley and Cash concert, but also arranged for various stars to appear on TV and radio in Midland-Odessa. In addition, "Pop" Holifield Sr. was also an advisor to Orbison about his would-be rock and roll career.
>
> Although there is only circumstantial evidence, it is strong that Holifield asked Cash to appear on KMID because he knew Orbison would also be performing. Whether the meeting was orchestrated or an accident, the result was the same. In spite of Orbison's thick glasses and rather bookish appearance, Cash was dazzled by his abilities as a singer and guitarist.[17]

After the KMID performance, Cash invited Orbison to the Midland High concert with a promise that he would meet Elvis. "Apparently, Cash also wanted Presley's opinion about Orbison's chances as a recording artist on Sam Phillips' Sun label. After talking with Orbison," Mills wrote, "Presley and Cash both agreed that the Wink native had the makings to be a musical success."[18]

The Rumor That Wouldn't Die

The wildest news in Midland during the 1990s concerned the supposed construction of a huge family entertainment venue, which was reported to have been in the works at a site along Interstate 20 between Midland and Odessa. As rumors go, this one was a doozy.

The headline of the day: *Disney Considering Theme Park in West Texas!*

Murmurs of the possibility that Midland would be home to a new Disney theme park grew fast and lingered for years afterward. New technology played a significant part in the story.

Part One: A Place with Character

A Few Fateful Words

It was 1996 and e-technology was just catching on. The *Midland Reporter-Telegram* operated a bulletin board, as they were known as in those days, called Basinlink. With a new way of communicating to constituents, Mayor Bobby Burns agreed to visit the newspaper to participate in a text Q&A, or chat session, with the bulletin board's users. At some point during the exchange, a user typed in the now-famous question, "Have you been involved in talks to bring a Disneyland theme park to Midland?" the screen read.

It seemed odd at the time. Then Burns responded. "Yes, I have been involved in discussions with people from Disney."[19]

The former mayor explained later that he had simply answered the question in the most honest way possible. He had just returned from a mayors' conference in Florida, where vendors and corporate representatives had set up display booths about their companies and products, courting the different city leaders. It's a practice not uncommon in the business world. Disney operated one of those booths, and Burns walked past during a break.

"There was some discussion about Disney looking for a desert location," Burns remembered. "I told them we had a great international airport, good land, and water, back when we actually had more water. It seemed to fit, which is why I had a meeting with them."[20]

Shortly after his return, Burns agreed to sit down for the Basinlink chat. "There was a story the next day on the front page, and before the end of the day, Big 2 [TV station KMID] wanted to talk about it on their newscast," Burns said.[21]

The Answer Is No

Within the next couple of months, though, Disney officials sent a letter to the mayor's office and told him the desert-themed project had been shelved. Goofy, Mickey, and Minnie would not be coming to West Texas. But by then, it was too late. The rumor had taken on a life of its own, and there was no stopping it.

About the same time that Burns received Disney's letter saying the project had been shelved, officials from *another* Disney division sent representatives to West Texas to lay the groundwork for a new Disney Store at Midland Park Mall. Word soon spread in Midland that Disney officials were staying at one of Midland's finest hotels, the Hilton Midland and Towers. Residents put two and two together, and before long, the rumor grew even larger.

"We told the media the story was over, that they weren't coming," Burns said.

Theatre, Music, and a Mickey Mouse Rumor

"But the public didn't believe it. They kept running with it. People would come to me and say, 'They have electrical that's been installed. I've seen water lines being laid. Roads are going in.' I kept hearing all this, and then I heard there were Disney reps staying at the Hilton."[22]

Burns said the city and chamber had been working together to encourage Disney to open one of its stores in the mall, and so the company was in town—just not for the reasons everyone hoped they were in town. In his three terms and nine years as mayor, Burns said he probably addressed questions about Disney a thousand times and speculated he fielded queries on average once a day.

"But You're Wrong, Mr. Mayor. We Have Information!"

"Every question-and-answer session I did for four or five years, I was asked about it," Burns said. "There were probably fifty Q&A's where citizens would tell me, the mayor, that I was wrong; it was happening and Disneyland was coming. Because they supposedly had the information. It no longer even mattered what I said."[23]

Burns said he never could figure out exactly why the rumor grew so huge. It got to a point where so many people told him they had information that Disney was coming, that "I actually started to question [whether] maybe I was wrong," Burns later joked. "I had no information suggesting they were coming, but I started to wonder myself."[24]

Even today, people insist that the park, had it ever been completed, was to have been located either on Highway 191 or Business 20 between Midland and Odessa, depending on which story you preferred. However, to no one's knowledge did a Disney theme-park representative ever actually set foot in Midland for a site visit.

People still talk about it as if it were a recent occurrence. Several users on a Midland history page on Facebook who were teenagers when the rumors swelled are disappointed it never panned out.

Another Facebook user said: "My father-in-law at the time worked construction, and they were looking at building it between Midland [and] Odessa. However, just the water bill alone was going to be astronomical, so they nixed the plan."

chapter 11

RACE RELATIONS IN MIDLAND

> *[A former student recently told me], "Miss Yarbrough, you know what I found out by leaving [Midland] and coming back? People in Midland, all they want to know is if you want to work and if you want to be a part of the town. It's not a black and white thing; it's a thing of 'I want to help.'"*
>
> —Barbara Yarbrough, longtime educator in Midland

No book on any American town would be complete or accurate without stories of its racial challenges and outright discrimination. Certainly racial prejudice has existed in West Texas since before the town of Midland itself was born, and there is no denying that race relations in Midland were strained during much of the twentieth century.

Midlanders will be among the first to say that although racism was less prevalent here than in many other cities, that still didn't make it acceptable.

In 2013 Midland County's race/ethnicity percentages were 52.2 percent Anglo, 38.7 percent Hispanic, 6.34 percent African American, 1.2 percent Asian American, and 1.4 percent other. Historically the county has comprised mostly Anglos and Hispanics, with a very small African American population.[1]

A Controversial Accusation in 1952

So few people had heard of Oscar M. Laurel in 1952 that an Associated Press wire story that ran in the *Midland Reporter-Telegram* on June 22, 1952, referred to him as Oscar Laura. At the time, Laurel, of Laredo, was the executive secretary and legal advisor for the League of United Latin American Citizens (LULAC). Scarcely three years later, he would be elevated to the position of LULAC's twenty-fourth president and soon came to be known as the best orator the organization ever had, according to former Laredo superintendent Vidal Trevino, a LULAC official.[2]

However, when Laurel took the podium at LULAC's annual convention in Corpus Christi in the summer of 1952, his words were anything but impressive to Midlanders. "Midland is a boiling cauldron of hate and discrimination," Laurel told the approximately 700 gathered at the state convention.

The single sentence was Laurel's only mention of Midland and its alleged racist tendencies, but in the days after the *Midland Reporter-Telegram* ran Laurel's comments, it was enough to generate heated conversation in coffee houses, barber shops, churches, and watering holes. Hackles were raised in town.

Two days after the original story, *Midland Reporter-Telegram* writer Harold Whittington wrote an article in response to the charges, under the headline, "Charge Midland Is 'Boiling Cauldron of Hate' Stirs Prompt Protests, Denials." Leading the pack of denials was A. V. Gutierrez, president of the Midland Council of LULAC, who said the city's instances of discrimination were problematic, but Laurel was "probably too strong in his indictment against the city," the *Midland Reporter-Telegram* reported.[3]

Mayor Perry Pickett spoke loudest, calling Laurel's comments "an injustice to the city, especially in that the speaker gave no facts to substantiate his charge."[4]

Another paragraph in that 1952 story read, "Latin Americans are not permitted to occupy seats on the main floors of Midland theatres, and there have been instances where they have been refused elsewhere. Nevertheless, it was conceded that while these factors exist here, they also exist in most other Texas cities." Today, more than sixty years after that *Midland Reporter-Telegram*'s story on Laurel's comments, many Midlanders would be disturbed if they were to read that statement, because it would awaken all-too-recent painful memories.

Gutierrez's words were even more pointed in the same 1952 account: "Our problem [in Midland] is in the city swimming pool, in the theatres, restaurants and barber shops. These things take years to solve and I have been unable to detect any progress here. But Midland is no worse than San Angelo and a number of other cities."

Odessa, it was pointed out, permitted Latin Americans to utilize its municipal swimming pool at the time.

Two of the city's pastors spoke as pointedly as anyone when hearing Laurel's indictment. First United Methodist pastor Luther Kirk charged that Laurel "simply doesn't know what he's talking about," while First Baptist Church's Rev. Vernon Yearby noted the church's work with Latinos.

"The charge is ridiculous," Yearby told the *Midland Reporter-Telegram*. "We have a Latin American mission which actually is a part of our own church. The mission is a building apart solely as a matter of convenience to the members and not as a matter of discrimination. Discrimination here is isolated, and the Anglo-Americans discriminate among themselves to a greater extent than they do among races. They discriminate on the grounds of economic and social life, often with greater determination than in those few cases of racial discrimination."

Midland's public schools were segregated until a federal lawsuit in the 1970s, however. One of the leaders of the movement to integrate Midland—and a party in that lawsuit—was a remarkable African American doctor from Louisiana.

Dr. Viola Coleman: Pioneer for Racial Equality

A pioneer in both medicine and civil rights, Dr. Viola Coleman arrived in Midland in 1951. To truly appreciate all she fought for and accomplished, we must follow her story back to the days before she came to West Texas, when she was unmarried and her name was still Viola Johnson.

Even her own sons knew nothing about her first major civil rights battle until after her death.

A Story Hidden in a Suitcase

When Viola Johnson opened her mailbox in New Iberia, Louisiana, she held out a slight feeling of hope that the letter inside would tell her that she had been accepted by Louisiana State University's medical school. Never mind that this was June 23, 1946, a time in our history when predominantly white institutions of higher learning did not admit students of color.

But the letter only confirmed what Johnson had suspected. "As you no doubt know," wrote James McLemore, then president of Louisiana State University, "the State of Louisiana maintains separate schools for its white and colored students. Southern University, located in Scotlandsville, in East Baton Rouge Parish, La., is the principle Louisiana university for negroes."[5]

Unintimidated by the bigotry and exclusionary practices of the time, Johnson immediately sat down at her manual typewriter and fashioned a response—but not to the school. Instead, Johnson wrote to Daniel Byrd, executive secretary of the National Association for the Advancement of Colored People (NAACP), in New York.

With her letter to Byrd, Johnson's pursuit of legal action against LSU began in earnest, and with the NAACP in her corner and future U.S. Supreme Court justice Thurgood Marshall serving as the association's special counsel, the wheels of the modern civil rights movement in Louisiana began to turn.

Johnson and the NAACP would ultimately lose their lawsuit in the Nineteenth District Court in Baton Rouge in an April 1947 judgment. Even so, historians in Texas and Louisiana say that what she represented and what she attempted, as well as the struggles she and her family faced in their lawsuit against LSU, were historically significant.

Adding intrigue to this chapter of Midland's history, when she died in Midland, Viola Johnson, who eventually became Dr. Viola Coleman, took the story of her historic challenge to the grave. Her two sons, Conrad, of Midland, and Reginald, of Dallas, both said their mother never spoke of her efforts to bring down the color barrier in Louisiana. "She never once sat us down and said, 'This is what I did,'" Conrad Coleman said. "I was just amazed when I started reading the letters."[6]

Viola Johnson's efforts to bring racial equality to Louisiana came some ten years before Dr. Martin Luther King Jr., Rosa Parks, and others began to gain national respect for their courage in advancing civil rights. Her trailblazing efforts live on today in the form of a fascinating series of letters that her sons found tucked in a suitcase inside a closet at her home on Midland's southeast side. That same home had also served as the location of her private medical practice.

It began in the summer of 1945, when Johnson wrote LSU requesting a course catalog. In the first return correspondence, the school's assistant registrar mistakenly referred to her as "Mr. Johnson." Five months passed before she received another letter. Finally, in March 1946, she wrote to LSU informing officials she was interested in applying for admission to medical school with their next class of students. Johnson received a letter from the university that foretold the unlikelihood of her gaining admission. School officials informed her bluntly that very few nonresident students were admitted to the school of medicine. By then, Johnson was attending Meharry College in Nashville, Tennessee. She ultimately received her medical degree from the Tennessee school.[7]

On May 31, 1946, Coleman received some good news. A letter from the

PART ONE: A PLACE WITH CHARACTER

NAACP advised her that the civil rights group would "consider it a privilege" to assist in her efforts to desegregate LSU's medical school.

"I assure you immediate action will be taken upon refusal of your admittance," wrote Daniel Byrd. The letter was carbon-copied to Thurgood Marshall. Marshall, of course, would himself make history by becoming the first African American justice on the United States Supreme Court in 1967.[8]

On June 6, 1946, Viola Johnson was notified by LSU that her application for admission had indeed been denied, and on June 23 came the second letter from McLemore, the chairman of the university's supervisors, leaving no doubt that she was not welcome at LSU.

It took the Nineteenth District Court in Louisiana more than six months to rule that Johnson was unsuccessful in her efforts against the university. A headline she clipped from the *New Orleans Times-Picayune* dated April 1, 1947, read, "Iberia Negress Loses Court Suit to Attend LSU."

Laurie Green, a history professor at the University of Texas with emphasis on civil rights matters, said whether Viola Johnson was successful or not is subjective depending on her ultimate goal. The crucial point, Green said, is that the Louisiana court's decision to deny her admission occurred at a transitional point in American history, when "separate but equal" was being redefined by the U.S. Supreme Court.

"The courage, stamina and determination that would have been involved for Viola, her family, her community, and the attorneys in bringing such a suit" are historically noteworthy, Green said. "So often, the only cases that get attention are the ones that win, but the ones that are lost can tell us just as much."[9]

There was an eight-month gap in correspondence between Dr. Coleman and the NAACP. The next letter arrived on Dec. 6, 1947, from the Louisiana Colored Teachers Association. It was accompanied by a $700 check from the Teacher-Pupil Welfare Fund, presumably to help Dr. Coleman with tuition at Meharry in Nashville.

She next received her penultimate correspondence from the NAACP in February 1948, a boldly worded letter of encouragement from Daniel Byrd:

> Please don't permit those persons whose attitudes and thoughts are dwarfed to the extent that they are antebellum in their philosophy and demeanor to alarm you. It is God's valiant minority who must wage war on the insidious evils; war on a double-barreled basis. In the one barrel aimed, sighted and cocked on the laws, practices, customs and usages that keep us walled in; and the other barrel, in a like manner, cocked on the members of

our group, who for a job or personal gain or for even a handout, would aid in the perpetuation of these evils.

Our hope is in the youth, whose minds are not enslaved to this inferior status.[10]

Byrd wrote one final letter to Viola Johnson, further encouraging her and saying that her efforts could be positively affected pending the outcome of a similar desegregation effort at the University of Texas, made by Hemon Sweatt, who challenged and finally desegregated that institution's law school. That last letter, found in her mementos, again made reference to Johnson receiving a $700 check by the "LEA," believed to have formerly been the Louisiana Colored Teachers' Association. Though no proof was ever found, it is believed that the State of Louisiana and the LEA funded Johnson's education at Meharry College, a victory of sorts, despite her technically losing the court challenge.

"Having known Dr. Coleman, I wouldn't think she would have considered it a victory," said Dr. James Fuller, a leader in Midland's African American community, a professor at Midland College, and a board member of the Midland Independent School District. "But I think her response was probably, 'I'll make the best of what I've got and go from there.' She did make the best of what she had in coming to Midland, picking up the mantle and addressing issues of segregation and some of the other issues she faced in her new hometown and state."[11]

Johnson's unsuccessful lawsuit was appealed to the Louisiana State Supreme Court, but the case was subsequently dropped on June 13, 1953, rendered moot because she had by then moved out of state, to Midland.

After graduation from Meharry, Dr. Johnson tried unsuccessfully to establish a practice in Louisiana, where Jim Crow was in full force. She attempted to secure a loan for $300 from a bank in Louisiana to start her practice, but the bank asked that she put up both her parents' house and her grandparents' house as collateral. It was then that Dr. Coleman and her husband, Raymond, a teacher, decided to board a train for the West Coast, where they had heard opportunities for and treatment of minorities were more plentiful and acceptable.

The train that carried the young married couple that summer of 1951 stopped in Fort Worth, where the young doctor ran into a friend and fellow physician. The man told the Colemans he'd heard about a possible medical position in a growing town just three hundred miles to the west. The train stopped again in Midland, where a brand-new hospital had just opened its doors.[12]

Part One: A Place with Character

Midland Welcomes Dr. Coleman

When Dr. Coleman and her husband stepped off the train in Midland, she went to Midland Memorial Hospital and asked medical officials there if they would grant her privileges to practice medicine there.

"And they said to her, 'Why wouldn't we?'" Conrad recalls his mother telling him.

Even though she had just arrived in town, Dr. Coleman was also able to obtain a loan from Murray Fasken, former president of Midland National Bank, based solely on her signature. Dr. Viola Coleman would use—and promptly repay—that loan to establish her medical practice on the city's southeast side. She continued tending to the sick through that practice until shortly before her death in 2005. Over her lifetime she left a lasting mark on the community and became one of the city's most revered citizens.

A Doctor Who Could Foresee the Future

Margaret Williams, a longtime nurse at Midland Memorial Hospital, spent several years working alongside Dr. Coleman and considered the doctor a friend. She recalls Coleman was an avid baseball fan who seldom if ever had a chance to attend games of the semiprofessional Midland Indians because she was "always delivering a baby." She was that rare medical professional who was a visionary, Williams said:

> It was like she could see into the future. She said, "One of these days there's going to be a hospital here that is going to lead the Permian Basin in treating all of these diseases that are killing people." She said we will have an open-heart surgery ability here, and when she said that, it was in the early 1960s and Parkland Hospital in Dallas was just introducing open-heart surgery procedures.
>
> We didn't have nursing homes in the 1950s, but she predicted that one day we would have a facility for elder patients who weren't sick enough for a hospital but who weren't well enough to be home. And of course we have a lot of those today. She predicted intensive care units, and that didn't come about until the early 1970s, and she predicted coronary care units, which we opened in 1971. She also knew that one day in the future, fathers would be able to go into labor rooms as their wives were having babies.[13]

In the 1970s, Coleman was also an instrumental voice in the movement for integrated schools in Midland, and a leader in the African American community.

Race Relations in Midland

Dr. James Fuller said Dr. Coleman's work in integrating both Midland schools and the city's hospital were representative of the type of challenges from which she never backed down. "The work of desegregating Midland Memorial and her work in bringing equity in education . . . she did that kind of work quite literally right up until the day she died," he noted. "[Dr. Coleman fought for] equity in terms of the eating facilities at the hospital, and moving patients of color from the basement to all floors of the hospital. . . . She was a woman of courage, perseverance, dedication, human sensitivity, and determination."[14]

After Dr. Coleman's death, her two sons donated their mother's letters and papers to the University of Texas of the Permian Basin, where the documents were used as part of a civil rights exhibit in 2009.

Personal Stories from Midlanders of Color

One of the best ways to obtain perspective on any social issue is to hear the stories of specific people involved. Hundreds of unique, sometimes contradictory personal accounts combine to form a composite picture. Here are brief narratives from several people in Midland.

Joe Chavez
"There's no more school for you after next week."
Joe Chavez is a Mexican American and a lifelong Midlander who is now in his eighties.

Joe Chavez described his experience in the Midland public schools in 1938:

> I remember being in the eighth grade. The school I went to was near downtown Midland, and I loved school. And I'll never forget how two days before I finished the eighth grade, my teacher came to me and said, "That's all. There's no more school for you after next week. But since you like school so much, you can repeat the eighth grade if you would like."[15]

Chavez was crushed. At that time Mexican Americans in Midland attended their own separate public school, which ended at eighth grade. It was not until 1946 that Mexican Americans were allowed to attend junior high and high school with white students and continue with their education through the twelfth grade. The first Mexican Americans graduated from high school in Midland in 1952.[16]

Another public school in Midland was just for African American students. Carver School, which opened in 1933, was later expanded and eventually included a junior high and high school. Its first twelfth graders graduated in 1943.[17] However, African American students were not integrated with white students in Midland until 1968.[18] (For more about Carver School and Midland's struggles with school integration, see Chapter 12.)

Chavez fought through the limited educational opportunities afforded him and others of his descent during those times. He and his wife raised three children, all of whom not only graduated from high school, but now have master's degrees. The Honorable Sylvia Chavez, a child-protection associate judge in Midland, is their daughter.[19]

Sid Trevino
"Give my sisters their money back."
Sid Trevino was the first Hispanic detective on the Midland police force, hired in 1953.

A frequent example of discrimination in Midland concerns minorities who were prohibited from sitting alongside whites in movie theatres in town, be it the Hodge, the Ritz, or the Yucca.

One theatre manager downtown made the mistake of keeping Sid Trevino's sisters out of first-floor seating at the Yucca one afternoon in 1954. As Trevino told the story:

> I have eight sisters. Three of them came for a visit on vacation that summer and asked what there was to do in Midland. I told them, "We have the Ritz Theater on Main Street or the Yucca Theatre." They got to the Yucca about three in the afternoon to see a movie, and they walked in the door and started to sit in the seats downstairs.
>
> The cashier told them, "You can't sit downstairs. You have to sit in the balcony." One of my sisters asked why. The theatre manager told them it was theatre policy.
>
> My sister told the manager, "Well, we want to sit downstairs. We don't want to sit in the balcony." The cashier told them again that they couldn't do that.
>
> My sister told the manager that she and the others wanted their money

back, and the theatre operator said, "Well, you can't have your money back."

One of my sisters got on the pay phone and called me. I was working with the police department by then. My sister told me, "This is your town. We came to visit you, and they are telling us where we can and cannot sit." So I ran down and talked to the cashier, who called the manager.

Two weeks earlier, there had been a burglary at the theatre, and the manager knew me. I had worked the case. He asked me if the three women were related to me, and I said, "Yes, they're my sisters."

And he said, "Well, it's okay, they can sit downstairs."

I told him, "They don't want to sit downstairs. They want their money back."

He said, "No problem, we'll get your money back. No problem."[20]

Barbara Yarbrough
"That little girl's mama told her she'd be raped in the hallways and the bathroom."
Barbara Yarbrough is an African American, a longtime classroom teacher, and the founder of the Barbara Yarbrough Parenting Center.

Barbara Yarbrough came to Midland in the 1950s. She was one bus stop away from turning around and going back to Houston because of how bleak she remembers West Texas being. Through the ups and downs of racism, she stuck it out and today remains happy for her decision to stay here. She calls Midland a place where "the possibilities are unlimited."

> Everything I was doing in my early days in Houston was grooming me to work in Midland. When I came here, the head of the art department was not a very nice person in my eyes. She'd talk about minstrels, and this and that. And I'm the only minority in the whole bunch at school. The rest were male coaches or white female art teachers. I told my principal I will not be responsible for what I do to this woman. My exact words were, "I am going to whip her ass if she says stuff like that again."
>
> When we clustered with Fannin and Burnet and South Elementary, the kids saw Mrs. Yarbrough. They didn't see a black teacher. Some of them might, but the masses in class saw "Miss Bro," that's what they called me. One student called me Crazy Lady. I called him Bossy Buddy. He still calls me Crazy Lady today. I had another one who was the bossiest little

Part One: A Place with Character

boy, so I named him Bossy Butt. These were kids with blue eyes, blond hair or brown hair, and they looked at me and saw "Miss Bro." So why shouldn't I look back at them and see another person, too? Working with children, they always see what they consider your goodness, and that's what they saw. Why shouldn't we see that in other people, too?[21]

It did take a while for people of different races to learn how to mix together acceptably after the desegregation issue in Midland in the 1970s. It was not an overnight adjustment. From Yarbrough's perspective as a teacher:

You have to think about those mamas at the time. It was the unknown that scared them to death. Every one of them sent their children to do what they [themselves] would not do. I thought they were terrible parents.

When the kids came over here to South Elementary from Fannin, I saw one little [white] girl dancing a jig one day, and I said, "Girl, what's the matter with you?" She said, "I need to go to the bathroom, but my mama said I'd be raped in the hallways and in the bathrooms." I had to walk that poor little girl to the toilet.

Soon enough, the children found out that the other children were just like they were. We're always afraid of the unknown, and we don't want our kids going to that school. Don't want them associating with those people.

I had emergency surgery in the spring the first year after the cluster system went into effect. It was the last Friday in April, and do you know who took care of me? My students. Not my black students. I would wake up and they were sitting on the side of my bed, my white students. They would tell their parents, "We've got to go to Miss Bro's house so we can see how she's doing." They would pick me up and bring me to the school. And their parents would ask, "Hey, Miss Yarbrough, do you need us to go to such and such?" They would come pick me up and take me places. I was their children's teacher. It wasn't about me being a colored lady, a black lady, whatever. This was 1978. Some of those parents, we're still tight today.[22]

Jose Cuevas
"I remember I was told, 'Black people don't do ceramics.'"
Jose Cuevas is a former Midland city councilman, the founder and CEO of the Jumburrito restaurant chain; presiding officer of the Texas Alcoholic Beverage Commission,

appointed by Texas Governor Rick Perry; and president of the Midland County Fresh Water Supply District No. 1.

In 1979, two years after moving to Midland from McAllen, Jose Cuevas purchased equipment to open a restaurant. By 2010 Jumburrito employed 155 people in six stores.

Cuevas has become an outspoken leader of the Latino community in Midland, has served as a Midland city councilman, and has been named the president of the Texas Restaurant Association.

President George W. Bush, who once frequented Jumburrito with close friend and former U.S. Commerce Secretary Don Evans, also from Midland, called on Cuevas to serve on a state board during Bush's term as Texas governor, but Cuevas was forced to decline because of prior obligations.

Like others in the Latino community, he has seen racism in his adopted hometown. He described his role in establishing a new community center in Midland's racially diverse southeast side:

> I remember we were in the planning process for Reyes-Nelms-Mashburn Park. [Longtime councilmember] Bill Williams knew the Hispanics in town didn't have the same opportunities to get facilities as in other parts of town. I remember sitting in a meeting with him and talking to the baseball board and telling them we were going to build T-ball and Little League fields. The board said nobody's gonna go to T-ball games there, and we said fine, that's where we're putting it anyway. Bill was with me. They were livid. But we stuck by it and built it. Now they use them all the time.
>
> The council hadn't done anything for the east or south side either. I told them I want to build a community center on the southeast side of town. They wanted me to use Community Development Block Grant money. I said I wanted to take unappropriated funds. So I called J. D. Faircloth and another council member and forced that vote, and now we have a Southeast Center over here in this part of town. One of the comments made during the planning process was that black people don't do ceramics. One of the other comments was, "Oh, they'll break the windows and have graffiti all over it." We've never had graffiti. No one has ever bothered it, because this was where their grandmothers were going [for craft programs].
>
> I'm disappointed that we don't have more Hispanic leaders stepping

Part One: A Place with Character

up and taking ownership. Father Tom Kelley, who pastored Our Lady of San Juan Church, now San Miguel Arcángel, on the south side, would tell everyone they are in charge of their own destiny. If the community you live in doesn't feel passionate enough and you are at a school board meeting, a county commissioners or a city council meeting, voice your concern. If you don't, you can't complain about it when things in your community don't happen.[23]

Pastor George Bell

"Midland is one of those God-blessed cities ... the most giving and caring cities." *Dr. George Bell, pastor of Greater Ideal Baptist Church on Midland's southeast side, has done a remarkable job in the last decade of rebuilding an area that has long been neglected.*

A 1986 closure of Lee Street at the railroad tracks along Front Street slowed the south-side economy and resulted in the closing of restaurants, Laundromats, barber shops, and entertainment venues. The city explained to the south-side residents and business owners that the street closure was because Lamesa Road had been enhanced and provided a more viable artery into and out of the community. Lee Street, however, suffered as a result, as Dr. Bell recalls:

> In the 1950s and 1960s, there were hotels, restaurants, gas stations, cab stands. The southeast side was self-sufficient. We had some of the greatest entertainers in the world come to Midland: Al Green, Ray Charles, Aretha Franklin. Some of the biggest names in show business came to Midland's southeast side. Lee Street was the main through street on the southeast side. You didn't come across Lamesa. Every business was thriving all up and down Lee Street, all of the nightclubs, churches, everything was thriving.
>
> The city cut off Lee Street and moved the main through street to Lamesa, which ended up being what we still have today. When that happened, you started seeing the end of some of the businesses.[24]

Bell's neighborhood revitalization efforts have resulted in the cropping up of numerous new businesses that have played a part in regrowing the community. Restaurants, revamped churches and parks, auto shops, and other businesses have grown as a result of the Greater Ideal effort.

Race Relations in Midland

Bell's grandfather is George Ellis, owner of Ellis and Sons Plumbing. Since 1958, Bell says, his grandfather's major form of advertising has been its signature orange vans, which served a dual purpose in the beginning:

> It was slow going starting out because many people weren't used to calling an African American plumber out to their house. A lot of Midlanders were working during the day, and when you call a plumber, you normally leave your door unlocked and you just have the plumber go in and do his business and he leaves a bill. That was a struggle for my grandfather in those days, and business was slow, but he overcame all the difficulties and made a great living for himself and his family, and left a great legacy for me and those who have come after me.
>
> My grandfather was one of the first African American plumbers in Midland, and you can imagine what it must have been like to start your own business as an African American in 1958. Things were very slow.
>
> I remember him telling us stories about when he started in the plumbing business he had a black-panel van instead of orange, and some weeks the phone wouldn't ring. He had a piece of plywood that he used to make signs for his advertising. One said "Ellis and Sons Plumbing" and the other said "Ellis and Sons Lawn Service, Peach Picking and Tree Trimming." If the phone wasn't ringing for the plumbing business, he'd switch the signs out and put the lawn mowing and peach picking and tree trimming sign out. He'd cut yards and all that, trying to wait it out until the plumbing business would build up. He did that for several years before he got a good foundation in plumbing.[25]

Bell doesn't deny that Midland has had its problem with discrimination through the years. Racism rarely if ever escapes anyone of color, regardless where they choose to call home. In spite of it, he has nothing but kind words to describe Midland.

> Midland is one of those God-blessed cities. It is one of the most giving and caring cities I have ever lived in all my life. Even growing up in Midland in the 1960s, which I did, I have to say I experienced racism and discrimination, but Midland hasn't been as bad as other areas of the country. Midland has a very generous heart and has always been generous for different cultures and races.[26]

Part One: A Place with Character

After almost fifty years, Bell came clean about a decision he made on the night he turned seven:

> I remember when James Brown came to town. My mom gave me a big birthday party, but my aunts had tickets to see James Brown. And the concert was at the same time as my birthday party. My aunts came over and snuck me out of my bedroom window to go with them to hear James Brown. It was the best of times and it was the worst of times, because my mother found out and came to the concert, and when she caught up with me, she got me in a bad way. I got to hear the opening song when he came out with his cape on and I saw him throw it before I got snatched up out of the building by my mother.[27]

Michael Williams
"The opportunities here are greater and more poignant than perhaps anyplace else."
Michael Williams, an African American, is a former Texas railroad commissioner and is currently the commissioner of the Texas Education Agency.

Michael Williams remembers well growing up in the last years of pre-integration Midland. Williams's school career parallels that of his mother, who left Midland for St. Peter Claver School in San Antonio because it was integrated, and all the schools in Midland were still segregated. Williams's parents sent him to Canyon City Boarding School in Canyon City, Colorado, because they did not want him attending school in a segregated district.

After he was away for a year, MISD schools finally desegregated. Williams returned to Midland and became one of the most successful students to graduate from Lee High School. He later graduated with bachelor's and master's degrees from the University of Southern California, as well as a law degree from the USC School of Law in Los Angeles. He was elected to the Texas Railroad Commission and currently serves as the Commissioner of Education with the Texas Education Agency in Austin.

Like George Bell, Williams remembers the changing face of the southeast side when traffic was routed to Lamesa Street as the main thoroughfare through the neighborhood:

> Was it controversial? Yes. Margie Titus and some of the other business owners in those first two blocks south of the tracks went to the city council

a couple of times to urge them not to do it, and there was even a petition drive at the time. It's awfully strange. I went back there recently, and it is still strange to see Lee Street with no traffic.[28]

Despite the imperfect world that is Midland, minority residents frequently say that the town provides opportunities that would be impossible elsewhere:

> I would daresay the opportunities here are greater and more poignant than perhaps anyplace else. There was no other place for me to be born and raised than Midland. I cannot imagine another city in this country that would have taken a kid who was black, who is out of law school by the age of twenty-five, and by the time he is twenty-seven would have served on the boards of directors for the United Way of Midland, the Midland Chamber [of Commerce], and the Midland County Housing Board. Where else could that happen?[29]

chapter 12

MIDLAND DEBATES KEY ISSUES IN THE HIGH COURTS

> *Things have changed a great deal in the last forty years. I believe there is a feeling on the part of everyone that we have made progress. I'm sure there are those who feel we haven't made enough.*
> —Charles Tighe, attorney and 1970s board member of the Midland Independent School District, in 2008

MIDLAND MADE NEWS FOR ITSELF in the late 1960s, when the United States Supreme Court took up a districting case that originated here. Another important federal lawsuit, about desegregating the public school system, would involve Midland in the 1970s.

Avery v. Midland County: A Lawsuit about Districting

In September 1962 Hank Avery, then mayor of Midland, petitioned the Midland County Commissioners Court to have voting districts drawn off in a more equitable manner. When his request was denied, he filed suit against Midland County that same month.[1]

One commissioner's district in Midland County included almost all of the City of Midland, while the remaining three were in rural areas. In 1963, when the case was first tried, the estimated population of the largest of the four districts was almost 68,000 voters. The three remaining rural districts had population estimates of 852, 414, and 828.[2]

Midland Debates Key Issues in the High Courts

A Commissioner Describes a Lopsided System

"I was the commissioner of Precinct One at that time," said longtime Midlander Bill Heck. "Precinct One had all the voters in the county, for all practical purposes. I had to fight to get the votes of half of the 68,000 . . . Alvey Bryant, the commissioner in Precinct Two, in the eastern part of the county . . . could have dinner at his house for all of his voters. The guy in Precinct Three was Clark Moreland . . . Lewis Osborne had the far west precinct, the airport area."

Heck said the abundance of voters in his precinct was only part of the problem. When commissioners cast votes in court sessions, the votes of all four commissioners were of equal value despite the discrepancy of the numbers of the electorate![3] If there was a tie, County Judge Barbara Culver would cast the deciding vote. On close votes, Heck said if he couldn't twist the arms of one of the commissioners of the rural precincts, he was "a dead duck."

"To get anything done, I had to pry one of them loose from their organization. For the first two years it was particularly tough. They were wedded to each other, and I couldn't get anything done. The main problem I had on the court was the solid front they could present to me and knock down anything they weren't in favor of. They could do anything they wanted to, and there was nothing I could do about it," Heck said.[4]

One of the worst transgressions in the disparity of votes came as a result of each commissioner being granted three miles of paving projects in his district each year. There was no justification as to why the paving was needed in a particular area, Heck said, and it was up to each commissioner to decide why his three-mile stretch deserved to be upgraded. The stretches of pavement would increase the value of adjacent land, and with the paving also came new fencing that ran alongside the newly paved roadways. Such upgrades were good for the rural commissioners.[5] "Alvey [Bryant] was probably the biggest offender," Heck said. "He would pave the road, build a new fence, and then he would buy the old fence and install it elsewhere in his precinct." Such maneuvering, Heck said, gave rural commissioners clear advantages. "If they had the stroke, they had the vote," Heck said. "And away they'd go." Moreland once came to loggerheads with Bryant, and the commissioners' schism ultimately meant Moreland sided with Heck on more issues, which made the court's votes somewhat more equitable for a time.[6]

Heck remembered a pump at a county-run barn that quit working one day. The maintenance man at the barn called Heck, who authorized the pump's repair.

Part One: A Place with Character

"The other commissioners wouldn't sign off on it to be fixed for about six months because I and another commissioner had already signed off on it. It was just little stuff like that."

Heck elected not to run again after his one term. He and his wife, Katie, became the first husband-and-wife team in Midland history to have both served in an elected capacity: Bill on the county commissioners court, Katie on the city council.

Avery v. Midland County Reaches the U.S. Supreme Court

The case was first tried in the District Court of Midland County, then appealed in the Texas Court of Civil Appeals and the Texas State Supreme Court before finally reaching the U.S. Supreme Court. Arguments were made before the high court on November 14, 1967, with Avery insisting that the disparity of population among the four districts violated the Equal Protection Clause of the Fourteenth Amendment. On April 1, 1968, the case was decided in favor of Avery, and the law was changed.[7]

Lawsuits about Desegregating Midland's Public Schools

The United States Supreme Court ruled on May 17, 1954, in *Brown v. Board of Education of Topeka*, that school districts providing "separate but equal" schools for students of different races violated equal protection of the laws guaranteed by the Fourteenth Amendment. The Supreme Court did allow time for states to make viable desegregation plans.[8]

Midland's First (Very Gradual) Integration Plan

Midland did not react with anything resembling swiftness with regard to the matter of integrating its public schools.

On August 14, 1956, the trustees of the Midland Independent School District (MISD) voted to integrate, beginning with the first grade, in September, and to add an additional grade upward each year. But under this plan, it would have taken twelve more years, until September 1968, before all grades were completely integrated. And in fact it took longer than that.[9]

Midland was admittedly not without its racist attitudes. Several days after the MISD trustees rendered their 1956 vote to integrate (however gradually), two six-foot burning crosses were planted on two different front lawns—terrorist acts that were ultimately dismissed by police as the work of pranksters. That same month, August 1956, the first African American enrolled in first grade at DeZavala Elementary, a virtually all Mexican American school. An African American second grader was denied admission there because second grade was not scheduled for integration until the following year, September 1957.[10] Not only had Anglo students been segregated from both Mexican American and African American students; these two minorities had also been largely separate from each other.

By the end of the 1956 school year, four African American students were enrolled at DeZavala School. In August 1957, school superintendent Harold Hitt said a total of thirteen African American first and second graders were expected to enroll at DeZavala School that fall, and MISD saw no reason to hurry its desegregation plans beyond this pace.[11]

A Lawsuit Foiled by an Attorney's Lapse

MISD's course of action was challenged by Dr. Viola Coleman and a group of intervenors in a July 1968 lawsuit. That September, MISD filed a motion to have the desegregation suit against it dismissed. Weldon Berry, the lawyer for the plaintiffs, failed to respond to the motion for dismissal or to show up in court, and on October 8, 1968, Judge Ernest Guinn, of El Paso's Western District Court, dismissed the suit because of Berry's lack of a timely response.[12]

Meanwhile, September 1968 had also seen the advent of secondary-school busing and the controversial closure of Carver Junior-Senior High School, a predominantly African American school whose students were now being bused to other Midland schools. But Midland's struggle with properly integrating its schools was just beginning.

United States v. Midland Independent School District

Less than two years later, on August 7, 1970, the U.S. Department of Justice, on behalf of the Department of Health, Education and Welfare, filed suit in Austin alleging that MISD and four other school districts in Texas continued to operate "racially dual school systems and had failed to adopt plans for a unitary, nondiscriminatory system."[13] The suit applied only to MISD elementary schools. By 1970 Midland's secondary schools had been integrated.[14]

"In the early 1970s, Midland was one of only five Texas school districts singled out for these lawsuits," recalled Joe Dominey, who served as president of the MISD trustees from 1976 to 1977 and was a board member from 1971 to 1980. "The others were Austin, Corpus Christi, Dallas, and Waco. These districts were chosen rather randomly. Ector ISD wasn't that much different than MISD on that issue, but they didn't go through the same legal process MISD did. Ector, though, had set up a system of magnet schools, and magnets drew on all parts of the community for students, and that satisfied the Justice Department's requirements."[15]

It was determined that, in singling out MISD, the Justice Department had considered evidence dating all the way back to the 1920s. Midland had opened a school for Mexican American students. On the front of the school was a sign that read "Mexican School." Dominey said, "That was *prima facie* evidence that we had a segregated school district.... We had a Negro School, too.... The Civil Rights Act of 1964 basically identified certain states as being segregationist-type states, and Texas fell into that category. Those states were treated differently than remaining states."[16]

United States v. Midland Independent School District shuttled back and forth several times between the U.S. District Court for the Western District of Texas (the lowest level of federal court involved) and the U.S. Court of Appeals, Fifth Circuit (the next higher level):

★ On September 1, 1970, Judge Ernest Guinn ruled in favor of MISD in the district court, claiming that Midland's school system was already unitary.[17]

★ On June 28, 1971, the court of appeals overturned this ruling and sent the case back to the district court, directing it "to require the school board forthwith to constitute and implement a pupil assignment plan" that complied with principles recently established in *Swann v. Charlotte-Mecklenburg Board of Education*,[18] another 1971 desegregation case.

★ The district court claimed a second time that MISD's existing plan already complied with the constitutional principles.

★ On August 28, 1975, the court of appeals reversed the district court's judgment a second time. Judge John Minor Wisdom held that "an overriding intent by the school board to segregate Mexican-Americans and blacks was demonstrated by the statistical evidence of record, including the fact that the seven elementary schools east of Big Spring Street have an average minority group enrollment of 81%, whereas the 12 elementary schools west of Big Spring Street have student populations averaging about 96% Anglo." MISD was ordered to "immediately ... dismantle the dual system in the elementary grades."[19]

★ MISD attempted to have the case reviewed by the U.S. Supreme Court, but that request was denied on February 23, 1976.[20] This rendered the August 1975 U.S. Court of Appeals decision final.

It was absolutely clear that MISD had to act. But the majority of Midlanders did not want to integrate the elementary schools. "So there were some strategies," Dominey said. "This time, people in the community were encouraged to come forward and, as neutral parties, help come up with some sort of plan."[21]

The Cluster System

One of those community members was Parker Humes, general manager of KCRS Radio and future board member and president of the MISD trustees. Another was attorney Pat Baskin, who would later become judge of the 142nd District Court in Midland. Together, Baskin and Humes arrived at a system that, while not necessarily ideal, at least equally inconvenienced everyone.[22]

It was called the cluster system. The plan affected students in fourth through sixth grades. Students would attend their neighborhood schools in kindergarten through third grade. Then all students in fourth, fifth, and sixth grades would be bused to schools in other parts of town. Minority students would attend a school in a nonminority area of town for a year. A second year, students in an affluent school, for instance, would attend a school on the south side or east side of town. The third year of the cluster system, students would remain in their home school while welcoming students from other parts of town.[23]

The plan satisfied the Justice Department's stipulations. Dominey and the school board signed off on it September 15, 1976, and the plan was enacted.

Reactions throughout the life of the cluster system were widely varied. Charles Tighe, a former MISD board member and local attorney, told the *Midland Reporter-Telegram* in 2008 that although support was far from unanimous, once people became used to the idea, most thought it was a good way to answer the stipulations of the Justice Department's call for Midland school desegregation.

Part One: A Place with Character

Robbyne Hocker Fuller, a Carver High School graduate, supported the cluster system because it fully integrated the district, and students throughout Midland schools were allowed to get to know each other.

Joe Dominey put it this way: "The argument in favor of the cluster system was students would have to ride the bus only two years out of seven. It was equal involvement for everyone. Everyone was inconvenienced—it didn't matter if you lived on the north side, the south side, the east side or the west side. Did it solve anything? The Justice Department was basically going to run the school district if we had not complied with the lawsuit. Theoretically, the board of trustees would have been removed, the superintendent would have been removed and the Justice Department would have come in and run the school district."[24]

Joan Baskin, wife of Pat Baskin, said the people involved in bringing on the cluster system were people who had a social conscience. As she put it in 2010, "I remember Margaret Cowden saying, 'The first bus that takes people to Edison Junior High School is going to have all of our children on it.' Margaret said, 'If our schools aren't good enough for our children, they're not good enough for anyone's children.' She took the point that we are the managers, we are the owners of our schools, and we have to take the attitude that the student from the single-parent home with no books is just as important as our kids are."[25]

The Closing of Carver School

Midland's transition to a fully integrated district did have a number of ups and downs, to be sure. One casualty was an educational facility that many people still remember with great fondness as a lifeline for the young African American community of Midland.

Joan Love-Davis, a business owner on Midland's southeast side, calls the closing of Carver School heartbreaking. The unique school united southeast Midland and bound together a way of life, creating and strengthening relationships, and serving the students who were unable to attend the city's white schools.

Carver School, opened in 1933, was the first public school for African Americans in Midland. (Before that, classes for students of color had been held in local churches.) The school opened in a three-room brick building in the 100 block of Carver Street. In 1943 Carver celebrated its first graduating class of two twelfth graders: one boy and one girl.

The school was later expanded to become a junior and senior high. Between 1940 and 1949, "enrollment increased from about 60 students to 550. Plans were then made for Midland's first high school building for African Americans. In 1950 a six-room brick building with a gymnasium-auditorium, a two-room office suite, a book room and a darkroom was completed."[26] In 1958 the school district spent $500,000 on remodeling and expanding Carver School again.[27]

"When we were going to Carver, the three Rs were really stressed," said Barbara Oliver Harris, a student. "The teacher was allowed to reprimand the students. They [the teachers] were there to train and to work. They were concerned about the mastery of subject matter. And nothing was ever said to the teacher who scolded or reprimanded the student into learning or into behaving. Parents had confidence in the educators. That made the difference."[28]

During much of its history, Carver students performed in an exemplary fashion in University Interscholastic League competition. Students were well prepared for school and for life.[29] But in 1968, everything changed.

On November 7, 1967, the U.S. Department of Health, Education and Welfare announced that segregated school systems in the South must be dismantled by the fall of 1969 or lose federal funding. The closure of Carver Senior High School was first proposed a week after HEW's ruling. The measure, though, called for Carver Junior High to remain open. On November 29, 1967, MISD trustees ordered the school closed at the end of the 1967–68 school year and students equally distributed between Midland and Lee High Schools, effective with the beginning of the 1968–69 term.[30] Calls of betrayal came from the southeast and northeast sides of Midland in April 1968, five days after Dr. Martin Luther King Jr. was assassinated, and two weeks after MISD superintendent Harold Hitt presented a proposal to close Carver Junior High. Hitt said distributing students between Austin and Edison Junior Highs while closing Carver Junior High would save the district $200,000 a year.[31]

"I remember my mother and the intervenors sat around our dining room table with poster boards, working on their own plans for integrating the Midland public schools," recalled Conrad Coleman:

> The first plan they came up with called for keeping Carver open. They proposed stopping the rural buses from east of town at Carver. Their thinking was we would not put any kids on buses that are not already riding a school bus. That plan was rejected because, according to my mother, one of the school board members said, "We can't bus white kids to your neighborhood."

Part One: A Place with Character

The second plan called for busing all elementary school kids. I remember several white community members coming to my mother's office to meet with her after hours. She later told me they pleaded not to bus first- through third-grade students. Many parents thought those kids were too young to be on buses.

The cluster plan was the solution arrived at so that first through third graders could stay in their neighborhood schools.[32]

Coleman said the feeling among many in the African American community was that the closing of Carver and Bunche Schools was punishment for wanting integration. "The closing of those schools almost killed the black community," Coleman said. "There were many empty houses, and there still are a lot of empty houses, so the south side that many experience today was a result of the schools' closings."[33]

All of the teachers employed in Carver and other schools in the African American community were reassigned. Head coaches at Carver became assistant coaches at other schools. Johnny Williams, the father of future Texas Commissioner of Education Michael Williams, was one of those coaches reassigned as an assistant coach.

On June 19, 1968, trustees voted 6–1 to close both Carver Senior and Junior High Schools and turn Austin and Edison Junior High Schools into freshman schools. When the 1968–69 school year opened on September 3, busing began without major problems, and Carver Junior-Senior High School was closed.[34]

"Carver offered so many opportunities that blacks haven't had since then," Dr. Viola Coleman told the *Midland Reporter-Telegram* in 1985. "Now, black students are a minute part of a larger environment. It's more difficult for them to make an impact in the larger environment." Coleman said MISD chose to close Carver and bus students because it was what she called "the easiest solution."[35]

The hallways of Carver School were filled with pride; students excelled and took advantage of extracurricular activities even though they were never given top-of-the-line materials with which to work. Love-Davis said the first band uniforms at Carver were white carpenter's overalls, and textbooks were handed down from Midland's white schools. No impediment, though, stood in the way of Carver's students and their belief that anything was possible.[36]

"When I came here it was Carver Junior-Senior and Elementary," Love-Davis said. "Everyone went to school together. We owe the spirit we had to our teachers and our parents. If you go back and talk to Carver students, the ones who live here and other places, we didn't know we couldn't do anything. We weren't aware that a certain job was only for white people because our teachers taught us we could do anything. If you listen to Barbara Yarbrough talk, you'll see that. We were well educated at Carver."[37]

Achieving Unitary Status

The district remained under the cluster system until May 24, 1994, when trustees voted 5–2 to seek unitary status, or freedom from court-ordered desegregation.[38] Achieving unitary status does not mean a school system has become exempt from federal desegregation requirements. Instead it means the district can prove to the federal court that those requirements have already been met, so that direct judicial oversight is no longer required. The court considers multiple factors, including "the composition of a student body, faculty, staff, transportation, extracurricular activities, and facilities. School boards that seek unitary status must prove that officials implemented their desegregation orders in good faith, that their plans were effective in eliminating all vestiges of school segregation to the extent practicable, and that they have not violated the U.S. Constitution subsequent to the original judicial decrees."[39]

Acquiring unitary status was a lengthy process and not granted until 1998. According to Rick Strange, now an Eleventh Court of Appeals judge:

> There was a three-year phase-out period where you had to undertake certain activities to achieve final unitary status [and] a mini-trial at the end of that where the trial court determines if [the district has] met performance criteria. [The Justice Department] looked at MISD's operations in practically every facet imaginable. When we came up for our initial mini-trial, we reached an agreement with the Department of Justice on that three-year transition period on the types of activities [the district] would undertake....
>
> For the most part, we were able to work everything out and ultimately when it came up for the final trial, the Department of Justice reached a settlement with the district. The intervenors objected and had a couple of concerns.[40]

The intervenors included Dr. Viola Coleman, Midland League of United Latin American Citizens (LULAC) Council No. 4386, and Permian Basin LULAC Council No. 4434. However, the trial court agreed with MISD, and the

PART ONE: A PLACE WITH CHARACTER

Department of Justice and U.S. District Judge Edward C. Prado entered the final order of dismissal.[41]

Some parents may still complain about racial unfairness or inequality in the Midland school system, but attorney and former MISD board member Charles Tighe believes their arguments would not hold up in court. "We have a policy where any student can transfer from a school where he is in the majority of a school to one where he is in the minority. So if a parent believes [a child's current school] is not the best place for her child and he qualifies [for a transfer], that's available," Tighe said.[42]

Throughout the process of desegregation, Dominey characterized the environment that existed between the intervenors and the school board as cordial. The process, he said, while maybe not the stuff of a Sunday-evening chat around a dinner table, was civil, professional, and productive.[43]

chapter 13

AN INFAMOUS MURDER

> [Attorney Carl Steckleberg] told me several years ago that Mr. Scharbauer came up before the start of the trial and told Marion's attorneys, "I want you to do the very best job you can to represent this man. He deserves it just like everybody else." Carl couldn't believe that.
> —Midland attorney David Lindemood, on Clarence Scharbauer Jr. at the trial of James Lee Marion in 1964

SOME MIGHT SUPPOSE that Midland's wealthiest families lead trouble-free lives in which nothing ever goes wrong. However, neither wealth nor professional success nor social position can protect people from tragedy or violence.

The period between April 1963 and February 1964 was a particularly grueling one for the Scharbauer and Turner families. Ruth Scharbauer, Clarence Jr.'s mother and the widow of Clarence Scharbauer Sr., died on April 30, 1963.[1] Both families' circumstances were about to get much worse in ways that neither of them could have predicted.

A Wealthy Oilman and His Family

Fred Turner Jr. was a multimillionaire in his mid-sixties. After discovering large gaps of land that had gone unleased in the Yates Oil Field near Rankin and Iraan, he had drilled in those gaps and struck it rich.[2] He and his sixty-six-year-old wife, Juliette, had two married daughters, Dorothy and Fredda, both of whom lived in Midland. Dorothy had married Clarence Scharbauer Jr. in 1949, and the couple

Part One: A Place with Character

lived less than three miles from the Turners.

Almost every year at about the same time, Fred Turner left his magnificent home on Missouri Avenue for an annual hunting trip at his ranch in New Mexico. When he left in late October 1963, he did not know it would be his last trip. He also didn't know that he would never again see his wife, Juliette. In fact, when Mr. Turner arrived home from the abbreviated excursion and learned of the details surrounding his wife's brutal death, he never again set foot in the mansion.[3]

James Lee Marion was a twenty-two-year-old short-order cook who had been released from prison less than four months earlier after serving time for burglary. He would later state that it was about 10:30 p.m. when he broke a window on a side door at the Turner home on Monday, October 28, 1963.

Upstairs, Juliette Turner was asleep, but she would not sleep much longer.

A Grisly Discovery

When Juanita Young, the Turner family's maid, arrived for work soon after sunrise Tuesday morning, she saw muddy footprints and broken glass by the door where Marion had gained entry. Immediately realizing that something was wrong, she ran across Missouri Avenue to the home of Mr. and Mrs. C. W. Chancellor, friends of the Turners. Juanita also phoned Clarence Scharbauer Jr. and his wife, Dorothy. He called Sheriff Ed Darnell, who quickly followed them to the Turner mansion.

The Scharbauers arrived about 8:30 a.m., before the sheriff and his deputy. While Dorothy Scharbauer waited on the first floor, her husband and Juanita Young made their way upstairs.

They found Mrs. Turner lying in a pool of blood in her bathroom. She had been beaten to death. Investigators would later estimate that she died sometime between 4:00 and 6:30 on Tuesday morning, October 29. As Clarence Scharbauer Jr. would later describe it:[4]

> Mrs. Turner had a .38-caliber pistol that Mr. Turner had given to her a long time ago. When [James Marion] broke the window downstairs and came up to her bedroom, she snapped it at him, trying to shoot him, but the ammunition was too old.
>
> She ran out on the balcony on the east side of the house. He followed her out, grabbed her, and dragged her back inside. He had a little .22 pistol

in his hand, and while they were scuffling on that balcony, it went off. Someone heard the shot, and the police went up and down the street, but they couldn't find anything. He took her in the bathroom and just beat her to death with that .38.

After Scharbauer Jr. and Juanita Young discovered Mrs. Turner's body, they walked downstairs to find that Darnell and one of his deputies had arrived.

None of them, however, knew one crucial fact: James Lee Marion was still inside the house.

Marion Attacks Dorothy Scharbauer

Marion would later tell a jury that after he killed Juliette Turner, he showered in one of the home's bathrooms and found a place to sleep for the night.

Marion was startled awake by the sounds of voices at the house and left the bedroom. He ran down a first-floor hallway to find Dorothy Scharbauer sitting in an entryway, where she had been since her and her husband's arrival several minutes earlier. The sight of Marion in the entryway frightened Mrs. Scharbauer, who was, at this point, still the only person at the mansion who knew he was still inside.[5]

Clarence Scharbauer Jr. remembered that Marion "walked right up to where my wife was sitting and beat her over the head with the pistol." Although Marion took just one swing at Mrs. Scharbauer, the blow he landed was vicious, causing a deep wound and profuse bleeding.[6]

"When we came back downstairs, Ed and his deputy came in the front door," Scharbauer remembered. "We went in to where Dorothy was, and blood was running all down her face. Marion came in right behind us. He backed us all up against a wall, and I yelled at him, 'Let me get her to the hospital, you son of a bitch, or she's gonna bleed to death!'"[7]

Darnell had no gun—he was known not to carry one—but even though his deputy was armed, there was little any of them could do. Marion had the .38-caliber pistol he had used to murder Mrs. Turner. Darnell, his deputy, Clarence and Dorothy Scharbauer, and Juanita Young were defenseless as Dorothy continued to bleed from her wound.[8]

However, the gun Marion was holding had jammed. Marion himself had temporarily forgotten this, and no one else had any way of knowing.

Part One: A Place with Character

Marion's Escape, Hiding, and Arrest

Marion suddenly broke and ran down the hallway. As he escaped, he pointed the gun he had used to kill Mrs. Turner at the sheriff and his deputy before running out the front door and east down Missouri Avenue. Apparently he suddenly remembered that the gun he was holding had proved useless when Mrs. Turner fired at him earlier.

He would evade capture and was able to find shelter, two blocks east of the Turner home, in the attic of an outbuilding behind the residence of Russ Craddick, father of Midland's future state representative Tom Craddick.

Marion might have continued to avoid detection had he not made one critical error: he had taken Mrs. Turner's wallet, and her identification fell out of his pocket onto the floor of the Craddick outbuilding, below where he was hiding. When Russ Craddick later found Mrs. Turner's ID, Marion was a sitting duck in the attic of the outbuilding.[9] As Tom Craddick later described it:

> The little outbuilding, or the servant's quarters as my dad liked to call it, was connected to our house. It was locked from the alley side, but from the front side you could just come through the fence and you could walk into it.
>
> My dad was at home, and I was at home—I was sick and was home from school and had been for quite a while. My dad was in the building out back, and there was a little cubbyhole that led into the attic portion of it.
>
> This guy had come down the alley and jumped a huge fence that's still there today, or he might have climbed on top of some trash cans to jump over more easily. The door was opened to this little building, and he went inside. My dad had been going outside to the building all morning, and I had been visiting him.
>
> Dad moved a box that was lying on the floor of the outbuilding, and he found Mrs. Turner's billfold and driver's license on top of the box. Marion had used the box to climb up into the attic, and he dropped Mrs. Turner's identification and billfold.[10]

Craddick said he and his father had heard about the murder the morning it happened. The neighborhood was swarming with sheriff's deputy patrol cars, all looking for the suspect. When Russ Craddick spotted Mrs. Turner's belongings, he went inside immediately and notified the police department.

"We didn't realize he was in that attic at that moment, not until we moved the box and saw the ID," Craddick said. "He was probably looking right down at us. We are probably lucky."[11]

Craddick said when police climbed to the outbuilding attic, Marion put a gun to the officer's head and pulled the trigger. But the gun did not fire. Police quickly took Marion into custody following the short manhunt.

The Media's Reaction

The murder made headlines far and wide because of the prominence of the Turner family, Fred Turner's history and reputation as a wealthy oilman, and the relative solitude and low crime rate of Midland. The headline on the story in the *Midland Reporter-Telegram* the day after the attack read, "Negro Relates Murder Details." Accompanying the story was a photograph of Midland police detective Wayne Gideon lighting a cigarette for the suspect during an interview Marion was giving to the newspaper's Cope Routh.[12]

"The 22-year-old, powerfully built Marion—he weighs only 158 pounds but it appears to be bunched in his broad shoulders—was being held in a solitary cell on the fourth floor of the Midland County Courthouse," Routh wrote in his story. "As Midland buzzed with talk of the bizarre slaying, police revealed that Marion had been arrested here on a traffic violation on October 19, less than four months after being released from the state penitentiary."[13]

The newspaper reported that in the days before the murder, Marion had told Wayne Gideon, who sent him to the pen in 1961 on the burglary charge, "Honest, Mr. Gideon, you won't find me in no trouble anymore. Man, I have learned my lesson."[14]

Marion signed a statement confessing the murder following his arrest, but questions remained in the immediate days that followed the vicious attack. He confessed that he had entered the house looking for money and found $11 and a billfold upon entering Juliette Turner's bedroom. He claimed also that he was unaware that anyone was home at the time of the break-in.[15] He told the *Midland Reporter-Telegram*, "I took the crowbar and knocked a hole in the door and when I did I heard somebody say, 'I'm gonna shoot.' When I went into [Mrs. Turner's bedroom] a shot was fired and I saw this woman standing on the balcony."[16]

Marion said he ran toward Mrs. Turner and wrested the gun from her after she fired at him. While he was searching through her dresser, looking for money, Mrs. Turner again lunged for the weapon that he had taken from her. After she retrieved it, Marion said he grabbed the weapon and hit her on the head.[17]

According to the *Midland Reporter-Telegram*, Marion described in chillingly calm narrative what happened in the next few minutes after he struck Mrs. Turner and she slumped back in a chair:

> "Did you see any blood then?" he was asked.
> "No."
> "Was she unconscious?"
> "No."
> Marion said he continued his prowling and at some point, Mrs. Turner lunged at him again.
> "She got up and got something in her hand. It was a cane or something. I took it away from her and hit her two more times with her gun."
> "What did she do then?"
> "She sat back down in the chair and then she slid to the floor."
> "Did you know she was dead?"
> "No."
> "Did you hit her any more?"
> "No."
> "What did you do then?"
> "I went back downstairs."
> "And what happened then?"
> "I went to sleep."[18]

Marion said he had not recognized Darnell as being the sheriff later that morning, and could offer no reason why he had fractured Mrs. Scharbauer's skull. Marion told detectives he chose to stay in the house for the night because the neighborhood was teeming with patrol cars, all searching the area for him after the initial shots-fired call earlier.[19]

Medical examiners concluded that Juliette Turner died from a skull fracture and massive cerebral hemorrhage. One report indicated that she could have died as late as 6:30 a.m., less than an hour before Juanita Young had arrived at the house for work. According to a published timeline, Mrs. Turner could have been alive for as long as two hours after the attack, though coroner Newnie Ellis speculated that she survived only ten to fifteen minutes after she was struck.[20]

Marion's statement that the shooting occurred shortly after he broke in at 10:30 p.m. on Monday night, October 28, contradicted police reports of the shots being fired at 4:12 a.m. on October 29. Marion said he lost track of time as he wandered around inside the mansion.

The Debate about Marion's Sanity

James Marion was promptly examined by two psychiatrists. On October 30, 1963, Joseph H. Mims, Midland County district attorney, announced that both had declared him legally sane.[21]

Following the issuance of the psychiatric evaluation, Marion's chances for winning even temporary freedom were substantially reduced when the State Board of Pardons and Paroles revoked Marion's parole on his 1961 charge of burglary, for which he had served two years of a six-year sentence. This time, freedom for Marion was out of the question, both because of the parole revocation and because a high bond had been set.

The *Midland Reporter-Telegram* reported, "It appeared unlikely the Negro would gain his freedom, even if it were somehow possible to post a $10,000 bond set by Justice of the Peace David M. (Doc) Ellis when [Marion] was arrested Tuesday afternoon on a charge of murder with malice."[22]

No one would step up and post bond for Marion, whose trial was set in Lubbock on a change of venue. Judge Perry Pickett made the venue announcement in January 1964. It would be impossible, Pickett told the Associated Press, for an impartial jury to be seated in Midland because of the widespread publicity and the prominence of the Turner and Scharbauer families.

Judge Victor Lindsey, of Lubbock's Seventy-Second District Court, set opening arguments for March 16, 1964. Mims asked for the death penalty, stating that Marion committed the murder while in the act of another crime, the burglary of the Turner house.[23]

Despite the evaluation of two Midland psychiatrists issued in the days following the murder, court-appointed attorney Garland Casebier said he would argue that Marion was insane when he committed the murder.

Part One: A Place with Character

The Trial

Longtime Midland attorney David Lindemood recalled the scene outside the courtroom before proceedings had started. Clarence Scharbauer Jr. insisted to the attorneys that despite Marion's crime he be given a fair trial. "He deserves that," Scharbauer said.[24]

The *Midland Reporter-Telegram* reported that the jury in the Marion murder case consisted of four Baptists, three members of the Church of Christ, two Methodists, a Presbyterian, an Episcopalian, and a Catholic. Professionally the panel included an auto-supply-store operator, two truck drivers, an office manager for a building-supply store, a bank clerk, the Czechoslovakian-born wife of a Lubbock attorney, the wife of a farmer, and an employee of the Veteran's Administration.[25]

After confessing to Midland police in the days following the crime, Marion suddenly turned sullen and noncommunicative in the early days of his trial. Casebier said his client "[is] unstable, has a very low intelligence and is totally unresponsive to questions about what happened. We found that we cannot rely on anything he tells us."[26]

On the first day of testimony, Marion broke his stoicism, laughing twice, first when his attorneys shared a humorous moment with each other and second, when Mims questioned Rev. A. L. Davis, the pastor of an African American Baptist church in Lubbock. Mims asked the preacher, a college graduate, if he felt Marion was sane at the time of the crime.[27]

"If I know Negroes, and I've been one for fifty-seven years, this young man couldn't have done this thing and then laid down and gone to sleep and be of sound mind," Rev. Davis replied. The reverend's statement prompted an uncharacteristic outburst of laughter from Marion, who had to be cautioned by Casebier to remain silent.[28]

Also testifying at the trial was Bobby Graham, the Midland police officer who pulled Marion from the attic of the Craddicks' outbuilding after discovering Mrs. Turner's identification. Graham found a small opening in the ceiling, climbed into it, and found Marion.

"He was lying partly on his left side," Graham said under oath. "He had a gun in his left hand. I told him to give it to me."

Graham told the court that he advised Marion that if he did not surrender his weapon, he would shoot him. The pistol Marion handed over was the .38 he had used to beat Mrs. Turner to death.[29]

The courtroom gallery, filled by Friday, March 20, 1964, heard Scharbauer Jr.'s testimony about the events that followed the murder, including when Marion briefly held him, his wife, Sheriff Darnell, his deputy, and Juanita Young in the lower floor of the mansion before making a run for it. Surprisingly, both Dorothy Scharbauer and her sister, Fredda Turner Durham, testified in Marion's trial on the final day of testimony. Mrs. Scharbauer recounted her exchange with Marion and how he waved both Mrs. Turner's .38 and his own .22 in front of her face before striking a blow to her head that rendered her unconscious.[30]

The *Midland Reporter-Telegram* published excerpts from the trial transcripts, including this passage of Dorothy Scharbauer's testimony:

"He walked up and said, 'What's the matter with you?' And I said, 'I'm frightened.' He said, 'Do you live here?' and I told him, 'No.'"

Mrs. Scharbauer said Marion then waved the two guns in front of her.

"You see these?" Marion asked her.

"Yes I do," she responded.

Mrs. Scharbauer told the court she thought Marion was going to "walk on past me and into the solarium but he hit me and I blacked out."

She next identified Marion in the courtroom as being the man who was in her parents' house and struck her the morning of October 29, 1963.[31]

The Verdict

As in many criminal trials, the testimony of different parties was contradictory. On Saturday, March 22, 1964, six days after jury selection had begun and less than five months after the murder of Juliette Turner, the eight-woman, four-man panel deliberated four hours before returning with a verdict of murder with malice, punishable by death in the electric chair.

"I don't have any feeling about it. I definitely don't think it is fair," Marion told reporters on his way out of the courtroom.[32]

Marion was transported to the state prison in Huntsville, where he began serving his sentence on death row. However, in 1972, the United States Supreme Court suspended all death sentences, including those already handed down.[33] The decision was the result of the Supreme Court's judgment in *Furman v. Georgia* that the death penalty was being imposed in an unconstitutional manner, in violation of the

Eighth Amendment to the U.S. Constitution. The visible suffering of Georgia death-row inmate Luis Monge during his gas-chamber execution on June 2, 1967, was judged to be evidence of cruel and unusual punishment. The Supreme Court's ruling meant Marion's death sentence was commuted to life in prison.

"Preston Smith, he was governor of Texas at the time, he called me and he called Lynn Durham, the Turners' other son-in-law, with the news about the Supreme Court," Scharbauer Jr. said. "He said, 'Clarence, I hate to tell you this, but . . . they're changing his sentence from death by electrocution to life in prison with parole.'"[34]

Marion served twenty-five years of his conviction for killing Juliette Turner. He was released from prison in 1989.[35] According to local law-enforcement officials, he still lives in Midland as of July 2014.

James Lee Marion's Final Victim

When James Lee Marion killed Juliette Turner in 1963, he effectively brought two lives to an end. Many would also argue that the crime hastened the death of Fred Turner, who never recovered emotionally from his wife's murder.

Fred Turner's Retreat to Brownwood

"When he came home from the ranch, he never went back to that house," said Scharbauer Jr. "I put him up at the hotel. One of his sisters came to Midland to be with him, and Lynn and Fredda, his son-in-law and daughter, I put them up at one of those motel rooms on Golf Course Road and Midkiff; it was brand-new then. He stayed there for a while, but then he moved to Brownwood with his sister. That's where he was born and had his farm."[36]

(Interestingly, another well-known figure would seek privacy and solace at the same ranch thirty-three years later. On December 12, 1997, Clarence Scharbauer III helped negotiate the sale of the Turners' 20,000-acre spread near Las Vegas, New Mexico, to actor Patrick Swayze, of *Dirty Dancing* fame. Swayze often sought refuge from the limelight and paparazzi at the ranch and spent much time there in his final days, suffering from pancreatic cancer, until his death in September 2009. He called New Mexico and the ranch his "healing place."[37])

Fred Turner was at his horse-breeding farm near Brownwood at the time of his death. Family members said he had been in Brownwood for ten days and had appeared in good health. A complete physical exam six weeks earlier showed no indication of a heart condition.[38]

Turner began feeling ill about five on the evening of February 4, 1964. He had returned from an inspection of his farm and complained to associates of feeling poorly. A doctor was summoned to the farm, and later that evening Turner underwent emergency surgery but was pronounced dead at 11:30 p.m.

The *Midland Reporter-Telegram* reported that Turner had been in virtual seclusion since Mrs. Turner's murder in October.[39] He did not live long enough to learn the verdict of James Marion's trial.

A Grandson's Vivid Memories

Clarence Scharbauer III was a thirteen-year-old eighth grader at San Jacinto Junior High when Marion committed the crimes against the Scharbauer and Turner families. His grandmother had been murdered, his mother gravely injured. "I was worried about my mom because she nearly died," Scharbauer III said. "She was in the hospital for a long time after the attack."[40] Dorothy Scharbauer would require a bone graft to replace a section of her fractured skull, but she did survive.

Scharbauer III thought of Fred and Juliette Turner, his maternal grandparents, as "royalty." He said, "We would go over and visit at Thanksgiving and Christmas. We'd dress up for Thanksgiving, spend the night. She had us over when my grandfather was gone. It was very formal."

The Parting Shot Never Fired

Scharbauer III also told a sad and revealing story about his grandfather: "When James Lee Marion was in the Midland County Jail, my grandfather [Fred Turner] got $10,000 cash from his bank account, grabbed a .357 magnum and went to the jailhouse. He plopped all that money on Ed Darnell's desk, and told the sheriff, 'All this is yours. All I need is about one minute. I'm going to go up there and I'm going to kill this guy.' Big Ed told him no."[41] Scharbauer III said his grandfather was serious about committing the revenge shooting because he "just didn't care anymore."

Despite his riches and the name he had made for himself in the oil industry's earliest days, Fred Turner literally and figuratively died of a broken heart.

chapter 14

Midland's Shift from Democratic to Republican

Ernie Angelo always used to say there was a flashing red light on LBJ's map because Midland would not conform to the rest of the state of Texas when LBJ was president. That was when we were just coming on, and we were voting more and more for Republicans [rather] than Democrats, and LBJ didn't like that.

—Lou Brown, former president
of the State Republican Executive Committee

Although it often seems that Midland politics have leaned Republican throughout its history, that's not so. About half the town's history was spent as a Democratic town. It wasn't until the 1950s and 1960s when everything changed, and Midland's axis tilted further to the right.[1]

To some degree, Midland's shift from Democratic to Republican can be attributed to changes in the two major parties themselves, which have evolved and redefined themselves over time.

In 1860 the Democratic Party split over the issue of slavery. After the Civil War, the Southern wing of the party defined itself as the "white man's party," which opposed Radical Reconstruction and the Republican Party's support of black civil and political rights. The Democratic Party dominated the South until the civil rights movement in the 1960s.[2]

In Texas specifically, "the Democratic Party evolved from a party closely identified with white racial supremacy to a coalition of groups that included African Americans and ethnic minorities, while the Republican Party slowly gained majority status as a home for social conservatives. Both parties today remain economically conservative, resisting tax increases and regulations on business, while promoting government support of business initiatives."[3]

A Hard Rightward Swing in the 1950s and 1960s

The voters of Midland County supported Democratic candidates in every presidential election between 1888 and 1948, but the county's loyalties shifted in 1952, when a majority of Midland County voters supported Republican candidate Dwight D. Eisenhower over Democrat Adlai Stevenson. Since 1952 Republican candidates have won in Midland County in every presidential contest.[4]

In 1962 the election of Midland Republican Bill Davis as State Representative in the Eighty-Second District was seen as a huge upset in state politics. There were only eight Republican representatives in the state legislature at the time. The outcome surprised statewide pundits, but not confident local Republicans. The Midland County party had organized down to the precinct, had decided on Davis as the candidate through a recruitment committee, and had a committed stable of volunteers.

In 1964 Frank Cahoon was sent to Austin as the Eighty-Second District's second Republican representative, an even bigger surprise because Cahoon would become the one and only Republican in the House. "It is quite unbelievable, considering that just over fifty years later we have over ninety Republicans in the Texas House," noted Ernest Angelo, a former mayor of Midland who later became a Texas National Republican Committee member and cochair of Ronald Reagan's 1976 Texas campaign.

Midland County also made a name for itself in the presidential election of 1964 when 56 percent of Midlanders voted for Barry Goldwater, the highest percentage in the state for the defeated candidate. Some saw the defeat of Goldwater as a big setback for party politics in Midland County. While many volunteers felt a harder fight was ahead, others quit.

Ernest Angelo: "Political Nerd" from Louisiana

It is not an exaggeration to suggest that the extreme rightward swing in Midland politics in the 1960s was due to the influence of Ernest Angelo, a self-described political nerd and registered Democrat from Bogalusa, Louisiana.

PART ONE: A PLACE WITH CHARACTER

In fact, some would say that he was largely responsible for the shift in political thinking of the entire state of Texas.

Angelo, a native of St. Paul, Minnesota, spent his formative years in southeastern Louisiana and later graduated from Louisiana State University with a degree in petroleum engineering in 1956. He voted as a Democrat in his first election simply because "there was nothing *but* the Democratic Party." When Angelo arrived in Texas, he was twenty-two years old and raring to go. He began work in Crane, lived in Odessa, and rarely saw the dinner table before the sun had done its work for the day.

In 1960 Angelo didn't much care for the presidential ballot. He was never fond of Richard Nixon and said he was "somewhat embarrassed" that John F. Kennedy became the first Roman Catholic elected president. Angelo, a Catholic himself, said, "I didn't care much for either one."

"I decided that this was not the way the country needed to be going," Angelo recalled. "There were some like-minded people my age in Midland, and we got to networking, whatever you called it in those days, and our families started having kids, and the Constitution Party intrigued me, and there were some people who were gung ho about it in Midland. One of them was Dr. Dorothy Wyvell. She was a very good speaker and she was knowledgeable, and I was enamored with that."[5] Angelo said he volunteered with the Constitution Party for a while before realizing that it wasn't likely headed for long-term success.

"In the early 1960s," Angelo said, "many of us who had been Democrats believed that the national Democratic Party was being dominated by liberal, big-government elements and that reversing that situation was nearly impossible. We thought the Republican Party, then dominated by Northeast moderates, offered a much better opportunity to promote the conservative, less-government, more-individual-freedom philosophy. The Texas GOP was the place to start even though the Texas Democratic Party still was relatively conservative."[6]

By 1962 Angelo had widened his base of acquaintances and found more and more that his professional and political circles consisted of people such as Bill and Douthea Shaner, Bill and Katie Heck, Bill Adam, Bill Davis, Jerry Clark, Bob Paxton, John Kirwan, Charlie Gillespie, and Doris and Van Howbert. While local Democrats weren't necessarily liberal, they weren't actively conservative, either. Angelo and his newfound friends felt they could build up the Republican Party and at least make it competitive with the Democrats, a thought that was itself somewhat radical in those days given the ineffectiveness of the Republican Party in Midland County and elsewhere in the state.

Midland's Shift from Democratic to Republican

Even in the early days, the Republicans suffered disunion, minor though it was, and nothing the party faithful felt they couldn't overcome, Angelo said. "We were fairly well united, though we did call it the establishment versus the conservative activists, which sounds familiar today because it's still going on over fifty years later," Angelo said.[7] As he explained it:

> The establishment is a catch-all term for elected officials and their supporters, such as business, special-interest groups, and prominent individuals.
>
> The conservative activists are the grassroots local leaders and volunteers, who sometimes are aligned with, or even part of, the establishment. However, often they want a more clear-cut philosophical difference . . . between the GOP elected officials and their [Democratic] counterparts, particularly in regards to domestic policy. This tends to create tension between the activists and the establishment, which we are seeing today. Very basically, the conservative activists want less government, while the establishment wants to make big government work better.[8]

Angelo said that in 1964 he quit his job at Sohio to become an independent oilman while devoting most of the workday not to petroleum but to politics. He admitted this was foolish considering that he was a father with young children at home.

The Young Republicans

In the early days of the party, Midland's first Young Republicans organization was formed and quickly grew to 300, even though, Angelo said, some members weren't technically of the age normally required to be considered "young."[9]

"We weren't that careful about watching a person's age," Angelo said. "We set up a mimeograph machine in Jerry Stevens's garage. Jerry had been instrumental in helping form the Young Republicans group. We would mimeograph stories from *Human Events*, *National Review*, *Time*, *U.S. News* [*& World Report*], whatever we could get our hands on, and put the articles out in a mailing to the 300 or so that had been identified as leaders in the community."[10]

The mail campaign turned out to be a hugely successful effort and played a significant role in helping grow the party. "There was a dearth of conservatism at the time, and we were proselytizing pretty hard by sending the articles out," Angelo said.[11]

Part One: A Place with Character

A Visit from John Tower

Future U.S. senator John Tower paid a visit to a Midland fund-raiser before his election in 1961. Angelo remembers that a dinner catered by Johnny's Barbecue fed an estimated 700 people.[12]

Tower was so popular with Midland Republicans that he was actually talked into making a guest appearance at a Summer Mummers production in the late 1960s. Several members of the county Republican Party leadership were active in the Midland Community Theatre and specifically in Mummers, including Bill Heck, a longtime character actor.[13] (For more on John Tower's appearance at Mummers, see Chapter 10.)

Added Angelo: "John was a funny guy in a lot of ways, very serious in most respects, but he had a good sense of humor. If you could ever get him away from the crowds and by himself, he was a real fun guy to be around if you could get a couple of Scotch on the rocks down him."[14]

Charlie Gillespie's Exit Leaves a Vacancy for County Chairman

Another person who did yeoman's work in building the Republican Party in Midland, Charlie Gillespie, was elected county chairman in 1962.[15] Then, in 1968, Gillespie decided to run for county commissioner. Friends and supporters liked what he had done for the party so much, though, that they wanted him to return as county chairman instead of serving as commissioner.

"We felt that [his running for county commissioner] was a mistake, and Charlie ended up falling out with us pretty badly," Angelo recalled. "He lost the primary. We didn't support Charlie in the commissioner's race, and he quit the party. He ended up going to New Mexico and buying some property that had some oil production on it, and it ended up making himself pretty well off, which he might have never done had he stayed in Midland County politics."[16]

Gillespie's decision to run for commissioner left a void for the party, and at the last minute it found itself with no candidate for county chairman in 1968. Angelo eventually stepped up to fill that role, but quickly found himself in an unenviable position. Midland County Republicans were trying desperately to find someone to run against Dorsey Hardeman, a Democratic state senator from San Angelo, representing the Twenty-Fifth District. So Angelo volunteered.

Midland's Shift from Democratic to Republican

As it turned out, Pete Snelson beat Dorsey Hardeman in the Democratic primary and was later elected to the state senate, though Angelo defeated him in Midland County. There was little or no chance Angelo would win out over the more seasoned Snelson, and when the votes were in, Angelo received just 40 percent of the vote. (For more on this election, and the role it played in reigniting tensions between Odessa and Midland as the two sparred over which town would become the home of a brand-new state college, see Chapter 15.)

In 1968 Richard Nixon was elected president, and nationally the Republicans entered into the destructive period of Watergate. Still, the Midland County branch of the party remained strong. Nadine Francis, a former committeewoman from Odessa, was an ally of Angelo's and helped him secure his start in the Republican Party of Texas by nominating him to the State Republican Executive Committee in 1971. A young legislator named Tom Craddick was reelected in 1970—and again in 1972—despite a strong challenge.

With Persuasion, Angelo Runs for Midland Mayor in 1972

Even though active with the State Executive Committee, Angelo turned his attention to local politics, and before he knew it, he found himself a candidate for mayor. As he later explained it:

> Several members of the Midland Republican Party came up with a slate of candidates to run for mayor because we figured Pat Baskin was going to run. He was a former Democratic county chair and was mayor pro tem, and would undoubtedly use whatever political stroke he had. So we felt we needed somebody to run for mayor against him. Martin Neal was going to run, but he decided he couldn't beat Pat, so he dropped out, and it was getting pretty close to the filing deadline.
>
> Budge McDonald, Frank Cahoon, Tom Craddick, and me, we all tossed out names, and no one could agree on anyone. Finally, someone said, "You need to run." I'd never even been to a city council meeting, and hadn't paid much attention to city government. I said, "No, no way I'm going to do that."[17]

A story in the January 12, 2011, *Midland Reporter-Telegram* noted that in 1972 Cahoon and his successor, Tom Craddick, encouraged Angelo to run for mayor of

Midland after incumbent Edwin Magruder announced he would not seek another term.[18] As Angelo described it, Craddick believed that "Baskin would use the office to try to derail Craddick's bid for a third term in the House in the 1972 general election."[19]

Still, Angelo's friends and fellow Republicans continued to push him to run, and he saw he had to devise a way to get out of the predicament in which he suddenly found himself. Meanwhile, when Cahoon decided against running for another term in 1968, many thought he, too, was done with politics. He had intimated as much.[20] So Angelo told his cronies that he would run for mayor only if Cahoon would run for an open position on the city council. Angelo was convinced it was his only way out of local politics.

Except for one thing: Cahoon agreed to run for council.

Angelo said he later found out that McDonald, Cahoon, and Craddick had actually planned the series of events earlier, and Cahoon had agreed to enter into the city-council race if it meant Angelo would run for mayor.[21]

Baskin Defeats Angelo! (Or Does He?)

When the returns came in on election night in May of 1972, it proved harrowing for Angelo and his friends, all of whom had encouraged him to run—not to mention the thousands who had voted for him.

The turnout in the 1972 election was over 10,000. Initial returns indicated that Baskin had defeated Angelo by 500 votes. Angelo was so upset he was ready to give what he called his Nixon speech. "I was ready to tell them all, 'You won't have Ernest Angelo to kick around anymore,'" he remembered.

State senator Hank Grover, who lost a run for governor that same year, advised Angelo not to make the concession speech. "Never do anything on election night when you are upset," Grover told him.[22]

"My kids had already gone to bed. It was after eleven, and they were all crying because I had lost," Angelo said. "Bob Monaghan, a friend of mine who was a huge part of the Republican Party in those early days, came over and he looked at the returns, and he turned to me and said, 'There's something screwy about these numbers.'" Monaghan pointed to a precinct where the number of votes did not match up with the number of voters. Both men were engineers; as a result, Angelo said, they were students of not only numbers but political numbers and politics.

"The numbers just didn't add up right," Angelo said, "We called [City Attorney] Joe Nuessle, who was also in bed by then, and Bob said, 'Joe, if you don't get down to city hall and get this straightened out, we're calling the judge and we're going to impound the boxes, and it's going to be an embarrassment for Midland.'"[23]

Nuessle made the late-night trip to city hall, and after making a quick canvas of the numbers, found a transposition error in the big precinct in question. Instead of losing by 500, Angelo wound up winning by 150. The numbers were changed and signed off on by midnight.[24]

Baskin's backers were in the process of toasting his victory when they received the news, which immediately brought an end to the hoorahs. "Pat won and then lost on the same night," Angelo said. "I lost and then won on the same night."

A Little Help from the Easter Bunny. Three days before the 1972 mayoral election, Angelo's wife, Penny, and a crowd of supporters stayed up late the night before Easter, making blue bunny door hangers that announced, EVEN THE GREAT EASTER BUNNY VOTES ANGELO!

The volunteers crisscrossed Midland late that night, hanging the door signs at many residences around town. Angelo said he didn't know for sure how many Easter Bunny door hangers were put out, but "When you win by 150, everything is a factor."[25]

Former Rivals Become Friends. At a press conference during the campaign, a KCRS Radio news reporter asked Angelo if he intended to step down from his spot on the State Republican Executive Committee since the position of mayor is supposed to be nonpartisan.

The next day, splashed across the front page of the *Midland Reporter-Telegram*, was Angelo's answer: "First, I'm not going to resign from the state committee, and my opponent [in the mayor's race] is a liberal Democrat. That's how nonpartisan it's going to be."[26]

"Pat and I ended up being friends," Angelo said. "He switched to the Republican Party at some point." Baskin was eventually elected as a Republican judge of the 142nd District in Midland.

"That's pretty much how the Republican Party evolved in Midland," Angelo said.

Angelo's Role in National Republican Politics

Angelo was named to the Republican National Committee and in 1976 was the co-manager of the Ronald W. Reagan Texas presidential primary campaign. In the 1980 Republican presidential primary campaign, Angelo was again state chairman for Reagan. He was deputy Reagan-Bush chairman under Governor Bill Clements as well as campaign manager of the 1980 general election campaign in Texas. At the 1984 Republican National Convention in Dallas, he was chair of the Arrangements Committee, and chair of the National Advisory Board for Reagan-Bush, and in 1980 and 1984, chair of the Texas National Convention delegation. He stepped down as Republican National Committeeman in 1996.[27]

Like others, Angelo believes Midland led the change in the way Texas voted in the 1960s and 1970s. "I think Reagan's campaign in 1976 was the final turning point for Texas Republicans to become the potential majority party," he said. "There has long been a huge majority turnout in Midland, and Midland was the first county in the state to outvote the Democrats in a [presidential] primary."

Surprise! Barbara Culver Is Elected County Judge

"They used to say if you were born in Texas you were born a Democrat," said Barbara Culver-Clack, one of those New Republicans who changed the face of Midland County politics. "There just wasn't any discussion about it."

Barbara Culver, as she was named then, grew up in a Democratic family and remained a Democrat until moving to Midland County. She was very much part of the conservative wing of the party, but the Republican Party's two other branches, moderate and liberal, were both growing rapidly during the 1960s.

Priding herself on her independence, something she has retained throughout life, Culver eased into the party by voting in the GOP primary and then attended her precinct primary during the years when the party didn't much resemble what it is today. In those early days, she said, Midland County Republicans were "just trying to scrape a few votes together. Party officials patched together a slate, and I let them put my name down for county judge, mainly to just get a little publicity."[28]

Culver-Clack remembers those early days as more a time of socializing and getting together with other like-minded individuals than anything seriously political. She referred to the party's would-be officeholders collectively as a "full slate of disposable candidates." Among them was a man named Bill Davis, a gregarious and outgoing geologist who worked for Exxon and frequently acted in Midland Community Theatre productions. Davis became the county's GOP candidate for state representative and was elected in 1960. "He was delightful and charming," Culver-Clack remembered of Davis. "Exxon thought it was fun for him to run."[29]

Then a funny thing happened on the way to the statehouse. Davis would become the only Republican representative in the Texas Legislature. Before long, Exxon no longer found it fun that one of its geologists was traipsing off to Austin with such frequency. The company ended up transferring Davis to Houston.

In 1962 Midland County Republicans continued to make waves with the election of Barbara Culver as county judge. The outcome was startling because a Democrat was supplanted by not just a Republican, but a Republican *woman*—unheard of in those days, especially in West Texas.

Tom Craddick: A Powerful Politician with a Vision for Texas

Toys first brought young Tom Craddick to Midland, Texas. Russ Craddick, father of the future government leader, was from Wisconsin. He visited West Texas, returned home, and in 1952—during one of the town's early oil booms—announced to his family he was moving them to Midland, where he intended to open what would become the first toy store between Fort Worth and El Paso.

"My parents moved down first, and my sister and I stayed behind to finish the school year while we lived with my grandparents," Craddick remembered. "My dad opened Craddick Drug. Then it was Tull's Drug Store, then Service Drug Store. Uncle Russ's Toy Store, which he also ran, was on Lamesa Road, next to B&W Grocery, across the street from the big funeral home on Lamesa. It eventually became Peyton's Toys and Bikes." Tom Craddick says today he was the first kid in West Texas to own a Schwinn bicycle.

Even with the entrepreneurial streak in the Craddick family, there was plenty of time for politics. One of Tom Craddick's great-great grandfathers was the head of the militia in a colony of settlers in Winston-Salem, North Carolina, and Tom Craddick's father dabbled in Democratic Party politics.[30]

Early Interest in Politics

"I guess I first became interested in politics in junior high in Wisconsin," Craddick recalled. "Dad was a Democratic precinct chairman in Midland after I got out of college, and when I ran for the legislature on the Republican ticket, he had to resign. He told me I'd never get elected, that the state was run by Democrats and that I was crazy to run as a Republican."

Craddick was in graduate school at Texas Tech when he was first approached about running for Frank Cahoon's seat in the Texas Legislature. After Craddick quit grad school for politics, he later learned Cahoon had in fact decided to run for a second term. Cahoon ran and won again, and Craddick went back to Lubbock to finish graduate school. Two years later, when Cahoon finally did step down, Craddick ran for Cahoon's vacant seat in Austin.[31]

"Back then they had a candidates committee, and they interviewed the prospective candidates," Craddick said. "Bill Heck was there, and he said to me, 'You look awful young. Can you lose twenty-five pounds to go on TV?' I lost seventy-five pounds and never gained it back."

A Groom Who Nearly Missed His Wedding

Tom Craddick's marriage to Nadine Nayfa of Sweetwater was not without a rough start, thanks entirely to politics. "Nadine moved to Midland in 1969, after I had already been elected," Craddick said. "We were married during a special session of the legislature. We had set a wedding date for September. But the governor, Preston Smith, called us back into session and I almost missed the wedding. I had driven home to Midland on a Friday and then drove to Sweetwater. Nadine was there and we had a rehearsal dinner that night. That next morning, I drove to Abilene and flew to Austin to vote on the tax bill, the whole reason the governor had called us back into special session."[32]

After the vote, Craddick had planned to take a flight back to Abilene and then drive to Sweetwater for the wedding. Unfortunately, the only flight to Abilene that night was canceled. Craddick was forced to take another plane to Midland and catch a ride with Jack Wilkinson, a member of his wedding party who had been forced to stay in Midland, unable to attend the rehearsal, due to the death of his father. Craddick and Wilkinson didn't make it to Sweetwater until forty-five minutes before the wedding procession began at the church.

A Wife Who Took to Politics

Fortunately for Craddick, his new bride "took to politics like cowboys take to hats," as she put it.[33] In the years since their wedding, Nadine Craddick has been a contributing member of the party in Midland County and the district, not to mention a visible presence in Austin when the legislature is in session.

Mrs. Craddick said that because she had come from Sweetwater, "in many ways Midland was a metropolitan area to me. And I was thrown into a life I had never been exposed to before. Fortunately, the folks who came before me in Midland, some older women and even some who were younger . . . all mentored me and I became involved in volunteering and getting to know Midland."[34]

Mrs. Craddick quickly learned that the political principles held in Midland were akin to her own. "The people who were here had a passion for politics and knew how to organize neighborhoods. We're the bastion of conservatism out here, and we think less government is better. I feel that way, too. Not everyone does. A lot of people would rather be independent, but with this can-do attitude we have here, there have been amazing accomplishments on every front."[35]

The Craddick-Midland fit has been perfect because of similar values and business philosophies, Mrs. Craddick said. "I believe you are put on this earth to do something. If you have an opportunity, you can either sit back and squander it, or you can have a vision. I think Tom has had a vision, not just for Midland but for the entire state, and not only for us, but long after we're gone, for everyone's children and grandchildren."[36]

Mrs. Craddick said her husband's work in tort reform, which limits frivolous lawsuits, will perhaps prove to be his most enduring legacy. She notes that 25,000 doctors have moved to Texas and established practices since tort reform has become law.

Craddick has served multiple terms between contested races on more than one occasion. West Texas judge Willie Dubose mounted a challenge early in Craddick's term in the House, but Craddick faced no serious competitors again until 2008. That year Bill Dingus, a somewhat controversial and outspoken yet popular former Midland city councilman, ran against Craddick but failed in a big way on election day. Dingus brought in just 35 percent of the vote to Craddick's 62 percent. In 2000 Gilberto Garcia, the Democratic candidate, was able to garner only 21 percent of the vote against Craddick, who found his toughest political challenge to be winning reelection to his Speaker post later in his career. Craddick remains hugely popular in West Texas, particularly Midland, the geographic, population, and business center of District Eighty-Two.

The Perfect Job in Politics

Craddick never envisioned that he would be involved in politics for the majority of his adult life.[37] When in Midland, he is a sales representative for a local oil-field supply company; he also owns Craddick Properties, a Midland investment business, and is president of Craddick, Inc. Without a doubt, though, his political contributions to the state and his beloved West Texas will long outlast his service to the statehouse.

Craddick, the first distinguished alumnus in the history of St. Ann's Catholic School in Midland[38] and later a graduate of Midland High and Texas Tech, said he always thought he might run for U.S. Congress, but marriage and children put those plans on hold permanently. He called his situation—as an elected official who is required to go to Austin only 141 days every two years—more conducive to life as a family man. "It was perfect for me," he said. "I could be involved in politics, go into business, coach YMCA basketball, and do what I needed to do with my kids."[39]

As his official biography notes, Craddick's time as a member of the Texas House has been marked by a series of landmark events. His initial years were focused on revitalizing the Texas GOP, but in 1971 he gained respect from both sides when he joined a bipartisan group of reformists dubbed the "Dirty Thirty," which pushed for changes in House Ethics. In 1975, Speaker Bill Clayton appointed Craddick as the first Republican committee chairman in 100 years. He continued to hold chairmanships under Clayton's successors, Gib Lewis and Pete Laney, and became the first Republican Speaker of the Texas House since the Reconstruction era, 130 years earlier.

He will long be remembered for the years he spent as Speaker, when Texas went from a $10 billion budget shortfall to a $10 billion surplus. The legislature also passed the largest property-tax cut in Texas history under Craddick's watch, and reformed a school finance system that had been ruled unconstitutional by the Texas Supreme Court. He has also appointed a record number of women and minorities, as well as twelve Democrats, to chairmanships.[40]

In a February 2005 profile of Craddick, *Texas Monthly* called him "an ambitious, uncompromising and intensely focused man" who was "respected, feared and loathed as one of the most powerful politicians in a generation. Lots of people are scared to death of him."[41]

"Tom Craddick is the most self-sufficient lone wolf I have ever seen as Speaker," an unidentified Austin lobbyist told *Texas Monthly*. "He really does keep his own counsel like no one I've ever seen."[42]

Bill Messer, Craddick's closest friend in Austin, called him one of the most competitive people he had ever met. "He fishes competitively," Messer said. "If we go fishing someplace and we come in at lunch, he wants to know how many fish I've caught and whether I won or he did. Go dove hunting and he wants to know how many shells it took you to get your limit compared to how many shells it took him to get his."[43]

Midland's Shift from Democratic to Republican

Midland County Republican Women

Texas Monthly proclaimed several years ago that you cannot win a political race in the state of Texas without appearing before the Midland County Republican Women. It is a powerful body, guided by strong leadership and financial backing. It does not veer from its principles. Rhonda Lacy, president of the organization in 2013, encouraged all Republicans to create their own business cards with information on the back that identifies them with those principles. Republicans, the card would say, believe in the U.S. Constitution, pro-life/family values, the right to bear arms, smaller government, a balanced budget/cutting spending, domestic oil production, decreasing regulations, supporting business, repealing Obamacare, and a true balance of power. With the exception of the repeal of Obamacare, the cards could have been carried in wallets and purses in Midland fifty years ago as easily as they could be carried today.

"The Midland County Republican Women has become the epitome of what we had always hoped Republican women's organizations would become," said Lou Brown,[44] president of MCRW in 1972, who also served as president of the State Republican Executive Committee from 1981 to 1983.

What has changed, though, is the local organization's influence on the state level. When the Midland County Republican Women first began, Brown said it had a voice at the state table but no power. "If anyone wanted to run for state office in those days, we always told them to go to the Dallas Republican Women, or the Concho Valley or Big Spring Republican Women. Those groups stayed organized between elections because they knew who had run and who hadn't run, and they knew where the skeletons were, and they were always organized. We told the state committee in the early days that Midland County could be a star organization because we have always been organized."[45]

Juandelle Lacy and the Texas Federation of Republican Women

When Juandelle Lacy and her husband moved to Midland from Tulsa in 1967, she made the Republican women's organization even stronger. In all her years with the Midland County Republican Women, she has made notable contributions, not the least of which is simply handing down the ideals of party politics.

When first approached, Lacy wasn't warm to the idea of joining the Texas Federation of Republican Women. The TFRW serves as a sort of umbrella organization for the smaller Republican Women's Clubs throughout the state, such as the Midland group.

"Virginia Streator . . . called to recruit me as vice president of membership with the TFRW shortly after I had moved back to Texas," Lacy said. "I told her I'd have to think about it because I didn't work well with women. I just wasn't sure I wanted to get involved. Plus, the federation didn't have a large membership. Now we have 10,000 in the state, and Midland is the largest club in the nation, with 600 members. Back then we were struggling to build a party, and women were struggling to be recognized as a source of not only hard work but finances and recruiting."[46]

Streator heard Lacy's ambivalence about becoming a member. "Virginia said to me, 'I think you're just what we're looking for.' Even then, you got to the point where it was a good-ol'-boy syndrome where you just have the same people serving over and over and over. People who serve sometimes get tired, but they won't give up. That's what they were trying to do back then at the TFRW."[47]

Lacy remains firm in her assessment of Republicans. It's the kind of toughness, she said, that needs to be practiced on a wider basis if the Republicans want to regain strength on the national stage. "We've got to get tough, and you've got to call an ace an ace. And when Democrats attack us, we can't say, 'Well, we're working on it.' Tell them to go straight to hell. And tell them what we believe in. The Democrats don't do that. We can't take that anymore; we have to call it like it is. If they're a liar, call them a liar. If they're a cheat, call them a cheat. And you can go get proof of it. You don't have to put yourself out there to be sued."[48]

chapter 15

THE LONGEST LOVE AFFAIR IN THE HISTORY OF MIDLAND

Hundreds of citizens and organizations donated time, talent and financial resources to provide the services and means to create a beautiful and functional campus which 25 years later is considered the gem of Midland. That love affair continues—the union of an aggressive and caring community and a college with a mission of service for all.
—Dr. David Daniel, third president of Midland College, 1997

MIDLAND'S LOVE AFFAIR WITH HIGHER EDUCATION goes back to the early years of the town and is still running strong.

Midland Christian College Opens in 1910

The city's first institution of higher learning, Midland Christian College, opened in 1910. Due west of downtown Midland and its historical district, remnants of the building's foundation can be still be found in Ulmer Park.[1] College Avenue received its name because it once led to Midland Christian College.

In the spring of 1908, trustees from Texas Christian University met to discuss the need for a new college in the western or southwestern region of the state. The proliferation of the ranching business in West Texas helped tip the scales in Midland's favor. "Trustees selected Midland, where ranching families came from hundreds of miles so their children could attend public schools. In December of the same year, interested Midland citizens met to select trustees and plan the proposed college," according to the Texas State Historical Commission.[2]

The college was chartered on January 19, 1909. Frank Elkin, an alumnus from Texas Christian University, sought financial assistance from his alma mater to help build the college. However, it turned out that TCU trustees didn't want the new campus that much: they offered only cooperation and an opportunity for the college to become affiliated with the Christian denomination.[3]

The history of First Christian Church of Midland credited the people of Midland with having the foresight to establish a Christian college here.[4] Midland citizens donated a 225-acre site, and the sale of 300 parcels of land established a financial base for the college. In May 1910 a three-story brick building, with stone trimmings and ornate Corinthian columns at the front and side entrances, was completed on a site 1.5 miles west of the Midland County Courthouse. All facilities for the college, from classrooms to dormitories, were in one building. One hundred and seven students enrolled for the first semester, which began in September 1910. The first president was Robert L. Marquis. He was followed by Henry R. Garrett, Franklin G. Jones, and John T. McKissick.[5]

Athletic programs consisted of football, baseball, and tennis. Midland Christian's football team, the Herefords, faced several area high school teams. The college published two journals: a monthly, *The Antelope*, and the school newspaper, *The Coyote*.[6]

A meningitis scare and scarlet fever epidemic closed the school for a month in January 1912, and although the school reopened, the closure foretold its ultimate future. Midland's small population, and the fact that many local ranchers were wealthy enough to send their children away to school, led directly to the demise of Midland Christian College. It had neither tax money nor endowment funds.

The school closed in 1921. With the permission of trustees, it moved about 200 miles east to Cisco and became Cisco Christian College in 1922 and, later, Randolph Junior College.[7]

How Midland and Odessa Fought Over One College, and Gained Two

Midlanders would not have another institution of higher learning within the county for almost another fifty years. Midland College was established in the early 1970s, but not until after Odessa won a high-stakes political battle in Austin to establish the

The Longest Love Affair in the History of Midland

University of Texas of the Permian Basin (UTPB) in Odessa. The years of wrangling in attempts to land the school that is part of the UT system proved costly in terms of the relationship between the competing cities.

Several months after Tom Craddick was first elected state representative from Midland in 1968, talks among the most influential Midlanders and Odessans about the establishment of UTPB were ongoing. At one of those meetings, Midlander Clarence Scharbauer Jr., forty-three at the time, offered to donate whatever land was necessary to build a four-year college that would be equidistant between the two cities.

It all started out simply, Scharbauer Jr. remembered. "When we started talking about building UTPB out here, there were eight of us from Midland and eight from Odessa, all leaders in the two towns. We met, as I remember, seven or eight times, sometimes in Odessa, sometimes here, and we were all pretty well in agreement: I offered to give them a section and a quarter, 671 acres, on Interstate 20, right over from the Warfield truck stop. It was nothing but open rangeland."[8]

Scharbauer was joined in the meetings by, among others, Midland power brokers Tom Sealy, Jno. P. Butler, and Paul Davis. Scharbauer said Sealy "had so much power as a member of the University of Texas Board of Regents" that the officials from the two cities figured the creation of the university on Scharbauer land was a done deal, and conversation about how influential the college would one day be had already begun. "We figured in twenty or thirty years, it would be another Texas Tech," Scharbauer said. "And we would have been right. But that's when politics got into it."[9]

A Democrat Says No in Austin

Dick Slack, the former Reeves County judge turned legislator and chairman of the powerful House Appropriations Committee—forever put his imprint on the future of education in the Permian Basin, all because of politics.

Slack, who died March 1, 2013, was a decorated war hero who returned to the United States in 1945, joined the Texas National Guard, and retired with the rank of colonel. According to his obituary in the *Midland Reporter-Telegram*, "He was instrumental in the establishment of UTPB and the Texas Tech Health Sciences Center in Odessa. As a legislator, he was a conservative, independent thinker with a wit and charm that broke down barriers."[10]

That charm and wit (and conservatism) were hard to see if you were a Midlander in the late 1960s. The tough-as-nails Democrat caught wind that Midlanders and Odessans were working on establishing a college between the two towns, one that would be located geographically in Midland County. It wasn't long before he weighed in with his decision when the plan hit his committee in Austin.

"I'll be damned if there'll be a college located in a county that sent a Republican to Austin," Slack said, according to Scharbauer Jr.

Scharbauer said he remembers Slack's attitude as being "it was over his dead body that his committee was going to appropriate $18 [million] to $19 million to a county that was Republican. And so he just killed it."[11]

Officials from the two towns thought Scharbauer's gesture of donating a section and a quarter for the school was more than generous. "It was a helluva lot more land than what they've got where it is now," Scharbauer said. The land he offered to donate was adjacent to what would be the site of the Texas Instruments plant at Farm to Market Road 1788 and Interstate 20. "When I offered to give a second quarter of land for the college, there was a lawyer in Odessa who said, 'Oh, them Scharbauers, they're just gonna give that land to make all their other land more valuable.' But we gave it because they needed it for the college."[12]

A Thwarted Backroom Political Deal

Politics had already played a role that was anything but positive, according to Ernest Angelo, who later became mayor of Midland and went on to fill several national campaign positions. (For more about Ernest Angelo's political career, see Chapter 14.)

In 1968 the Midland County Republican Party was trying to find a suitable candidate to run against Dorsey Hardeman, a Democratic state senator from San Angelo, representing the Twenty-Fifth District. "We thought we had a chance to beat him," Angelo said. "And Odessa was in the same state senate district as we were in Midland."[13] After a series of closed-door meetings, local Republicans decided that if Odessa found a candidate to run against Dorsey, it would strengthen the party throughout the region, since Republicans were already strong in Midland.

One day before the filing deadline, Angelo and other Midland County Republicans learned that not only had Odessa's Republicans failed to find a candidate, but they were, according to Angelo, discouraging people from running against Hardeman. "We believed they were publicly negotiating with Midland to make [the college] a joint deal between the two towns, but behind closed doors they were working with Hardeman to have [UTBP] put in Odessa," Angelo said.[14]

Meanwhile, Midland Democrat Pete Snelson, a relative newcomer, filed to run for the District Twenty-Five State Senate seat at the last minute. If Snelson won the

The Longest Love Affair in the History of Midland

Democratic primary, Angelo knew he didn't have a chance in the general election.

"Still, I wasn't going to let it get by that Odessa had neglected to get a candidate because they didn't want to screw up the deal they had made with Hardeman," Angelo said. "So I filed to run for senate at the deadline."[15]

Snelson defeated Hardeman in the primary, temporarily blowing up any deals that were being made to put UTPB in Odessa.

Although the feud between the two cities had existed throughout the towns' histories, Angelo says it became even more heated over the Hardeman controversy. Doug Henson, now president of real-estate development company SBC, LP, and a longtime respected Midland businessman, remembers those times well. The rivalry between the two towns, Henson said, started out much like one between two high school football teams and quickly escalated when the two sides began playing tackle.

"There was always a challenge there in the early days, but no hatred," Henson said. "It became a true obsession to go out of your way to make them fail because of UTPB. The airport had something to do with it later, from Odessa's side. I think their viewpoint was, 'Whose ox is getting gored?' Have we made strides to get past it? No. There's been lip service, but right now I think Odessa's leadership is on point, and they seem to be paying some firms to move to Ector County [of which Odessa is the county seat]. But I don't think that money should be used to move anybody from one county seat to another. There's no net gain, and a lot of money wasted."[16]

Henson likened the relationship between the two cities to that of two quarreling brothers: "If we don't look out for each other, then the rest of the state is damn sure not gonna look out for us," he said. "We're in the desert, we don't have enough population to be recognized significantly, and it's foolish we don't have one sales team, and that we don't just have one of a lot of things. It's sad. But there's too many skeletons with regard to the college and anything else that has evolved that we both had a chance at. There's just no need in risking friendship or a chance of success because of all that."[17]

Odessa Finally Gets UTPB

When the political maneuvering was over, UT–Permian Basin was bound for its new home in northeast Odessa. Euell McKnight, from Odessa, wound up selling the land to officials who began working on the establishment of the university, Scharbauer said.

According to Dr. Jess Parrish, second president of Midland College, "Midland got left totally out of the UT–Permian Basin equation. Totally. And it made a lot of people very unhappy."[18]

Midland's Battle to Create Its Own Tax District

In virtually no time, the Tall City's response to losing UTPB was the decision to establish its own college, far from an easy task. Midland had been part of the Permian Basin Junior College System since 1969. If Midland wanted its own college, it would have to create its own community college district, with its own authority to issue bonds and levy taxes.[19] "We were in the Permian Basin College District when Odessa got UT–Permian Basin, and so we decided we wanted our own college over here," said Ralph Way, an original board member at Midland College. Odessa voters, though, overwhelmingly voted to keep Midland in the Permian Basin College District. "That just meant they wanted to get our money and keep their college over there both," said Way.[20]

Eileen Piwetz, who began her career in the nursing program at Midland College and became executive director of the Midland College Foundation until her retirement in 2011, recalls hearing about the anger and frustration resulting from Odessa voting against building a Midland campus as part of the Permian Junior College District. "The rivalry is strong here in Midland-Odessa, and it's about more than just football," Piwetz said.[21]

Odessans fought hard to keep Midland in its taxing district, but ultimately the powers that be in Austin granted Midlanders' request for their own district, which finally provided for the new school. Dr. David Daniel, third president of Midland College, wrote in his introduction to *Midland College: The First Twenty-Five Years* by Karen Lanier and H. A. Tuck:

> The shackles of a district administration and the recalcitrance of a larger voting district that included the citizens of Odessa prohibited the creation of a permanent campus for Midland. President Langford and a determined group of trustees and supporters launched an all-out offensive to see that a new community college district was created, splitting with the former district. This small, determined army of Midlanders camped out in Austin and perfected a strategy that brought victory to Midland. Attorney Reagan Legg and Dr. Langford were generals of persuasion and clout who led the charge day after day, and when Gov. Preston Smith signed the bill creating the Midland Junior College District, Midland College was born.[22]

The Longest Love Affair in the History of Midland

Midland College Opens in 1972

It is no small coincidence that Midland College opened its doors in the fall of 1972, a full year before UT–Permian Basin began classes in September 1973. Beating their neighbors to the west served as a nice remedy for losing UTPB. As it has turned out, though, Midland College has been anything but a consolation prize.

The school has experienced tremendous growth throughout most of its first forty years, and the rivalry between the two cities has taken on a decidedly calmer tone.

During the campaign for the passage of a $41.8 million bond package that brought multiple additions and renovations to Midland College in 2005, Dr. Daniel summed it up best when he was asked about the college's standing in the community.

"The longest love affair in the history of this community is between the people of Midland and this college," Daniel said. "It was born out of necessity and controversy. Midland College lost no time in surpassing early enrollment projections and the community quickly embraced the college with uncommon support."[23]

"Young Lady, I Told You, Midland Takes Care of Its Own"

One of the primary movers and shakers who brought the college from concept to reality was Al Langford, who later had the school's state-of-the-art multipurpose event venue named in his honor: the Al G. Langford Chaparral Center.

Langford is remembered as a powerful force in Midland and Austin who had a persuasive way of debating for what he wanted. Langford was a one-time administrator with the Permian Basin Junior College System and was in charge of anything and everything related to Midland College in its formative years, at a time when classes were held in banks, in churches, and wherever rooms could be rented and space found.[24]

Langford led a group of supporters to Austin as the effort continued to try to get Midland released from its commitment to the junior college system Langford had once directed. When Governor Preston Smith signed the bill calling for the establishment of the Midland Junior College District, the search was on for land, architects, and designers that would forge the establishment of the college.[25]

"I loved watching Al Langford in action," Eileen Piwetz said. "I'll never forget when we went to Austin to talk to the Board of Nurse Examiners for the State of Texas, he gave them his Chamber of Commerce speech and he was really, really good at it. And when one of the BNE members said, 'Now, Dr. Langford, you're going to sit there and tell us that this is going to happen and that is going to happen, but what assurances do we have that it is, in fact, all going to happen the way you say it is?' Dr. Langford got up and leaned across that table and said, 'Young lady, I told you, Midland takes care of its own, and it will!'"[26]

Years later, Piwetz said, when she returned to Austin as a newly appointed BNE member by Gov. Bill Clements, she met up with the same woman whom Langford had addressed during the contingent's original visit.

"She said to me, 'I remember when you came down with your president and he assured us that Midland takes care of its own,'" Piwetz said. "When we started that nursing program at Midland College, we had a 100 percent pass rate for years. We were top dogs in the state. And Dr. Langford was right. And she knew he had been right all those years."[27]

Midland College is a fixture in the community and has been since its earliest days. In 2013 the board announced it was adding a three-phase master plan with a $50 million price tag. New academic and community facilities on the drawing board include the construction of an Early College High School, an expansion of the dining hall at the Scharbauer Student Center, the creation of a retreat complex, the relocation of the Petroleum Professional Development Center, and the construction of a fourth residence hall. Dr. Steve Thomas said the facilities' construction would be financed through existing reserves, private donations, and a capital campaign.[28]

Midland voters have been generous in approving capital campaigns for the college, including the $41.8 million bond that passed by an overwhelming 62 percent of the vote in 2005.

Midland College hit an all-time high in enrollment of 6,344 in 2010. The college, which measures growth in five-year increments, experienced its greatest growth rates between 2000–2005 and 2005–2010. Enrollment fell to 5,268 in 2013, a reflection of a good economy.[29] "When the economy is good, community college enrollment tends to drop because everyone is working and not going to school," said Rebecca Bell, dean of community relations and special events. And Midland's economy was indeed good in 2013.

A Mount Rushmore of Midland College Presidents

Eileen Piwetz has been an outspoken champion of Midland College, and one of the few individuals who has witnessed firsthand the school's success during all four of its presidents' terms. As she described it:

The Longest Love Affair in the History of Midland

I think what has happened is that there has been a president for each season. We had to have the chamber glad-handing, the charismatic, all-encompassing energy and outgoing personality of Dr. Langford to get it started. He was such a great cheerleader. He could go out and play a round of golf and come back with hundreds of thousands of dollars and promises for even more.

Jess Parrish came in and provided stability and growth during his time. The college was about ten years old when he came in, and that's the time when we did so well in sports, our Spud Webb time, the time when our health sciences program grew, and those were big parts of his presidency. Dr. Parrish pretty much gave us free reign to bring in whatever curricula we determined the community needed.

Dr. Daniel came in when we were about twenty-five years old, and he provided a great period of growth. He was a visionary, and it was his vision to create the Advanced Technology Center and Cogdell Learning Center. He had the vision to expand the college with new state-of-the-art facilities, and he knew that we needed residence halls. And how important that part of student life is if you are, for instance, a parent in Iraan and you want your daughter living in a dorm and not an apartment.

When Dr. Daniel retired, Dr. Steve Thomas came in, and his philosophy has been all about outreach to a whole new generation of college students and low-income residents who might not otherwise be encouraged to come to college.[30]

Exciting Lectures and Performances, Free to the Public

Piwetz said one of the highlights of her years at Midland College was overseeing the Davidson Distinguished Lecture Series and the Phyllis and Bob Cowan Performing Arts Series. On the surface, the two series were opportunities for Midlanders and West Texans to hear gifted speakers or talented performers. Yet, as she would tell you, it's about much more than offering free programs to the public:

> One of our committee members came to one of the performing arts performances that featured Chinese acrobats. He got out of his car and next to it was this old beaten-up vehicle, and eight people crawled out of it. He couldn't believe it. They all came in to see the Chinese acrobats. One of the wealthiest men in town was there, too. Those eight people and this

affluent individual all got to see the Chinese acrobats for the same price. And that's what the Cowans wanted.

The neat thing about Ballet Folklorico de Mexico was that it was a turning point for the Hispanic culture. There were grown men in the audience crying and singing along. Chaparral Center was filled, and it was wonderful for those who came.

After that, the Hispanic people in Midland came to a lot of the performances. It didn't matter if it was the Ten Tenors from Australia or Marvin Hamlisch; we continued to get a lot of calls from the Hispanic community because music, performance, and dance transcend language. You don't have to understand or speak English to appreciate music and dance and song.[31]

Piwetz said when the public voted on the $42 million bond package, it is highly likely that the Davidson and Cowan series made a difference in the outcome. While Piwetz isn't sure whether the two series helped increase enrollment, she is sure both brought the college to the surrounding community and welcomed everyone.

chapter 16

"We'll Never See a Bank Like That Again"

An old, faithful hand in West Texas is in trouble. Everybody needs to get behind it. Something needs to be done to turn things around.
—Goodrich Hejl, about First National Bank

A MIDLAND REPORTER-TELEGRAM STORY that ran on the morning of October 15, 1983, said it all: "And word spread quickly: the King is Dead, the King is Dead. Long Live the King."[1]

The story, on the front page of the sports section, was datelined Odessa, and told how the Midland Lee Rebels finally defeated the Odessa Permian Panthers in high school football. But sportswriter Terry Williamson's lead paragraph could have just as easily applied to what had happened the day before back in Midland, something that no doubt had an impact on the families of many of the players on that winning football team.

The Failure of First National Bank

Representatives with the Federal Deposit Insurance Corporation stormed the doors of First National Bank in downtown Midland an hour before the football game's kickoff on Friday, October 14, 1983, bringing an end to an institution that had provided financial assistance, business support, community leadership, and as hundreds would still say today, a friendship with tens of thousands of Midlanders in its ninety-three-year history.

Lana Cunningham's account of the events of the late afternoon of October 14 was descriptively and emotionally telling. "Dozens of navy-suited men carrying briefcases and wearing tags saying FDIC walked into the bank from the Colorado Street entrance. About 6:45 p.m., sad-faced and teary-eyed employees poured out that same entrance, refusing to make comments to the waiting media. One concerned shareholder, not told of what was being announced to the employees, also waited outside the door trying to find answers from the workers."[2]

Jno. P. Butler was ordered to remain silent, advised by the FDIC not to speak with the media. All he said to an inquiring reporter at the time of the takeover was, "I don't care what it is; I'm not going to say anything."[3] Other local officials with the bank, not just Butler, were ordered not to speak to the media. An announcement on the bank's status never did come from any local director, but from the FDIC.[4]

First National Bank's death was officially blamed on huge energy-loan losses, and the condition that led to the bank's last breath could be seen coming for nine months. Losses due to failed energy loans had reduced First National Bank's reserves to $862,000. Just ten months earlier, at the end of 1982, those reserves had been $122 million.

FDIC spokesperson Dean Debuck issued a statement void of the emotion many were feeling that day: "The lack of available funds to meet depositor demands caused a liquidity crisis, which necessitated a declaration of insolvency by the acting comptroller."[5]

The size of the bank's failure was second only to the October 1974 closure of Franklin Bank of New York. At its height, Franklin had counted assets at $3.6 billion, $2.2 billion more than those of First National in Midland. First National's deposits totaled $600 million, the third largest amount in the country behind Franklin's $1.4 billion and the U.S. National Bank of San Diego with $932 million. U.S. National failed in 1973. FNB was the largest bank ever to fail in Texas and the second largest in the country.

RepublicBank's Takeover Bid Accepted

First National Bank was declared insolvent by the U.S. Comptroller of Accounts, H. Joe Shelby, at 6:13 p.m. on Friday, October 14, 1983. After RepublicBank was declared high bidder and purchased the bank from the FDIC for $51.1 million, it reopened as RepublicBank First National Midland on Monday, October 17, 1983. The purchase by RepublicBank meant the FDIC would avoid having to pay off

76,400 accounts. It would also prevent possible loss to customers who had deposits in excess of $100,000, the FDIC's maximum guaranteed amount.[6]

The bid offer by RepublicBank was one of fourteen. Although preference was given to in-state banks, RepublicBank's offer of purchase was not only the highest but also clearly the best for the bank, its shareholders, its depositors, and the community.[7]

"That's fantastic," bank customer Jerry Fullinwider said. "It's the best news I've had in a year. I was scared to death an East Coast bank would get it. Republic is our kind of folks; they're big in oil and run by Texans."[8]

RepublicBank chairman James D. Berry attempted to salve a variety of community wounds when he told the *Midland Reporter-Telegram*, "What we have bought is essentially a brand-new bank. This is the No. 1 bank charter in Midland with an unusually strong and loyal base of customers. We will begin as a clean bank and with the clear expectation of soon becoming a billion-dollar bank. RepublicBank recognizes Midland as the cornerstone of the energy industry and despite recent difficulties we are convinced that the energy business is here to stay and will get better."[9]

When First National Bank closed and then reopened Monday under new ownership, *Midland Reporter-Telegram* writer Lana Cunningham, in a story on how the waiting game was finally over for anxiety-ridden customers and local residents, wrote, "It was like watching an eagle die and a phoenix rise from the ashes."[10]

Lynn Durham Jr. walked through the bank's lobby shortly after rumors became reality, noting many others there who looked as if they were bidding farewell to an old friend at a funeral Mass. "We'll never see a bank like that again," Durham told the *Midland Reporter-Telegram*. "I hope Republic recognizes the goodwill First National had and tries to maintain it."[11]

Underlying Causes of First National's Failure

The failure of First National Bank was not the first in West Texas in 1983: National Bank of Odessa had closed September 30 and later reopened as the First State Bank of Odessa, and Metro Bank of Midland had closed July 29. It would later reopen as Mid-Cities National Bank.[12]

At one time in First National's history, it held an incredible two-thirds of the city's total deposits Only a few years earlier, the bank had been doing so well that it added sixteen more floors, which opened in 1978. But the bank and the citizens

Part One: A Place with Character

watched the institution's slow destruction as it lost $120.8 million in the first nine months of 1983, which virtually wiped out all stockholder equity.[13]

David L. Smith, executive director of the Abell-Hanger Foundation, worked at First National Bank earlier in his career. He remembers clearly the moves, well intentioned though they were, that ultimately led to the demise of the institution:

> I think there were some mistakes made at the bank, and when it started coming unraveled, there was no way to stop it. In the end it was a classic case of a run on a bank, and one of the things that Midlanders who have lived here a long time and have been in a boom period and have seen the success and the money and the oil, will tell you: it's a dad-gum drug is what it is, and it clouds your thinking, and you begin to think this is never going to end. You think it's always going to be like this and I'm the master of the universe.
>
> And of course it never continues on like that; it always calms down and something causes the price of oil to drop, which it did at the end of the Arab oil embargo, virtually overnight. But the boom fueled all sorts of drilling and business activity, and the bank wanted to be a part of making that happen. People were saying that the price of oil was going to hit $100 [a barrel] because we had to import it, and all the conventional wisdom confirmed that price, and the bank was trying to position itself to help the local independents, contractors, and service companies. With strong loan demand, the local deposits were not enough to meet that loan demand. So when that happens, you have to go outside the area to get the deposits so you can lend the money.[14]

The late 1970s and early 1980s were a time of very high interest rates. The bank would obtain money to lend at 14 to 16 percent and turn around and charge 21 percent. It had to "get that money out the door, and their lending got a little sloppy, much like the recent mortgage crisis," Smith said.[15]

"What happens then is you have a little ripple, or concern in that money from the outside, and when that money leaves, the deposit-to-loan ratio gets all out of whack and everybody gets nervous, and then more and more people begin to withdraw. There was nothing [bank president] Charles Frazier could do to stop it at that point. Charles made the decision to offer those brokered CDs and to bring that money in, because at the time it was a good strategy because you could help more people and lend more money and be more successful."[16]

Smith said no one ever dreamed that the price of oil would drop off as precipitously as it did, from more than $40 a barrel in 1982 to less than $9 a barrel in 1986. "Panic, fear, and chaos began to reign," Smith said. "That's what brought the bank down." With the ensuing panic, Smith said customers began drawing money out of the bank at alarming rates.[17]

Impact on the Community

More than thirty years after its demise, Midanders who were around at the time still remember the bleakness of the day First National Bank collapsed. As many others would, Judge John Hyde ranked it on his list of top ten most significant events in our history. He called the collapse of the economy and the closing of First National "a defining event in this community":

> There are few adults in this city who do not recall painfully the demise of First National. The decline of oil prices in the early 1980s was worrisome at first. Many financial plans were made in anticipation of oil reaching $80 a barrel. But when the price of crude oil dropped below the expense to lift it from underground, the worries turned to fatalistic anguish. Some people had enjoyed the prosperity of the oil boom to the point of living as if there were no tomorrow. Gone forever were the halcyon days of the great independent financial giant that had seen Midland through good times and bad. Gone, too, were the festive holidays of wassail and gingerbread. Life, as the saying goes, does go on. But for Midland, life would never be quite the same without First National Bank.[18]

David L. Smith said, "Alan Trobaugh, a former [First National Bank] director, came to bank employee Wayne Merritt and said, 'Who's drawing money out? I want to know. Why are they abandoning the bank? I want to see the list.' Wayne told him, 'Mr. Trobaugh, I can get you the list, but I promise you do not want to see it, because there are people you have been involved with and you go to the country club with. And if you see it, it will forever change how you see those people, and you're not going to stop them from doing it because they are scared.'"[19]

Joe Mabee was a board member at the time the bank was taken over. He remembers the failure hurting many and, although he survived, he remembers

Part One: A Place with Character

being not very happy about the way things played out.

"We were sued by people who said we didn't loan them enough money and sued by people who said we loaned them too much," Mabee said. "Every bank, every board member, we were all looked at by the IRS very hard. We were looked at like we were a bunch of damned criminals. They wanted to know how many cattle I had in one of their compliance reviews. Every one of us they looked at, but they could find nothing wrong with any of us. But it was hell to go through. Everybody passed. Nobody was a crook."[20]

Guy McCrary, president and CEO of the Permian Basin Area Foundation, and a former Midland County Commissioner, came to Midland in 1979 and immediately went to work for First National Bank. McCrary said working for the bank in those years was a real thrill for a twentysomething. But he remembers the disillusionment of the time when the bank changed hands and became part of the larger RepublicBank of Dallas, which would also subsequently fail. McCrary said he was never comfortable with how the whole process took shape and the old bank "exited the world without much spin."[21]

Because of all First National Bank had done and everything it stood for, his disappointment was made more profound. In its final days, McCrary said there wasn't enough money in the world to pump into it to satisfy the office of the controller of currency. In his words:

> That was new territory to the regulators. And in retrospect, they could have been smarter about the cyclical nature of things. They had absolutely no concerns about how that bank affected our community. A book I read called *The Great Texas Banking Crash* by Joseph M. Grant, about Texas American Bank, talks about the ripple effects and how the guys in the decision-making seats at various banks as well as the boards were very frustrated with the government regulators. Deals could be made and then ignored or invalidated up the bureaucratic chain of command without any fallout. Nobody saw the failure of these banks coming, and nobody could have done anything to prevent it.[22]

McCrary, too, says First National's failure couldn't be blamed solely on the bank's generous loan policy and its quickly dwindling assets in 1982–83. A real irony existed with regard to the timing of the financial downfall and the political scene of the 1980s and President Ronald Reagan.

"October 1983 brought some dark times," he said. "It would prove to be the beginning of what ultimately became a very serious bust across Texas. It was a down business climate with oil and gas, and real estate all in a decline. And if you remember, in the early 1980s Reagan was president, and the new tax structure really changed the oil and gas business. Some of the changes in the tax code did not bode well for the oil and gas industry, which is built on capital, both then and now."[23]

Midland and Odessa Attempt at a Last-Minute Rescue

Several days before First National failed, three Midlanders organized a pledge drive to help rescue the institution. That same week, another group organized a community rally to give citizens the opportunity to come together to show their support.

"That bank should not be allowed to go under by members of the community," said Margaret Captain, who helped organize the pledge drive with fellow Midlanders Ken Lough and Goodrich Hejl. Lough told the *Midland Reporter-Telegram* the three of them were just cheerleaders, helping to ensure an eleventh-hour turnaround. Hejl said he pledged his support of the bank in spite of occasionally getting mad at it.[24]

Although Midlanders pledged millions of dollars, it was, of course, too little too late. Still, the effort of a pledge drive was another example of Midlanders coming together to try to help make a bleak situation better, a dark day brighter. Midland's history is full of these kinds of episodes.

The show of support for the bank at the Midland Center was termed "Midland's finest hour."[25] The night was made even brighter when Odessa community leader Steve Late announced he had raised $500,000 to be deposited at FNB. Democratic governor Mark White made a surprise appearance at the rally, telling the 1,000 supporters the state of Texas was behind the troubled institution.[26]

An editorial in the *Midland Reporter-Telegram* commented:

> How often have residents of a community joined hands and forces to show their support for and confidence in a bank in trouble, most of them not stockholders, many of them not customers, some of them even competitors? How often have citizens facing a similar situation come forward with deposits of any size, not to mention the magnitude of what has been pledged here in only two days? How often have residents of a

PART ONE: A PLACE WITH CHARACTER

competitive sister city with a history, admittedly with help from us, of having engaged in a longstanding feud, raised a large amount of money for deposit, not to their own banks, but to one of ours?"[27]

In full support of the Odessans who, within two hours actually produced a half million dollars for deposit, the *Midland Reporter-Telegram* editorial board said it was one thing for a sister city to pledge support and pass resolutions in show of same, but it was quite another for them to put their money where their mouth was.

"It was a cataclysmic event," remembered Mary Lou Cassidy. "The pep rally before the fall . . . it was surreal. They had the Lone Star Brass, a marching band, cheerleaders, and a lot of rah-rah speeches. I was sitting in the back just thinking, where is *Texas Monthly* when you need them? They really need to be seeing this. It was absolutely the most bizarre Midland event I have ever seen."[28]

"Good-bye, Old Friend"

In his daybook, on the calendar page opened to October 14, 1983, Jno. P. Butler wrote, "Good-bye, old friend."[29] Those three words perfectly summed up not only Butler's relationship with First National, but the community's feelings toward the institution that had championed it for ninety-three years, and toward Butler himself.

His daughter and four grandchildren witnessed how the bank's failure affected him.

"Kim, my late husband, and I went over to Father's house on the day [the bank] collapsed," Jane McAbee said. "When we walked in the door, he was sitting in his bathrobe, watching Jim Palmer's Baltimore Orioles defeat Steve Carlton's Philadelphia Phillies to go up two games to one in the World Series. Mother was pale and practically had to go to bed. She was terribly upset. But we went in, and there he was watching baseball, and I asked him how he was doing and he said, 'I'm doing fine. We saved the depositors their money.' And they did. That board, by putting up their stock, made such sacrifices for the investors."[30]

Butler's granddaughter Katie Spriggs said:

The best way to say it was that it just broke his heart. It just damn near destroyed him. He lived his whole life and career for that bank, and to see it go down in such a disastrous fashion hurt him horribly.

"We'll Never See a Bank Like That Again"

My grandmother had a 16mm home-movie projector, and when the bank was being built, she went to that site every day with a tripod on it and filmed it in time-lapse motion, and gave it to him for Christmas one year. She kept reels of all of us growing up, which amounted to fifty years of home movies, and every year at Christmas we would pull out one or two and watch home movies. One Christmas, after the bank failed, we pulled out the one that grandmother had filmed of the bank being built and watched that. It was the only time I ever saw my grandfather cry.[31]

Jno. P. Butler's New Role at RepublicBank

So sterling was Butler's reputation, and so solid his rapport with the community and its citizens, that he remained on at RepublicBank after it took control of First National Bank. "He knew everyone, or it seemed everyone, personally," said Spriggs:

After RepublicBank took over, his main job was to stay in contact with his long-term customers, many of them elderly or widowed. When their accounts came up for renewal he would call them and say, "Mrs. So-and-So, we need to talk about what to do with all this money you have."

And all these widows trusted him completely and they would say, "Well, Mr. Butler, what do you think I should do with it?"

He would tell them something like, "Personally, I think we need to roll it over into an IRA, and that way your money will be safe for another year."

And they would always say to him, "Well, if that's what you think I need to do, then that's what we'll do." Republic kept my grandfather on because all those people trusted him, and they all stayed on as customers with the bank because of him.[32]

chapter 17

TODDLER'S RESCUE BRINGS MUCH-NEEDED OPTIMISM

We were in a depression because of the oil bust and the failure of First National Bank. [Jessica McClure's rescue] was something that everyone rallied around, and it brought the morale of the whole town up.

—Dr. Debbie Reese

THERE ARE CERTAIN EVENTS IN OUR LIVES that, even forty or fifty years later, we can look back and say with certainty what we were doing at the time we heard the news. The assassinations of John F. Kennedy and Martin Luther King, Jr. The explosion of the space shuttle *Challenger*. The death of Elvis Presley. 9/11. And the entrapment of eighteen-month-old Jessica McClure in an abandoned well on October 14, 1987, and her rescue fifty-eight hours later. Many who remember the story recall where they were when the announcement was made.

"Baby Jessica," who became "America's Baby" and later "America's Sweetheart," accomplished at least two things few others have: She took people's minds off of high school football, if only for a few moments. And she arguably changed the course of cable news coverage.

Wednesday, October 14: Jessica's Fall, and the First Hours

Jessica fell twenty-two feet down an abandoned water well the morning of October 14 while playing in her aunt's backyard. The well was only eight inches wide. Jessica's mother, Reba Gayle ("Cissy") McClure, was in the backyard watching her daughter play with several other children that morning, and when she returned

Toddler's Rescue Brings Much-Needed Optimism

from answering the phone inside, she saw several of the children in the yard looking down the hole. But she didn't see Jessica.[1]

Shortly after rescue operations began at about 11:30 a.m., word spread quickly about the unfolding drama under way in southwest Midland. The first words from officials came from police spokesman Jim White, who told reporters Jessica was "very upset, but we can hear her."[2] Early media accounts of the incident told of how police and fire officials heard the young girl talking and crying from inside the shaft. When workers from the Department of Highways and Public Transportation used a drilling mechanism to try to free her, the resulting vibration caused Jessica to inch farther down the well.

The Rescue Plan

James Roberts, Midland's fire chief at the time, still says there were serious doubts that rescuers would be able to pull the child free from the well in time. It was determined that the best way to free Jessica would be to drill a shaft parallel to the well where she was trapped.

It was a remarkable coincidence that the toddler had fallen down a well in the Permian Basin, an area filled with more drilling engineers and oil industry professionals than any other rural region in the continental United States. Yet the workers who actually drilled the hole parallel to the well came in from a highway construction crew near Albuquerque, New Mexico, assisted by a federal mine safety official, also from New Mexico.[3]

Concerns about the toddler's condition grew, and local doctors feared dehydration as the rescue operation continued and the baby's entrapment grew to a full day, but hope never seemed to wane.

According to Roberts, three of Midland's wealthiest families assured officials, "Whatever you need, just ask." Those three families—and scores of other people—collectively represent the spirit of Midland during that ordeal.

Thursday, October 15, 1987

The *Midland Reporter-Telegram* described how the chipping away at the hole was being done. "Underground diggers—on their knees and wielding 50-pound air

Part One: A Place with Character

hammers—are using a three-step process while picking away at the rock. First, diggers are drilling small starter holes in the rock using smaller star bits. Then, using larger cross bits, workers next begin to drill away at the areas between the starter holes, and then when a large portion of rock has been excavated, chisels are used to pick out the rest of the areas between starter holes."[4]

By Thursday morning, workers turned their drill bits sideways and upward, inching slowly toward the youngster. The *Midland Reporter-Telegram* article added that Jessica "might not be reunited with her mother, Cissy, until 6 p.m. this evening."[5]

Officials reported Thursday morning that the toddler had spent some of the overnight hours sleeping. A crude mini camera dropped down the hole showed fuzzy images of her head, and her legs drawn up to her chest. And she was breathing.

A local physician told the media that Jessica could likely last three to four days without water, depending on her overall health, and acknowledged that the young girl's cries indicated she was doing well.[6] As Thursday dragged on, Jessica became more and more agitated with the shaking being caused by the nearby drilling. Reba McClure remained secluded in her sister's house on Tanner Street, where the rescue effort was ongoing. Chip McClure, Jessica's father, publicly thanked rescuers. He was eighteen years old and worked as a housepainter.[7]

Workers began moving at a quicker pace toward reaching Jessica after switching to a pneumatic drill. The quick rate at which workers progressed necessitated a more careful approach as they neared the child.[8]

Chief Roberts remembered one late night during the ordeal when he and then police chief Richard Czech were on a brief break, sitting on the bumper of one of Czech's squad cars:

> You know how brilliant the stars over West Texas can be. We were sitting on the back of that police car, and I said, "Dick, do you realize what we're trying to do here? I mean, do you really realize?"
> And he said, "Yeah, we're trying to get a little girl out of a well."
> I shook my head. "No, no, just look at all this," I said to him, gesturing toward the galaxy of stars overhead. "What makes you and me think we're so damn good that we can do something like this? We're not even a little speck in this whole thing."
> But Dick was always positive.[9]

Toddler's Rescue Brings Much-Needed Optimism

Friday, October 16, 1987

On Friday diggers reported that the subterranean conditions in the hole were hot and dusty. More than a hundred drillers had by then taken part in the operation.

When rescuers chiseled their way through the solid rock and could see Jessica, they noticed that one of her legs was wedged against the interior well wall. Doctors had been constantly monitoring the situation and the baby's condition by listening through a microphone that had been lowered into the hole. Emergency-room physicians from Midland Memorial Hospital said she was not seriously injured and appeared to be in good condition.[10]

Carroll Thomas, Midland's mayor at the time, recalled in 2011 how an increasing concern had crept into his optimism in the hours before Jessica was lifted out. "I told them they needed to make an extra effort to get her out," Thomas said. "I don't know how that little girl could survive; she was bound to be under stress and shock. I have never really said this publicly, but they were trying to be really gentle and careful, and I said, 'You need to do what you need to do to get her out of there. We can repair a broken limb or a pulled joint, but if we lose that little girl—we don't want that to happen at any point.' They got her out eight to ten hours after that."[11]

Friday Evening: Rescued at Last!

When Jessica was finally eased upward to safety by tired workers, the owner of an oil-field service company came forward and offered to pay every dime of the baby's medical expenses. With Jessica swaddled in her arms, Dr. Debbie Reese hurried the baby to a waiting ambulance and rode with her to the emergency room at Midland Memorial Hospital.

"She was covered in dirt and tar," Dr. Reese said. "She was awake but she had [a big patch of skin scraped off her forehead], and injuries to her extremities. And she was very dehydrated, but I thought she would probably be okay when I took her. Local surgeon Dr. Terry Tubb devised a way to expand the skin that remained on her forehead. He put a balloon on her forehead and let it gradually stretch the skin so it could close over that defect that had formed in the hole."[12]

Dr. Reese said Jessica's young age, and the resilience that often comes with such youth, played a role in her survival.

Part One: A Place with Character

Medical Concerns During the Aftermath

On the morning of Saturday, October 17, 1987, any Midlander who had gone to bed before 8:30 p.m. on Friday, or had not attended a high school football game, awoke to welcome news. "Jessica Free, Under Doctor's Care," the headline read.[13]

The jubilant announcement, however, was somewhat tempered by news accounts written by Ramona Nye, one of at least five local newspaper reporters who had handled pieces of the stories along the way. "Gangrene, a 15 percent loss of body fluids and a possible need for plastic surgery remained concerns for newly freed Jessica McClure, who emerged wide-eyed Friday night after 58 hours in an abandoned water well."[14]

Anxious family members, friends, and rescuers would have to wait several days before doctors could determine whether it would be necessary to amputate her right foot, where gangrene development was most feared. Ultimately, the toddler did not lose a foot, but did have a toe amputated because of gangrene. Throughout her childhood and adolescence, McClure would have fifteen surgeries but no recall of the event that drew international attention.

While hospitalized in the days following her rescue, she received intravenous fluids for dehydration, and doctors treated abrasions on her forehead they likened to bedsores for having been pressed up against the wall of the well for so many hours.

"Considering everything Jessica's been through, she's a very spunky little girl, and she's doing great," Dr. Carolyn Rhode said.[15]

Dr. Rhode was assisted in Jessica's care by Dr. Debbie Reese, who six years earlier had been the pediatrician for Jenna and Barbara Bush, twin daughters of President and Mrs. George W. Bush. Dr. Reese was concerned about Jessica's enzyme levels, which were heightened because of the nature of her crush injuries. "Her CPK enzyme level was something like 12,000," said Dr. Reese. "Whenever you crush a muscle or tissue, enzymes are released, and it can shut your kidneys down. A normal CPK reading is in the 100s, so Jessica's level was my main concern."[16]

The Media Phenomenon

When the news of Jessica's fall first broke, CNN's Larry King looked into living rooms across the country and informed everyone that a baby was stuck in a well in Midland, Texas. America gave a collective shudder. To comfort ourselves, many of

Toddler's Rescue Brings Much-Needed Optimism

us stayed glued to the television for much of the next two and a half days.

Cable news was in its infancy then; never before had there been continuous coverage of a story that unfolded over an extended time period. When we couldn't be around a television because of our work or routine chores, appointments, or kids' sporting events, we called loved ones for updates. There was no texting then, no cell phones either, so reaching out for the latest information was more difficult than it is today. Access to television coverage was a must in order to keep abreast of the latest about the trapped child. In 1995 *The New York Times* reported:

> CNN was quickly on the spot, and the event helped make (its) name. If a picture is worth a thousand words, then a moving picture is worth many times that, and a live moving picture makes an emotional connection that goes deeper than logic and lasts well beyond the actual event. This was before correspondents reported live from the enemy capital while American bombs were falling. Before Saddam Hussein held a surreal press conference with a few of the hundreds of Americans he was holding hostage. Before the nation watched, riveted but powerless, as Los Angeles was looted and burned. Before O. J. Simpson took a slow ride in a white Bronco, and before everyone close to his case had an agent and a book contract. This was uncharted territory just a short time ago.[17]

Coverage of Jessica McClure's rescue represented more than what the *Times* depicted it to be: it was the first time Americans collectively and simultaneously shared their fears and hopes together in the form of almost wall-to-wall news coverage that remained mostly live at the scene. The phenomenon of live news coverage had one recent and memorable event that it had covered with vigor: the *Challenger* disaster, which occurred January 28, 1986, almost two full years before the baby in the well. The *Challenger* explosion was tragic but short lived, and the only live coverage was of its aftermath. It was not an ongoing live news event.

The drama and eventual rescue of Jessica McClure brought a nation together, if only for two or three days. During that time it was the only topic of conversation for many people. Whether for good or bad, "Continuous live coverage" was born in Midland with the Jessica McClure story.

"Even Ted Turner said the story was one of CNN's first great efforts that put the cable news network in the limelight," said Tom Barnett, a former media professor at Midland College and Odessa College. "The world was watching us, that's for sure."[18]

PART ONE: A PLACE WITH CHARACTER

"Another thing I remember is, I went to pick up my cleaning, and darned if they didn't have the TV tuned to the rescue. Everywhere I stopped, up and down Andrews Highway, they had the news tuned to it. Every employee was watching coverage of it wherever I went," Barnett said.[19]

"You talk to CNN and they'll tell you that's the event that made them," Chief Roberts said. "They celebrated that event for years and years because they really do feel that that was the birth of CNN. They were on the scene twenty-four hours a day, and they were the only ones that were for a while. They said that made CNN News."

A few weeks after Jessica's rescue, the country continued to latch on to the story and wouldn't let go. There was an Oprah Winfrey taping at the Midland Center and later a Movie of the Week.

Winfrey's taped broadcast featured rescuers, family members, and Jessica herself. Years later, *Everybody's Baby: The Rescue of Jessica McClure* aired with Beau Bridges as Police Chief Richard Czech, and Pat Hingle playing Fire Chief James Roberts.

The Celebration

Jessica was finally freed from the well during the middle of Friday-night football games, which are almost a religion in West Texas. Game announcers around the country made a call they likely still remember as they passed along news that Jessica had been rescued and was going to be all right. People stood and cheered. Action stopped. Fans watching small-town games from cars parked in end zones honked horns and flashed headlights.

Tom Barnett also remembers church bells ringing when McClure was lifted from the well shaft.[20]

Vice President George H. W. Bush paid the McClure family a visit in the days following her rescue, and the family received a call from President Ronald Reagan. More than 300 plush teddy bears arrived in town for the child in the days immediately following her rescue, and the hospital switchboard was overrun with calls, at the rate of fifty per hour, from people concerned about Jessica's welfare.[21]

"I don't get tired of saying her condition over and over," said Darla Tucker, a volunteer with the hospital auxiliary. "We've had people call and it's long distance and they can't talk because they're crying so hard. It breaks your heart is what it does."[22]

Toddler's Rescue Brings Much-Needed Optimism

On October 28, two weeks after Jessica first fell down the well, she was introduced by her mother, Reba, to waiting news media. The famous toddler wore an orange jumper and said "trick or treat" to the collected journalists as her mother announced she would dress as a cat for Halloween. The next day, an estimated one-third of Midland turned out to honor the rescuers and Jessica at a parade she watched from her room at Midland Memorial Hospital.[23]

The *Midland Reporter-Telegram* suspended its policy of not publishing poetry. Nine poems and one song written about the girl and her rescuers were published in a special edition that summarized the events of the week in October. One poem came from Hoffman Estates, Illinois, and noted family columnist Bob Greene devoted a column to the rescue.

"When 18-month-old Jessica McClure was pulled out of that hole in the ground Friday night, you would have to have been very callous indeed not to find yourself wiping your eyes and feeling something catch in your throat," Greene wrote.[24] "What the volunteers in Midland—and the volunteers who traveled to Midland from various points around the United States—showed us was that, even when we are feeling as if we might be entering our darkest and gloomiest days, the heart of this nation is as strong and as true as it ever was."

"There was a lot of doubt she was going to get out safe," admitted fire chief James Roberts. "It was a miracle, and there were a bunch of us that worked together to do that, and it really did show what a group of determined people can do. I'm very proud to have been able to participate in a miracle."

In a special section, the *Midland Reporter-Telegram* published thirty-seven letters to the editor, a sizable number for a community newspaper. The letters came from sixteen states—Arizona, Tennessee, New York, Florida, South Carolina, North Carolina, Virginia, Michigan, Oklahoma, Illinois, Georgia, Louisiana, Colorado, Minnesota, Massachusetts, and Texas.

What Jessica's Rescue Did for Midland

Jessica's fall occurred exactly four years after the collapse of Midland's beloved First National Bank—coincidentally, to the very day. The city was still reeling from the effects of the oil bust that had brought that collapse. But the overwhelming community support during Jessica's crisis did a great deal to restore Midland's hope and optimism.

Part One: A Place with Character

"I don't know how we would have made it through this ordeal without everyone's help," said Jessica's father.

Dr. Debbie Reese said she will never forget how the rescue lifted the morale of the entire city. "I think Jessica kind of gave the community a little boost," she said.[25]

"I do truly believe that the closer you get to the frontier, the more you depend on your friends and neighbors," said Mayor Carroll Thomas. That spirit, he said, lies predominantly in the western part of the country.[26]

In the October 18, 1987, edition of the *Midland Reporter-Telegram*, Thomas published an open letter to the people of the town:

> We have just gone through a tremendous test of the true character of our community; a test not only of Midland but of our state and nation and of our faith in God. We will always remember these days among the proudest moments in our history. Now let's move forward with thanksgiving and renewed spirit toward the bright future we face because we are Midlanders."[27]

Today McClure and her husband live in Midland County.

For Some, the Silence Afterward Became Tragic

While the communitywide show of support for the rescuers who worked tirelessly to free Jessica was just the booster shot the people of West Texas needed, the future for Midland was not all rosy, and the warm feeling brought by the coordinated effort of many Midlanders gave way to a chill in the years ahead.

Robert O'Donnell

In 1995, eight years later after the last network camera went dark and production trucks pulled away, Robert O'Donnell, one of Jessica's rescuers, killed himself at his parents' ranch. O'Donnell's death was attributed to the inability to handle the absence of the limelight that came when the bright lights went dark.

Chief Roberts was O'Donnell's superior at the Midland Fire Department. "The spotlight burns very brightly, and when it goes out, it's very cold," Roberts said.

O'Donnell, famously photographed as the rescuer holding Jessica tight to his chest as he helped pull her out of the well, numbed the pain that came in the aftermath of the rescue with prescription drugs, a substance that he soon began taking at levels that friends knew amounted to substance abuse.[28]

"I used to tell Robert after the event, when he couldn't make a living as America's Hero, that there was no living to be made. I told him five years from now I was [still] going to be sitting behind the chief's desk, and he better be standing on the other side of it and not out in the cold."

Eight years later, O'Donnell was dead.

Andy Glasscock

In 2003 Midland police sergeant Andy Glasscock, one of the first responders on the scene, pleaded guilty to drugging and raping a 53-year-old Odessa woman, and to federal charges of possession of child pornography. Glasscock said after the excitement of the rescue diminished he substituted that adrenalin rush with doses of excitement and Internet pornography.[29]

Ironically, it was Glasscock who would comment on the death of Robert O'Donnell:

> Friends say he never really recovered from the quicksilver fame he won as one of Jessica's rescuers, fame which vanished not long after the network news crews left town. Four years after the rescue, his marriage ended in divorce. A year later his career at the Midland Fire Department collapsed amid allegations of prescription-drug abuse. Once the adrenalin [subsides], you go into a major depression. Robert never came out of it. We saved a little girl, but we've all lost a friend.[30]

Dr. Debbie Reese

Even Dr. Debbie Reese suffered, though not nearly to the extent of O'Donnell or Glasscock. "I was desperate to run away from [all the publicity] myself," Reese said. "People were bugging me about it and I just didn't want to talk about it anymore. I went to New Orleans for a medical conference right after it was over, and when people asked me where I was from, I told them Houston just so they wouldn't bother me."[31]

Twenty-five years after Jessica's rescue, Dr. Reese clearly recalls that she was made out to be "a witch" for advocating a controversial rescue plan if it could mean getting the toddler out quicker. "I told them it was okay to break her leg, and the news media sensationalized that," Reese said. "She had been down there for three days! Who cares if her leg is broken? Just get her out."[32]

Part One: A Place with Character

Steve Forbes

The other rescuer who played an integral role in rescuing McClure was Steve Forbes, a paramedic and a man Roberts said handled the aftermath and the glow of fame more admirably than anyone. Forbes has never shared details of his story with the media.[33]

chapter 18

MIDLANDERS ON THE NATIONAL POLITICAL SCENE

Midland is a place where you make lasting friendships. It mattered a lot to me during the presidency that these good folks were my friends prior to [my] going into politics and remained so during the time I was governor and president. Friends really helped keep Laura and me grounded and remind us of the important things in life.

—President George W. Bush,
in correspondence with the author, February 2012

ONE OF MIDLAND'S HALLMARK CHARACTERISTICS is that, for a town of its modest size, it has been home to a remarkable number of people who go on to do bigger, better things on the national stage.

Tommy Franks, a 1963 graduate of Midland Lee High School, was commander of the coalition forces in Iraq during Operation Desert Storm. His classmate Tommy Lee Jones became one of the most respected actors in Hollywood, perhaps most notably playing Captain Woodrow Call in one of television's most honored miniseries, *Lonesome Dove*.

Susan Graham, another graduate of Midland Lee High School, went on to become a highly renowned classical singer who performs in opera houses all over the world.

But no field shows this trend more abundantly than politics. The Tall City can make a unique claim to having been home to two U.S. presidents, two first ladies, and two governors.

Midland is also home to a shrewd businessman who found that he didn't belong in politics after all.

Part One: A Place with Character

Clayton Williams Jr.

While Clayton Williams Jr. was becoming a West Texas oil magnate, he was also respected and accomplished in real estate, telecommunications, farming, ranching, and teaching. A good thirty years before his infamous run for Texas governor in 1990, he sold life insurance.

Singing "Like a Full-Blooded Mexican"

At least one man in Midland still remembers the image of the slight-of-build man who first showed up in Midland in the 1960s with a briefcase, a fondness for beer, and a way with Mexican ballads. Sid Trevino, in his eighties now, is the former owner of Club Granada on West Wall Street. Trevino was Midland's first Hispanic police detective and is still Williams's head of security at ClayDesta Plaza.

"When he made his trips up from Fort Stockton to Midland and Odessa back then, he didn't have all that he has now," Trevino said. "Back in the 1950s and 1960s, he used to carry this little suitcase. He'd come into the club and ask me if he could leave his suitcase in my office. After he'd had a couple of beers, he'd say, 'Sid, you mind if I sing along with the band?' I'd always laugh and tell him, 'Well, the band is kinda picky. They don't want just every drunk getting up there and singing with them. Most drunks, as soon as they have a couple of drinks, they think they're movie stars.'"[1]

Trevino talked to the band about Williams's request to sing with them. The club owner and would-be balladeer soon became fast friends. Making the decision to let the future tycoon join in was, as it turned out, not such a bad decision at all. "If you were just sitting at the bar listening to Claytie sing during those days," said Trevino, "you would think you were listening to a full-blooded Mexican singing. He had a great voice for that, and he was very good."[2]

Williams continued his bar singing as a hobby, and over the years parlayed his professional life into a West Texas empire. He is one of Midland's truest characters, and his exploits, adventures, and experiences could fill volumes.

Controversy over a Historic Building

He did not, however, make a favorable first impression when he bought the Gulf Building (aka the Hogan Building) in downtown Midland. Williams's attorneys negotiated the purchase of the building in 1973 with the sellers, who were also negotiating with C. J. Kelly and First National Bank to sell them the same building. When Williams's attorneys spoke with Kelly's, they advised Williams that they were convinced First National Bank officials might be upset with the deal but were unlikely to file suit if the purchase went through.³

"I went over to see Mr. Kelly to thank him for being so considerate in letting me buy the building," Williams said. "C. J. blew his top and ran me out of his office. Even an Aggie could realize he had not intended for me to have the building."⁴

In *Claytie*, Michael Cochran's biography of the oilman, Williams is quoted as saying that he attempted to prevent "the God of the oil field" from becoming angrier after the encounter, but Kelly actually did become angrier and filed suit against the young upstart. Williams's response was typical Claytie. "I acquired the largest Texas A&M flag I could find and raised it from atop the Gulf Building's flagpole—directly across from First National. It was my battle cry and my response to the lawsuit."⁵

Williams took occupancy of the building, moved his people into the historic downtown structure, and let his lawyers work through the details and cope with the storm still brewing in the First National offices. Calmer heads eventually prevailed. Years later, Williams said the entire affair could have been settled were it not for "the hardheadedness of C. J. Kelly, and to a lesser extent myself."⁶

A Notorious Political Blunder

Always quick with a quip, Williams has proved expert in almost all of his endeavors. There was one notable exception: politics. Looking back on his gubernatorial run against Ann Richards in 1990, he admits to having learned one critical lesson.

"To keep my mouth shut," Williams said.⁷

Although his now infamous "If it's inevitable, relax and enjoy it" statement, supposedly a joke about rape, proved to be a gaffe that singlehandedly destroyed his chances for the state house, he acknowledged the error in his words and apologized at a news conference days after the story broke. Williams told the media he had been worked over "like you can't believe" by his mother and daughters for his attempt at humor, admitting that his mother told him, "I didn't raise you that way."⁸

"I feel terrible about this," Williams said at the news conference. "I had no intention in my heart to hurt anyone, especially those women who had been traumatized by rape. Looking back, I realize it was insensitive and had no place at the campfire setting or in any setting. People who know me and who know what I've been saying in my campaign know that I feel strongly about criminals who roam our streets inflicting violence on innocent citizens. Rape is one of the most violent crimes we are faced with today and it will be met with a firm hand if I am elected governor."⁹

Williams lost the election despite outspending Richards two to one and being ahead by as much as eleven points three months before the election.¹⁰ In hindsight, Williams admitted that he was perhaps not cut out for political office, though he continues to remain an influence in the Republican Party.

Williams said that former U.S. senator Phil Gramm (R-Texas) "told me once I wasn't mean enough for politics. I'd say that's basically true. I've been in fistfights, yes, but I was raised in a Christian family. I think politics may have more meanness than what it took for me to be involved in. I remember I came in like a small battering ram, but I'm the one that took the battering at the end."¹¹

Williams still thinks that had he won the Texas gubernatorial race, he could have gone on to become president. As it turned out, however, too many things worked against him as the race progressed. Though he doesn't blame the media, he thinks they did turn on him:¹²

> The media is like apples. There are good ones and there are bad ones.
>
> I think there is definitely bias in the media politically, and it is very real. The media were taught to write, but nobody ever taught them to think. I was a political cowboy businessman, and the media really liked me at first because I created things for them to write about. When it came down to it, they were basically liberals and that came out at the end. If you're going to be successful in politics, you've got to deal with it better than I did. I made a few mistakes, absolutely.¹³

Ambitious Oil and Gas Tycoon

Williams's humbling defeat, which featured a less-than-flattering photograph of him pulling at his ears on the cover of *Texas Monthly*, should not negate his many accomplishments outside the political arena.

In 1957 he and friend John May started May and Williams, an oil and gas company. In 1959 the duo drilled a successful well in Coyanosa, and from that well, started a natural-gas company and planted the seed for Clajon Gas Company, founded in 1961. Clajon became the largest independently owned gas company in the state.

In the mid-1970s, Williams made his biggest strike. The Gataga No. 2 well blew in with such force that the nearby town of Mentone had to be evacuated. It became one of the largest wells in the Permian Basin, producing 32 million cubic feet of gas

Midlanders on the National Political Scene

per day. Williams had become one of the top natural-gas wildcatters in Texas, and in May 1993 he took Clayton Williams Energy public on the NASDAQ.

In early 1998, Clayton Williams Energy's oil production continued to rise as a result of drilling long, record-breaking laterals and soon after established a world record for horizontal length drilled in a twenty-four-hour period.

Williams has organized many other companies, including WilGas Company, NGL Service Company, Natural Gas of Mississippi, Century Royalty Company, Williams Ranches, Williams Brangus, Williams Farms, ClayDesta Corporation, ClayDesta National Bank, Hunters Africa, ClayDesta Communications Company, Warrior Gas Company, Maverick Mud Service, and W&G Partnership.[14]

One of his favorite Claytie-isms would be in direct contrast to the astute businessman Williams really is, a fact verified by his many accomplishments. He says he runs his energy company the way Christopher Columbus ran his famous expedition that led to the discovery of America: "When he left Spain, Chris didn't know where he was going," Williams said. "When he got over here, he didn't know where he was. And when he got back to Spain, he didn't know where he'd been. But we both did it on borrowed money."[15]

While Williams was running for governor, one anonymous supporter offered him a half million dollars. All he had to do was take the money. Not wanting to be obligated to anyone who gave him $500,000 sight unseen, Williams joked that had he known he was going to lose the governor's race, he would have taken it.[16]

Williams has met most every challenge that has come his way and has seldom, if ever, been a man of few words. Modesta, the woman he married in 1965, said her husband has a quick mind. "It's amazing to all of us that he has so many pieces to the pie, and he can just pick one out and go from one to the other to the other to the other. And I'm the one who picks up the pieces from what he does," Mrs. Williams joked.[17]

The Bush Family

Two Midlanders who have arguably accomplished the most on the national stage are George H. W. Bush and his son George W. Bush.

George Herbert Walker Bush was a Connecticut Yankee who brought his family to Midland in the 1950s. He later became the forty-first president of the United States, occupying the White House from 1989 to 1993 along with his wife, former

PART ONE: A PLACE WITH CHARACTER

First Lady Barbara Pierce Bush, herself a transplant to West Texas.

George W. Bush was a future governor of Texas and forty-third president of the United States, from 2001 to 2009. His wife, Laura Welch Bush, was a native Midlander who graduated from Midland Lee High School and Southern Methodist University in Dallas.

President George W. Bush's younger brother, Jeb, who also spent a portion of his childhood in Midland, would be elected the forty-third governor of Florida, and serve from 1999 to 2007.

Like many others, the Bushes came to Midland because of oil. When they arrived in town, they moved into a small home at 405 East Maple Avenue. Three years later, another move would land them at 1412 West Ohio Avenue.

President George W. Bush has expressed fond memories of his childhood home, which was officially dedicated as a museum on April 11, 2006. It has become a popular attraction for out-of-town guests and Midlanders alike. More than 30,000 visitors, from every state and sixty foreign countries, have come to see it since its opening.

George W. Bush

Before becoming president, George W. Bush was governor of Texas. Before that, he was majority owner of the Texas Rangers Baseball Club. Though born in Connecticut and educated at Yale in New Haven, Connecticut, Bush remains Texan through and through. His memories of Midland are among his fondest, and his sincerity was obvious when he emotionally told tens of thousands of people assembled in twenty-degree temperatures in Centennial Plaza in January 2001, "This is my home!"[18]

A Flyover by Air Force One

Many Midlanders fondly remember the rally to show support for President Bush, as he began the first of two presidential terms. The event remains on many Midlanders' lists of their fondest memories. Tens of thousands of people huddled together in sub-zero wind chills on that January day as Bush insisted Midland be his last stop on the way to Washington. Eight years later, he returned to an equally exuberant crowd numbering well into the tens of thousands again, as Air Force One made a flyover, not so high above the downtown crowd below.

"You know, I don't know about Air Force One and why it flew over Midland," the president said. "You'll be pleased to know I did not decide the flight path for Air Force One. I'm sure what the pilot wanted to do was to let people see that majestic plane that carried Laura and me around the world. It's a marvel to look at, and I'm sure it was a thrill for the thousands that had gathered there."[19]

The president said he decided to come to West Texas en route to Washington in 2001 because he still considered Midland home, even though it had been almost fifteen years since he had resided here. George W. and Laura Bush left Midland in 1987 to help work on his father's presidential campaign.

> Midland was where Laura and I were both raised, Midland was where we established the principles that guided our lives, Midland was where we had a lot of friends. And so therefore it was a kickoff, a time to say good-bye to Texas.
>
> But as I made it clear in that speech, I said I wasn't going to leave the values and principles behind even though I was moving temporarily to Washington. I retained what I learned in Midland, so when the presidency was over, I thought it was a good way to complete the circle and go back to where we started. It was a very symbolic decision to leave from Midland and go back to Midland.[20]

Bush's parents took him regularly to First Presbyterian Church during his childhood. He said that solid religious upbringing helped plant seeds of moral values that admittedly "took a while to take root and grow." The president mentioned the time spent in Community Bible Study when he lived in Midland as an adult, adding that he still recalled CBS as a means of reconnecting him to his Christian faith.

"I think Community Bible Study helped me get back into religion in a way that focused my mind and eventually focused my heart," he said.[21]

The president lived in Midland twice, first during his adolescent years in the 1950s, when the family came out because of oil and President George H. W. Bush began his own oil company, and then in the 1980s, when the younger Bush started an oil business of his own. In 1981–82, President George W. Bush served as campaign chairman of the United Way of Midland.

Bush's Enduring Friendships with Many Midlanders

It was during his second stay here that a great number of friendships were formed

PART ONE: A PLACE WITH CHARACTER

that he continues to maintain today. As he explained:

> I've got a lot of friends from Midland. Robert McCleskey is my accountant. He and I grew up together. Mike Proctor grew up across the street from me on Ohio Street; he and I have remained friends forever.
>
> Charlie Younger is a dear friend of mine. He was older than I was, so I don't remember him during elementary school, but when I moved back to Midland, Charlie and Donnie Evans and I became great pals. We used to spend hours running together or sitting in Charlie's doctor's office shooting the breeze and having fun.
>
> Joe and Jan O'Neill did introduce me and Laura in their backyard. We remained close all of these years. I've got a lot of friends in Midland.[22]

Joe O'Neill. One of the Midlanders who knew the president both as a boy, and later when Bush returned to Midland, was Joe O'Neill. He still remembers introducing the future president and first lady:

> I was sitting in my office one day and got a call from the front desk. The receptionist said, "George Bush wants to see you." I walked to the front, and it was the same guy I had known when I was nine or ten.
>
> We were probably thirty then. Jan and I were married, and this was probably 1974. Laura and Jan knew each other from high school, and they had roomed together with Susie Evans down in Houston in the late 1960s. Then Laura left and got her master's degree in Austin.
>
> Jan knew Laura was coming to town. Laura's parents lived just two blocks from us. George was the only single man in our group, so we tried to set him up with her and she said no, she didn't really want to make this out as a dating thing.
>
> We asked her a couple more times, and the two of them finally went out together. And when they finally did, it was all over but the shouting. He was smitten. He stayed out with her until 12:30 that night, and he never stayed up past nine.[23]

O'Neill speculates that he probably gave as many as 250 media interviews during Bush's presidential campaigns because of his lifelong friendship with Bush. A people person, O'Neill called him—the type of person who would frequently study others.

Midlanders on the National Political Scene

Charlie Younger. An orthopedic surgeon in Midland, Charlie Younger said that when he and Bush rekindled their friendship in the mid-1970s, upon the president's move back to Midland, they did so by jogging together at lunch during the workday. They weren't designed, preappointed jogs, but rather they simply jogged at the same time daily and often, through chance, they would meet and end up running together.

Soon, though, those jogs led to a longtime friendship.

"I actually saw him more when he was president than I've seen him since he's been in Dallas," Younger said. "Sometimes he would have groups to the White House on his birthday or for Christmas, or some other special event. Even though he was running the country, he was very good about keeping up with his friends. I think his old friends were often a safety net for him, a pop-off valve with whom he could let his guard down and relax for a couple of hours."[24]

Younger still finds one occasion particularly memorable. He had been in nearby West Point for a meeting. When it had ended, he went to Washington to spend some time at the White House, at President Bush's invitation:

> President Bush asked me, "Do you want to go to the movies?" There was a movie being screened downstairs at the White House. It was a private showing of *We Were Soldiers*.
>
> We go down and have a nice dinner before the movie. It was my wife and me, Dick Cheney, Colin Powell, Donald Rumsfeld, Condoleezza Rice, all these people who are involved in defense and national security. Hal Moore, who the movie was about, was there, along with Joe Galloway, the famous journalist who was in Vietnam, and then all the actors, Mel Gibson, Greg Kinnear. It was kind of surreal to watch the movie with the cabinet members, the actors, and the president and first lady.[25]

Like many others who knew the president, Younger insists that he is the same person today as he was when he knew him in the 1970s.

"He enjoyed being president until I guess about the last two months," Younger said. "He really did wake up every day, truly relishing being the president of the United States. His values, his work ethic, his beliefs, have all stayed the same. He hasn't changed to this day. I don't think he'll ever change. He just happened to be the president."[26]

Part One: A Place with Character

K. Michael Conaway. Another close friend and former business partner, U.S. Representative K. Michael Conaway, can't speak at length about President Bush without becoming emotional over his friend's generosity.

"When my first wife was diagnosed with leukemia, George would come over and get our boys and take them to Midland College basketball games," Conaway remembered. "He didn't have to do that. He couldn't do anything about Julia's treatment, but he could come by and be with the boys, and that's what he did."[27]

Conaway jokes about his former business partner when the two ran Arbusto Energy, saying he would have rather been business partners when Bush was owner of the Texas Rangers.

"I'd have made a lot more money," Conaway joked. "He invited the boys and me up after Julia died. He had us as his guests at the last game the Rangers played in their old stadium and the first one in the Ballpark in Arlington. We were standing there watching batting practice before one of the games, and he walked up behind us and said, 'This is my own personal field of dreams.'"[28]

Some media outlets today have written that the only reason George W. Bush entered the political arena was that he was unable to land the job he really wanted: that of Major League Baseball Commissioner. The rumor sprouted wings again when current commissioner Bud Selig announced he would retire in 2014. Bush's name is on the top of some speculation lists of possible replacements for Selig.

Conaway said the president enjoyed being in office until about the last year in the White House. He still recalls with fondness how he watched his friend grow before being molded into the person who would later become the forty-third president.

"I'm not the least bit surprised at how well he did as president," Conaway said. "His presidency will be looked upon more favorably with each round of historians who look at it, and in two to three generations I think it will be looked at as one of the top presidencies in United States history."[29]

Conaway watched regretfully as his friend was repeatedly stung by the national news media, which often painted him a warmonger and someone lacking the tools to be president.

"You cannot be a human being and not have it sting," he said. "He did a good job of not exposing himself to more of that. He went to bed early every night, never watched Leno or Letterman. He didn't listen to all that nonsense. He wasn't swayed by all the silliness that surrounds any president."[30]

chapter 19

THE CITY'S BOLD PROGRESS CONTINUES

Even with the big hits we have taken, Midland still progresses and has the ability to take charge of the things it does. Ever since I've lived here, I have always thought Midland was going to succeed no matter what. We've always had the ability to make things happen.

—Bobby Burns, former mayor of Midland

EVER SINCE THE 1920S, MIDLAND has been associated with the skyscraper. The term "Tall City" itself came from the city's penchant for developing tall buildings and other projects on a grand scale.

It began with T. S. Hogan's construction of the twelve-story Hogan Building, which opened in 1929. (For more about its construction and the vital role it played in Midland's development, see Chapter 5.) The Petroleum Building, as the Hogan Building has come to be called, didn't reach its full potential until after the Depression.

Jack Wilkinson's Wilco Building instantly became Midland's tallest structure (twenty-two floors) upon its 1958 opening. It was proudly advertised as the tallest building between Fort Worth and Phoenix. Twenty years later, the First National Bank Building—which became the RepublicBank Building in 1983 and later the Bank of America Building—grabbed that distinction when it was expanded to twenty-four floors, surpassing the Wilco. The bank has remained the tallest structure in Midland ever since those upper sixteen floors opened in 1978.

ClayDesta Business Complex, though it contains no building that comes close to skyscraper status, broke ground in 1982 and became a go-to business location with several structures of six or more floors.

Part One: A Place with Character

Some of Midland's most impressive building projects in recent years have included a major hospital addition, a highway loop full of attractive retail businesses, and a magnificent sports stadium.

The New Patient Tower at Midland Memorial Hospital

Although the eight-story Dorothy and Clarence Scharbauer Jr. Tower is technically not a skyscraper, it represents a significant achievement in the growth of Midland's medical reputation.

A project six years in the making, the new patient tower at Midland Memorial Hospital was opened on December 18, 2012. A $115 million bond issue was approved by Midland voters in 2009, a decision that helped—but was not completely responsible for—the tower's existence. That number would have had to be much higher if not for $65 million in private donations—including $25 million given by Clarence Scharbauer Jr. alone.

"The opening of the tower concludes a journey that began in 2006, with the initial work on a plan to resolve the many long-standing facility challenges facing Midland Memorial," hospital CEO Russell Meyers wrote in the *Midland Reporter-Telegram*. "Despite our limited resources, the hospital's aging and obsolete infrastructure demanded radical improvement if we were to properly serve the community in the years ahead." Meyers said that despite a down national economy in 2008–2009, the worst since the Great Depression, Midlanders chose to invest in their community's health care. "It's amazing to recount how much has happened in the six years since the planning work began," he wrote.[1]

Unexpected cost savings in construction and equipment allowed the hospital to build an even larger garage than had been planned, new operating rooms, and two additional floors.

How to Ask for $25 Million
In the early going, volunteer fund-raiser Rosalind Grover said the project had its share of detractors, and had she listened, there would be no new patient tower. As she described it:

> Everybody told me, "You can't get that done." There were certainly doubters. And I would always tell them, "Of course we can." I'm a dreamer. I always

The City's Bold Progress Continues

look at something and say, "We can get this done. It is a mountain, but we can climb it."

I thought that we could get this done even before Clarence Jr.'s donation. I knew there was always going to be somebody who would give the seed money. And I knew that seed money was going to come from Clarence Scharbauer Jr. . . ., The Scharbauers, that family, as many things that have their name on them, they are really very low-key people."[2]

Grover said the Scharbauer family had earned the right to have the first chance to provide the seed money for the patient tower "because they helped found Midland Memorial and have been its biggest supporters ever since." If the Scharbauers had not made that gift, Grover said she would have approached other potential givers. But, she added, "I had no doubt" the Scharbauers would be the ones.[3]

The meeting that would end with a pledge of $25 million by Scharbauer Jr. deserves a place in Midland's wheeler-dealer hall of fame, if there ever is one. Grover still remembers how it all came to be.

As Rosalind Grover later explained, "Clarence first called me and left a message on my answering machine. He told me he was going to give me $10 million. I remember thinking, 'Well, that's just not enough. We can't make it if he doesn't give $25 million.'"[4]

The phone message, Grover said, was literally, "Roz, I know you're doing this and I want to help, and I'm going to give $10 million. You just let me know what the payment program is and I'll sign up."[5]

When Grover heard the message from Scharbauer Jr., her first thought was that Scharbauer didn't want to talk in person about the gift. She called a childhood friend, longtime Midlander Tevis Herd, a philanthropist in his own right and a local attorney, thinking that if the two of them were to approach Scharbauer Jr. together, it would look better than if she went solo.

"At the meeting . . . I had a piece of paper on which I had put what the naming opportunities were," Grover said. "Twenty-five million was the [highest listed] naming opportunity on the tower. We had two $10 million opportunities, then a $5 million, and a $3 million. So I took this piece of paper and I said, 'Clarence, I want to talk to you. This is such a great gift and I am very grateful.'"[6]

Grover then slid the slip of paper across the table toward Scharbauer Jr. She said the two of them continued to dance around the bottom line. As she described the conversation:

> I kept talking about it, and I would say all that we intended to do, and I intended to get this and that, and he'd nod his head yes. It became a sort of staged pirouette. He was waiting for me to ask, and I kept delaying it. Finally I asked, "Clarence, would you do the $25 million for me?"
>
> And he said yes, just like that.
>
> Nobody in this town, I promise you, ever gives as graciously or as generously or with as much style as Dorothy and Clarence Scharbauer. And if he's not interested in your project, he will tell you right off, "I'm not interested." They would never lead you on.[7]

With $25 million in hand, Grover's job of selling the bond package to the people became instantly easier. Scharbauer's donation allowed her to approach others and say, "This is what's going to happen," with a confidence she had not been afforded earlier.[8]

Getting Voters to Approve a Bond Package

The plan at that point, Grover said, was to get the hospital's board of directors to approve a $115 million package to present to Midland voters and let the remaining $60 million of the project's $175 million cost be handled by private donations.

"They finally agreed to do that," Grover said. "It took a little persuading. One of the hospital commissioners, the one that represented my district, said, 'You know, Roz, I just don't think people will vote for this. It's too big a tax increase. I don't think we can go to them with that.'"[9]

Grover said it was the job of the directors and the administration to explain to voters what quality health care would cost. Those who championed the hospital's improvements must deliver to the voters a message of "Do you want this Class A health care or do you not?"

"If they rejected the bond issue," Grover said, "it wouldn't bother me one bit. That [would] just [mean] people don't want that kind of quality health care, and so then we would go to them and say, 'Okay, this is what Class B health care costs,' and if they rejected that, we would go to Class C health care—however far down they wanted to go."[10]

Midland's Choice: Top-Quality Health Care

As it turned out, voter approval of a $115 million package—for top-rate health care—was overwhelming.

Grover said her most memorable moment during the fundraising campaign came when she was sitting at a traffic light in town. An old, beat-up pickup truck advertising an independent plumbing business, driven by a Mexican American, pulled up next to her. On the side of the man's toolbox was the hospital bond issue's official bumper sticker, which read, I SUPPORT THE HOSPITAL BOND BECAUSE IT MATTERS.

"It proved my point," Grover said. "Just because you don't have the resources doesn't mean you're dumb or can't tell what's in your best interest. You may simply be the victim of circumstances. And the voters knew that having a good hospital was in their best interest."[11]

How generous is Midland? Grover said donations were "left on the table." An overage of donations was pledged. More than twenty individuals or families pledged at least $1 million. "It was an incredible outpouring of support," Grover said. "These people in Midland, they get behind things and they get things done."

Bobby Burns: A Mayor with Big Projects in Mind

When he moved to Midland in 1978, Bobby Burns knew he wanted to make a difference in his new hometown. At the time, he may not have known exactly how much of a difference he would make.

Born in Oklahoma City to Southern Baptists—his father, Arvy Burns, was a Baptist preacher—Burns received an undergraduate degree from Baylor University, and when he completed his classwork for his master's at Oklahoma University, he moved to Midland.

A lot of people, Burns said, come here unable to see anything but flat lands and the brown skies sometimes caused by dust blowing in from the prairie. All Burns could see was opportunity. Midland fit Burns's vision for what he had in mind for his life, a vision that the town and its residents helped happen.

"Midland has that character," he said. "We know how to figure out how to make things happen. We feel like we're a big city, but we're still small, so we get the good of a small city without the bad of a big city."[12]

Burns has had to repeatedly try to convince his lifelong friends in the Southwest that Midland isn't the dusty outpost many believe it to be. Midland, they tell the former mayor, is too far away, almost exotic. Those same friends, he said, won't think a minute before driving five or six hours to Dallas or Waco or Austin or Oklahoma City, but they would never consider driving to Midland.

"That's what helps give us that feeling of remoteness," he said. "We rely on each other here and we take care of each other, and we aren't afraid to try. And as history will show, we have had our massive successes and our massive failures."[13]

Bobby Burns was mayor of Midland from 1994 to 2001. When he was sworn in, oil was still low—below $15 a barrel in the first quarter of 1994—but people had begun to believe in themselves again. "It wasn't a booming economy, but that didn't stop Midland," Burns said. "We still progressed."[14]

Loop 250

One of the more significant pieces of development Burns helped make happen was Loop 250, a semicircular, highwaylike thoroughfare that curves across the northern half of Midland, connecting its extreme east and west points. (The southern half of the loop has yet to be built). As recently as the early 1990s, the loop did not exist in its present state. The land between the north and south service roads was there, dedicated to the eventual establishment of the road as it is today, but it was mostly undeveloped rangeland. Some businesses existed: there was a magic shop at North Midland Drive and the pre-loop service roads. But Walmart, Target, Best Buy, and Barnes & Noble were still the stuff of Burns's dreams as he took office.

When Burns became mayor, he said he realized Midland had never really been a town with full-scale regional appeal. The loop changed that, and it gave city coffers substantial revenue increases. After years of construction work in the 1990s, the loop was dedicated on August 30, 1999.

"We had never really given people from Andrews or Lamesa or Big Spring or Odessa a tremendous reason to come here and shop as a regional hub," Burns said. "But all of a sudden, there came Target and On the Border, more choices of restaurant and retail. Sales-tax revenues just blossomed. Midlanders wanted choices, and as mayor you give them what they want, even though it created a lot of challenges getting it done."[15]

Interestingly, every vote the council took on zoning changes that would help create Loop 250 passed by just a single vote.[16] It was critical that every time a vote was held regarding a zoning change on the loop, he knew exactly where each council member stood. One more vote against Loop 250 at any time during that development phase, and the dominoes would have fallen. Burns said it was his job to make sure those dominoes stacked up. Allowing the project to fall through would have impeded progress and sent a message around the state that Midland was not ready to grow. The council understood that, and made that progress happen.[17]

Former assistant city manager Glenn Hackler, now the city manager in Andrews, Texas, was crucial to Burns's road map for development in the 1990s—so crucial, in fact, that Burns said loop development might not have been done without Hackler. Burns still calls Hackler "one of the best city managers in Texas."[18]

Without a doubt, the two biggest accomplishments Burns can hang his hat on in his three terms, aside from loop development, are the construction of the Scharbauer Sports Complex and the new Midland International Airport terminal. He says of his time as mayor, "We didn't just go to council meetings and raise our hands."[19]

Even as Burns said the council was trying to bring loop development, "the whole time, in my hip pocket was the stadium idea."

Bobby Burns's 100 Speeches

The mayor sold the loop development, the new Midland International Airport terminal, and construction of the sports complex to the public by making appearances around town and ensuring Midlanders they could have whatever they needed without having to raise property taxes, which Burns had promised he would steer clear of as mayor. He called his whirlwind tour his 100 Speeches. Some were to a dozen people, others to a thousand. But all of them focused on five attainable projects.

Burns's five projects were the Scharbauer Sports Complex, the new Midland International Airport terminal, development of Loop 250, the Wagner-Noel Performing Arts Center, and an expo center (the Horseshoe). All five projects have become reality. (For more about the construction of the new terminal at Midland International Airport, see Chapter 8.)

"The goal was to raise vision and the thinking of the people, and I think we did it," he said. "If you want a new football stadium, we can do it. If you want a new baseball stadium so we can keep the Angels [now the Rockhounds], we can do it. There's a way to have a new performing arts center [now the Wagner-Noel Performing Arts Center], a new expo center [now the Horseshoe]. If you want a new Midland Center, we can do it."[20]

While people wanted most things he said they could have, a feeling soon rose that people were not behind a new Midland Center. On all other issues, Burns said there was support for a sort of "Midland wish list." By listening to the people's questions and by looking them square in the eyes, Burns said he began to get a sense of what the people had the will to do.

Part One: A Place with Character

"I thought a downtown stadium would really launch a revitalization effort, but I began to see early on it would mean having to take out Carter Furniture and a number of other businesses, and that's not the Texas way. If everyone was willing to sell, that's one thing, but to take their land away, I don't think Midlanders like that much," Burns said.[21]

The Scharbauer Sports Complex

On the west side of Midland, rising up from the flatness of the nearby desert, stand two structures built of rough-hewn desert limestone, each enclosing an emerald-green playing field. This is the Scharbauer Sports Complex, where Midlanders enjoy their favorite sports: football first, of course, followed by the Class AA Texas League Midland Rockhounds and professional soccer. Sports in West Texas set us free from the workaday routine in the oil patch and the hardscrabble effort it has often taken through the decades to simply survive.

The Scharbauer Sports Complex is considered by more than a handful of Midlanders to be one of our grandest accomplishments. Developers built the facility on a patch of land that is impossible to miss for travelers coming into the north side of Midland from the airport. Making the complex a reality took some doing by city leaders in the 1990s.

Burns stated that of everything he did as mayor, he probably invested the most energy and emotion in the sports complex. "I was really wanting to do something meaningful for Midland," he said.[22]

Midland's History of Winning Athletes

Midland has produced winning athletes throughout its existence. We have had state championship football teams dating from the thirties through 1999 and Texas League championship teams, including one that was partly claimed within the white lines of the minor league baseball field at the complex.

Midland has seen its share of athletes grow up here and move on to noteworthy careers or accomplishments on the college or professional level. Former Major League Baseball infielder Randy Velarde and NFL running back Cedric Benson are perhaps the two most well-known Midland athletes in their respective sports. Save for a brief injury rehabilitation appearance by Velarde with the Rockhounds during the 2002 season, his last, neither he nor Benson ever played at the Scharbauer Sports Complex.

Throughout its history, Midland has experienced impressively large, even frightening dust storms, which often usher in strong weather fronts. Pictured is a dust storm of February 20, 1894.

Dust storms carry tons of topsoil, and when the winds subside, a blanket of brown earth settles on cars, people, and even home interiors.

Midland's first Texas & Pacific railroad depot, photographed circa 1895. The railroad was crucial to Midland's early development.

The original First National Bank building, seen here in the 1910s. The bank was opened in 1888 and chartered in 1890.

The first Llano Hotel, photographed circa 1885, on the northwest corner of what are now Main and Wall Streets, was a popular gathering place in nineteenth-century Midland.

A fire on April 8, 1909, destroyed the Llano Hotel and several other businesses in downtown Midland, including First National Bank, on the extreme left. The flames were so intense that they gutted the entire hotel.

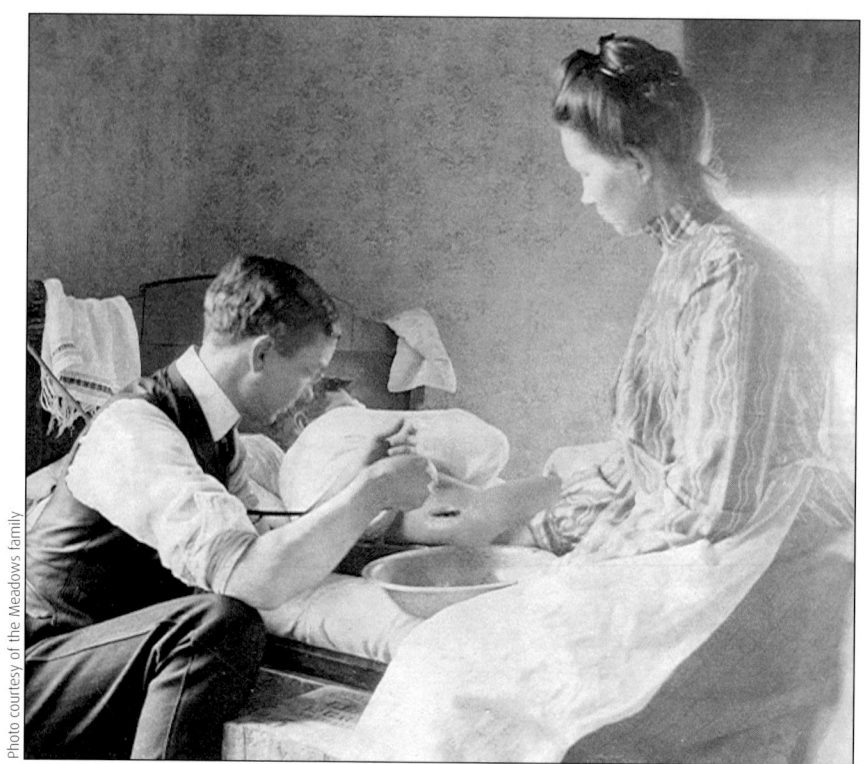

Dr. John B. Thomas performing the first kidney surgery in West Texas. The woman is probably Josephine Guly, Thomas's nurse for years. An early medical pioneer in Midland, Thomas opened a hospital wing on the second floor of the rebuilt Llano Hotel and later devoted a floor to hospital care in his own Thomas Building.

Facing page: Three of Midland's most important buildings from the late 1920s helped establish Midland as the oil capital of West Texas. Clockwise from top left: the Thomas Building, 1928; the Hogan Building, 1929; and the Scharbauer Hotel, 1928.

The Thomas Building

The Hogan Building

The Scharbauer Hotel

This modern photo of the Petroleum Building shows more detail. The structure was a marvel of early-twentieth-century architecture when built by T. S. Hogan.

Photo by Karen J. Patterson

Cadets at the Midland Army Flying School use practice bombs in their physical training exercises. A total of 6,627 bombardiers were trained at the school from April 1942 to January 1945.

Midland mayor Marvin C. Ulmer, on horseback, greets Brigadier General Isaiah Davies, first commanding officer of the Midland Army Air Field, at the official opening of the World War II training school.

Midland County Courthouse, with the Petroleum Building in the background. Few people ever thought the Petroleum Building would stand longer than the downtown courthouse, scheduled for demolition in 2015.

The Midland Tower Building (foreground) opened in 1948. Behind is the Bank of America Building, the tallest structure in Midland since 1976.

Benson, who led the Midland Lee High School Rebels to three-straight state Texas Class 5A high school football championships (1997–1999), played his college ball at the University of Texas, and bounced around the NFL for eight seasons before becoming an unsigned free agent at the outset of the 2013 NFL season. Run-ins with the law during both his collegiate and professional careers always seemed to slow Benson from reaching his full potential.

Working to Keep Midland's Minor-League Baseball Team

What drove the construction of the new complex, at least in its early days, was the fear that Midland might lose its minor-league baseball affiliation unless it gave its team a nicer home. Max Christensen Stadium, on the city's northeast side, had served as a useful, functioning facility since the Midland Cubs first played in West Texas in 1972, but the team and the fans outgrew the ballpark where on a hot summer day, it was impossible not to burn your hide in the aluminum seats. Even the façade of the press box was all metal, still a step up from the wooden enclosure that served the media until the stadium's remodel in the early 1990s. A common visitor to the press box at one point in the late 1980s was a future U.S. Congressman, Mike Conaway, who helped keep score during Midland High School Bulldog baseball games.

"Miles Prentice, owner of the Angels/Rockhounds, never demanded or put pressure on us at all to build a new stadium," Burns said. "I remember he simply asked if there was a chance of Midland building a new stadium. I told him, 'I'm working on it,' and that was when I began to lay out the concepts and designs. Miles helped on the political side and looked into planning. These are the kinds of things that make Midland. I would hate to have lost the baseball team without really trying [to keep it]."[23]

For Burns, the complex was a no-brainer. If you know you can help your school district and save baseball at the same time, Burns remembered, how can you not do it?

"Of all the projects we did, that was probably the most challenging," he said, adding that most electorates would rather put their money into education or parks and find sports facilities a tough horse pill to swallow.

The election went smoothly and the complex passed with roughly 65 percent of the vote. A sermon Burns heard in 1998, about taking risks, proved to be the final piece of the motivational puzzle he was searching for. When he walked out of church, the pastor's message still fresh on his mind, Burns knew that, first, he was going to go after a big-ticket item like the stadium, and second, he was going to catch hell for it.

Part One: A Place with Character

Bobby Burns seldom beats around the bush. He says what he's going to do, and then he does it. Most notable was overseeing three huge projects—the sports complex, airport, and loop development—without once raising property taxes. (Perhaps the football stadium's greatest fan base can be found within the walls of the Midland Independent School District, since the stadium was financed by the city and so has never been a financial drain to MISD.)[24]

Showdown Over a Metal-Skinned Cinema

Burns recalls what happened when he was once tested by a builder who did not deliver on a promise.

Representatives of Hollywood Theaters had been notified that if they wanted to build an entertainment complex on Loop 250, they could not provide a building with a metal exterior. Such buildings are generally considered less visually appealing than those made of a sturdier substance, Burns and the council had already called for a higher building standard when businesses along the loop began popping up, and Hollywood agreed in council chambers to follow the standard.

"When they built it," Burns said, "they conveniently forgot that. I was in South America with the Sister City program, and city attorney Keith Stretcher called and said, 'Bobby, we have a problem. We accidentally approved this building at city hall, and they have the wrong skin on it.'"[25] The representative said Hollywood could not comply as the council requested, because it would cost an additional $50,000.

Burns described his follow-up conversation with the theater representative:

> I told him, "If you think you're moving into that building the way it is, you're wrong. You're not getting in there without a new skin."
>
> He said, "You can't stop me."
>
> I told him, "I can and I will. It will be red-tagged, and you'll never see the light of day."[26]

Burns said Hollywood Theaters threatened to take the city to court. Unshaken, Burns said he'd gladly go to court but insisted again Hollywood would not be allowed to occupy the building until it met the agreed-upon code that called for something of higher quality than an exterior metallic skin. "You can't lie to the Midland people," Burns told Hollywood.[27]

Finally, Hollywood agreed to put a new skin on the theater that served as a compromise. It cost the company $50,000, and while it is still a steel structure, it is adorned in such a way that it looks somewhat better, and it did not bring down the quality of loop building standards.

"It was still a steel building without brick, or Dryvit, or reinforced skin," said Burns, "and it's not the way I wanted to go, but the point is you have to raise the quality of the loop to where it's taken care of."[28]

The kicker?

"I had fun because I was totally bluffing," Burns said. "I would have admitted the city's mistake of okaying it with just a metal skin, and [I would have] followed the law. The Hollywood Theaters representative knew the rule [about no metal skin], though, and he did it anyway. He just flat-out lied in council chambers. And he couldn't take the risk that I might not be bluffing. So Hollywood honored their earlier agreements in the end, which is all I was asking [them] to do."[29]

chapter 20

How the Wolfberry Changed Midland

> *The Wolfberry will ultimately recover about three billion barrels of oil, making it the largest discovery in the Permian Basin in the last fifty years.*
>
> —Jim Henry, founder of Henry Petroleum and member of Permian Basin Petroleum Museum Hall of Fame

Eighty years after oil was first discovered in West Texas in 1923, and just over a half century after it was first extracted in Midland County in 1945, the hydrocarbon returned with a powerful punch at the turn of the twenty-first century. These are unprecedented times in West Texas, and for the oil industry in particular.

The Wolfberry has brought heretofore unforeseen levels of prosperity to Midland, but also daunting challenges and adjustments in the way a once quiet town lives and thrives. The city's infrastructure is under strain. Roads and highways are under siege. There are shortages of classrooms for students, a disturbing increase in fatal traffic accidents, a severe housing shortage, and skyrocketing real-estate prices. In many ways in West Texas, these are the best of times and the worst of times.

What Is the Wolfberry?

The Wolfberry is a combination of two geologic drilling zones: the Wolfcamp and the Spraberry, thus the term "Wolfberry." The Wolfcamp has long been known to contain oil and gas but has always carried with it the reputation for providing speedy yields that slow to a quick trickle, according to Summit Petroleum CEO Dennis Johnson, former president of Henry Petroleum.[1] The Spraberry is similar. Discovered in West Texas in the 1940s, Spraberry wells have never produced gusher-worthy barrels of oil, but instead yield at slower yet still economic amounts.[2]

The Four Factors That Made It Possible
What made the West Texas economy take off this time around? Jim Henry, founder of Henry Petroleum, cites the convergence of four events that brought on the discovery of the Wolfberry: The realization that Wolfcamp wells were better toward the edge of the Midland Basin, the development and evolution of new hydraulic fracturing techniques ("fracking" for short), service companies' construction of the necessary equipment to carry out the fracturing, and sustained higher oil prices.[3]

While oil-industry analysts and insiders watched the effect of global politics on the price of a barrel of crude, it became increasingly apparent that still other factors—who was in the White House, the threat or reality of drought, and the endangered status of a tiny indigenous lizard[4]—would play a part in just how long fracking could be sustained.

Still, the always fluid oil price continued to affect the overall economy, as prices dropped to $77.70 on June 28, 2012, an eight-month low. That price neared the $70 per barrel threshold that industry professionals and economists say makes drilling in the Wolfberry no longer economical. The petroleum industry, though, remained optimistic about the long-term production of the Wolfberry and other oil-rich fields, including the Wolfbone and Wolffork in other regions of West Texas and southeastern New Mexico.

George Mitchell, the Father of Fracking
Hydraulic fracturing was developed in the mid-1980s by a Galveston native who made a large portion of his fortune in the oil fields outside of Fort Worth. George Mitchell has been called the Father of Fracking. He developed and built an entire town in southeast Texas, The Woodlands. He never lived or worked in West Texas, but his advancements and discoveries in petroleum led *The Economist* to say of him, "Few businesspeople have done as much to change the world."[5]

Henry Petroleum and the Wolfberry
Jim Henry founded not only Henry Petroleum but Henry Resources and the Henry Companies as well. He is widely considered to be the Father of the Wolfberry in the Permian Basin.

Henry started in the oil business in the late 1940s and was widely considered one of the original pioneers of the Spraberry as well. What Henry and his staff of engineers, geologists, and support personnel first discovered in the late 1990s would never have been possible had it not been for Mitchell's invention of hydraulic fracturing techniques.

A decade after his discovery became noteworthy in the 1980s, Henry Petroleum began to adopt hydraulic fracturing technology to develop the Wolfberry in the Permian Basin. The result has produced a great increase of wealth in West Texas.[6]

In the early 2000s, the commingling of the two zones led to what is now commonly referred to as the Wolfberry. (Commingling of exploration zones had previously been prohibited by the Texas Railroad Commission, the state regulatory body that governs oil and gas.) A few years after the technique's discovery in the Basin, eighty companies were vying for undeveloped Spraberry acreage.[7]

Henry Petroleum, led by Henry and Johnson, put together forty-two prospects and 250,000 acres before the lease rush began. Other companies lagged behind in early exploration of the Wolfberry. By the end of 2010, industry analysts estimated that 8,952 wells had been drilled, and many more prospects were simply there for the taking.

Henry gives credit for the Wolfberry's development to Dennis Johnson; Dave Feavel, a geologist; and consultant Dennis Phelps, a former ARCO Permian engineer turned independent who had moved from West Texas to near Tyler.

Jim Henry's Predictions of the Wolfberry's Yield

On April 8, 2010, while speaking to a joint gathering of the Permian Basin Petroleum Association (PBPA) and the Society of Petroleum Engineers (SPE), Henry uttered a statement now famous to those in petroleum circles: "The Wolfberry will prove to be one of the most important events ever in the Permian Basin."[8]

On January 19, 2012, less than two years after his pronouncement at Midland Country Club, Henry one-upped his bold view of the future, telling the Society of International Petroleum Earth Scientists that the Wolfberry would eventually recover about 3 billion barrels of oil.[9]

In the years that have followed his discovery, Henry has revised his prediction of what lies beneath us and now says there may be as much as ten times that amount—or 30 *billion* barrels—yet to be recovered in the Permian Basin alone. Many other energy experts hold the same opinion.

How Long Will the Current Oil Boom Last?

Oil production in the Permian Basin peaked at roughly 2 million barrels a day in 1973. Today, even with total production down to 1 million barrels a day, the West Texas economy still rides squarely on the backs of the oil and gas industry because of the increase in the price of a barrel of oil.[10]

Dr. Diana Davids Hinton, a petroleum historian at the University of Texas of the Permian Basin, says the Wolfberry stands the chance of holding as much historical significance as the Spraberry. "Probably," she said, "although we're not looking at the same thing as opening up the Spraberry.... What's happening now is not your old wildcatter, seat-of-the-pants-type oil boom where somebody has a hunch and drills a well and gets rich. [We now have] a boom tied to new [hydraulic fracturing] technology and 3D seismic and horizontal drilling."[11]

Aside from the historic levels of discovery in our midst, Hinton often reminds students in her petroleum history classes just how important petroleum-based products themselves are to our daily lives. "[Petroleum] impacts us thousands of ways every day, starting with the basics of how you are going to get to work, and continuing on to how many of the objects around you get to you, and what a lot of them are made of, right down to the miracle of petrochemicals in a lot of what you eat. It's hard to think of anything in our world one way or another that is not impacted in an economic sense by the oil industry."[12]

The Good and Bad Wrought by Prosperity

As with the Spraberry in the late 1940s and early 1950s, Midland and the surrounding area experienced historic growth that stretched local infrastructures to the limit in the 2010s. Water, housing, transportation, retail, and restaurants in West Texas—Midland in particular—are all dealing with unprecedented demand brought on by an oil source that Jim Henry says will not go away in our lifetime. Henry points not to day-to-day production of oil, but the net worth of that production when economic factors and current conditions are factored in.[13]

Very Low Unemployment Rate
Long before the discovery of the Wolfberry, Midland has been a perennial presence on the list of communities with the lowest unemployment rate in the nation.

Part One: A Place with Character

The Bureau of Labor Statistics reported that the unemployment rate for the city of Midland fell to 3.0 percent in April 2013, less than half the statewide unemployment rate of 6.4 percent. Since the advent of the Wolfberry era, the jobless rate in Midland peaked at 6.4 percent (June 2009). In April 2014, the rate sat at 2.7 percent, or, in real numbers, 2,629 people without work.

The June 2012 edition of *Forbes* magazine listed both Midland and Odessa atop the publication's annual listing of best cities in which to find work. Odessa was first and Midland second on the overall list.[14]

Odessa-based economist Ray Perryman said in 2012 that the oil and gas industry is largely but not solely responsible for the booming economy and jobs numbers:

> We have set the stage for long-term performance well above most of the nation. While the state is certainly facing its share of challenges, at least we have notable economic growth to help us work our way through. There's more to it [than oil and gas]. There are plenty of other areas with large natural resource deposits but poor economic performance. The upbeat employment news has a downside, though. It is frequently heard in Midland that if someone without work can't find a job, it's because he or she is not looking hard enough or simply doesn't want to work. The fact remains there are more jobs here than people to fill them.[15]

One man, after hearing that there were jobs in Midland, hitchhiked here all the way from eastern Georgia. When he arrived, he found a job within two hours, after he met a man in a Walmart parking lot who needed help fixing his truck.[16]

Midland's Population Explosion

In the 2010 census, Midland's population stood at 111,147.[17] Population numbers being used by city officials in the spring of 2014 show 140,000 in the city of Midland, according to Mayor Jerry Morales—an increase of virtually 17 percent in just over three years.[18]

"We predict the population of Midland will be at 200,000 in 2028," said Jerry Morales, who became Midland's mayor in 2014. "If that happens, it will be the biggest increase since Midland grew from 21,713 people to 62,625 from 1950 to 1960. Helping somewhat with that influx of people will be an expansion of Midland's city boundaries through the annexation of almost fifty square miles, from seventy-four square miles presently to over 120 square miles by 2024."[19]

That dramatic increase could be almost solely attributed to the Wolfberry. People are coming to Midland in droves because of the available jobs in the oil industry. But, as the adage goes, if you live and work in West Texas, you are in the oil industry, whether you are an engineer, a roughneck, a nurse at the hospital, or a clerk at a convenience store.

Scarce Housing

Other factors have become concerns in the local economy, issues that would have astonished Midlanders just ten years ago. In 2012 apartment rentals in Midland had increased by 40 percent over 2010 lease rates, and only 148 single-family housing units were on the market in March 2012. "It's not uncommon for a seller to receive multiple offers within days of listing a home and often at least one of the offers come in over the asking price," a Permian Basin Realtor said.[20] Shopping for homes at websites like Craigslist was a phenomenon.

Some families who relocated to the Permian Basin brought their own homes with them in the form of recreational vehicles. One man moved his family from Tyler to Midland in the family's camper trailer, hoping when he arrived he and his family would soon be able to find permanent housing. Seven months later, that man was still looking for a long-term residence and had upgraded his smaller camper to a thirty-seven-foot trailer he called his "own little apartment."[21]

In 2012–2013, it became virtually impossible to find a hotel room in Midland. When there was an available bed, room rates could easily run as high as $259 a night for a simple, nondescript business economy hotel, and $599 a week for a room in an extended-stay hotel. The Tradewinds area of Midland saw six hotels go up during a two-year period, from 2011 to 2013.

Morales added that there were 4,716 single-family lots and apartment units built in 2013 alone. In 2014 residential construction is expected to top 2,175 single-family lots and 1,052 apartments, a drop of about 30 percent from 2013 to 2014.[22]

Traffic Congestion

Midland's traffic and roadway issues posed serious concerns with no apparent letup in sight. A workable solution, if there is one, may not even be yet known.

One area of remarkable traffic growth has been Loop 250. "When I came to Midland in 2003, the traffic counts on Loop 250 for a one-day period were 42,000," said James Beauchamp, director of the Midland-Odessa Transportation Alliance.

Part One: A Place with Character

"The latest counts we have are 72,000 automobiles using Loop 250 every day. Waco's traffic counts on I-35, by comparison, are about 60,000 a day."[23]

One obvious contributor to the shape of the roads and increase in accidents is the growth in energy-sector jobs. Kirk Edwards, former chairman of the Permian Basin Petroleum Association, estimated it takes 1,100 trucks—the equivalent of 8 million cars on the road—to bring a well from spudding to completion. The wear and tear on the roadways of West Texas—which accounts for 75 percent of the state's crude oil—is significant.[24]

State Highway 191, the roadway between Midland and Odessa, has undergone a manageable growth rate of 4 to 5 percent in traffic counts since 2003, the year the Wolfberry was discovered. More noticeable is the traffic congestion on Business 20, the roadway lined with industrial warehouses and distribution centers that connects the two cities, some two and a half miles south of Highway 191. The growth in usage of that major artery was particularly noticeable in 2011–2012.[25]

Morales said, "To alleviate some of the in-city traffic, several roads will be expanded or created, including new and extended arterials to the north and northwest. Fairgrounds Road will be expanded from a two-lane to a four-lane road to keep heavy truck traffic off of Texas Highway 349 North. Midland's long term goal is to establish an outer loop to get commuters from downtown to the growing north side of town. This will also help with the ingress and egress of a reenergized downtown. These are really exciting times with a lot of challenges, but they do come with a very expensive price tag."[26]

Major Downturn in Road-Surface Quality

Wes Perry, a native of Midland and its mayor from 2008 to 2014, said a recent traffic study conducted on Midland's west side showed the potential for alarming growth in future years.

Part of the problem is that the kind of growth Midland and West Texas have experienced was never anticipated. In 2012 Midland's growth rate was 8 percent—six and a half times the yearly anticipated level in Midland. Don Szczesny, manager of Fort Worth–based Dunaway Associates, told the *Midland Reporter-Telegram*, "I've done traffic studies throughout North Texas and I've never seen anything like what's going on in Midland."[27]

In October 2012, a third-party study conducted by the Dunaway Group showed that if the city did not take proactive steps soon, the Tradewinds Corridor (on the west side of Midland, west of Loop 250, north of Thomason Drive and south of

Highway 191) would quickly become one of the city's most congested areas.[28] If this type of growth continues, the Tradewinds corridor could have 2,462 multifamily housing units, 3,337 single-family residential units, 587 hotel rooms, and nearly 3 million cubic feet of office and retail space. The study showed that traffic counts would total over 8,500 vehicles during the morning peak hours, 7:15 to 8:15 a.m., and 15,100 vehicles for evening peak hours, 5:15 to 6:15 p.m.[29]

Perry says the study also showed that, to effectively handle the influx of higher traffic counts, Thomason Drive would have to be widened from five lanes to nine.

Traffic Accidents

The Texas Department of Transportation reported that highway drivers in the Odessa District, which covers Midland and Odessa, were three times more likely to die in an automobile accident than anywhere else in Texas in 2013. Similarly, transportation officials in West Texas reported that one person died in a traffic accident in Midland County once every six days in the first half of 2013. In the first five months of 2014, that number improved only slightly. With eighteen fatalities through May, the fatality rate was one death every 8.3 days on Midland County roads.

In 2012 fatal traffic accidents occurred at an alarming pace in Midland. Wes Perry attributed the increase to two things: workers traveling from one oilfield-related job to another, or to those who are at the end of a lengthy shift and fatigued as they leave the jobsite. And in 2013, a disturbing total of forty-four fatalities—a record high number for any year in Midland—were reported because of automobile accidents.

Although the accidents themselves often do not include oil-field equipment, Beauchamp said the increase in the number of mishaps is directly related to the growth and traffic counts in the area. Perry said people like to blame the transients who have moved into town for the increase in traffic problems, but the mayor doubts that is the case at all. "We are all just too busy at this point," he said. Perry said fatigue and rushing from one job to another are two recurring causes in many accidents that were plaguing Midland in 2012–2013.[30]

"Midlanders are the friendliest people on earth until they get behind the wheel of a car," Perry said. "They'll run red lights [and] stop signs, text and drive, and it's not something the government can solve. We have laws against distracted driving. We all know not to run a red light—it's against the law—but I saw it twice this morning driving to work. It's a real problem."[31]

Part One: A Place with Character

Protecting Small-Town Values in a Burgeoning City

Wes Perry has been the city's most visible spokesman through its economic heyday. He has seen his hometown go from a quaint, small town, ideal and safe for its youth, to a city bursting at the seams and unable to control its growth. As he said:

> That's what keeps me up at nights. Are we going to lose what we love about Midland? We have to be really careful [to protect] the culture we have. I'm not saying that we need to be like we were in the 1950s, but one of the best things about Midland is it's family-oriented, and it's friendly, and we take care of our neighbors. We're a pretty good-sized city, yet with small-town values.
>
> That's something we need to keep, and I think it's important—at least it has been on my watch as mayor.[32]

chapter 21

WATER PRECIOUS AS OIL

Droughts are unlike other natural disasters. They creep in slowly with no need for the dramatic services of the Red Cross, martial law or the state police, and in the end, everybody loses.
—Walter Prescott Webb, University of Texas historian and noted water expert, 1953

OUR CURRENT LACK of beneficial rainfall, until recently thought of as "not as bad as the drought of the 1950s," began to turn heads in the summer of 2013. By then, more and more old-timers began to make comparisons many feared: that our current drought may be approaching the severity of the near-biblical dry period we had six decades ago.

Judge John Hyde pointed out one certain fact: no other drought in Midland has affected as many people as the twenty-first-century dry spell.

An Old Question: What If We Run Out of Water?

"For a community that averages 12 to 14 inches of rainfall a year," said Hyde, "the 0.11 inches of precipitation Midland received from January through June 2011 engenders a challenge no less than the question faced by Coronado and Captain Marcy when they first trod this land: What happens if we run out of water?"[1]

The weekly drought monitor at the University of Nebraska–Lincoln showed Midland and Ector Counties to be in extreme drought conditions as late as September 10, 2013. Only small portions of eleven other Texas counties north of

Part One: A Place with Character

Midland and Odessa were still experiencing a dry spell as extreme as those between Interstate 20 and Interstate 40 in the Panhandle. However, numerous West Texas counties and elsewhere—in Central Texas, the Rio Grande Valley, North Central Texas, and East Texas—remained in the throes of extreme drought in late 2013.

Rainfall Measured by Decade

Locally, Mike McGregor, who served as city manager in Midland during the 1990s and 2000s and whose specialty is water, painted bleak numbers over longer time periods. As project coordinator at High Plains Underground Water Conservation District No. 1, McGregor was once tasked with conducting a study for a client in the region who asked about a decade-by-decade rain total. McGregor's study showed that in the decade of 2001 to 2011, the Lubbock area received 41 inches less rainfall than the average in any of the preceding nine decades.

From 2000 through 2009, Midland received a total precipitation of 138.2 inches. In 2001 Midland recorded 9.85 inches of rain. As a side note, each of the three years preceding 2001 also saw fewer than ten inches (9.65 inches in 2000, 7.60 inches in 1999, and 5.14 inches in 1998).

Not surprisingly, Midland's driest decade on record since weather officials began keeping totals in 1931, was 1950 to 1959, when 120.6 inches fell.

Midland Rainfall Totals, by Decade

1931–1939	138 inches
1940–1949	153 inches
1950–1959	120 inches
1960–1969	140 inches
1970–1979	142 inches
1980–1989	165 inches
1990–1999	135 inches
2000–2009	138 inches

Source: Colorado River Municipal Water District

There was a noticeable drop in rainfall during the twenty-year period from 1990 to 2009, when a total of thirty-four fewer inches of rain were recorded compared to the twenty-year period from 1970 to 1989.[2]

As Dry as the 1950s?

Midland's driest year on record is 1951, when just 4.24 inches of rain fell. During the drought of the 1950s, a total of 64.34 inches of rain fell from 1950 to 1956, an average of 9.19 inches a year. West Texans who survived the drought of the 1950s are hesitant to compare the current dry spell to that one, and it is easy to see why, despite the seemingly longer duration of the current drought. From 2001 to 2012, Midland has recorded a total of 162.9 inches of rain, an average of 13.57 inches a year, 4.38 inches (48 percent) more than the annual average during the 1950s drought.

What remains troubling is this: from 2010 through 2013, Midland recorded a total of 42.84 inches of rain, an average of 10.71 inches per year. Factored out for the entire decade, Midland is on pace to record just 107.1 inches of rain from 2010 through 2019. If those numbers hold, the 2010s will go down as the driest decade since officials began keeping records in 1931.

"Climatologists say these droughts can last as long as twenty to thirty years," McGregor noted. "No one wants to speculate when it will end."[3]

Ed Magruder, a former mayor of Midland, said the current drought isn't like the one Texans and Midlanders suffered through from 1949 to 1956, but in the summer of 2013 he said it was getting close. "I've read horrors stories about thirty-year droughts. I don't know what man will do. We still have an appetite for beef, and our population is growing, and we are fast depleting lots of water supplies that are devoted to irrigation and raising cattle and human feed. I don't know how we're going to replace that water."[4]

Spring and Summer 2011: Brutally Hot, Dry, and Fiery

Although it is difficult to pinpoint the day, week, or even month the current drought started, John Nielsen-Gammon warned that Texas could be in the midst of its worst drought ever. Nielsen-Gammon, the Texas state climatologist and a professor of meteorology at Texas A&M University, pointed to 2011 as the year the current drought came into full swing. In fact, 2011 was the year that the two periods from March through May and June through August set all records for lowest rainfall totals across the state. Nielsen-Gammon said the only comparable drought to the current one was in the 1950s, but no single year during that drought was as dry as 2011 in the state of Texas overall. He added that Midland received only 0.18 inch

Part One: A Place with Character

of rain from January 1 through August 10, 2011, a time span when the city's average rainfall had been 11.40 inches.

Water Restrictions

The City of Midland's water usage, as agreed upon with the Colorado River Municipal Water District (CRMWD), was not to exceed 24.71 million gallons per day. During the week of April 17, 2011, that limit was exceeded by 3 million gallons one day and by over 1.5 million gallons another day.[5]

Residents failure to comply, utilities director Stuart Purvis said, would likely bring a stricter plan that would include fines of up to $500 for watering during a non-approved time. Those stricter fines did, in fact, come. Lawns died, personal wells were installed, xeriscaping was introduced on many lawns, and water rates skyrocketed.

In June 2011, the Midland City Council approved a new drought contingency plan by a 6–0 vote and began enforcing tougher restrictions, which permitted citizens to water outdoors for a set number of hours only on two selected days of the week.

At the council meeting enacting the plan, Purvis announced that the city had exceeded its limit with the CRMWD on seven different days during the period from June 1 to June 12, 2011. City Manager Courtney Sharp said, "We have an immediate drought that we need to fix," and John James, a Midland city councilman, reminded residents of what brought the restrictions, urging them not to let it happen again. "We missed an opportunity a month ago to get ahead of this. We're not missing it again," he said.[6]

Frequent newspaper accounts about the water restrictions did nothing to help people feel secure about their water future. On an up note, those same articles may have gone a long way to change public perception about how critical it was for everyone to conserve. "Midland went from not caring about their water usage to turning in their neighbors if they watered on the wrong day," said Berry Simpson, former city councilman.[7]

A Series of Devastating Wildfires

The worst wildfire in the history of Midland County started on April 9, 2011. Two flash points grew together to become the Hickman Fire, a blaze that burned 18,000 acres and destroyed twenty-four structures. This may have marked the nadir for many Midlanders who endured the drought. According to the *Midland Reporter-Telegram*, the raging flames "took not just a few minutes or a few hours to extinguish, but several hours just to get under control. Fire Marshal Dale Little said wind and dry weather worked together to spread not only the Hickman Fire but other smaller fires that broke out as well."[8]

Less than two months later, on May 24, 2011, another 5,000 acres went up in the CEED Fire. That day also marked the 244th day since the last rainfall of more than one-tenth of an inch in Midland. Only six days of measurable rainfall had been recorded during that spell. On nine other days, only a trace of moisture had been measured. Investigators found that a piece of metal that had fallen off a car started the April 9 Hickman Fire, and a burning cigarette had started the May 24 CEED Fire.[9]

Other factors exacerbated an already bleak situation: wildfires were not confined to Midland County. Firefighters battled a blaze in the high Davis Mountains that same spring season. And to the east and southeast came even more bad news. Rev. Hubert Wade, pastor of the Catholic churches in Bronte, Robert Lee, and Ballinger, reported that his parishioners had suffered fires where over a hundred head of cattle were burned and had to be euthanized with a shot to the head. In another fire east of Midland, over a hundred head of deer became trapped in a pen, unable to escape, and burned to death near Maryneal.[10]

On Texas Highway 67 between Ballinger and San Angelo, another wildfire was said to have begun when the sun refracted through a soda bottle that had been tossed out a car window. The heat brought by the refraction caused a roadside spark-up that, though not a significant blaze, showed just how dry conditions had become throughout all of West Texas.[11]

To make matters worse, a heat wave in late May compounded the hellish conditions. May 27, 2011 saw the mercury at Midland International Airport reach 107. From May 27 until September 23, 2011, there were sixty days of 100-degree temperatures or higher, one of the most brutal summers on record.[12]

Dry Lakes and Dead Fish

People of many, if not all, faiths prayed regularly for beneficial rainfall. On July 24, the *Midland Reporter-Telegram* showed that conditions in the region could—and had—become worse, when it published a cover photograph of a dead fish on a cracked, dried lake bed. The fish had once called San Angelo's Lake O. C. Fisher Reservoir its home, but that lake dried up entirely. Hundreds of fish were dead as a result.

To the north came the total evaporation of Lake Meredith, northeast of Amarillo in the Texas Panhandle. In June 2011 the *Houston Chronicle* posted photographs online showing a completely empty lake.[13] Twelve years earlier, Meredith's lowest point had been fifty feet deep.

Other startling images could be found of Lake Ivie—Midland's main water supply. By the late summer of 2012, Ivie had fallen to a scary low 11 percent—particularly alarming given its size at capacity: 19,149 surface acres and 119 feet deep.[14] Hard as it is to believe, 89 percent of the water that had been in the reservoir earlier was just gone. It had disappeared because of usage or evaporated in the heat, and not been replaced by rainfall. People could literally drive into the now dry lakebed.

The condition of this once large lake prompted CRMWD's executive director, John Grant, to say all lakes in West Texas were going dry. It was not the first time within recent memory that lakes in West Texas had dried up and permanently disappeared. When pioneers first arrived in Midland in the late 1800s, there were five sizable bodies of water in and around Midland County, but none of them survived.[15]

A Much-Needed Rainfall in September 2012

But then in the middle of the worst conditions, something wonderful occurred. A rainfall bordering on the miraculous visited the region on September 28, 2012. The historic event came not only to Midland-Odessa, but also to the water sources in the Upper Colorado Municipal Water District, of which Lake Ivie is a part.

The single-event rainfall was the most since 1988 and came from clouds that had veered away from Hurricane Miriam, which pushed into the region from the Pacific coast. It didn't come with the ferocity or intensity of the 1968 flooding rains. The rainfall of late September 2012 fell at moderate rates, but it fell throughout much of the day, providing relief for vegetation in Midland and increasing Lake Ivie storage by fifteen feet—enough rainfall in a single weather event to extend Midland's groundwater supply by eighteen months, according to Mike McGregor, who had been watching the levels from his High Plains Water District Office in Lubbock for years. The lake rose from being 11 percent full to 26 percent following the rainfall.[16]

Alec Lyster, a meteorologist with the National Weather Service, attributed the rainfall to the convergence of two weather systems over West Texas. The remnants of Miriam, which came in from the west, were joined by a flow of moisture that brought additional rain up from the Gulf of Mexico. When the two systems came together, Lyster told the *Midland Reporter-Telegram*, it made the difference between the scant but still welcome one-inch rain events that are sporadic in Midland to the all-day rain event that the Tall City recorded, an almost unheard-of natural occurrence, but one that was desperately needed. West Texans welcomed it with a vast sense of relief, having hoped and prayed for a beneficial rain for more than a year. The September 2012 rain was one of the top ten ever recorded in Midland:

TOP TEN RAINFALLS IN MIDLAND COUNTY
(from 1931 through June 30, 2014)

5.32 inches	August 24, 1934
4.75 inches	May 9, 1968
4.45 inches	September 28, 2012
4.10 inches	July 21, 1961
3.95 inches	June 24, 1940
3.60 inches	September 5, 1944
3.59 inches	October 17, 1985
3.59 inches	July 18, 1988
3.29 inches	September 4, 1986
3.23 inches	June 26, 1938

Source: National Weather Service

Making the September 2012 rain even more unusual was that, with West Texans being so unaccustomed to such buckets full of rain falling in a short time, Midland Independent School District dismissed classes for the day. Midlanders have occasionally heard of snow days, but a rain day was perhaps a first. Midland Emergency Management Services reported twenty-one water rescues in the county.[17]

Did Midland Almost Run Dry?

How close had Midland come to running out of water when the 4.45-inch miracle of September 2012 came? From his Lubbock office in July 2012, McGregor expressed his own fear for his former hometown a full three months before the September deluge.

"[In May 2012, Lake] Ivie was 14 percent full," McGregor said. "A year ago, in April [2011], it was at 29 percent. In 13 months we used 15 percent. In 13 more months there'll be another expected 15 percent use. Realistically, Ivie could have fallen to 5 percent, based on those calculations. You begin to see how close a call it is. I know residents have cut back, and the way water is priced now, they're probably

Part One: A Place with Character

using a little less. It's just a close call. An extremely close call. And it all depends on the weather."[18]

According to John Grant, executive director of the CRMWD, the rainfall "basically put us back to where we were, water-wise, in June 2011. If we hadn't gotten the inflow, we would have run out of surface water by June 2013."[19] That prediction meant that the T-Bar water supply, which came online in May 2013, would have been available with literally no time to spare. Until the September rain, CRMWD had begun to look at limiting water deliveries in the winter of 2012–2013 to help extend the supply.[20]

The T-Bar Pipeline: A Race Against Time and Evaporation

In that sweltering summer of 2011, Mayor Wes Perry, something of an eternal optimist, hinted that although we were still somewhat far from resolution, there had at least been movement in the right direction toward solving our water woes. "There are new possibilities," Perry said. "I think we'll have plans that will not only provide additional water and options for Midland in the next few years but also for decades."[21]

When the city of Midland bought the T-Bar Ranch in the 1950s, it executed the contracts for surface rights, including water rights, that would allow them to proceed with construction of a pipeline bringing the ranch's underground water source (between 70,000 and 80,000 acre-feet) whenever necessary. The additional supply Perry alluded to in 2011 was the Clearwater Ranch, a second source of underground water from Winkler County.

But the main underground supply, which would ensure Midland would have enough water for fifty years, came from the T-Bar. Once the decision was made to move water to Midland, the race was on to get the T-Bar pipeline online before Lake Ivie dried up completely. Crews from Garney Construction, and Black & Veatch Contractors, began in earnest to build the seventy-eight-mile pipeline from the T-Bar Ranch to Midland. Overseeing the project was local construction firm Parkhill, Smith and Cooper.

Why Midland Used Lake Ivie's Water First

Considering Midland's close call in 2011, some might wonder why the T-Bar pipeline wasn't completed years earlier.

Midland did evaluate the option of going to the T-Bar in the early 1990s, and tying in to the surface water of Lake Ivie later, but knew the underground T-Bar water was not evaporating or disappearing and would be secure. Surface water, on the other hand, will evaporate if it is not used. Fred Poe and Mike McGregor both concluded, along with council at the time, that it was better to pump water from Lake Ivie rather than let it dry up. As McGregor put it, "The available lake was full, and we knew the groundwater at T-Bar was safe and not going anywhere."[22] Lake Ivie has provided Midland with water now for over twenty years.

McGregor observed the development and completion of the T-Bar pipeline project in an unofficial capacity, after retiring as city manager of Midland and moving to Lubbock in 2001. He and former city manager Fred Poe worked on the CRMWD contract in its early days. When McGregor left, he said he never dreamed a line to the T-Bar wouldn't be in place by 2006 at the latest. "All the projections said we needed both of those sources of water," he said. "We just elected to do Ivie water first."[23]

Ongoing work to secure the project never stopped. From the mid-1980s to the mid-2000s, city staff had continually protected the water source from mineral developers and tested its quantity and quality. Conflicts between mineral developers and the city regarding oil and saltwater seepage into the groundwater supply continue today.[24]

Magruder told the *Midland Reporter-Telegram* that if the city had used the T-Bar twenty to thirty years ago, it would have taken huge amounts of money to drill and lay the pipe. The technology during those earlier years did not exist as it does today, Magruder said. As late as 2006, city staff considered the T-Bar field a "last card to play."[25]

The T-Bar Goes Online in 2013

When the T-Bar was completed, $200 million had been spent for its development, a number significantly reduced by the foresight of a city council that had paid $750,000 for 20,000 acres in Winkler and Loving Counties in 1965. That vision came thanks to former mayor Hank Avery, Ed Magruder, Curtis Inman, Preston Lea, Hugh McCullough, and Joe H. E. Ward.

On May 31, 2013, three men did the honors to signify the opening of the T-Bar pipeline: Wes Perry, mayor of Midland; Ed Magruder, a former mayor who had been instrumental in the project; and Jose Cuevas, president of the Midland County Fresh Water District No. 1. As they turned the valve, water symbolically rushed out into a 550-gallon tank, and the assembled crowd applauded enthusiastically. At the conclusion of the ceremonies, Magruder termed the project a miracle.[26]

The City of Midland had numerous contingency plans in case the rains didn't come. Mayor Perry said that the T-Bar pipeline was the "short-term solution, a minimum of fifty years." The city's purchase of the Clearwater Ranch added an additional supply of quality water, enough for approximately fifteen additional years. To meet needs after that, Perry and the mayors from Abilene and San Angelo began working to secure surface and underground rechargeable sources of water. At the end of the day, Midland has 100 years of water.[27]

chapter 22

MIDLAND: A CITY OF CHARACTER

Character is the mainstay of this community.
—Gary Painter, Midland County Sheriff, 1985–

Midland has long been known for its hard work and its generous help. We do both with a passion. We're proud of our town and the buildings in which we work, but more people care about how they can help than what floor in the skyscraper the elevator takes them to each day. That passion for people has paid off in countless ways. But more importantly, it has shaped who we are.

John Hyde, former district judge
"A man's word is his bond. If two men shook hands over a barbed-wire fence, it was iron clad."

When the Honorable John Hyde died on January 2, 2012, the *Midland Reporter-Telegram* published front-page stories for four consecutive days about one of Midland's most recognizable and enduring figures. Hyde grew up in Abilene, attended Baylor University, and began practicing law in Midland in the 1970s. He instantly began building a legacy based on fairness, honesty, and integrity. In 1990 he was chosen by voters as judge of the 238th District Court.

Hyde was an unflinching champion of Midland, its go-to historian, and a favorite citizen. Few others have enjoyed such a sterling reputation. Even those he sentenced remembered him positively. It was not uncommon to see this district judge, a man who trusted in people and believed in their goodness, helping his wife, Sharon, shop at a local supermarket. He rarely spoke a discouraging word.

Part One: A Place with Character

- ★ On Midland's attorneys, many of whom practiced in his courtroom through the years: "You can count on one hand in this town the number of lawyers on whom you cannot rely. The rest of them, over 300, they can tell you something on their handshake, and you can believe it."

- ★ On two of Midland's signature families: "The Scharbauers and Cowdens and so many others who settled here saw something about Midland. They weren't just here to make money. They were here to build a community. It was not like in the old movies where a community was run by a local land baron. We didn't do that here. We were a giving people even back then, and that shows a lot about Midland. That flavor of giving still exists here."

- ★ On the rescue of Jessica McClure: "I daresay there was a time when more people knew about Midland because of that little girl falling in the well than for two presidents coming from here. That event helped define the character of Midland. People came from everywhere to offer help for that child."

- ★ On Judge Pat Baskin: "Judge Baskin told me [that] in his mind there were really three great people who came to Midland that he got to know and who he thought really reflected Midland: C. J. Kelly, Martin Allday of Lynch-Chappell, and Kenny Jastrow. Kenny was understated, a great philanthropist and as kind as he can be. When I think of the character of Midland, I think of people like that. Or Joan Baskin. In a way, Pat sort of stood in her shadow. Pat described Joan as a world-class organizer, and she is. She has done so much for this community. But she's not alone. There have been so many, too many to name."

John Hyde could tell stories about Midland and its people all day long. It was one of the things people liked about him. His favorite subject, aside from his family and his belief in the court system, was Midland and its character. Hyde said scores of people have come to Midland who have simply been willing to contribute to the community without asking for or expecting recognition.

The definitive thing about this community in my opinion is not the economy; it's the quality of the people that live here. I really believe that. I think I see a mirror reflection of the early people who settled here and the kind of people here now. And you see it in any number of different ways.

Midland is a community that never needed tort reform. Midland juries do not give large plaintiff verdicts; they never have. That, I think, is a reflection of the people who settled here. If you fell and hurt yourself, you had to get up and keep working. If your horse bucked you off and you broke your leg, you set it and the next morning you were out riding fence.

I think that is a reflection of the handshake deal that is a man's word is his bond. If two men shook hands over a barbed-wire fence, it was iron clad. I see it so many times in the courtroom. If you close your eyes and went back a hundred years, you could hear the same things.

This is a unique town. It's always been very conservative minded, and yet Midland juries don't give real harsh punishments in criminal cases. They value liberty, and they take it very strongly. They're not going to take away people's liberty too quickly.

"The greatest asset of Midland is the quality of people that come here, punch holes in the ground, and pull out oil. You've got to have good people who come here and have the common sense to do that. It's remarkable." Hyde attributed much of the quality of people to West Texas itself.

You can't move into Tyler and instantly become part of the fabric of that town unless your grandparents are from there, too. It's not an easy town to get into and contribute to. That's not true of Midland. If you come here, no one says, "Tell us about your ancestors." Nobody ever looked at me when I moved here and said, "You didn't grow up here." It doesn't make any difference. It never has.[1]

Roger Robles, businessman, community leader
"We all want the same thing: great opportunities for our families, an education for our children, better jobs, better housing."

A Realtor and a longtime leader in Midland's Hispanic community, Roger Robles is a former president of the Hispanic Chamber of Commerce. He believes race relations in Midland have improved a great deal:

PART ONE: A PLACE WITH CHARACTER

> I remember a long time ago there used to be a Woolworth store, and my Hispanic friend told me they wouldn't serve him there. They told me Hispanic kids weren't allowed in the white person's bathroom. I started making waves. It didn't sit too well with me.
>
> Same thing happened at the Hodge Theater. They had said if we let blacks or Hispanics in here, we lose our business. I was a grown man at the time. I told them that was wrong. I guess it's human nature to want to stay in your cubicle and not make waves.
>
> I love Midland. Race relations have definitely gotten a lot better. I see it in the paper, too: Those honor rolls at the high schools, there are so many Hispanic kids' names there. So many excelling in academics nowadays. Before, Hispanic kids couldn't relate, because there were no Hispanic heroes.
>
> People have a preconceived notion about people, but we all want the same thing: great opportunities for our families, an education for our children, better jobs, better housing.[2]

President George W. Bush
"My dad showed our family what it's like to take risks, to be independent, and to dream big."

One of those who came and contributed and moved on to even bigger things was President George W. Bush.

> I think one reason why Midland is a place from where some have gone on to achieve recognition is probably ... that we were raised in good families. In my case, I think it was because not only was I given unconditional love by my parents, but it took an extraordinary man and woman to decide to leave the East Coast to move out to the desert of Texas. In other words, my dad showed our family what it's like to take risks, to be independent, and to dream big. I'm confident it's one of the reasons why I decided to run for president. It may be part of the reason others have succeeded as well.
>
> In my book [*Decision Points*] I spoke about the American Dream, and I did have Midland in mind. Because I think Midland is the kind of place where you can show up with nothing, work hard, have a dream, and end up making something out of yourself. There are very few barriers to entry

in the oil business. The oil business has always been a place for dreamers and doers.³

Gary Painter, sheriff of Midland County
"A lot of millionaires were made here based solely on their word. That was just the way it was."

Gary Painter, sheriff of Midland County since 1985, remembers how many fortunes were made in Midland on the basis of a signature alone:

> A few years before I first moved here in 1982, over 3,000 millionaires lived in Midland. You could walk in and tell [bankers] you had a wildcat prospect, and Jno. P. Butler would sit down with you, and if he liked the idea, you could get yourself the money to develop it on your signature. A lot of millionaires were made here based solely on their word. That was just the way it was. Bankers would look at you and judge your character, and if you were a person of character and if you were honest, you could get any kind of loan you wanted or needed.⁴

Joan Baskin, community leader, volunteer
"We don't care about where your mother is from; we care about you."

Right after graduating from college in 1952, Joan Baskin came to Midland. She has been here ever since, championing any number of causes, not the least of which was the city's centennial celebration in downtown Midland, and the town's "Vision" projects, which call together community volunteers every ten years to "dream big" and recommend projects to improve Midland.

> I [had] just finished the University of Texas, where everybody is a faux sophisticate, and we came out here to find this wonderful Western atmosphere and an attitude of, "Whatever needs to be done, let's get it done." We don't care about where your mother is from; we care about you.
>
> The prevailing thought in Midland has long been, "It's a challenge, but we can do it." We have a citizenry that cares and is smart enough to make suggestions for it. Let's have our Disneyland or let's build a big lake. You might not be able to have those things, but we can still take them to

Part One: A Place with Character

the Vision committee that makes big dreams possible, and the people of Midland all talk about those ideas for six months.[5]

Grant Billingsley, executive director of the Scharbauer Foundation
"There are more than 200 churches in Midland. You cannot have that many churches for this many people without people being committed to supporting them."

Grant Billinglsey was manager of public affairs for Wagner & Brown from 1988 to 2011. In 2012 he was named executive director of the Scharbauer Foundation, a philanthropic entity that promises Midland's spirit of giving will go on for decades upon decades. Billingsley moved to town in 1975 and went to work as public relations director with the Midland Chamber of Commerce. There were challenges in those early days: economic-development projects that didn't pan out, the loss of the Supercolliding Super Conductor project. The loss of the SSC, a particle-accelerator project that ultimately went to Waxahachie, was said to have been because of Midland's lack of a political power base. Ultimately, the federal government ended up shelving the project and Waxahachie, like Midland, also found itself without a potentially huge economic development project.

The bust of the 1980s, Billingsley remembered, brought even more difficult times to Midland:

> We went from tent city with people living everywhere, to being written up in *Town and Country* magazine as being some high-flying, fast-growing boom town, to how things had gone really, really bad. Companies went under, but we worked in economic development to continue to bring businesses to the community.

Through countless up cycles being followed by down cycles being followed by up cycles, Midland's continued effort to fight on and return to a prosperous and thriving community has set it apart from other communities its size:

> My instinct tells me Midland is different in a number of ways. Maybe it's the boosterism. Maybe it's the pride.
>
> One of the most telling things, as I recall, was when an editor from a British newspaper visited Midland. He came here because he wanted to understand who George W. Bush was, and he wanted to understand why

this president was so clear about his faith and made his faith such a big part of his life.

There are more than 200 churches in Midland. You cannot have that many churches for this many people without people being committed to supporting them. People in Midland make their religion a very important part of their lives here.[6]

Barbara Yarbrough, educator, community leader
"If your children don't have anything to do in this town, it's because you are not the kind of parent you are supposed to be."

A longtime educator in the Midland schools, Barbara Yarbrough talks about her years in Midland, including the bus ride through West Texas when she first arrived from her native Houston:

> When I got to Stanton, I thought, "If Midland looks bad, that would not be good." If the next stop hadn't been Midland, I was gonna catch the bus and go back to Houston. I had $15 left. It was so desolate coming from Houston, and you look out the bus window and see nothing but caliche. I thought, "Ooh, my lord, I have died and gone straight to hell, and I am walkin' upright."

As an educator, Yarbrough is particularly attuned to Midland's opportunities for youth:

> Midland is a place where the possibilities are unlimited. Is Midland more accepting than other places? Personally I think so. I'll tell anyone, I've lived here over 50 years and raised my children in Midland, and I would do it again.
>
> My cousins used to come out. They would send their sons to me every summer. Those boys—their parents are chemists and attorneys in Houston—they say, "Our fondest memories from when we were growing up were coming to Midland." They would beg to come to Midland every summer. They got involved in baseball at the YMCA.
>
> One of the kids came out here and got involved in our summer youth programs. I said to him, "Out here people are sports-minded because of

their children. They know if they have activities for the kids, the kids are gonna stay off the streets." If your children don't have anything to do in this town, it's because you are not the kind of parent you are supposed to be.[7]

Wes Perry, former mayor of Midland
"People here have been blessed with things, and they want to give back and start their own legacy of giving."

Wes Perry, a native Midlander and mayor from 2008 through 2014, says the number of charitable organizations and churches in Midland speaks to its entrepreneurial spirit. "People here have been blessed with things, and they want to give back and start their own legacy of giving," Perry said.

He recalled, too, the outbreak of wildfires in the spring of 2011, and noted there was a lack of news about responses to victims by the American Red Cross, which covers Midland. The reason? People were already taking care of their own before the Red Cross had the chance to be notified there was something to respond to:

> You didn't hear from the people who were affected saying how they were struggling. Their workplaces and the churches they attend were already taking care of them. That kind of help rarely gets into the public eye.

Perry also shared the story of John Crisman, president of Apache Corporation, a Midland-based independent oil company. In that same fire season of 2011, Crisman sat down after work one day, turned on the news, and learned of the fires that were raging in the parts of the county that were underequipped to handle the outbreaks:

> The next day, John called Dale Little [emergency services coordinator for Midland County], and John wrote a check for $180,000 to cover the cost of needed fire equipment in the Northeast Volunteer Fire Department and Greenwood Volunteer Fire Department.
>
> At the end of the day, John and many others like him in Midland simply say, "I've got to help take care of my neighbor." Apache wasn't even in Midland a year before this happened.

Perry also told the story of an employee of a local Albertson's grocery store who had lost her house to fire:

Midland: A City of Character

> I went into the store and found that the employees there were collecting money for this person—the next day. There was nothing on the news about that. They just found a place for her to live.
>
> It's just that kind of mentality in Midland. I don't care if you are Clarence Scharbauer Jr. or the manager of a local Albertson's location. Those kinds of stories here just go on and on and on.[8]

David Mims, former community leader
"People come here and learn how to like it and import their own character to contribute to the rest of us."

David Mims, longtime insurance man and community leader, was heavily involved in community activities and in his church before his death in 2011. He was thankful the town has turned out the way it has:

> Before I came to Midland, I was involved in volunteer stuff in our church, and there were people of character there. Did that characterize that community? I don't know. But it does characterize Midland. Midland is a melting pot in a lot of ways. People come here and learn how to like it and import their own character to contribute to the rest of us.[9]

Felipe Morales, businessman
"Our son bought the Ritz Theater. I just thought, it's funny how you can buy a piece of property where you used to be told you could only sit upstairs."

Morales is the founder of Casita Gerardos restaurant and the co-owner of Morales and Maes Insurance and Financial Services. Here he talks about how much things have changed in the Hispanic community in just one generation:

> When Celia and I were dating a long while ago, I took her to the Ritz Theatre downtown. They would always tell us to go upstairs to sit. We were originally from San Antonio so we'd never experienced anything like that.
>
> Many years later, our son Novert bought the Ritz Theater. I just thought, it's funny how you can buy a piece of property where you used to be told you could only sit upstairs. It made me feel very good when Novert bought that building.

Part One: A Place with Character

> Midland has been so good to our family. Our daughter is doing well and has her own business. Jerry is mayor. But you have to get involved. Success doesn't grow automatically. A long time ago at the restaurant we would have Jerry or Novert's team over after the games for free sopapillas. Before we knew it, the restaurant would be filled with families. That was our form of advertising. It was a lot of hard work. But it was worth it.
>
> Clarence Scharbauer Jr. once told me, "I admire you, Felipe, for having your family all in the same place."[10]

Fred Poe, former city manager of Midland
"If you can get people to stay here for six months or a year, it's hard to run 'em off."

Midland's appeal is not obvious to newcomers. It takes a while, as former city manager Fred Poe once said. Once people have a clear understanding for the place, though, West Texans often become lifers. It happens frequently throughout West Texas, of which Midland has served as an unofficial capital in some ways:

> If you can get people to stay here for six months or a year, it's hard to run 'em off. But it's hard to keep 'em that first six months. You come out here and you can see as far as the eyes can see. People aren't used to that, and they think, "Goodness, there's nothing out here but wilderness." But soon enough, people fall in love with the people and with the land, and with the climate.[11]

part two

People of Integrity, Past and Present

A few of the Midlanders who have helped make us who we are

Part Two: People of Integrity

George and Gladys Abell
by David L. Smith

George Abell moved to Midland in 1927 and entered the petroleum business. He married Gladys Hanger, the daughter of a pioneer Tarrant County family, in 1939.

George Abell was active in many civic, community, cultural, and educational activities, including the Midland Independent School District, Midland Memorial Hospital, and the Permian Basin Petroleum Museum. Gladys Abell was active with Midland Presbyterian Homes (Manor Park) and the Museum of the Southwest, as well as the Petroleum Museum.

Mr. Abell summed up his attitude about business and success in this way: "Sure, men like to be successful, not just for the money, but because of what they can do for their community, their country, and for mankind. Business success provides the opportunity to do some of the things most of us dream about doing for our community and its various institutions, organizations, and agencies."

In 1954 George and Gladys Abell established the Abell-Hanger Foundation, a private charitable foundation, to carry out their philanthropic work after their deaths, which did not occur for more than twenty-five years. Aided by the unexpected increase in the value of their oil and gas properties because of the 1974 OPEC oil embargo, their respective estates left $35 million (George) and $45 million (Gladys) to fully fund their philanthropic dream of 1954.

Since that time, the Abell-Hanger Foundation's holdings have grown to $175 million, and it has donated more than $200 million to charitable causes. The vast majority of those grants have followed their donors' original intent and life-giving record by making Midland the epicenter of their generosity.

While I never had the pleasure of knowing George Abell, I did work for Gladys Abell for nearly six years, until her death in 1988. Often I would visit with Gladys at her home to review some of the funding requests we were considering. The purpose of those meetings was to gauge her interest in those funding opportunities. I vividly remember one exchange with her concerning the Palmer Drug Abuse Program. Gladys was in her eighties at the time and had no experience with drug abuse or point of reference for it. She understood alcoholism well, having seen that problem in society, but the drug problems were a little bit of a mystery to her. As I endeavored to explain that to her, she said, "I just want these people to straighten up and have a good life."

I said to her, "Well this is the way to help them do that."

Sitting on the couch beside me, she patted me on the knee and said, "Well then, let's help them out!"

That exchange with Gladys Abell was indicative of the Abells' approach to citizenship: if there is a problem, we want to be a part of the solution. I believe that the Abell-Hanger Foundation has lived up to the faith and vision of its two founders when they established it nearly sixty years ago. As Gaylord Nelson said, "The ultimate test of a man's conscience may be his willingness to sacrifice today for future generations whose words of thanks will not be heard."

David L. Smith is executive director of the Abell-Hanger Foundation.

Part Two: People of Integrity

Ernest Angelo
by Juandelle Lacy Roberts

I first met Ernie Angelo in 1968. My husband and I and our family had just moved to Midland from Tulsa, Oklahoma. Being involved in politics for years and hearing that Mr. Angelo was a candidate for state senator, I walked into his office and asked if he needed any help. His answer was unequivocally YES! He didn't win the race, but he never gave up. Ernie is a man of many talents. He loves his family, his community, the United States, and God. I have respected him all these years for his honesty and integrity.

Ernest Angelo is "Mr. Republican." He was mayor of Midland from 1972 to 1980. Angelo has joked that he took office as mayor during a downturn in the West Texas oil industry and "my leadership and the Arab Oil Embargo got Midland booming."

Let me share a true story about Ernie that you may not know. In 1976 he was campaign manager for Ronald Reagan's Texas presidential primary campaign. Now, Texas was still blue and had not yet turned red throughout the state. Through the efforts of Ernie and two other co-chairmen, Ronald Reagan won the Texas delegates for the nomination at the 1976 Republican National Convention. With that Texas win, the door was open for Ronald Reagan's 1980 nomination and his winning the presidency by a wide margin. We can thank Ernie for his belief that Ronald Reagan was the man for America. Credit has been given to Ernie for the courage to buck the Republican establishment at the time and support Reagan. Without Ernest Angelo and the support he raised in Texas, we might not have had Ronald Reagan. And the rest is history, thanks to Ernie. He also served the Republican National Committee nationally as Texas's committeeman for twenty years.

If anyone needs any advice on the political issues of the day, we all go to Ernest Angelo. His wisdom, experience, and knowledge are unquestionable. He remains committed to Republican affairs as a behind-the-scenes consultant with comparatively little attention focused on him.

Much can be said about Ernie serving on many other boards and committees, such as Texas Parks and Wildlife Commission, chairman of the Texas Public Safety

Commission, and the Texas Society of Professional Engineers as Permian Basin president and also state director. He has also been named Permian Basin Engineer of the Year and received the John Ben Shepperd Award for Outstanding Texas Leadership.

As a petroleum engineer he took a position from 1956 to 1962 with Gulf Oil; then from 1962 to 1964 he was affiliated with Sohio Petroleum. In 1964 he formed his own company, Discovery Exploration, with partners Don Sparks and Webb Farish.

I certainly could not share this information without mentioning his passion for hunting (one of his favorite pastimes). He is a firm believer in the U.S. Constitution, especially the second amendment. "The right of the people to keep and bear arms shall not be infringed."

Juandelle Lacy Roberts is a longtime member of the Republican Party and the Midland County Republican Women.

Part Two: People of Integrity

Joan Baskin
by Jack Swallow

There is no question that Joan Baskin deserves the equal space given to the others of recognition in this wonderful book evidencing Midland's character. I have known Joan for over fifty years, and to provide a profile for my friend is putting my life at great risk. In short, she shuns, she detests, she flees from public accolades of her decades of good works within the Midland community.

However, I will take the risk because an historical anthology of Midland's finest folks simply cannot be written without inclusion of Joan Baskin. The height and depth and breadth of her undertakings in her sixty years as a Midland citizen are simply remarkable.

Since arriving in the Tall City in the 1950s, Joan developed a reputation as a selfless leader who sought excellence and results over credit. She was a leader in the arts (Midland-Odessa Symphony & Chorale, Midland Community Theatre, Phyllis & Bob Cowan Performing Arts Series, and Arts Assembly of Midland), business and philanthropy (Midland Chamber of Commerce, Helen Greathouse Charitable Trust, Rea Charitable Trust, Permian Basin Area Foundation, and the Midland International Airport), as well as community interests (Midland Junior League, Leadership Midland, Midland Vision 2000 and Beyond, and Midland Centennial Commission).

At the forefront of her accomplishments has been her pursuit of quality public school education in Midland. Having raised four children who excelled in Midland public schools, Joan was always there to lead in PTA responsibilities, to trumpet the need for new and improved school facilities when the district needed a champion, or along with her husband, to help shape the Midland schools' integration plan of the late 1960s and early 1970s. That plan paved a successful and peaceful path to quality education and equal access for all of Midland races.

She served on the Midland County Library Board, wrote plays for youth, chaired an after-school child-care task force, led the inaugural Davidson Distinguished Lecture Series, and mentored hundreds of college scholarship students, many of whom attained the first college degree in their family.

No doubt Joan's husband, the late Judge Pat Baskin, receives equal billing for the things to which she brought favorable improvement. They were each other's best counsel, and lights burned late in their home when they were on board for something to make Midland a better place.

In the late 1990s, Joan cochaired Midland's Vision 2000 and Beyond, that decade's edition of the ten-year goal setting for the community. Hundreds of involved citizens broke into task forces representing all aspects of community life to prepare a blueprint shaping community development and infrastructure, the economy, human services, recreation, arts and culture, and civic affairs. By the end of 2010, the accomplished goals included the Scharbauer Sports Complex, the expansion and updating of Midland's secondary schools, additions to Midland College, the sweeping improvements and additions to the city's parks and recreation facilities, and the construction of the Midland Horseshoe Expo Center.

Joan is a woman of firsts. She was honored as the first Outstanding Female Student at the University of Texas during her senior year in 1951. She was the first female president of the Midland Chamber of Commerce. She was the first female elder elected to the Session of the First Presbyterian Church of Midland. But, for all of these firsts as a female, she was not selected for any of these responsibilities to be a standard bearer for women's equality. She was just the best person for the job each time.

Joan Baskin arrived in Midland already stamped "successful leader." Midland's contribution was welcoming willing community leaders like Joan and others in this book to make a difference. When asked to serve, she did, demonstrating a passion for organizing, a talent for recruiting, and a gift for inspiring others.

Joan Baskin never sought election to public office. If she had, she could easily have been selected by the Midland electorate. She likely would have served as the school board president, mayor, or even as a state or national legislator.

But that has never been her style. The greatest character trait she exhibits in each of these undertakings is pure altruism. She has no desire whatsoever to achieve personal gain. Her sole intent is to merely make all aspects of Midland better for current and future citizens, and for six decades, she has delivered.

Jack Swallow was born in Midland. He is a community leader, a philanthropist, and director of The Swallow Group.

Part Two: People of Integrity

Dr. George Bell

George Bell learned how to be a businessman from his grandfather, George Ellis, founder of Ellis and Sons Plumbing. But business was not all he learned. Ellis taught his grandson that getting along with others and treating them with respect are as important as marketing in any successful business.

Bell grew up attending church regularly. His earliest memories of being in the church remain with him today. When he graduated with a business degree from a university in California, Bell remembers feeling a sense of accomplishment. What was missing, he said, was satisfaction, something that didn't come with his education.

Bell knew there was more that God wanted him to do, but even then he had no particular designs on becoming a minister. He wanted to be a Wall Street tycoon. He moved to Chicago and went to work for Sears. Before he accepted that position, he had promised his grandfather that should he ever be needed to run the family business in Midland, he would return home.

When George Ellis was diagnosed with prostate cancer, he called his grandson. "Remember that promise you made me?" Ellis asked Bell. "I'm getting ready to step down." Bell fulfilled the promise he had made and moved back to Midland. And in the "God works in mysterious ways" department, right about the time he made that decision, Sears, downsizing at the time, closed his division.

Bell and his family returned to West Texas and began attending New Jerusalem Baptist Church. John Campbell, the church's pastor, made Bell a deacon. Two years later, Campbell fell ill one Sunday. The church's assistant pastors were out of town, and the task of preaching a sermon at New Jerusalem fell to the young deacon and former Sears division head.

A church employee recorded Bell's sermon and took the cassette tape to Campbell. The pastor was astounded at Bell's preaching style and his words, and he implored Bell to "quit playing with what God gave you." In other words, it was time Bell gave a serious look into life as a minister.

After studying and becoming ordained, Bell didn't take the normal route. He started something called New Jack Ministry, in an apartment complex near Big

Spring and Golf Course roads. Midlander Ken Craft paid rent monthly on an apartment that Bell used as his church. Tenants weren't receptive to Bell. When knocking on doors, looking for potential congregants in his apartment ministry, Bell and his daughter were cussed out. Rocks were thrown at them, dogs snapped at them, and doors were slammed in their faces. But they never gave up.

In January 1999, Bell delivered his first sermon at Greater Ideal Baptist Church, on the city's southeast side, a section of town people often refer to as the Flats, although the name is not just derogatory but also incorrect. The Flats is actually the Flat, and is literally no larger than a single block of southeast Midland where people often congregated.

And then George Bell moved into the neighborhood. Through his community outreach program, Bell has almost singlehandedly rejuvenated the neighborhood that had once fallen victim to difficult economic times brought on by societal biases.

Businesses have sprung up after would-be entrepreneurs have been nurtured and brought along by Bell and the church. Restaurants, beauty shops, a tax-preparation service, and many other offices have risen from the once barren plains in the formerly beleaguered part of town. Bell has been the prime mover in literally reshaping an entire part of Midland. Pride has returned to the area.

Bell and the church have also started Miracle on Tyler Street, an outreach that gives children in Midland a "snow-covered" Christmas setting and a chance to experience a Christian holiday they may not otherwise experience to the degree they can now.

Bell's philosophy on why Greater Ideal has worked miracles is simple, as he told the *Midland Reporter-Telegram* in 2008:

> We are really trying to minister holistically to people in the community. People have more than just spiritual needs. If you are going through financial difficulties, the church should be there and it should be able to teach you how to manage your money. If you need marriage counseling, the church should be there to sit down with you and help you. If you need a job, the church should help you. I believe a church ought to be an organization that ministers to the entire person. That's really what's made the difference here. We not only preach the Bible. We teach it. And then we walk what we teach.[1]

—*Jimmy Patterson*

Part Two: People of Integrity

Irma Bueno
by Dr. Steve Thomas

During Irma Bueno's senior year at Midland High School, her father was diagnosed with renal failure. Irma knew that the most important thing she could do for her father—who never advanced any further in his education than elementary school—would be to complete high school. She persisted and graduated with honors in 2008.

Since 1986 the Legacy Scholarship has provided tuition assistance to Midland County high school graduates who attend Midland College. The scholarship is built on the legacy left by four great Midland families—Gladys and George Abell, Helen and Barney Greathouse, Harriet and J. Harvey Herd, and the Clarence Scharbauer family—who invested their time and resources to help build Midland into the community it is today. The philosophy of these community builders ensures that graduates of Midland County high schools are able to continue to take advantage of higher education at Midland College. In return for the scholarship, which pays their tuition and fees, students volunteer community service hours with an approved Midland nonprofit organization.

"It was at Midland High that I learned about the Legacy Scholarship," explained Bueno. "I wanted to go to college, but there was no way my family could afford it. I was already a member of Midland High's Students in Philanthropy [SIP] club, and I knew about the importance of giving back to nonprofit agencies. The forty-hour volunteer requirement did not deter me in the least. I volunteered at the soup kitchen and with Christmas for Our Troops." Bueno continued to volunteer with the nonprofit agencies throughout her two years at Midland College and transferred her SIP membership there.

While she was at MC, Bueno became involved in student activities, made good grades, and enjoyed college life. She was able to finance her college tuition through the Legacy Scholarship and the Bill Pace Cogdell Scholarship. Her father was undergoing dialysis and was awaiting a kidney transplant. Then, suddenly, during Irma's last semester at MC, the same disease that affected her father's kidneys spread to his lungs; he was hospitalized and removed from the kidney transplant list, with little hope for recovery. "There were times during that last semester when I didn't think I could continue with my studies," said Bueno.

Bueno credits her parents, siblings, and friends, and the MC faculty and staff, with giving her the love and encouragement to continue that last semester. She received an associate of arts degree from Midland College in 2010 and transferred to the University of Texas of the Permian Basin (UTPB). Because of the connections she made while at Midland College, Bueno was able to fund her studies at UTPB with the Bill Pace Cogdell Scholarship and the Abell-Hanger Foundation Education Continuance Scholarship, both of which are awarded to deserving Midland College students in order to continue their studies.

Bueno said, "I don't think people realize the opportunities provided by starting their higher education at Midland College. Had I not gone to Midland College, I might not have had the resources to complete my baccalaureate degree, or at the very least, I would probably be starting my career owing money in student loans."

During her senior year at UTPB, Bueno worked as an intern for Casa de Amigos. She now works as a client advocate for Safe Place, where she assists victims of domestic violence and their children. Bueno stated, "The minute I stepped in the doors of Safe Place for that initial interview, I knew this was the place for me."

She continues to live in Midland with her parents. Her father recovered from his lung illness, and in April 2012 he received the long-awaited kidney transplant from an anonymous donor at Baylor Medical Center in Dallas. Irma's mother is employed as a housekeeper.

Irma's two older siblings, Ruben and Ana, are also products of Midland College. Irma said that after almost having lost her dad, the family members feel blessed to be able to continue to be together.

"My parents are my true drive," continued Bueno. "They are my rock and my strength. Neither of them graduated from high school, and they always wanted more for their children. Despite my mom working long hours and my father being sick, they never missed attending my school events and high school and college graduations. They participated in everything—even the SIP fund-raisers! My diplomas are as much theirs as they are mine."

Dr. Steve Thomas is president of Midland College.

Part Two: People of Integrity

Bobby Burns
by Wes Perry

I've often thought Bobby Burns had a knack for being in the right place at the right time. That was certainly the case during his three terms as mayor of Midland. One need only look at his service in the 1990s to understand just what all he helped accomplish that has paved the way for where we are today: a significant renovation at Midland International Airport, a new sports complex, and the development of Loop 250 as a major business and retail corridor in Midland. He improved our parks system, invigorated our sister city program, and reduced the tax rate in Midland not once, not twice, but six times.

Bobby oversaw the building of two new fire stations, turned Wadley into more of a major thoroughfare and less "Rio Wadley" by improving the drainage system, and helped improve relations with our neighbors in Odessa.

In short, Bobby Burns changed the face of Midland.

When he and others oversaw the construction of the sports complex, what they were doing by bearing a portion of the expense on the project was to become the only city in the state of Texas to help bear the brunt of an enormous expense that MISD would otherwise likely be handling by itself.

Those are the accomplishments that many Midlanders are aware of. What many are unaware of may surprise some, but not those who know Bobby. He would often drive the streets of Midland in the evenings or during his off hours, his wife Denise with him as his almost constant companion, and together they would check for needs the city had: streets that needed potholes patched, alleys that needed to be graded or cleaned, streetlights that needed bulbs replaced. The small stuff that can often take up a mayor's time as well as the valuable hours of city staff.

Bobby was adamant about those big-ticket items that he helped push through: the stadium complex, loop development, and airport renovations. But, as Denise told me, Bobby loved helping Midlanders, especially when they least expected it.

When Bobby began his time as director of the John Ben Shepperd Leadership Series, based in Odessa, his absence in Midland during the workday was often felt.

Part Two: People of Integrity

Now that he is back, Bobby is accomplishing more good for Midland in his position as CEO of the Midland Chamber of Commerce.

In more ways than one, Bobby has provided a sort of template on how to be mayor during a time of growth and change in a city. I know I have learned from him. I, as well as all Midlanders, owe him a debt of gratitude for all that he has done for our town.

Wes Perry *served as mayor of Midland from 2008 to 2014.*

PART TWO: PEOPLE OF INTEGRITY

Laura Bush

Laura Bush, who grew up Laura Welch in Midland, wrote in her book *Spoken From the Heart* that even though she left Midland, Midland never really left her. Many other well-known people who grew up in Midland feel the same way. Mrs. Bush tells it like she remembers it in the book, but her hometown undoubtedly left a long-lasting impression on her.

Midland "was not just the pan-flat arid land that we were leaving behind with each mile of road but a way of being and of speaking," she wrote in *Spoken from the Heart*. "People in West Texas believe that they think differently, and to a large degree they do. There is a plainness to the way West Texas looks that translates into how people act and what they value."

Mrs. Bush has often been seen and referred to as one of the most gracious First Ladies to have ever occupied the White House. Congressman Mike Conaway, in fact, calls her "the classiest First Lady I've ever been associated with. You can't say enough good about her."

Those sentiments would appear to be the feelings of many Americans. A *USA Today*/CNN/Gallup poll published in February 2006 found that 82 percent of Americans approved and just 13 percent disapproved of the job Laura Bush was doing as first lady. In 2005 her Gallup rating was even higher—at 85 percent.

Mrs. Bush owns the distinction of appearing in the same 1962 yearbook as retired U.S. Army general Tommy Franks and actor Tommy Lee Jones, all three of whom attended Lee High School at the same time.

Mrs. Bush, who graduated from Southern Methodist University and would go on to become a schoolteacher and librarian before meeting husband George W. Bush, has always had the concerns of children foremost in her mind. She embraces reading initiatives and has even authored children's books. Following the September 11, 2001, terrorist attacks on America, she wrote a letter to the young people of America:

> On September 11, 2001, many Americans lost mothers, fathers, sisters, brothers, and friends in a national tragedy. Those who knew them are

feeling a great loss, and you may be feeling sorrow, fear and confusion as well. The feelings and thoughts that surround this tragedy are as plentiful as they are conflicting. I want to reassure you that there are many people—including your family, your teachers, and your school counselors—who are there to listen to you. September 11 changed our world. But with each story of sorrow and pain comes one of hope and courage. As we move forward, all of us have an opportunity to become better people and to learn valuable lessons about heroism, love, and compassion. As we mourn those who died, let us remember that as Americans, we can be proud and confident that we live in a country that symbolizes freedom and opportunity to millions throughout the world. Our nation is strong, and our people resilient. We have a well-earned reputation for pulling together in the worst of times to help each other.[1]

—Jimmy Patterson

Part Two: People of Integrity

President George H. W. Bush
by Ed Magruder

I am fortunate enough to be friends with both George H. W. Bush and George W. Bush, Midland's two U.S. presidents.

George H. W. and I used to play touch football up at the Midland Country Club when it was on Cuthbert, between Golf Course Road and A and D Streets.

I think even today you can still go to the YMCA in downtown Midland and see both my name and George H. W.'s name on a plaque listing the directors when that facility was first built.

We had an office at one time on Colorado Street. I used to sit in board meetings with George H. W. Bush. He was always a very level-headed guy. He had a good sense of humor. He and Barbara were members of the social scene here, and they came to Midland, I guess, from Odessa. The little house where they lived in Odessa sits right behind the Presidential Museum.

George H. W. is just a man of high character, stamina, and guts. He has got all three qualities.

He always proceeded with caution when making important decisions. He was instrumental in the gathering up money for the YMCA. He brought a lot of money down here from the East and invested it in the oil business. George and Bar—her name was Barbara but everyone just called her Bar—they were real people. They never tried to outshine anybody.

I know he sky-dived on his ninetieth birthday.

I've known his son George W., and Laura too, since they were little kids. Laura's father was a builder and developer here and he was honest to the core.

When George W. came back to Midland in the 1980s and was in the oil business, I would go to the Y every day at noon, and he went to the Y and ran on the streets with his friends Doss Rogers, Doug Christensen, and some other guys, such as Corby Considine. They would run six miles during lunch. George would come back in, and after we had showered, I'd be putting on my shoes and socks, and I'd look up and he would already be fully dressed ready to go back to work, and he'd pass by me when he walked out of the locker room, and he'd always look at me and say, "Adios, Eduardo, hasta mañana."

He's a good man. Just as honorable as his father.

Ed Magruder, mayor of Midland from 1968 to 1972, was named the tenth recipient of the Top Pioneer Award by the Permian Basin Petroleum Museum Pioneers in October 2013.

PART TWO: PEOPLE OF INTEGRITY

President George W. Bush
by Dr. Charles Younger

In the early 1950s, when a young family moved into a middle-class neighborhood on Ohio Street, no one imagined that the modest dwelling would be the home of two future United States presidents, two governors of prominent states, and a first lady of America. The family was one of a handful of "Yorkies" who moved to Midland from the eastern United States to explore the opportunities in the booming West Texas oilfields.

George W. Bush spent his early formative years in the neighborhood as one of many peers who was the beneficiary of an idyllic environment. Life was safe and simple. Neighborhood kids played sports and games in the local park and rode their bicycles freely throughout the town. Time was spent outdoors playing games until we were called home for supper.

Midland in the 1950s was a progressive city blessed with dedicated civic leaders determined to provide quality educational and recreational, cultural, and religious opportunities for the citizenry.

George grew up in a home where unconditional love prevailed. Influenced primarily by family, friends, teachers, and coaches, he developed many of his core values during his formative years in Midland. Lessons learned at a young age would serve him well and were the bedrock values that guided him in a life of public service. It was during this time that a myriad of character traits such as honesty, a sense of humor, responsibility, accountability, integrity, discipline, athleticism, and faith found their early roots.

Moving from Midland in the late 1950s, he returned in 1975 to pursue a career in the oil business. He arrived in blue jeans, a white T-shirt, and an old car. His first housing was a back-alley, one-room efficiency apartment barely fit for human existence.

Eager to learn, he methodically called on old and new acquaintances. First as an independent and later forming his own operating company, George immersed himself in the petroleum industry. He was known as an honest, ethical, and frugal operator who was not particularly successful at finding oil. Investors were given a fair opportunity for success in his dealings.

His life changed dramatically when he met and married Laura Welch and fathered their two daughters in Midland. In the early 1980s through the influence of friends, church, and Men's Community Bible Study, he had a spiritual awakening that transformed his life. During this time, he realized that alcohol was depriving him of a portion of his energy and productivity. He abruptly turned to a life of sobriety.

Moving away from Midland with his young family to pursue additional opportunities, he continues to call Midland home. From the town square, he left a group of loyal supporters in 2001 to become the forty-third president of the United States. Following two terms, his final flight on Air Force One brought him back to Midland in 2009 to the same loyal admirers who gave him unconditional support in his life of public service as a governor and president.

Recently he was asked by a Chinese official, "You are from Midland, Texas, in the middle of nowhere?" George replied that Midland might be in the middle of nowhere, but it certainly is on top of something. Indeed, Midland is on top of something, and a favorite son is a gleaming portrait to the world of that "something" that makes Midland special.

Charles Younger is a noted orthopedic surgeon in Midland. He and President George W. Bush remain close.

Part Two: People of Integrity

Jno. P. Butler
by Katie Spriggs

My grandfather loved two things: his family and the First National Bank of Midland. I'm not even sure in which order!

My grandparents came to Midland in 1927 with my mother, who was just a few months old. Evidently they drove their Model T Ford across the West Texas landscape—much of the driving off-road, dodging mesquite trees. The move to Midland in 1927 was so that my grandfather could take up a teller position with First National Bank. He rose through the ranks, watching and helping Midland and Midlanders build their community, and helping make their dreams come true for more than sixty years.

When he "retired," he was honorary chairman of the board at First National and was so respected and valuable to the bank and community that subsequent bank owners retained his services for a number of years. There are so many stories about his brand of banking, which was based on fair dealings, integrity, and mutual trust with his customers.

He and my grandmother Alva were married for nearly seventy years. At their fiftieth-anniversary party (at the bank, no less), he announced to the guests and my grandmother, "Alva, I've decided to renew your contract."

My grandmother tried valiantly to encourage my grandfather to take vacations. She loved to travel, while he thought every day at First National was vacation enough for him. (He would even visit the bank on Saturdays and allow us to play on the escalators, which he would turn on for our entertainment while he worked for a while.)

Eventually my grandmother decided that the only way to get him to leave the bank behind was to take him on long worldwide cruises. No phones or mail! Having been on a few of these trips with them, my brothers, sister, and I would be sworn to secrecy about where he would disappear to every day. Upon embarking on any ship, he would immediately seek out the captain and negotiate a daily ship-to-shore call to his secretary at First National! He always started each call with, "What were the deposits yesterday?" I don't think my grandmother ever knew about these subversive phone calls.

The saddest day of his life was on October 14, 1983—the day First National failed. Evidently the last entry in his office diary was, "Good-bye, old friend." He could just as easily have written, "Good-bye, best friend."

Katie Spriggs, a former Midlander, now lives in France.

Part Two: People of Integrity

Frank Cahoon

Before the inroads made by Barbara Culver-Clack, a path in Midland County politics had been cleared by Frank Cahoon, who was elected in 1964 to the Texas House of Representatives. Cahoon was elected after Bill Davis's term was complete, but a greater distinction is that he preceded Tom Craddick, who served as Midland's state representative from 1968 to the present day.

Cahoon was active in the Midland Republican Party when Davis chose not to run for reelection in 1964. Davis was instructed to find a suitable replacement on the GOP ticket. Ultimately, local party leaders determined that Cahoon himself was the ideal candidate. He achieved his greatest political distinction when he won the seat by a margin of just 1,500 votes over his Democratic opponent, according to House historic records. With the win, Cahoon became the one and only Republican to have a seat in the Texas House of Representatives. That seat was placed symbolically in the middle of the house floor. He was a member of the House Labor, Public Health, and Revenue and Taxation committees both terms, serving from 1964 to 1969.

Cahoon's win came the same year Democrat Lyndon Johnson and running mate Hubert Humphrey swept the electoral votes from Texas, and two of the Republicans who had been serving Texas in the U.S. House of Representatives were unseated by Democratic challengers. The only Republican who remained in office in 1964 was U.S. senator John Tower, who ran uncontested that year.

Tom Craddick still remembers Cahoon's response when he learned Craddick was going to be running for the District Eighty-Two representative spot in Austin. "He said to me, 'Thank God, they told me I was going to have to run again if I couldn't find anybody. You're it,'" Craddick said.[1]

When news spread of Cahoon's death on January 31, 2013, Craddick told the *Midland Reporter-Telegram*:

> I could always count on Frank for advice, encouragement and support. He was a tremendous advisor and helpful to me when I ran for the legislature

and every year since. I will miss visiting and strategizing with him about the legislative process and how to best serve Midland. While he gained the respect of many for his professional achievements in the oil-and-gas industry, he will be remembered for his many accomplishments as a public official and community leader that helped shape Midland. He always kept the best interest of our community in mind. Nadine and I will forever remember Frank as a thoughtful friend and a true statesman.[2]

Cahoon was one of those quality Midlanders who helped in as many ways as he could during his time here. He served on the Midland City Council and on volunteer boards with Midland Memorial Hospital, the Commemorative Air Force, Midland College, and the Greathouse Charitable Trust, and he was a driving force in establishing the Chaparral Gallery at the Permian Basin Petroleum Museum.

—*Jimmy Patterson*

PART TWO: PEOPLE OF INTEGRITY

Art Cole
by Mary Lou Cassidy

I am not sure when I realized Art Cole was not just an ordinary theatre director, but it was probably when he spent two hours stippling blue and red dots on my face and a latex tip to my nose to transform me from age twenty-one to eighty-six for the role of Grandma in *The American Dream*. That he was doing my makeup was not what was extraordinary. It was where it was happening. The year was 1965, and Art and I were sitting in the dressing room of the opera house in Monte Carlo, Monaco, awaiting Midland Community Theatre's performance as the United States representative in the International Amateur Theatre Festival. Art and his wife, Ruth, watched our performance from the royal box as guests of Her Serene Highness Princess Grace of Monaco. He reported that the princess (former actress Grace Kelly) quizzed him on how to start a children's theatre in the principality. I was impressed that MCT was in Monaco, and I was impressed by the man who put us there.

I have been a ham actor all of my life. A major person in that development was Art Cole, the founder of Midland Community Theatre. He helped me subdue my native West Texas twang as a kid in children's theatre and made sure I spoke loudly enough for the old lady on the back row to hear clearly. His near-professional productions fascinated me as I grew up. (I never missed an MCT production from the fifth grade until I went to college.) When I was a young adult, he taught me the tricks of comedy timing and how to punch up a laugh. I listened to every note he ever gave me after a rehearsal. Please realize it was all criticism. He never praised anyone. You listened, you learned, you got better ... maybe. I confess I was terrified of Art Cole, all five foot four inches of him, until the day he died.

Art was a brilliant teacher. Almost none of the actors on his stage came in as theatre majors, but he molded the clay. You may not believe this, but he never cast one of his shows. Three volunteers were designated as a casting committee, and he accepted their decision. Those geologists, housewives, engineers, clerks, secretaries, and kids became whatever the playwright and Art intended. Offstage he designed, built, and painted the sets with volunteers learning beside him. He was equally effective in the front of the house. Ruth designed and ran the membership campaigns and the box office.

The couple early on learned the business of theatre—budgets, funding, accounting—matters that have killed many a new theatre. Art and Ruth became master fund-raisers. They tapped the growing oil business through the major companies and the prosperous independents. Their efforts through the years earned enough to build two theatre buildings, the first near Dennis the Menace Park on Indiana Street in the late fifties and the Wadley complex in 1978. By the way, Art designed each of those theatres himself. A Renaissance man? A genius? I vote yes.

He was a little guy from Ohio. World War II brought him to Midland. He stayed nearly four decades, produced memorable theatre, built his monuments, and then he left town. He lived another thirty years but seldom returned. Nevertheless, he is the most important figure in the cultural and entertainment history of Midland.

Art Cole took advantage of geography—Midland was a long way from any other entertainment. He built a nationally acclaimed theatre with multiple facilities, an amazing program, and a fund-raising event (Summer Mummers) that is the envy of nonprofits everywhere. But he did more than that. He trained audiences to come to MCT and expect to have a great evening of theatre—not amateur theatre, but "real theatre." His success empowered other arts organizations to pursue that same audience. Many of those who enjoyed an evening of theatre also attended the Midland-Odessa Symphony & Chorale, Midland Festival Ballet, and Midland Opera Theater as those organizations emerged later. Culture is not a dirty word in Midland, Texas. Art Cole made it acceptable to enjoy the arts in this unlikely place three hundred miles from anywhere.

Mary Lou Cassidy is a Midland attorney and longtime volunteer and actor with Midland Community Theater and the Maverick Players.

PART TWO: PEOPLE OF INTEGRITY

Dr. Viola Coleman
by Conrad Coleman

My mother, Dr. Viola Coleman, moved to Midland in 1951 to set up a medical practice. She had recently finished her internship in New York after graduating from Meharry Medical School in Nashville, Tennessee. Her dreams of practicing medicine in her hometown of New Iberia, Louisiana, proved impossible when she was unable to borrow money from the bank to set up an office. Midland banks, on the other hand, were eager to loan her money to start her practice.

Midland Memorial Hospital was just as eager to grant her staff privileges at its brand-new facility. The young Dr. Coleman and her new husband set up her medical practice in Midland's south side, where my father worked as her first "nurse" and receptionist until they could afford to hire someone.

The most important things to my mother were her faith, her family, her patients, and education. Some in the family would say that at times the patients came before family. Her office was right next to the house and many patients would ring the doorbell after the office had closed because they knew that she would take care of them. So either my brother or I would have to get up from the dinner table to go and open the office and tell the patient she would see them after she had finished her dinner. My parents insisted that we all have dinner together as a family, and the dinner table was where my parents got updates on our schoolwork and our lives in general. Sometimes we felt like we were on trial because they would ask us things about our day that they already knew the answers to. My father taught science at the school we attended for a couple of years, and our other teachers were usually patients of my mother's. My parents believed that it takes a village to raise a child, and everyone seemed to know everyone in our neighborhood. We did not get away with much, growing up in this close-knit environment.

That same dinner table was also the center of many great debates: political and otherwise. My mother loved to entertain. I can remember dinners that went on for hours with guests and family members defending their views on a variety of topics that my mother would throw out. We never knew if she believed what she was saying or just playing devil's advocate to get us to think about things from a different perspective.

My mother played the piano and organ at our small neighborhood church for many years. Throughout the years she was very involved in the church, and she was always bringing or inviting someone to church or Sunday school, sometimes showing up with a car full of kids to make sure they attended Sunday school to learn about God.

"Doc," or "Doctor Vi," as many referred to her, was always running behind in her office, mostly because she would spend a lot of time with her young patients, making sure they were doing well in school. She was concerned not only with her patients' physical well-being, but also with their spiritual and psychological well-being. She spent many a day telling young people to stay in school and not give up on their education. She was always saying that no matter what happens to you in life, the one thing that can never be taken away from you is your education. My mother's passion for education may have led to a quote that she was known for: "You can accomplish anything in life if you are willing to pay the price."

Conrad Coleman *is a Midland native and a healthcare professional in West Texas.*

Part Two: People of Integrity

Bill Collyns

Few men in Midland history have been as congenial and kind as Bill Collyns. The former editor of the *Midland Reporter-Telegram* went to work at First National Bank following his newspaper career. He was one of the most respected residents in the town's history—so respected that he even had a day named after him on the occasion of his receiving the *Reporter-Telegram*'s Annual Energy Award for a lifetime of service and dedication to the Permian Basin on May 16, 1996.

He was known as Mr. Midland, Mr. Permian Basin, even Mr. West Texas during his time in Midland. His friends say, Collyns was a down-to-earth person who rose to the respectable place he still holds in all the hearts of those who knew him, and everyone in town knew who he was.

Collyns was the manager of the Midland Chamber of Commerce before being named editor of the newspaper. He used his position as the *Reporter-Telegram*'s editor to further champion the town he loved so much.

Bobby Burns, then mayor of Midland, declared that May 16, 1996, would be Bill Collyns Day. An enthusiastic *Midland Reporter-Telegram* editorial in support of this special holiday said "During the long years in which he headed the editorial side of the newspaper, Collyns' loyalty to Midland never wavered. On the contrary, it went far beyond the city's borders. Midland County and its people and welfare were equally important. So was West Texas. His service to the entire region has been recognized through the years with a number of honors and awards bestowed by prestigious organizations."[1]

The same editorial spoke of a list "too long to name" that contained the names of the numerous organizations Collyns had helped. In the nearly sixty years Collyns served Midland in some capacity, there "was probably no effort directed at Midland's welfare that Bill Collyns did not participate in or, more often, play a major role [in]."[2]

Collyns came to Midland in 1935, when Humble moved its headquarters here. As chamber boss, he directed the city's efforts to relocate a number of oil companies here and is also credited with securing the deal that brought Continental Airlines to begin Midland service. He was also instrumental in bringing the town its first airport before he left for World War II.

When Collyns returned, he was named editor of the *Midland Reporter-Telegram*, a chair he filled like no other, remaining until 1980, over thirty years.

When he was eighty-nine, Collyns spoke to *Reporter-Telegram* correspondent Lana Cunningham. She put into words just how important his contribution to the airport was to Midland and its people:

> Collyns learned that Continental Airlines was planning to start service from Denver to San Antonio with stops in Hobbs, N.M., and in Big Spring. He also learned the president of Continental would be visiting Hobbs. Collyns drove to Hobbs and introduced himself. "I suggested Continental stop in Midland instead of Big Spring and they said they weren't going to change their mind." That didn't stop Collyns from giving them a brief he prepared on the advantages of landing in Midland. A week later, the Continental delegation visited Midland and switched the route's stop from Big Spring. With one major airline under its wing, Midland would then find it easier to attract others.[3]

American Airlines and Trans Texas Airlines soon followed Continental, and Midland suddenly had itself a major airport because of Collyns's hard work.

Collyns never lost grip on his trademark humility. After working with others to establish groups like the United Way of Midland, Girl Scouts of the Permian Basin, the Salvation Army, and many others, he often found himself a member of charitable organizations' boards of directors in a list that was indeed too numerous to count.

When he was once recognized for his hard work in the community, his response was not surprising.

"I wonder if I deserve any of these awards," he said. "I feel I've been overly honored. A lot of other people worked very hard."

—*Jimmy Patterson*

PART TWO: PEOPLE OF INTEGRITY

K. Michael Conaway
by Bill Bain

Congressman Mike Conaway and I were ordained as deacons together at Spring Valley Baptist Church in Dallas when we both lived there. I remember thinking, "They're going to ask me some hard theological question and I'm going to be embarrassed, and my wife and mother are here and they will hear that I don't know." The church leaders finally came to Mike and asked him what he thought of when he thought of a deacon and he said, "Oh, gray hair, about seventy-five."

That's one of my favorite memories of him. We both still recall that one of our strongest bonding times together was when we had a revival in our church and we were asked to find a prayer partner we could pray with every day. Mike and I were each other's prayer partners, and the revival was during tax season. I wasn't in public tax accounting at the time, but he was. He still made the time to call every day so that we could pray together over the phone, even as busy as he was. It was something that obviously strengthened our friendship over the years.

Mike's first wife, Julie, passed away twenty-five years ago. I remember when he married Suzanne, at the rehearsal dinner, three or four men got up to speak and they all said they felt Mike was probably their best friend. I always considered him by best friend, too. When you have a friendship like Mike and I have, that person supports you completely, and when that happens, you know that person is your best friend.

Mike calls those kinds of persons his "clod fight friends." He would always explain that when he grew up in Odessa, there were two kinds of people: People who would come up during a clod fight and say, "Mike, what's going on? What caused this?" and those who came up and started throwing clods alongside you and at some point would say, "Hey, Mike, why are we doing this?"

When he is back in town, we always have to go to the same Mexican restaurant. One time we got the check and we were trying to divide up a little $21 check, and I couldn't help but wonder what people thought when they saw this U.S. congressman trying to divide up a tiny check like that. That might explain why he's chair of the House Ethics Committee. He's also on the House Agriculture, Armed Services, and

Intelligence committees. He just exemplifies the core values of West Texas—family, faith, personal relationships, with both personal and fiscal conservative principles.

These are all noteworthy accomplishments and represent a commitment to his family, his profession, and his community, but what I value as much is Mike's sense of right and wrong, his sense that we are all required to do the right thing.

He cares about the people he is representing. When he is out visiting with people, going from town hall meeting to town hall meeting, one of the toughest jobs is to keep him on schedule. If you've ever been to one of his town hall meetings, at the end of the day, he will stay and talk as long as there are people there who have questions. In the middle of the day, his district director will plead with him about how they have to go in order to make a one o'clock in Sterling City, for instance. But he's not inclined to walk away when he's talking to someone and thinks you don't understand something. Both Mike and Suzanne have committed a tremendous amount of personal time to listening to the concerns of people in West Texas whom he has represented since 2004.

Bill Bain is a Midland accountant and Mike Conaway's best friend (or one of them).

Part Two: People of Integrity

The Cowden Family

While the Scharbauer family has been rightfully described as the current that has carried Midland through its many years, the Cowden family can be described as the calm in or out of the storm. The family has developed a reputation for the serene way in which it approaches both good news and bad. While impending gloom understandably rankles many, the Cowdens have always seemed to have the ability to weather whatever condition West Texas has tossed its way.

Rosalind Grover tells a story about Frank Cowden Sr. that epitomizes the family's calmness.

> Frank Cowden Sr. would often go down to the Scharbauer Hotel and gather around his friends at the spittoon and tell stories. They were frequent visitors to the Scharbauer, and when it was demolished by a wrecking ball, they just all moved down to the First National Bank where they could go for coffee every morning. They met there for several years, right up to when the bank failed and was taken over by the FDIC in October 1987.
>
> Someone one day asked, "Oh, Mr. Cowden, isn't this terrible about the bank?"
>
> And Mr. Cowden said, "Well, we all saw it coming. We thought that with our usual can-do attitude, we'll just put all our money in the bank and keep it there, and then the comptroller of the currency will listen to us and he'll see our money there, and he'll just let the bank stay open."[1]

After the comptroller of the currency came and did *not* let the bank stay open, Mr. Cowden had a response to that as well:

> He told me, "Oh honey, these banks, they come and they go. I was there in aught seven when the Midland National failed. All that matters is your money. You have to pay more attention to your money and let the bank pay attention to the business. Maybe that's what happened to the bank.

Maybe that bank got in trouble because it didn't pay sufficient attention to its business."²

The Cowdens came to West Texas from Scotland by way of Tennessee and Palo Pinto County, Texas, bringing with them cattle and the hope for grass, open country, and the opportunity to buy some of that land.

The family, like many others, toughed it out during the lean years before the discovery of oil. But the Cowdens endured and have become one of Midland's most respected families. Their work ethic and devotion to philanthropic efforts are just two reasons for that well-earned respect.

—Jimmy Patterson

Part Two: People of Integrity

Tom Craddick
by Ernest Angelo

In 1968 Midland was a Democratic town, but a small, dedicated group was working to change that. In 1962 we elected a Republican state representative, Bill Davis, and in 1964 Frank Cahoon had been elected as the only GOP representative in the Texas House. Since he had declined to run again, our candidate recruitment committee was looking for someone who could be a contender for us.

That was how I first met Tom Craddick. After his interview, I commented that he was too young (twenty-four) and too overweight to be elected. Now that he has won election every two years, including 2012, my evaluation has proven somewhat lacking.

Tom quickly became an influential member of the Texas House and in 1971 was part of the "Dirty Thirty" that brought much-needed ethical reforms to Texas state government. His mastery of the rules and his steadfast commitment to conservative principles gained him an ever-increasing ability to pass good legislation and kill bad.

As Republican numbers continued to grow in each succeeding election, Tom's responsibilities also increased. By 1975 he was chairman of the Natural Resources Committee, becoming the first Republican committee chairman in more than 100 years.

When Republicans achieved majority status in the 2002 election, significantly due to Tom's relentless recruitment and campaigning for GOP candidates, Tom was elected as speaker of the Texas House. He was the first Republican in that office since Reconstruction.

In his first term as speaker, the state faced a $10 billion budget shortfall. Through his leadership and skillful cooperation with the governor and lieutenant governor, the legislature passed a balanced budget that covered state responsibilities without a tax increase, thereby laying the foundation for the Texas economy to lead the nation. Tom served three terms as speaker, from 2003 to 2009.

Over the years, Tom has done much to advance the energy interest in Texas.

His leadership has enabled good legislation and prevented untold damaging bills from being enacted. In the same manner, he has promoted the conservative philosophy of government across the board.

For the Permian Basin in general and Midland in particular, Tom has been responsible for huge gains in educational and medical facilities for Midland and Odessa. The University of Texas of the Permian Basin would not be what it has become without his constant support. Suffice it to say he has been an exemplary legislator for his district and for the state of Texas.

Speaker Craddick is also a successful businessman. He holds both a BA and an MBA from Texas Tech University.

Tom married Nadine Nayfa in 1969. They have a daughter, Christi, now a Texas railroad commissioner, and a son, Thomas Jr., who is in the oil and gas business. For nearly forty years, Tom and Nadine were our neighbors. We are godparents for each other's children. It would be difficult to find better friends.

> ***Ernest Angelo*** *was the mayor of Midland from 1972 to 1980 and was later active in national Republican politics.*

Part Two: People of Integrity

Barbara Culver-Clack

Barbara Culver-Clack's integrity can best be measured through a personal story. In 1947 she married John Culver, whom she met at Texas Tech University. Mr. Culver was a veteran of World War II and disabled. A concussion damaged his central retina, and he was legally blind. To help John Culver navigate his way through law school and eventually earn his jurisprudence degree, Barbara Culver read law books to him that he could not otherwise read.

When the two graduated in 1951, they were faced with unique and not ideal circumstances: between them they had two law degrees. One would-be lawyer was sight impaired. The other was a woman. There was no demand for either in 1950s Dallas.

After being confronted with an option of practicing in Mount Pleasant—a town John considered too small—they opted instead to move to Midland.

John and Barbara lived off John's pension while waiting for work. When the two moved here, it was during one of Midland's mini boom eras, in the 1950s. The Spraberry had recently been discovered and the town was crowded. There was no office space or housing, and rumors were rampant of people sleeping in tents and under bridges.

The Culvers had no special way of attracting clients, but they went to work and eventually built a practice for themselves.

Barbara Culver became active in Republican politics in Midland, despite being born and raised a Democrat. She was part of the conservative arm of the party before becoming an independent and ultimately a guiding force in the early days of Midland County Republicans.

Culver-Clack has always enjoyed working in the juvenile court system. In the 1960s she had a say in the revisions made to the codification of the Texas Family Law Code, participating in that document's rewrite. Her experiences in family and juvenile court, and in revising the Texas Family Code, would lead her to become a leading authority on divorce and custody issues. She served as a county court-at-law judge in Midland County for fifteen years and for ten years on the district court level.

"Bill Smith, John Hyde, and a lot of other fine lawyers practiced in my court. A lot of my baby lawyers, as I called them, cut their teeth on my desk," she said.

After serving on the county and district benches, she was named a member of the Texas Constitution Revision Commission, a task she recalls with fondness.

"We had leaders from all over the state working on that, and we did a bang-up good job on it, but then it was sent to the legislature and they turned it back into hash and took it to the voters, and it was defeated."

When officials with the county came to her and said they wanted to name a building after her for her accomplishments, Culver-Clack said she was pleasantly surprised and suggested perhaps a structure that was devoted to youth.

"My prime interest has always been juveniles," she said. "I liked the feeling that you could help one out of ten or twenty or a hundred, so that when they turned seventeen, they wouldn't go to the penitentiary. Most of the time you got your heart broken, but sometimes we did some good."

—Jimmy Patterson

PART TWO: PEOPLE OF INTEGRITY

Dr. David Daniel
by Eileen Piwetz

In 1991 a legendary character, David E. Daniel, came to West Texas to a land, a people, a spirit, and a lifestyle to which he quickly adapted and came to love passionately. Daniel wasn't looking for a new job; however, he had agreed to be interviewed for the presidency of Midland College. After he completed his interview, he and his wife, DeeDee, boarded the plane to return to Pennsylvania when he was called off the plane and hired by the college's board of trustees, right in Midland airport. Armed with degrees from Furman University, Colgate-Rochester Divinity School, and North Carolina State University, Dr. David E. Daniel would serve as the Midland College President for seventeen years, making the college a shining star within the community.

Already known nationally for being an activist and staunch advocate for community colleges, Daniel quickly embarked upon making Midland College one of the premier community colleges in the United States. An incredible visionary, his steady and wise leadership at Midland College culminated in a fifty-three percent enrollment increase; an Advanced Technology Center shared by college and Midland public school students to provide an educated technical workforce; the Petroleum Professional Development Center to support the area's major industry; and the Williams Regional Technical Training Center in Fort Stockton to reach students who were geographically limited.

Daniel created a legacy and set a new standard for Midland College's fiscal future when he encouraged the Midland College Foundation Board to establish the Chaparral Circle Endowment Fund, which would prevent the college from suffering from the roller coaster ride of Texas's economy. Midlanders generously responded and subsequently Midland College would rank within the top ten community college endowments in the nation. Daniel would later thank Midland voters for passing an expansion and improvement bond for college facilities.

During his tenure, the Davidson Distinguished Lecture Series and the Phyllis and Bob Cowan Performing Arts Series were established, reaching and enhancing the lives of tens of thousands of area residents. A community builder, Daniel recognized the need for a minority outreach center in southeast Midland, and hence the Cogdell Learning Center was established. In addition to several new and renovated academic buildings, Daniel introduced residence halls allowing students to have a full college experience. He had a clear understanding of the whole interlocking process of getting things done.

This charismatic president, with his intelligence, sharp wit, physical presence, and booming voice, created the "Midland College Family." He was a master at giving the staff tremendous independence to achieve their highest level of excellence; empowering the employees; and leading by example, frequently bending over to pick up pieces of trash that had blown onto campus. Daniel strongly encouraged students as well as employees to pursue their dreams through education. His productive leadership yielded an exceptional community college family.

Eileen Piwetz is executive director of the FMH Foundation, former vice president of Midland College, ,and executive director of Midland College Foundation.

Part Two: People of Integrity

Ed Darnell

In its more than 125-year existence, Midland County has been protected by twelve sheriffs. Only Ed Darnell has served longer than Gary Painter. The county's top lawman from 1941 to 1976, Darnell was a West Texas sheriff befitting the stereotype: a tough guy with a heart.

Almost forty years after he last pinned on his badge, stories still circulate about Darnell and his methods. Sheriff Painter is the purveyor of many of those stories of his predecessor. The former sheriff lived in an apartment on the fourth floor of the Midland County Courthouse, the same floor where the jail was located.

"A couple of times at Christmas, Big Ed would open the doors to the jail and send all the prisoners home on furlough and tell them to all be back in two or three days," Painter said. "He'd just let them go so he and his family could enjoy Christmas together. And the prisoners would all show back up when he told them, because they all had enough respect for him. You can't do that nowadays or you'd wind up in jail yourself."

Not only was Darnell a sheriff, he was an astute and established businessman. "Before he was sheriff, Ed had a hamburger shack down on Rankin Highway," Painter said. "His motto was 'We may doze, but we never close.' Oilfield truckers often came through at two or three o'clock in the morning, and Big Ed would get up and cook them something to eat. That's how people got to know him, and that's how he got elected."

Darnell had no prior law enforcement background when he was elected, but he quickly came to realize the importance of cultivating resources, much to the dislike of some Midlanders.

"A long time ago Midland was dry, and people had a hard time buying liquor," Painter said. "There were a lot of places on the south side and southeast side of town that would sell alcohol anyway, and law enforcement wouldn't do anything to them, mainly because they would provide a lot of information to law enforcement. There was just certain information the people had about everyone, and they'd get to drinking and talking. That was how sources were developed by law enforcement."

Part Two: People of Integrity

It wasn't just Darnell who helped keep the prisoners on the straight and narrow. His wife got in on the action, too. In 1972 an inmate at the county jail tried to escape, but Mrs. Darnell, wise to the attempt, shut and sealed the doors on the jail level and thwarted the man's getaway.

"Ed was a good sheriff," Painter said. "He took care of the people. A lot of people might not agree with the way he did it, but he did it in such a way that crooks had enough respect for him that they didn't mess with him. People had respect for law enforcement back then. Now they don't."[1]

—*Jimmy Patterson*

Part Two: People of Integrity

Newnie Ellis

Newnie Ellis came to Midland in 1881.

His son Newnie Ellis followed, just a few clickety-clacks of the T&P rail wheels later. Newnie Ellis, son of Newnie and grandson of Newnie, followed in 1919.

When you ask about Newnie Ellis, don't be surprised to hear the response, "Which one?"

Each of them was as vital to Midland history as the other two.

Newnie H., or Newnan as he was formally known, came first, bringing his family to Midland from Refugio County via the town of Pecos, where Ellis was the town pharmacist. When Newnie H. landed in Midland, he opened an apothecary, practicing from a small building on Main Street. He was not a doctor, but that didn't stop folks in Midland from calling him Dr. Ellis.

The Ellis family, particularly Newnie W. Ellis and Newnie W. Ellis Jr., were best known in the Midland community for the operation of Ellis Funeral Home, which was founded by Newnie H. in 1892. Two years prior to the formal opening of the funeral home, Newnie H. saw what he considered a natural fit. From Nancy McKinley's *The Pioneer History of Midland County, Texas: 1880–1926*: "Due to the nature of his calling and its near proximity to sometimes accompanying death, Ellis placed, in the rear of his store, a supply of coffins. He provided coffins upon request and began rendering additional services to the dead. Thus was established the present day Ellis Funeral Home."[1]

Newnie W. Ellis, son of Newnie H., was for a time the youngest known funeral-home operator in the state of Texas. Newnie W. was involved in the community of Midland in a number of ways. He served as city clerk, county tax assessor-collector, and justice of the peace.

Certainly Newnie W. Ellis Jr. is remembered by most Midlanders today. Born in 1919, Ellis attended Midland High School, Tarleton College, and Texas A&M. After enlisting in the service during his senior year at Texas A&M, he served as an air traffic controller with the Army Air Corps in the China-Burma-India Theater during World War II. When the war was over, he returned to Midland to help his mother in the operation of Ellis Funeral Home, while continuing to serve his country at Midland Air Field.

As a friend once wrote, Newnie Ellis had a calling from God to ease people's pain as their loved ones made the transition from this earthly life to the next—a calling to help those around him. And those around him will tell you that no man was ever better suited for that job. In 2001, the Newnie Ellis family was inducted into the West Texas Heritage Hall of Fame for their service and contributions.

Newnie met Charlotte Jane Posey of Monticello, Arkansas, in 1946. They married in 1947 at Highland Park Presbyterian Church in Dallas, where Newnie was attending Dallas Mortuary School. They returned to live in Midland in 1948 and had two daughters, Angela and Priscilla. Newnie started bird hunting as a boy and shot his last bird at age ninety. He was a hunter, fisherman, skier, and sailor, and he had a passion for training English setters.

Newnie was an avid reader who loved and appreciated literature and poetry. He often quoted Rudyard Kipling. According to his obituary on October 26, 2011, he and Charlotte could frequently be found dancing at a dance hall somewhere in West Texas.

In a story in the *Midland Reporter-Telegram* on the occasion of his death, Ed Todd told the story of Ellis's good-heartedness, quoting the beloved West Texan:

"When I pass through this vale and someone happens to remember my name and wants to make my ghost happy, wink at some pretty girl and forgive some sinner," Ellis was reported to have said. "And if you really want my bones to jingle jangle in mirth, walk over to the dance-hall wall and ask a not-so-pretty girl to dance."[2]

—*Jimmy Patterson*

PART TWO: PEOPLE OF INTEGRITY

Donald L. Evans
by Dr. Charles Younger

Donald L. Evans was born in Houston on July 27, 1946, to Sam and Betty Evans. Don was blessed to be the product of a Christ-centered, loving family environment.

He entered the University of Texas in 1964 and graduated with a BS in mechanical engineering in 1969 and an MBA in 1973. He was a student leader and a member of the prestigious service organization the Texas Cowboys. He never dreamed that in later years he would be honored by his alma mater as a Distinguished Graduate of the College of Engineering and inducted into the Red McCombs School of Business Hall of Fame. He is a Distinguished Alumnus of U.T. and has served as chairman of the Board of Regents.

Don moved to Midland in 1975, encouraged by his wife, Susan Marinis Evans, a native Midlander. Don's career in the oil and gas industry with Tom Brown, Inc. (TBI) was on a fast track, and he quickly ascended to the office of president. As young Midlanders, Don and Susie balanced their family and professional lives with leadership in a myriad of civic and volunteer endeavors.

TBI grew from a small drilling company into a $2 billion market cap company with 1,200 employees. With the collapse of the oil commodity price in the mid-1980s, the liabilities of TBI suddenly exceeded its assets. It was a depressing time for Don, but he remained grounded in faith, trust, hope, perseverance, and a deep-rooted integrity. Don and TBI eventually emerged once again whole and a leader within the industry.

Don served as the head of multiple successful state and national political campaigns for his close friend and fellow Midlander George W. Bush. Departing the private sector in 2000 at considerable personal sacrifice, Don answered the call as the thirty-fourth secretary of the United States Department of Commerce. In this capacity, he was a close and trusted adviser to President Bush. Known as a man of his word, Don gained the admiration and respect of many national and world leaders.

Part Two: People of Integrity

Since his return to Midland in 2004, he has remained active in all arenas of life. He currently serves as chairman of Energy Future Holdings and chairman of the George W. Bush Foundation for the George W. Bush Presidential Center. He is pending induction into the Texas Business Hall of Fame. Locally, Don has earned almost every honorary award within the nonprofit community and petroleum industry.

Honors and professional accomplishments do not define the man. He is a self-described optimist who feels that one's highest calling is in service to others. He is a trusted go-to friend in all seasons. He has blessed many people, young and old, with heartfelt words of support, encouragement, and sound advice.

A devout Christian, he starts each day in the Bible and in prayer.

He will readily admit that his greatest earthly accomplishments involve his family. Don and Susie are mutually loving spouses, with three outstanding children, a son- and daughter-in-law, and four precious grandchildren.

By example, Don and Susie pass on the legacy of a lifetime of service to God, family, community, and country.

Dr. Charles Younger *is a Midland native and an orthopedic surgeon.*

Part Two: People of Integrity

Murray Fasken
by Bob Jones

I've worked for and with Murray Fasken since the 1960s, and he was both my friend and my boss. He always called me "boy," but to me, it was a term of endearment.

Murray was a known but unknown quantity in Midland for many years. He would do things for people out of the goodness of his heart. I remember one time when an individual asked for help to pay her electric bill. When we looked into it a little bit more, we discovered that the woman actually didn't need the money for her bills; they were all up to date. Murray, who had already reached into his personal pocket to help her, just said, "Don't worry. She'll be able to use it for something else."

Murray was like that. Often, if people were turned down by the loan committee at Midland National Bank, he would pull them aside later, write them a personal check, and give them the money they needed. He would verbally work out payment arrangements, and as far as I know, everyone who came to him always paid him back as they agreed. I imagine there were some people who didn't, though, because Murray helped a lot of people that no one ever knew about.

One of my favorite stories about Murray was the day a young doctor moved to Midland in 1951. Viola Coleman, who had moved here from Louisiana, approached the bank asking for operating expenses to start up a practice. Of course, it was the first clinic run by a black doctor, man or woman. When she came into the board meeting, Murray asked her, "Why did you choose Midland?"

Dr. Coleman said, "Well, sir, I just got off the train, looked around a little, and thought Midland was a place that could use a black doctor."

Murray asked her, "Are you any good?"

And Dr. Coleman told him and the loan committee, "Yes, sir, and I aim to be better."

The loan committee gave Dr. Coleman the loan she needed, based solely on her signature and her word. No collateral was offered or asked for.

After Murray's banking career he established the Fasken Foundation, and I worked with him there. Its objective has always been to help fund the college education of young people who might not otherwise have a means to go to college.

All the foundation asked was that students complete twelve hours a semester with a C average. Murray's philosophy was always "We don't need a bunch of brains, we need workers." That's just the way we ran it. If a young person had a problem and didn't pass, we would meet and find out what the problem was. We'd tell them, "You know the rules. Since you weren't able to pass this class, you go out and take twelve hours on your own, and if you pass them all and turn in good grades to us, we'll put you back in school."

There were many stories about the legend of Murray Fasken. Most of them are true. One time, his housekeeper, Minnie, who just hated to fly, boarded a plane with her husband. They had been invited up to Ruidoso to spend Christmas with the Fasken family. Lynn Durham, who also worked at Midland National Bank, was on the plane too. When he saw Minnie get on board, he said, "Minnie, why are you on this plane? I thought you hate to fly."

And she said, "Mr. Lynn, have you ever *ridden* with Mr. Fasken?"

Murray, an Aggie, was also a straight shooter. When his fellow Aggie Clayton Williams was stinging from his now infamous quote about rape, made during his campaign for governor of Texas, Claytie walked up to Murray and said, "Murray, I really messed it up, didn't I?"

Murray looked at Claytie and said, "Yessir, I'm afraid you did."

Bob Jones *is longtime director of the Fasken Foundation.*

Part Two: People of Integrity

Herman Garrett

While many Midlanders in this book were known for their accomplishments and for things they created, changed, improved, or left behind, Herman Garrett deserves recognition simply for being here.

Garrett was not just here; he was among the first and is widely considered to have been the first permanent resident of Midland when he came here seeking tall grass on which his sheep could graze. When he arrived, he met a man named Lum Medlin, a barefoot antelope hunter—thought to be the most proficient antelope hunter of the plains—but it was Garrett who deserves mention for coming and staying.

Already a well-traveled man before settling in Midland, Herman Garrett was born in Cook County, Illinois, August 6, 1849. His parents, Sam and Malinda Garrett, moved the family to New York City, then traveled by boat around Cape Horn of South America, before heading up the West Coast and disembarking in San Francisco.

When he was thirty-three, Garrett set out for Midland after hearing a series of reports about grazing lands, even-tempered weather and year-round ranching. "The idea made his pioneer spirit restless and he decided to give it a try," wrote Nancy McKinley in her book *The Pioneer History of Midland County, Texas, 1880–1926*.[1]

What made Garrett's life and accomplishments all the more courageous is that everything he achieved after he came to Midland was with the benefit of just one arm. Garrett had lost part of his left arm in a combine accident when he was a wheat farmer in Sacramento. It was the loss of the arm that made it difficult for Garrett to farm and propelled him to adventurously strike out on his own as a sheepman.

When he set out for Texas from California, he did so with two others who had an equally pioneering spirit. His traveling companions—his brother Jim and friend John Cutler—stayed in El Paso for a while. So Herman took his share of the sheep and followed the railroad east. "For no other reason other than he liked what he saw, Garrett finally stopped at Midway Station," according to Gus Clemens, author of *Legacy*.[2] When he reached the Pecos River, railroad workers laid boards over the river so that his animals could pass safely.

Part Two: People of Integrity

Garrett set up a camp at what is now the corner of Wall and Main Streets. It was at the very site of Garrett's camp that First National Bank was later built. After camping downtown the first night, Garrett later found his permanent settlement at, coincidentally, Mustang Draw, where Captain Randolph Marcy had himself set up camp on his way back to Fort Smith, Arkansas, in the midst of staking out what one day became known as the Marcy Trail.

Garrett did not become the first Midlander without a certain amount of sacrifice. Many early pioneers left their wives and families behind in order to establish themselves in places largely unsettled. When the men arrived and determined the safety and viability of their new town, they would often next send for their families. Garrett was one of these men. Many waited until the railroad stretched to Midland before sending for their loved ones.

Garrett was one of the men who established First National Bank on June 16, 1890, and he was named one of the bank's first two vice presidents. By the time he died on June 16, 1933, Midland was no longer a wilderness, but a town.

The Garrett family holds at least one other distinction: forty years later, in 1973, Elizabeth Garrett died at age ninety-two. "Lizzie," as she was known, was the daughter of Herman and his wife, Lucy Ann Bohannon Garrett, and was the first white child resident of Midland County.

—*Jimmy Patterson*

PART TWO: PEOPLE OF INTEGRITY

Susan Graham
by John Rutherford

Deemed "America's favorite mezzo" by *Gramophone* magazine, Susan Graham has achieved success in a field that most people would not have foreseen from her background or her dusty hometown.

I met Suzy at Goddard Junior High School when we were both in the eighth grade. She was pretty typical for a kid living in Midland during that time. Most of us were just one generation removed from a farm or ranch, and our dads were college-educated in technical fields and employed in the oil and gas business. Suzy's dad, Pete Graham, a geophysicist, moved his family to Midland in 1974 to join Dawson Geophysical. He and his wife, Betty, both grew up on ranches in southeastern New Mexico.

Music lessons were common among baby boomer children, and Suzy started playing piano at the same time she started learning to read. She studied piano with Joy Finley and voice with Ruth Ann Griffin. Both of us sang in the choir at Lee High School under director Doug Brown. (So did my future wife, Deanna.)

Suzy claims to have been a "piano nerd" during high school, though the record shows she was an outstanding student in all respects. Her vocal performance debut occurred during our senior year, when she sang the lead role in the Lee High School production of *The Sound of Music*. Prior to her professional opera debut, she went on to star in musical and opera roles at both Texas Tech University and the Manhattan School of Music.

Suzy says that Midland's slogan, "The Sky's the Limit," really did shape her dreams and aspirations. Opera caught her interest, primarily because it seemed a nearly impossible goal. Inspired by the fact that she knew of no one who had pursued opera as a career, the effort became a clean canvas onto which she could paint her own color. "I knew that it was a rigorous and unforgiving genre. My thought was, 'If I can sing opera, it will really be something.'"

Now that she has received worldwide acclaim for numerous opera roles and her signature repertoire of French music, her West Texas sensibilities create a unique contrast in the opera world. I would say she is the contradiva: a genuinely nice person in a field rife with big egos and temperamental personalities.

With a Grammy and a Legion of Honor to her credit, Susan performs in all the great opera houses in the world, for celebrities and potentates from every continent. She sang for George H. W. Bush's presidential inauguration and at the funeral of Senator Ted Kennedy.

True to her upbringing, Suzy doesn't appreciate a condescending comment about her home. After singing at a gala at the Royal Opera in London, she stood in a receiving line backstage to meet Prince Charles. She was introduced to him as "Susan Graham, our American singer this evening."

He was fiddling with his cufflinks as he asked her, "Um . . . and what part of the States are you from?"

She curtseyed in her self-proclaimed "spangly" concert gown and said, "I'm from Texas."

He eyed her up and down and said, "Oh. One would never have guessed."

She was severely tempted to lift up her skirts and say, "Did'ja expect tuh see *boots* under this here gown, and fer me to sing mah *eye*-talian with a *drawl?*" She didn't, but oh, how she wanted to.

It may seem out of place for an opera star to rise out of the heat and mesquite of West Texas, but it isn't. The same attributes that drive success in any life pursuit drive success in opera. Things like work ethic, technical competence, innovation, creativity, and authenticity move people to the top of every endeavor.

Over the years, I've witnessed a number of Suzy's opera performances and recitals. No matter how they dress her up and no matter how storied the venue, a really nice girl from Midland, Texas, still shows through in every performance. Suzy loves to talk about her passion for her chosen profession, about the arts, about inspiration and our basic human need for expression. Creativity is really just the assembly of congruency and contrast in fresh and unique combinations. That is exactly how I would describe Susan Graham.

John Rutherford, a landman and horse breeder, moved to Midland in 1971. He and Susan Graham have been friends since 1974.

Part Two: People of Integrity

Barney and Helen Greathouse
by David L. Smith

Helen Maddox Greathouse was born in 1908 in Graford, Texas, one of five children. Barney R. Greathouse was born and raised in Blackwell, Texas. They met and married in 1929. Shortly afterward, in December of that year, the couple moved to Midland, where they bought the inventory of a failed drugstore and opened their own drugstore downtown. Helen supported this new business endeavor by baking pies and cakes for sale at the drugstore. Together they worked side by side for more than thirty-seven years, building their business.

As Midland grew and expanded in the 1950s, the community built a new hospital. Barney and Helen followed by building a new drugstore adjacent to the hospital. Barney gained a wonderful reputation of offering free medicine to all children whose families could not afford it. Over the years, the Greathouses expanded their store inventory far beyond that of typical drugstore, eventually selling household items, appliances, toys, sporting goods, and clothing. They were so successful that they labeled their enterprise "Texas' Largest Drug Store." Nearly twenty-five years later, they sold to Walgreen's and became the largest individual shareholders of the corporation. Barney was very active in the community with the chamber of commerce, banking, church affairs, and Midland Presbyterian Homes (now known as Manor Park).

After Barney's unexpected death in 1973, Helen became quite an accomplished philanthropist, focusing on the needs of children, especially those with developmental or physical disabilities. Despite not having children of her own, in this way she became a nurturing mother to many children. One hallmark of her generosity was that she often initiated contact with agencies rather than waiting to be solicited. She was described by one of her favorite nonprofits as strong-willed, proud, humble, frugal, determined, fun-loving, willing to take a risk, and a woman of great style.

Like many entrepreneurs who took risks and succeeded, Helen and Barney were both very generous during their lifetimes and then left a lasting financial legacy. Helen established and funded the Helen Greathouse Charitable Trust in 1997. She found that the ultimate way to give back was by creating a permanent philanthropic entity that would meet the needs of the community in perpetuity. Since its inception, the Helen Greathouse Charitable Trust has donated more than $27 million to charitable causes, the majority of which has directly benefited the citizens of Midland.

Helen passed away in 2001, but a lasting legacy of the generosity of Barney and Helen Greathouse lives on. A good example of the impact of their philanthropy is the $1 million capital grant made to the Wagner Noel Performing Arts Center. Today citizens from Midland, Odessa, and the outlying areas are able to enjoy a venue for a wide variety of performing arts, partially because of the generosity of Barney and Helen Greathouse.

David L. Smith is executive director of the Abell-Hanger Foundation.

Part Two: People of Integrity

Rosalind Grover
by Russell Meyers

Approaching sixty years of age, Midland Memorial Hospital's original building was increasingly inadequate to meet the needs of a modern medical community. With six-foot-wide corridors, seven-foot ceilings, tiny patient rooms, and plumbing caked with decades of Midland water's mineral-rich sludge, the old place was groaning toward the end of its eventful life. The hospital did not have two pennies to rub together, but its visionary leaders embarked on an ambitious plan to replace the old facilities with a beautiful, modern leap into the twenty-first century.

The excitement of the new hospital planning process was tempered by its nine-digit price tag. With minimal cash reserves and a substantial debt load, the vision of a new hospital was never going to be realized without an unprecedented capital campaign—double, triple (sextuple?) the biggest fund-raising effort Midland had ever seen. The sages of the board of governors knew there was one person with any hope of pulling off such a monumental task: Rosalind Redfern Grover.

You can't go far in the hospital without running into evidence of John Redfern's influence on its history, but his daughter, Roz, had spent her time on many other worthy endeavors. She would go on to become one of the most important people in my life, but when I first talked with her about leading our capital campaign, I did not know her well. Not long after our first conversation, I let myself be quoted in the local paper, telling a half-baked version of our plans for the new facility. I immediately had my first experience of Roz's laser focus: if she was going to run this campaign, we were going to carefully manage our story and never deviate from the script. Appropriately chastened, I was thrilled she said yes, and from that point on I never doubted who was in charge of the Campaign for Tomorrow!

For over two years, Roz (and her beloved husband Arden) lived and breathed our capital campaign. She developed the story, fretted over the details, influenced every element of facility design, and put her dynamic persuasive talents at our disposal. It was vital that every person of influence in Midland understand, and support, the hospital project. We established a comprehensive storytelling method, including sixty-five hospital tours and dinners at the Grovers' home for more than 500 local opinion leaders.

The Campaign for Tomorrow was a breathtaking success. Private donors gave nearly $67 million for the development of our new hospital, and those influential dinner guests helped us pass a record $115 million bond issue with almost two-thirds of the vote. At the end of 2012, the new Midland Memorial Hospital opened, on time and under budget, at its new address: 400 Rosalind Redfern Grover Parkway.

During the course of our campaign, I must have heard Roz say this a thousand times, but it still illustrates her passionate commitment to our hospital and our community better than anything I could write:

> You know, you can go to Houston for your cancer treatment, you can go to Dallas for your knee surgery, you can go to New York for your face-lift, but when you have your heart attack or you have your stroke or your child or grandchild is in an automobile accident, Midland Memorial Hospital is where you are going to go. So when the doors of that emergency room burst open and it is YOU on the gurney, how good do we have to be?

We had to be the best, and Roz would accept nothing less. Nobody I know can say no to Roz, but there is an appropriate one-word response to all she has done for Midland Memorial Hospital and our community: Thanks.

Russell Meyers is president/CEO of Midland Memorial Hospital.

Part Two: People of Integrity

Frank Haag

There is surprisingly little information in Midland County history annals about Benjamin Franklin Haag, yet he is a significant person of influence in Midland history.

At the time of his tragic death in a 1933 car accident northwest of Sterling City, it was thought Haag was being groomed for a run for the governorship of Texas, although he was still a relative newcomer to the state political scene.

Haag was born February 6, 1886, on a farm in Jack County, Texas. He attended a country school and went to high school first at Jacksboro before graduating from Bellview. In 1910 he moved to Andrews, purchased the *Andrews County Times*, and was its publisher for several years. In 1915 he moved his family to Midland, where he began an intensive study of law at his home, and was later admitted to the bar by the El Paso Court of Civil Appeals.

At the time of his death on July 13, 1933, Haag served as a state representative for Midland. The mark he left on West Texas is immeasurable, from roads to commerce to water. He served in practically every civic role possible and he was in service to West Texas—returning to Midland after meeting with the Texas Highway Commission to lobby for more roads in the region—at the time of his death.

Haag had the kind of foresight that Midland's brightest leaders have always possessed. He knew oil would make a huge impact on the regional economy, but only if the proper road and highway system were built to handle the traffic and weight load of the heavy trucks that were necessary to make it all happen.

Haag was the first president of the Midland Chamber of Commerce, and his business acumen led him to become an instrumental figure in the founding of numerous small town chambers of commerce in West Texas. He was also instrumental in securing an ample supply of water, recognizing that it would be a hard to find commodity for years to come, even all those years ago.

Interestingly, Haag, who accomplished many notable firsts for Midland and West Texas, accomplished one more first upon his death. According to a letter written in a Rotarians' newsletter by John Howe, president of the Midland Rotary Club, Haag was the first of the club's members to die. Howe wrote:

> The daily life of Frank was exemplification of the very motto of Rotary: "Service Above Self." It was not only his desire but it was his will and privilege to serve his fellowman.
>
> We share with the citizenship of this region the loss of a noble, upright, God-fearing and God-loving public servant. As Rotarians we are parted from one whom we all loved and whose efforts for the promotion of the individual and collective good will be sorely missed.[1]

—Jimmy Patterson

Part Two: People of Integrity

Henry Halff

Shortly after the dawn of the twentieth century, the Henry Halff family moved to West Texas from New York. Remembered fondly by Rabe Preston, a former employee on Halff's famed Quien Sabe Ranch, Henry Halff was widely respected in the region for his honesty, integrity, and work ethic. The Halffs were also Midland's first millionaires, according to historian Nancy McKinley.[1]

Born in San Antonio on August 17, 1874, Halff was educated at the Staunton Military Academy in Virginia and at Eastman Business College in Poughkeepsie, New York. When he moved to West Texas with his new bride, Rosa Wechsler, he oversaw the operation of ninety of the almost 600 sections of land on the Quien Sabe.

The family clearly had wealth, McKinley stated in her book, and "lived like millionaires . . . [with] a French maid, a German governess for their children, a chauffeur and other servants . . . [but] they were not at all stuck up. When they gave a party, everyone was invited."[2]

Renowned for his cattle-breeding techniques, Henry Halff ran as many as 20,000 Herefords on the ranch, and his bulls were known and desired by many throughout the Southwest. Halff also loved polo ponies and once won an international polo competition.

Probably his most important contribution to the area's development, however, was his use of underground water resources. The Texas State Historical Association hails him as a pioneer in irrigation, stating that Halff's irrigation methods produced a sufficient amount of water to grow grapes, melons, grain, and cotton. A well Halff drilled on Cloverdale Farms, five miles southeast of Midland, later became a critical source of the town's water supply.

Midland author Patrick Dearen, who researched and wrote about the family, calls Henry Halff "the most dominant figure in Midland history, whose contributions to the community secured for it an international reputation."

—*Jimmy Patterson*

Part Two: People of Integrity

Jim Henry
by Ellen Hopkins

Jim Henry wanted to be an engineer like his father, James, who had worked his own way through college by throwing newspapers. James later worked as a mining engineer in Colombia, South America, where Jim was born.

With his own $1,500 savings from throwing papers during high school, Jim graduated with two petroleum engineering degrees: a bachelor's, followed one year later by a master's. He worked for Humble Oil every day and wrote his thesis at night.

Jim recalls, "I never had a burning desire to become wealthy; my immediate plan after college was to work for a large oil company and acquire training."

Humble, the Air Force, Skelly, and Solar provided that training before Jim paired up with Bob Landenberger, whom Jim calls "the best geologist I've ever known." They once said to each other, "We can do this, so why don't we start our own company sometime?"

The partners had years of experience, young families, and an abundance of drive and determination. The only capital they had was the equity in their mortgaged homes. After working as independent consultants and completing a Spraberry study for Skelly Oil, the pair became known as Spraberry experts. "From our study in 1970, we predicted thousands of wells would be drilled in the Spraberry," Jim says, "and we were right."

After Bob retired, Jim continued the business on a growth path that never gave away interest in the company. He asked brother-in-law Dennis Johnson to join him in 1980. Always one to give credit where it's due, Jim credits Dennis with many innovations that helped Henry Petroleum reach an income level of $1 million a month by 2000. Although it took nearly thirty years to achieve that, within five more years the company's Wolfcamp development, coupled with high oil and gas prices, dramatically increased company revenue. Jim credits a handful of key employees for discovering these potential reserves and developing them with his and Dennis's full support. This development is responsible for the Permian Basin oil boom since 2009.

Part Two: People of Integrity

"Some companies drill a successful well but they only see a small picture," says Jim. "At Henry, the Wolfcamp has evolved such that we acquired additional acreage before others did. We'll keep many rigs busy for years to come."

Smart decisions—such as keeping company debt low, hiring multitalented employees, selling part of the company in 2008, and placing heavy emphasis on giving back to the community—have combined to propel the Henry Companies into its fifth decade. Jim has received numerous awards for his community involvement, philanthropic efforts, and impetus to further the industry worldwide.

"When Jim first began volunteering with United Way, he wanted to see how the process worked by starting at the bottom," said his wife, Paula. "His engineering background and need to know how everything works convinced him to begin this way. Ultimately, he wound up being president of United Way twice."

Ellen Hopkins is a freelance writer in Midland. She has written about the Henry family, Henry Companies, Johnny Warren, and the Yates family, among others.

Part Two: People of Integrity

Harvey and Harriet Herd
by Tevis Herd

My father, Harvey Herd, was born in Post, Texas, and moved to Midland in 1937 with Standard Oil of California. In 1940 he married Harriet Daniel, who had grown up in Temple, Texas. They were married for sixty-four years.

Dad was always quiet. He was a photographic officer in the Army Air Corps, ending his service with the rank of captain. He didn't talk much about his combat experiences in World War II, or even about his business. When he came to Midland, he was an oil scout, back when oil companies would hire people to sit on wells when they were being drilled to see what was going on. They wouldn't dream of doing that today.

Dad always said, "The harder I work, the luckier I get." He had a close association with John Redfern, and for seventeen years the two of them ran an oil business, Flag-Redfern Oil Company. After all those years together, John wanted to make the company larger, but Dad didn't. He went out on his own. They always remained friends and had an amicable parting of ways in the oil company.

In 2001 Dad was recognized for his work in the oil business when the Petroleum Pioneers Association named him Top Pioneer. He joined both the Midland Memorial Hospital board and the YMCA board. (Just by coincidence, those are two of my favorite causes to support as well.) But Dad never really sought any attention for all he did.

Mom received all sorts of accolades and deserved them all. She and Ibby Hardie were the cofounders of Family Counseling Services, which is now Centers for Children and Families. She also started the Ballet Association and the National Young Artists' Competition at Midland College. Mom was very organized. I think if she felt like she was wasting time, she felt like she was cheating the community.

The phone at the house was always ringing, and it was always for Mom because of all the things she was doing in the community. I still remember one time when I was in high school, one night we were eating dinner and the phone rang. And it rang again. My dad walked over and picked up the phone and said, "We closed at five!"

Part Two: People of Integrity

Mom died in 2004. She's still a legend at the Junior League. Whenever I meet a member of the Junior League, they'll always ask me if I am related to her. She was just a beautiful lady.

Mom and Dad were a part of that group of people who came to Midland, or came back to Midland after the war, pitched in, and started things like the hospital or Family Counseling Services. And a lot of people did those kinds of things, and together they have literally made Midland what it is.

During Midland Memorial Hospital's first capital campaign in 1946, I know my parents contributed to every single campaign—buildings, renovation, equipment, everything. In 2011, the year he died, Dad established the Herd Family Endowment Fund so that people could make memorial tributes.

I guess more than anything, my mom and dad left me with a sense of service to the community.

Tevis Herd is an attorney, philanthropist, and community leader in Midland.

Part Two: People of Integrity

T. S. Hogan

As Midland visionaries go, there may not be a more unlikely candidate than T. S. Hogan. From his home in Montana, where he served as a state senator, he predicted that the center of the Permian Basin oil business—still several years ahead on the West Texas calendar—would be Midland.

With that knowledge, derived by studying engineering and geological logs, Hogan moved to West Texas by way of Denver and began to make plans for what would be one of the two most significant structures in early Midland: the Hogan Building. (The other was the Scharbauer Hotel.) As Judge John Hyde wrote on June 4, 2011, in the *Midland Reporter-Telegram*:

> [Hogan] was a visionary who saw the great importance of the petroleum industry, so he came to where the activity was strong. Beginning in 1928, he had the landmark Gothic architecture building constructed at Colorado and Texas streets. The twelve-story T. S. Hogan Building, later known as the Shell Building and more recently as the Petroleum Building, was one of three major assets enticing oil companies to station their headquarters in Midland. First, the Texas and Pacific Railroad already was here to transport crude oil out of the basin; second, the interstate highway system adjacent to the railroad tracks made Midland accessible and inviting as a capital city for the petroleum industry. The T. S. Hogan Building became the third asset, providing much-needed office space for the oil companies. This historic structure helped to make Midland an important part of the emerging petroleum industry."[1]

As John Howard Griffin stated in his book *Land of the High Sky*, Hogan "proved his faith in Midland by building the handsomest office facilities between Fort Worth and El Paso at a time when only belief in the future warranted such an investment."[2]

He made trips to East Coast financiers and wrote articles touting Midland's potential, calling it the future oil capital of West Texas. In speeches he made to

Part Two: People of Integrity

women's clubs, he urged them to turn Midland into a city of flowers and parks.

For a year, Hogan had been keeping his sharp eye on West Texas and its petroleum growth. When Christmas morning dawned in 1927, Hogan and his son had purchased a full-page ad in the Midland newspaper. It read:

> Men of vision, common sense and courage will profit by the growth of the city. Others will tell their grandchildren what they might have done if they had bought this or that piece of property. We have been watching the development of West Texas for the past year. Being primarily interested in the oil business, our investigations have convinced us that no other area in North America contains greater petroleum deposits than the district within 125 miles of Midland. This fact guarantees long continued development on an enormous scale.[3]

By virtue of his confidence in Midland's future in the oil industry—a future that is sustained even today, almost 100 years later—the building that bore Hogan's name stands among the tallest accomplishments recorded in the city's history.

—*Jimmy Patterson*

Part Two: People of Integrity

Judge John Hyde
by the Honorable Dean Rucker

I was faced with a very difficult case decision. John Hyde had always been my go-to judge for advice and counsel, and he was an excellent sounding board, always giving me the benefit of calling shots just the way he saw them. This time, however, he was away from the office, and I was about to leave on a short trip, so I left him a note detailing the help I was seeking.

When I returned that weekend, I found a note on my desk he had written in response, imparting his usual sage advice. I called him at home to thank him for his help. He told me he'd had a "touch of the flu" the week before but was feeling well enough to travel to Austin in the coming week to teach the state's newly elected and appointed trial judges at the College for New Judges. I told him they could find someone else if he was not up to the travel, but he protested that he had promised to be there and he was going to see it through.

Although I was not at the College for New Judges, I am told by those who were with him that John's presentations were outstanding, given with the vigor, passion, and wisdom we had all come to expect of his teaching over the years. As the week came to an end, I received word that John had returned home and been hospitalized to undergo some aggressive medical treatment for what was later discovered to be cancer of the brain lining.

Only after his hospitalization in those final days did I learn of the gravity of John's condition. Despite not feeling well for several weeks, John exhibited no outward signs of illness to his friends and colleagues. Belying his condition, he continued to show up for work as usual, offered the assistance I had sought from him, and fulfilled his commitment to teach the state's newest judges. Less than one month later, Midland learned of the death of one of its favorite sons, on January 2, 2012.

Not once did John refuse to help, complain about his situation, or allow illness to interfere with what he perceived to be his duty to the electorate and those to

PART TWO: PEOPLE OF INTEGRITY

whom he had made commitments of his time and talent. Such was the selfless, caring nature and sense of duty of this loyal, stalwart, and stoic man. He gave fully and freely of himself to the end. His life, his work, and his sterling character are an inspiration to generations to come.

> ***The Honorable Dean Rucker*** *is a lifelong Midlander and judge of the 318th District Court in Midland. He was one of John Hyde's closest friends.*

Part Two: People of Integrity

C. J. Kelly
by Arlen Edgar

I'm a member of Grace Lutheran Church, which originally met in a little building on Wall Street. We were outgrowing it in the late 1960s, so we decided to buy a lot in the north part of Midland and build on.

The church's financial review committee decided what we could spend on the building, and it turned out we needed to borrow the difference. One of our members was the vice president of Cactus Drilling Company, and he and I were delegated to go over and talk to C. J. Kelly about a loan. I gathered all the information I could think of—site plans, budgets, financial statements, everything.

We went in and sat down, and C. J. came out and said, "What can I do for you boys?"

We said, "We'd like to borrow some money."

He asked us how much we needed.

I said, "Two hundred sixty thousand dollars."

He asked us, "Well, how much interest do you want to pay?"

And we said, "Well, we thought you would tell us."

C. J. said, "Okay, how about 6 percent?" That was kind of the going rate at the time. We said that would be fine.

C. J. told us to go see the bank attorney and he'd draw up the papers.

I asked him if that was all.

C. J. said, "That's it."

He didn't even want to see all the information we had brought with us, and I asked him why.

He said, "I'll tell you why. This bank has financed almost every church congregation in Midland. We've never had a default, and I don't think you are going to be the first one."

We were in talking with him for about five minutes, and probably another fifteen with the attorney.

Years later Grace Lutheran had grown to the point where we had to expand

Part Two: People of Integrity

again, and we came up with the need for a $1.3 million project. We went back to the bank, and they had gone through several presidents by this point. We sat down and talked to the new president, and he told us what all we were going to have to do to get the loan.

I said, "I can't believe we are having to jump through all these hoops!"

And he said, "I'm sorry, but that's the way it is."

I told him the C. J. Kelly story, and he said, "That's a great story, but we can't do that anymore. The feds won't let us."

***Arlen Edgar** is a longtime independent oilman in the Permian Basin.*

Part Two: People of Integrity

W. W. Lackey

One of early Midland's most innovative and progressive figures was W. W. Lackey, the first superintendent of the local school system after its formation in 1907.

Some longtime Midlanders remember Lackey as somewhat of a polarizing figure because of his renowned flamboyant style and unorthodox teaching methods, while others recall Lackey as being "one of the greatest leaders of our times."[1]

In 1950 Mrs. Mabel Glass, the daughter of Midland rancher O. B. Holt, wrote a history of Midland that she presented to civic organizations in town. Her paper is currently archived in the Haley Memorial Library. In it, she called Lackey one of the most prominent educators in Texas. "Through Superintendent Lackey's forethought and ability," she wrote, "and with the cooperation of the townspeople, Midland public schools attained a recognition superior to all others in the state with two possible exceptions. The school was the hub of the town. Every cultural and educational activity was centered by and on the public schools."[2]

Nancy McKinley's *The Pioneer History of Midland County, Texas, 1880–1926* noted that Lackey was named superintendent of Midland schools after local educators deemed the schools in such a condition that "something drastic had to be done."[3]

Lackey wrote and published four volumes of original poetry and organized and directed a citywide Christmas cantata, presented annually. The *Midland Reporter-Telegram* noted that Lackey, a native Texan and the son of a Baptist preacher, moved to Midland after earning bachelor's and master's degrees from the University of Texas and an LLD from Hardin-Simmons.

"A student in Midland High School during Mr. Lackey's administration received a cultural and musical background second to none," Mrs. Clinton Myrick wrote in the *Midland Reporter-Telegram* in 1976. "The entire student body repeated from memory literary selections and complete chapters of the Bible in unison."

Lackey served as superintendent of Midland schools until 1941.

—*Jimmy Patterson*

Part Two: People of Integrity

Dr. Al G. Langford
by Stan Jacobs

"Someday, Midland College will have its own campus, including a fine arts building, and over 3,000 students."

Al Langford made that prediction when he interviewed Midland College's first prospective art instructor in the dining room of the old Scharbauer Hotel in the summer of 1971. The fabled hotel was the energy headquarters of the "Emerald City" at that time. The young artist from Kansas believed him—and so did the voters of Midland when they overwhelmingly approved Midland College's first bond election for $5.1 million in December 1972. In March 1973, Midland College purchased 114.87 acres of land just north of Wadley and Garfield from the city of Midland for $114,870, and ground was broken that fall.[1]

Dr. Langford had been dean of the Midland campus of the Permian Junior College System, which included Odessa College, since 1969. After successfully enabling legislation, a nine-member board of trustees was elected, and Dr. Langford became the founding president of the new community college in Midland in 1972. Ken Peeler, one of the original nine board members, still serves. According to Mr. Peeler, Reagan Legg, and other members of the board, Midland College enjoyed a "honeymoon" with the citizens of Midland. That honeymoon has continued, and even now Midland College is referred to as "*your* college" when Midlanders speak to current or prospective students there.[2]

In 1976, when enrollment surpassed 2,000 students, a second bond election for $6.3 million was called, and once again the voters approved by more than a 2–1 margin. In 1978 Midland College completed an addition to its Occupational-Technical building as well as the Allison Fine Arts building (only five years after it was predicted) and the 5,000-seat multipurpose Chaparral Center. According to *Sports Illustrated*, Chap Center was the "finest community college basketball arena in the country."[4] It now bears the name "Al G. Langford Chaparral Center."

Dr. Langford would give credit to so many for the success of Midland College but the man in the pilot's seat was Al Langford.

A certain community leader once said, "Al Langford, for a college president, does not seem very scholarly." Bold, persuasive, arm-twisting, clever, impulsive, and charismatic are words that describe him. He was a West Texas storm cell that did not lose force as he moved over the city, raising money and support in both good times and bad. He could be found in bank boardrooms, governmental chambers, public schools, oil-company offices, golf courses, and wherever Midlanders gathered to work or play.

When a committee was formed to fund the landscaping of the new Midland College campus, the college received checks from $2 to $10,000 for that purpose. The campus now has well over 1,000 trees[4] and is known as one of the most beautiful campuses in the country.

But it was not just about buildings and trees. Dr. Langford always put students first, and he included those who teach and serve students. He said that his door was always open—to anyone who was a friend of education and the community college concept. He was both an idealist and a pragmatist. He frequently referred to Midland College as the Impossible Dream, and one could often hear the chimes from the Hodge Carillon Tower playing the song of the same name from *Man of La Mancha*. He knew when to stand his ground and when to compromise. He listened to the board members, the public, the students, and the faculty. When he thought the college needed more faculty members with doctoral degrees, he not only hired them, he also grew them. He established an incentive program in which faculty members working on a doctorate could take a year's sabbatical at half salary to complete their degree.

In 1981 Dr. Langford retired as president of Midland College and entered the oil industry.

In the 1970s Sam Prendergast, former columnist for the *San Angelo Standard-Times*, called Midland College the "miracle on the greasewood plain." Dr. Al Langford laid the foundation for that miracle. Today his legacy remains secure.

Stan Jacobs, the first art instructor at Midland College, has been employed at the school for more than forty years. He is a former associate vice president of instruction for academic transfer courses, a Fulbright Scholar, and a veteran of the U.S. Navy.

Part Two: People of Integrity

The Mabee family

Guy and Ruby Mabee arrived in Midland in 1943 after a trek through several states with their young son, Joe. Along the way, Guy had tried his hand at several kinds of work. As Joe Mabee explained it:

> My parents got married in 1927, when my dad was eighteen and my mom was only fifteen. He was a farmer in Missouri, raising corn to feed their hogs, which was the cash crop. But in 1931, during the Depression, the price of hogs fell to zero, so we went broke.
>
> Dad heard there were jobs in Oklahoma City, so he hitchhiked there with my mother and me when I was very young. My dad went to work for his uncle, John, in Oklahoma City, who was in the contracting business. Dad started in drilling contract work and as a roughneck in Oklahoma in 1931.[1]

The Mabee family later moved several times during the next few years: Kansas, Indiana, then Illinois in 1936. That was where Guy Mabee bought into his first oil rigs. "He was working for a company in Illinois, on the Wabash River," said Joe, "where they were drilling shallow wells right on the river beds. Someone in the company told my father he needed to get to Midland, where he said the next boom was going to be."[2]

So the family picked up stakes once more and came to Midland in 1943, right about the time oil turned around in the Permian Basin. By then Guy had gone into business for himself as a drilling contractor, and he did well in Midland. Later, when the Spraberry came in, the family prospered even more. "We could drill a Spraberry well in Midland County and probably put it in the tanks for $100,000 back then," Joe Mabee said. "Nowadays, that wouldn't even get you started."[3]

Joe Mabee became a well-known Midland rancher who now also helps direct the Mabee Foundation, a philanthropic organization. He knew many of the Midlanders who made the town, including George Abell ("You could not have met a nicer man") and Jno. P. Butler ("He was for Midland, period. He was a gentlemen, a fine man, and a good banker").

Mabee was one of the board members at First National Bank who worked with Butler during the darks days of October 1983. "[The bank's closure] hurt a lot of people," he said. "It hurt me. I survived it, but I wasn't very happy about it. We didn't have any crooks running that bank. I think if they had just left us alone, we could have saved it."[4]

—Jimmy Patterson

Part Two: People of Integrity

Ed Magruder

Edwin "Ed" Magruder was born in Mississippi but got to West Texas as fast as he could. He settled in Midland in 1949, a year after his graduation from the University of Mississippi, where he majored in business. Once here, he became a professional landman and a fixture in leadership and community volunteerism circles. A member of the Greatest Generation, he had been a naval aviator during World War II.

Magruder's volunteer efforts in Midland include the Midland Chamber of Commerce, the Museum of the Southwest, Casa de Amigos, the Permian Basin Centers for Mental Health and Mental Retardation, Midland Memorial Hospital, the old Midland Fair and Rodeo Association, and the Boy Scouts' Buffalo Trail Council. In 2010 he was honored with the Buffalo Trails Council's Distinguished Citizen Award.

He served as Midland's mayor from 1968 to 1972. He had been Midland's mayor only a few months when the town received its famous 300-year rain on May 9, 1968: nearly five inches of rain in two hours. But Magruder knew a little about municipal management, making him the perfect man to be in a leadership position.

Magruder recalls that there was only one lawsuit filed after the storm because of the inferior drainage system that Midland had at the time.

"It was all my fault," Magruder said with a chuckle. "I was the mayor. We expected all kinds of lawsuits. Only one person sued us. He lived on Bedford, and what he did was make the mistake of opening his back gate, and the water came rushing in through the backyard. The water then broke out his sliding glass door and ran through his house and into the Wadley-Barron Park."[1]

When the flood hit, there was no drainage ditch that ran east to west just north of Wadley Avenue, as there is now. Wadley *was* that ditch, Magruder recalled. When the floodwaters subsided, the city of Midland commissioned a study by the Army Corps of Engineers in Lubbock to study a drainage plan for Midland. The recommendation of the corps was to construct a box culvert under Wadley that was the width of Wadley. The culvert would measure 90 feet wide by 8 feet high and run from Garfield to Lamesa. The price tag on the system was $6.5 million.

"We didn't have $6.5 million, and I don't know if the residents of Midland would have voted for a $6 million bond issue for just that one area after something that had been termed a 300-year flood," Magruder said.[2]

Ed Gideon, then city finance director, found almost $700,000 worth of unappropriated street bond funds, but there was no provision in the wording that they could be used for construction of a drainage ditch. Instead, after the rain of 1968, the city designated a thirty-foot street on each side of the drainage ditch, on A Street from Big Spring through the airpark.

"We surveyed the drainage, and it was at about a percent gradient, so when it does rain a lot, it fills up pretty high," Magruder said. "It drains off through the Tanglewood subdivision and ends up where the Corps of Engineers' box culvert would have ended up, at Lamesa and Wadley Streets."[3]

A second drainage deposit was built where the Scharbauer Draw intersects the Midland Draw and comes across Highway 80, just east of the Midland County Exhibits Building, near Fairgrounds Road. Magruder explained:

> We designated that thirty-foot street on each side but we never paved the street and instead we used the money to dig that ditch. We dug that lateral ditch off the end of Wadley, to the northeast into the draw that comes down out of Kimberlea, and it comes behind Ainsley and those streets to the north and goes through the south end of what is now Midland College.
>
> Just east of where it intersects with that drainage ditch, we cut off the end of Wadley Street to relieve the water from going down behind I Street as much as possible. It goes across the runway and then turns northeast and up through the airpark, and as you enter the airpark on Airpark Drive, you will drive right through that ditch. It goes on northeast and turns southeast under Big Spring and down through the Tanglewood subdivision. It was a pretty cool way of getting around what we were supposed to spend money for and benefit the whole town.[4]

—*Jimmy Patterson*

Part Two: People of Integrity

Randolph Marcy

When Randolph Marcy first laid eyes on what eventually became Midland, he was not impressed with its beauty. Far from it. After that first visit, Marcy would say, "It is not fit for man or beast." Not exactly a glowing remembrance.

If it's any consolation, Marcy didn't much care for Santa Fe either, calling it a "miserable group of low flat houses all huddled together inside a mud wall."[1]

But Midland served Marcy's purpose. He was tasked with finding the straightest route for a railroad between Fort Smith, Arkansas, and Santa Fe, New Mexico. He is believed to be the first white man to set foot in the Midland area.

When he had arrived at Santa Fe, Marcy's orders were to return to Fort Smith via a more southerly route. So he took off toward El Paso, and then, just north of that city, he and his men turned east, and soon found themselves traveling across the Trans-Pecos region. Just past what later became present-day Midland, Marcy and his men came upon a draw. Many aged hoofprints led into and out of the water. The sight of the hoofprints led him to believe it was a permanent resource, so he named it Mustang Pond.

Marcy's lack of affinity for the region did not matter in the history books. (He also once called the area the Great Zahara of North America.) But his discovery of the ideal railroad route along what was later called the Marcy Trail had a direct impact on the formation of Midland as a railroad town. Had Marcy gone elsewhere on his way back to Fort Smith, had he even deviated slightly from his route, Midland might have not come into being, at least not at its present location.

—*Jimmy Patterson*

Part Two: People of Integrity

Len "Tuffy" McCormick

Longtime Midland attorney Lloyd McDonald tells a good story about Tuffy McCormick, a former Midland city attorney who left many good stories behind:

> One day at Vatican Square in Rome, in a sea of thousands and thousands of people, two men step out onto the balcony where the pope gives his audiences. One guy in the crowd turns to another and asks, "Hey, who's the guy up there in the funny hat?"
>
> The second guy responds, "I don't know, but he's standing with Tuffy McCormick."[1]

It's a good story. Lloyd McDonald is not the only one who has told it through the years.

Tuffy McCormick, it seems, knew just about everyone. He was a pallbearer at J. Edgar Hoover's funeral and a friend of Frank Sinatra, President George H. W. Bush, T. Boone Pickens, hotelier Barron Hilton, actor James Garner, and just about everyone else. He once owned Big Bend Ranch State Park, a huge spread of land northwest of Big Bend National Park.

Despite his stature and seemingly unending circle of friends and acquaintances, he has also been able to retain a certain amount of humility. Told that he would be included among a list of Midland's all-time characters in an upcoming book, and that the late John Hyde had recommended his inclusion, McCormick responded with a certain amount of emotion, a tear, and the question, "There are actually people there who still remember me?"[2]

Despite being gone from Midland for over half a century, he still spoke about the town with the highest praise. "There's no way for me to ever say how grateful I am to Midland and what a great part of my life it was. It's probably one of the great cities of all time."[3]

When McCormick graduated from Baylor Law School, he became a major in the judge advocate general's corps during the Korean War. Right after the war, he came to Midland, where he served as Midland city attorney. He also played on the

Part Two: People of Integrity

Midland Misfits, a ragtag group of men that played football against teams from other towns.

Judge Hyde said McCormick was widely admired. Calling him one of Midland's last true characters, Hyde noted that the scuttlebutt out of Hollywood was that the 1963 James Garner movie *Wheeler Dealers* was based on McCormick's exploits as a wildcatter in Midland and West Texas.

During an interview at his home near Houston's Galleria in November 2010, McCormick fondly recalled his former West Texas home. "I made and lost a bunch of fortunes out there," he said. "Ruth Scharbauer was one of my favorite people. I remember the old Midland Country Club was right near downtown, and we were out playing one time, and when we teed off she'd make me stop by and see her."[4]

McCormick also recalled his days teaching Laura Bush's mom and dad in Sunday school classes at First United Methodist Church in Midland. "George H. W. Bush and I were in a lot of ventures together, too," McCormick said. "We were on several bank boards together. When I had a blowout and went broke, George stayed with me."[5]

Longtime Midland philanthropist Rosalind Grover clearly remembers McCormick's days in Midland. "He was mesmerizing," Grover said. "I never met anyone who didn't like Tuffy. They might have lost some money to him, but they always liked him."

Remembering another of his favorite stories, McDonald said:

> I would see people at cocktail parties in Indiana, Nebraska, anywhere, and when they found out I was from Midland, they'd ask, "Do you know Tuffy McCormick?" He knew people everywhere. He was reportedly known at the hotels in Las Vegas so well that when [the late millionaire oilman] Fred Turner went into one of those hotels and tried to cash a check, they said, "If you can get Tuffy McCormick to approve it, we'll cash it."[6]

McCormick died August 20, 2012, at age eighty-nine. He was buried in Eldorado, Texas, the same small oilfield town in which he was born.

—*Jimmy Patterson*

Part Two: People of Integrity

Nancy McKinley
by Ed Todd

Petite in stature at five feet even, but valiant and dauntless in action, Midland historian-preservationist Nancy Elizabeth Rankin McKinley trumpeted Midland's heritage in the 1900s and into the next century, until her death at age ninety-seven in 2011. Eventually her frail body yielded to the years, but never her mind and spirit.

She was kind, gracious, and forthright in her West Texas mannerisms. And, when needed, she could be stern and demanding, wary of compromise. In honoring the "Midland Country" heritage, McKinley declared: "You just get right on and do what needs to be done. As time goes on, you've got to work the angles. It is important to know and to appreciate your heritage."

McKinley honored her birthright as a Daughter of the American Revolution, Daughter of the Republic of Texas, and Daughter of the Confederacy. She was at the forefront in securing Texas Historical Commission landmarks throughout Midland County, including those for the majestic twelve-story T. S. Hogan Building and the adjoining Yucca Theatre, both dedicated in 1929.

Nancy McKinley had moxie well beyond her roles of heading up the MCHS and the Midland County Historical Commission and as curator of the Midland County Historical Museum. Dressed to the hilt with her flaming red hat and her generous eyeglasses framed in red, she would march confidently down the aisles of the Midland County Commissioners Courtroom. Quickened by her resolve, the commissioners would sit bolt upright in their elevated seats, like West Point cadets under severe scrutiny.

Eventually they abided by her fervent wishes: she prevailed in convincing the commissioners to build the Midland County Historical Museum. It stands virtually in the shadows of the downtown Midland County Public Library. By the early 1990s, the museum's artifacts and archives had been moved to the new museum from their "dungeon" in the library's basement.

"Nancy McKinley was a beautiful lady, . . . a kind and gracious history mentor of Midland, and must always be remembered well," reflected the esteemed Midland historian-jurist Judge John Hyde. "She was smart. She was informed. She loved Texas." Like McKinley, Hyde was steeped in the history and lore of Midland, both the town and the surrounding county. He called Nancy McKinley an "irreplaceable icon."

"Nancy was history, the history that we all relied on to understand the community," said Midland County judge Mike Bradford. "I used to kid her that I saw her in some of John Wayne's movies with wagons" passing westward through the West Texas plains and mountains and on to the Pacific.

A native Midlander, McKinley was born to Porter and Julia Estes Rankin on June 4, 1913. (The Rankin community south of Midland is named after her grandfather.) She was characterized as "independent" in the 1931 edition of Midland High School yearbook, *Catoico*.

In preserving Midland's heritage through the written word and in photographs, McKinley was chairman of the MCHS's book committee in publishing the 1984 book *The Pioneer History of Midland County, Texas, 1880–1926*;[1] in co-editing with West Texas historian Bill Modisett the MCHS's 1998 *Historic Midland, An Illustrated History of Midland County*;[2] and was book chairman in publishing the 1890–1990 history *The First Christian Church (Disciples of Christ)*.[3]

McKinley was vigorous "in intellectual stature in regard to the legacy and heritage that we [in West Texas] enjoy," said Pat McDaniel, director of the Haley Memorial Library and History Center. "She was fun to be around. She could get your blood pumping. And she encouraged you without discouraging you," especially in matters of honor and heritage. "She truly believed that honesty and integrity are two of the most important intangible assets you could possess."

Ed Todd is a longtime columnist and writer for the Midland Reporter-Telegram.

Part Two: People of Integrity

Henry Meadows
by John Meadows

Many good things can be told about my father, Henry Meadows. He served as an example for all who knew him and never had a negative thing to say about anyone.

Born in 1912 in Comanche, Texas, he attended high school in Waco, where he played football under the coaching legend Paul Tyson. Henry went to college at the Rice Institute, where he was chosen as president of his freshman and junior class and graduated with a civil engineering degree. In the 1930s he began his career with Humble Oil and met two lifelong friends, Matthew Lynn and Clovis Chappel, who later moved to Midland along with Henry. Both men had a major impact on Midland: Dr. Lynn as minister of the First Presbyterian Church and Mr. Chappel as an attorney extraordinaire.

Prior to moving back to Midland with Humble, Henry worked in Crowley and New Orleans, Louisiana, as well as in Houston and McCamey, Texas. In Midland, he was introduced to the daughter of Dr. and Mrs. Jno Thomas. He married Read Thomas on August 23, 1937. They had four sons: Henry Jr., Thomas, Robert, and John. Henry was a loving and caring son, husband, father, father-in-law, and grandfather.

Henry Meadows was always a faithful Christian. He was a pillar of the First Presbyterian Church in Midland who practiced "the quiet hour" every morning, studying the Word of God and the Bible, often taking notes for the Bible classes he taught. His faith, his character, his theology are pretty well summed up in a verse found often in his writings: "O give thanks unto the Lord, for He is good: for His mercy endureth for ever." Dr. Matthew Lynn, the former minister of Henry's church, once said of Henry, "his faith in the goodness and the mercy of God, it was more than that, it was also his response to that faith ... he expressed his thanksgiving by his life, by his compassion for other people, and by his extreme generosity to so many."

For his beloved First Presbyterian Church, Henry Meadows was a teacher, chairman of the Board of Deacons, Ruling Elder, and Elder Emeritus. He also chaired the building committee for the then-new sanctuary.

Part Two: People of Integrity

Mr. Meadows was often referred to as a man of sterling character and great integrity. He was also a quiet man. He did not say a lot, but when he did, you really listened. He was not assuming. He was sensitive to the needs of others in a humble way. He was a very good writer, often offering great advice and counsel to his children. Seldom has a community had such a faithful, compassionate, and loving husband, father, and friend.

Henry spent much time in his early years being outdoors, often at his ranches in Crockett County. In Midland, he served on the Planning and Zoning Commission and the Board of Equalization, and he was chairman of the Highway Committee of the Chamber of Commerce. He also served on the Education Committee of the Chamber of Commerce and Midland County Historical Commission. West Texas history was a passion of Mr. Meadows, who was often asked to speak to various groups.

Other Midland area activities included his service as president and chairman of the YMCA and the High Sky Girls Ranch, where he chaired their building committees. He also served as head of the building committee for the Midland and Lee High School youth centers, the Permian Basin Petroleum Museum and Hall of Fame, the Midland Country Club, and the Humble Building, all during periods of expansion. He served on the board of directors for many organizations. Henry was the West Texas recruiter for Rice University for many decades.

It was not at all unexpected when in 1968 Henry was presented the Golden Deeds Award by the Exchange Club of Midland for his dedication to the services of his community. Mr. Meadows did not know how to say no when his family, church, or community came calling.

Henry retired from Humble Oil in the mid-1960s as engineering coordinator for the Permian Basin but remained active in civic affairs. He died in Midland in 1991.

John Meadows is an attorney in Austin and the son of Henry Meadows.

Part Two: People of Integrity

James Mims
by Ed Todd

The good-heartedness of James Mims has pervaded his life. "It is a good day, but all days are good," Mims reckoned in his ninetieth year, ripe with goodwill and gratitude. "Just some days are better."

Mims considers himself "extremely fortunate" to be blessed with forebears and then children of sterling character. He was born into a dynamic family in 1923. His grandfather, Joseph Mims, was an early-day city marshal. His father, Percy Mims, was an enterprising insurance executive and a quintessential community leader who embraced the First Baptist Church, the Midland Chamber of Commerce, the Midland Rotary Club, and highway expansions. Percy Mims soldiered in France in World War I with the American Expeditionary Forces (AEF). By 1919 he was American Legion commander in Midland. James said his father "never said anything bad about anybody. He loved people, and it showed."

James's mother, Maurine Littlejohn Mims, was a schoolteacher steeped in the classics who settled in Midland in 1922 and promptly introduced home economics and the Parent Teacher Association to Midland schools. As the tale goes, Percy Mims, age thirty in 1922, came a'calling at the Rhea Cottage, a downtown boarding house, to romance the teachers, including Maurine Littlejohn. He was smitten, marriage followed, and James Mims appeared in October 1923.

James attended the Midland schools when W. W. Lackey was superintendent. Lackey offered a classical education and required recitation of heartening classical works and scripture. "I couldn't get away with anything because Mother knew all the teachers," Mims recalled. "If we [Mims and his sister, Margaret] were in trouble, she knew about it before we got home."

A scholarly, talented, and handsome student, Mims played saxophone in the band, sang in quartets and in the glee club, played the Henry Aldrich role in *What a Life*, and was the yearbook cartoonist. "That's all I wanted to do was to be a commercial artist," he declared. "It wasn't to be."

Part Two: People of Integrity

After Pearl Harbor in 1941, while Mims was a freshman at Texas A&M University, he entered the Army and served as a staff sergeant in combat in the Pacific Theater. "That's an experience I don't care to repeat," Mims said of war. Afterward Mims returned to Midland, entered his father's insurance business, and married his sweetheart, Mary Bell.

Their son, David Mims, was "a lot like my daddy," said James. "He was a wheelhorse," an exemplary community leader and churchman, "a mighty fine man." David died at age sixty-two in 2011.

James and Mary's daughter, Martha Manulik, also blossomed into a person of ennobling character, forthright and plainspoken.

Like his Midland forebears, Mims is a community builder, sustainer, and one who encourages others. "Most of us need to be encouraged, not bad-mouthed," he says. Steeped in scripture, he is mindful of the exhortation to be "kind to one another, tenderhearted, forgiving one another."

Self-effacing and endowed with a charming wit, James Mims allows that "everyone has skeletons in their closet" and most of his are buried. As he put it, "What I say goes because I've outlived all the witnesses."

"We've got some wonderful pioneers who built this Western country," Mims said. He believes Midland today is a "good place to live," but that the community "does not now have the typical [West Texas] small-town characteristics and charm, the charisma, the intimacy, the flair of innocence without pretense. It is too big, and that goes with the territory."

As storyteller-historian, he delights in Midland folktales, including one dating to the late 1920s after brothers Samuel and Harvey Sloan had opened a flying service at Sloan Field in 1927.

An Army Air Corps major had flown over Midland, mostly a ranching-farming town of about 5,000 folks, and "hadn't seen anything" in his approach to Sloan Field, Mims said in recounting the tale. "It was a little old town in those days."

As the story goes, Kenneth Ambrose, chairman of the Midland Chamber of Commerce's aviation committee, happened to greet the major.

"Mr. Ambrose," the aviator asked, "how big is Midland?"

"Oh, Major," Ambrose replied with candor, "it's about the size of Chicago. It just hasn't filled out yet."

Ed Todd is a longtime columnist and writer for the Midland Reporter-Telegram.

Part Two: People of Integrity

The Morales Family

When Jerry Morales was elected mayor of Midland on November 5, 2013, the victory represented a culmination of more than fifty years of work and civic involvement by one of the most recognizable family names in the West Texas Hispanic community.

Morales, the first Hispanic mayor in the history of Midland, will point to his parents, and his aunt Paula, as being among the most important pieces to his and his family's achievements and successes in Midland.

While Morales's mother, Celia, taught him all she knew about business finance, and his father bestowed the importance of ethics, hard work, and how-to, none of the Morales family's achievements would have been possible were it not for Paula Muñoz's decision to move from Chicago to Midland in the 1950s. When she did, she opened El Nopal, at the time the first Tejano record shop between El Paso and Fort Worth. Morales called his aunt the Casey Casem of Hispanic music. Artists in the business sought her out and considered her endorsement of their music as high an honor as they could achieve.

When Paula Muñoz convinced Felipe Morales, his wife, Celia, and even other Morales family members to move to West Texas, that's when the family reputation began to grow.

Before long, the Moraleses operated three businesses at Big Spring and Neely—Aunt Paula's record shop, Felipe Morales's first insurance company, and a beauty shop co-operated by Paula and Celia.

Today the family is best known not just for the family insurance business, run now by Jerry's sister, Cynthia Maes, and her husband, Greg, but even more so for Gerardo's Casita, one of the longest-standing Mexican restaurants in Midland. When the eatery opened in the 1960s, it was one of only three in town, but the family made sure it did its research before cooking its first burrito. The Moraleses literally drove from town to town in Texas for a year, asking those in the industry how they ran their restaurants. When they had heard enough answers, they returned to Midland for good and opened what was, at the time, Gerardo's Casita.

Part Two: People of Integrity

Jerry Morales still remembers driving around the state when, as Celia said recently, fuel for such a trip was five or ten dollars a tankful.

The interesting thing about the Morales family was they admit when they developed the idea to open a Mexican restaurant, they knew nothing about how to do it. After that one year, though, they had all they needed to turn it into one of Midland's longest continuously operated businesses, restaurant or otherwise.

Potential investors said before they could approve a business loan, the Moraleses needed a business plan. That's when the road trip that would change their lives became reality.

Novert Morales, Jerry and Cindy's brother, remains the only Morales family member who lives elsewhere—he is an attorney in Austin—but still visits family here frequently.

Both Jerry and Cindy have taken the traits instilled by their culture-rich family and used them to better the community. While Cindy remains a successful businessperson, Jerry's political aspirations took root in 2008 when he ran and lost in his first race to be on the Midland city council. He won his second race for an at-large position, and was elected mayor in 2013.

Morales said the biggest challenges that lie just ahead for Midland are effectively handling its population surge and dealing with offshoot issues such as available housing, adequate roadways, and infrastructure.

Almost fifty years ago, Felipe Morales endured slurs because of his willing involvement with and in the white community. Today, the Morales's son serves as mayor, their daughter is a noted insurance representative, and their other son is an attorney. The Morales successes make for a happy pinnacle to a family that has devoted itself to all communities in Midland.

—Jimmy Patterson

Part Two: People of Integrity

Joan Nobles
by June Cowden

Joan Stocks Nobles and I have been close friends since we first met around 1948 as brides of ranchers living near Midland. I had moved here from a ranch near Tuscola, after marrying Frank Cowden Jr., and was living on the M Bar ranch near Goldsmith. Joan moved here from Kent and the Stocks family ranch near Fort Davis, and had recently married Gerald Nobles. She was living northwest of Midland on the Nobles' L Bar ranch. High Sky Children's ranch was once part of the Nobles ranch. Frank and Gerald were first cousins.

As young ranching couples, we gathered socially on the weekends—the men held roping contests—and we all visited and caught up on life since our last gathering. We ended the day with a big "supper" in the evening. Mary and Buster Cole, Harriet and Roy Parks (later Harriet Faudree), and the Wyches were among other ranching families who were always in attendance along with all the children.

Joan was always a country girl at heart and loved being in the country, especially down around Fort Davis, where she ended up living for a while as an adult. She loved horses from the moment she learned to ride at three years of age. She was rounding up cattle with her brother Banky at the age of five on their family ranch, and she always owned a horse and loved teaching her children to ride. Resilience, fortitude, and a love of the outdoors are traits that all remind me of Joan.

Joan is a fabulous cook. My family always looked forward to Sunday lunch at their home on Cuthbert, where we dined on her homemade rolls and ice cream. My daughter and I use her recipes to this day. Later in life she owned restaurants in San Angelo and Fort Davis and was director of the Midland Woman's Club at Hogan Park. Joan was always generous with her time and culinary skills.

Many of the ranching couples eventually moved into town and still gathered with their families on the weekends for fun. Picnicking at Hogan (the only park at that time) and playing softball were the primary forms of entertainment, and all the children joined in. There were no softball fields; we used boxes and rocks for bases.

Part Two: People of Integrity

The biggest social season of the year was rodeo time early every June. Everyone rode in the parade through downtown Midland, and many rode in the Grand Entry, which began each evening's events. Of course Joan was always front and center. Ranching parties might include "son-of-a-gun stew" if the rancher had recently slaughtered a calf—a very rich stew similar to menudo, which was cooked all day long over an outdoor fire.

Joan is strong, independent, and caring, and is always there if you need help. She is devoted to her family and especially to her grandchildren. She never missed a camp meeting at Bloys Camp Meeting near Fort Davis. She had a family cabin and was there every August for the week of long nondenominational prayer meetings, Bible schools, and services in the open-sided Tabernacle. Camp meetings originated when ranchers lived too far from churches to attend services regularly. Once a year a traveling preacher came through an area, and all the ranching families gathered to hold weddings, christenings, and church services.

When I think of Joan, I think of strength, horses, and great food.

June Cowden is a longtime friend of Joan Nobles.

Part Two: People of Integrity

Gary Painter

History is made every day. Much of it goes unnoticed and too much of it unrecorded. Yet Midland is in the midst of a truly historic time, and not just because of the energy industry and the benefits of its most prosperous economy ever. With each day that Midland County sheriff Gary Painter climbs into his cruiser, drives to the jailhouse, and punches a time clock, we are living during one of the longest reigns of any sheriff in the history of Midland County. But it almost didn't happen.

In the early 1980s, Painter was hired as a jailer by Dallas Smith, who was then sheriff. He worked in the jail for four months, moved to criminal investigations, and later became a patrol lieutenant before resigning in February 1984 to run against Smith, a man Painter said was "hard to get along with."

"I prayed about it for quite awhile and decided the best thing I could do was to run for the office," Painter said.

Painter called County Judge Bill Ahders and informed him of his intentions to run. It was the last day of filing for the 1984 elections. Bill Shaner, Midland County Republican Party chairman, also worked in the oil business, and on that last day he was 160 miles away on an oil rig.

"I went by the sheriff's office and told the dispatcher I quit, that I was running for sheriff," said Painter. He handed over the keys to his cruiser, climbed into his car, and drove 160 miles to see Shaner on this drilling unit. Painter arrived well after five p.m. to inform the chairman that he wanted to file to run for sheriff. A law enforcement newcomer in Midland County, Painter had submitted both his filing fee and application. Shaner told Painter he had missed the five-o'clock deadline. "When I got to the drilling site, Shaner told me he wasn't sure if he could accept the filing papers," said Painter.[1]

Painter called the State Bar of Texas and hired an attorney who specialized in election law, paid him $5,000, and filed a lawsuit against Midland County because Shaner refused to accept his application and fee. The basis for the lawsuit was Shaner's being unavailable to potential candidates on the last day of filing.

Part Two: People of Integrity

Ultimately, the lawsuit was fast-tracked because of time sensitivity. When it went before the Texas Supreme Court, justices found in Painter's favor. "They ruled that somebody had to be present to accept the application," Painter said. "If they weren't there and that prevented me from running, that would have been a violation of my constitutional rights."[2]

In the next legislative session in 1985, the legislature passed a law stating that political party chairmen or secretaries had to be present in the elections office until the deadline on the last day of filing.

Painter's legal action led to the new law being created, and because of that, the publicity that resulted over the next thirty days would play in his favor with the voters of Midland County. Painter beat Smith in the 1984 primary. Smith later lost to Painter again in the general election that same year after supporters waged an unsuccessful write-in campaign for Smith.

"The night of the election in November 1984 after I had won, I got in my car and drove around until three or four o'clock in the morning, to the county line north, then south, then east, then west, just to get the full breadth of what I had gotten myself into. It wasn't anything I wasn't comfortable with."[3]

—*Jimmy Patterson*

Part Two: People of Integrity

Jess Parrish
by Delnor Poss

On January 16, 1977, I was hired as head basketball coach/athletic director at Midland College by Dr. Al G. Langford. Dr. Langford told me my primary objective was to build the top community college athletic program in the nation. We immediately set out to accomplish this objective. When Dr. Langford retired in 1981, I felt a great deal of uncertainty about the future of the college's athletic program.

However, when Dr. Jess Parrish was hired as college president, he made it known immediately that he wanted to continue with the building of a National Junior College Athletic Association (NJCAA) program. He wanted to be a national power in all sports. At my first meeting with Jess, as he preferred to be addressed, I found him to be down-to-earth and easy to communicate with. It was clear from the outset that under Jess's leadership we had a direct line of communication from our office to his office. His management style was relaxed, and each person with a leadership role was given a job to do. Jess let you do the job with your individual management skills. His gentle but firm West Texas personality allowed him to integrate into the Midland community in a quick, solid way.

Jess soon became a friend as well as chief executive officer of the college. He was adept in setting up planning sessions with all of his departmental heads, both in groups and one-on-one with him. Jess and his wife, Norma, were our number one fans of Chaparral Athletics and attended National Championship events with enthusiasm and gusto in all sports. Norma is intelligent, personable, and gracious. She has undoubtedly contributed to her husband's success by being extremely supportive of all his endeavors.

Jess was dedicated to every sector of the educational process at Midland College in academic and vocational programs as well as athletics. He implemented a sense of cohesiveness in his faculty and staff on every level and in every sector of the college. He was receptive to his employees' ideas and readily changed his view if one of his employees had a better idea or solution.

Jess stressed to all of us the need for community involvement on all levels. He himself served as chairman of the Midland Chamber of Commerce and as chairman of the United Way of Midland, as well as serving on the boards of many important community-oriented endeavors.

We as employees felt that Jess was "one of us," but we never doubted who the boss was at all times. He was a great president to work with because you always knew how you stood with him. Jess is blessed with a very active sense of humor and a quick wit. He had an ability to correct you without your realizing you had been corrected. No matter what, he was loyal to you and your cause.

Jess is a true West Texan. He grew up in Ballinger through high school, taught elementary school in San Angelo, received his degree at Texas Tech University, and was very much involved in the development of Midland College as it is today. Jess was instrumental in beginning the college's nursing program in the facility that now bears his name.

Today Jess and Norma Parrish remain good friends of ours, and I am honored to have served at Midland College under his very capable leadership.

Delnor Poss is longtime athletic director and golf coach at Midland College.

Part Two: People of Integrity

Wes Perry

When Midland native Wes Perry was elected mayor in 2008, many people did not realize that he was not only stepping into the time-consuming position he had rightfully won, but he was also becoming the city's interim, volunteer city manager.

Midland was without a city manager at the time of Perry's election. It was after Rick Menchaca left Midland and before the hiring of Courtney Sharp when Wes walked in to his partners at EOG Resources and told them he needed to take a leave of absence. Perry ended up being away from his day job for almost six months so that he could tend to matters of the city. Getting off to a good start was imperative for the newly elected mayor.

Perry served two terms as mayor after he had served a three-year term as city councilman. His devotion to the city is as obvious as his engaging personality. Many Midland mayors have represented much over the years, but if the example we wish to convey is that we are a friendly bunch, Wes Perry is indeed the face of our elected officials.

He guided Midland through good times, challenging times, and heartache. After the horrific train accident in November 2012, Midland was at one of the lowest points in its history. The accident had taken the lives of four veterans who were in town to be honored for their sacrifice to our country. Perry told a city councilman he didn't want the community to fall apart and he didn't want the national media to portray Midland in a negative light. He took charge of the city and its collective morale at that dark time and provided perhaps the finest example of leadership a mayor had done in recent town history. During the days following the accident, Perry said that the city was going to stay strong, pray together, and stay together as one big family. He led those prayers himself and provided the leadership needed by a town that had suffered a critical blow.

Perry did not escape his tenure unscathed, though. He was on the receiving end of criticism for appearing not to be on the side of the oil industry during debates on drilling within the city limits when he voted on the side of surface owners. He has also been criticized for his real estate holdings but has repeatedly abstained from

Part Two: People of Integrity

votes that would directly affect any of his personal or business holdings.

The stories of leadership in local government do not include the stories of his integrity, or his Christian beliefs and actions as an individual, husband, and father. His business character and personal character are one and the same. Perry and wife, Roni, choose to keep private all they do for charitable organizations, churches, schools, and suffering individuals. What they do for those they help, though, often has lifelong positive implications.

Roni and Wes Perry have invested in the educations of countless young people who otherwise would be unable to attend college. But Perry and his wife do not simply write a check. They invite the students they help to their home, and when their educations are completed, the Perrys attend the students' graduation ceremonies.

There are few stories of integrity and generosity in Midland quite as all-encompassing and well-rounded as the example provided by Wes Perry and his family.

—Jimmy Patterson

Part Two: People of Integrity

Frank Pickrell

Frank Pickrell was not among the first pioneers who moved to Midland to help forge the upstart railroad town. In fact, Pickrell wasn't from Midland at all. He was a businessman from El Paso, but his importance to Midland as the community it would one day become is immeasurable.

It all began when a man named Rupert P. Ricker, intent on making a name for himself in the oil business, gave up. Ricker was fresh out of the U.S. Army when he moved home to Big Lake. By visiting wealthy businessmen in Fort Worth, he attempted to obtain financing to drill for oil. He needed just over $43,000, an amount that would allow him to drill on 431,360 acres in Crockett, Reagan, and Upton counties. After three weeks, though, Ricker had not found a single investor. In fact, he was not only rejected, but laughed at and scorned as well.

Discouraged by his inability to find funding, Ricker headed to the train station in Fort Worth to hop aboard the first train home. It was there that he ran into Frank Pickrell and his business partner, Hayman Krupp. Not twelve hours before Ricker's chance meeting with the two businessmen, Pickrell and Krupp had each made the conscious decision to seek their fortunes in the oil business. The two men had just returned from Burkburnett and were on the way to Ranger to investigate drilling opportunities. Ricker had been Sgt. Pickrell's commanding officer in the company in which they served together during World War I. But on this day, it was the actions of the man with fewer stripes on his uniform sleeve—Pickrell—who would change Ricker's fortunes forever.

Pickrell and Krupp pooled their money, bought Ricker's 431,360 acres of University Lands, and formed Texon Oil & Land Company. Together the two men drilled a test well, and it became the famed Santa Rita No. 1. The well became the birth of the industry in West Texas and brought a great deal of revenue to the University Lands system, whose lease fees have allowed the University of Texas System and the Texas A&M University System to be among the world leaders in higher education.

Pickrell, according to *Santa Rita*, published by the Texas State Historical Association, was either lucky, clever, or both for his decision to put a well on the

Part Two: People of Integrity

3,000-acre spot west of Big Lake in what became the company camp of Texon.

"Frank Pickrell's feat certainly ranks with those of Dad Joiner in East Texas, Col. Humphries at Mexia and perhaps A. F. Lucas at Spindletop. He brought wealth to the University of Texas and, if truth is a part of education, that institution should be the first to acknowledge—merely as a matter of history—the truth," said David O'Donoghue, a Fort Worth geologist.[1]

Pickrell liked to note that geologists and oil companies that preceded him condemned West Texas. His foresight and financing of the Texon Oil and Land Company, and the drilling of the Santa Rita wells, he said, allowed him to "pioneer in ideas as well as accomplishment."

Born in Ennis in 1890, Pickrell was orphaned as a young boy. He went to work for an uncle in his soda fountain, but the work didn't appeal to him, so he found work more suited to him at the First National Bank in El Paso. It was truly Pickrell's investment money that led to the discovery of the Santa Rita, and as a result, placed him among the most prominent members of Midland's long history. He would later admit, "There is one thing you must understand: I had never seen an oil well. I did not know what an oil well was. I knew they flowed but I did not know what you did with them. I did not know how you got the oil, what you did with it, how you sold it. I did not have the slightest idea."[2]

In 1968, forty-five years after Pickrell and Krupp's investment in Reagan County came in a gusher, Pickrell became the first person to be elected to the Permian Basin Petroleum Hall of Fame.

—*Jimmy Patterson*

Part Two: People of Integrity

Eileen Piwetz
by Joan Baskin

Because Eileen combines efficiency, talent, and versatility, she makes doing many jobs at once look easy. Her leadership guided our first-class Midland College School of Nursing.

Recognizing her unique abilities, the college named her vice president (of everything). Her main duty was "development": the fine art of identifying, encouraging, and appreciating donors. And did she do a bang-up job! When President David Daniels and Eileen called on you, you might as well start writing your check.

After Midland College was established in 1972, the college waited more than thirty-five years before returning to the voters for a bond to build needed facilities. In the interim, more than a half-dozen structures (classrooms, dining hall, dormitories, a chapel, even a bridge) were added to the campus, all paid for by private donations.

And guess who was pivotal in raising that money? Our Eileen.

Eileen organized and oversaw the highly successful Davidson Lecture and Cowan Performing Arts Series, and made sure it was generously funded by adding the Friends of the Series donors. She planned the various celebrations for college birthdays, instituted the program for "First in the Family to Attend College," and helped launch the Advanced Technology Center.

Every new and exciting future plan for Midland college seemed to end up in Eileen's portfolio, and she took on each new effort with her usual enthusiasm and graciousness.

My husband, Pat, liked to say that the marriage between Midland College and Midland citizens was the longest and happiest on record. Eileen Piwetz was undoubtedly the magic matchmaker.

Joan Baskin is a longtime community volunteer and philanthropist in Midland.

Part Two: People of Integrity

Foy Proctor
by Pat McDaniel

Foy Proctor and his wife, Hahl, were among those who chose to invest in their community and ensure that it prospered.

Foy Proctor was born to L. C. and Rieta Proctor on September 28, 1896, in Runnels County. The Proctor family made its way west into Midland County in 1907. Foy and his older brother, Leonard, attended Midland schools. Leonard graduated in 1911 and Foy in 1913 from Midland High School. Foy also went on to the newly opened Midland Christian College for another year.

The brothers Proctor then began their ranching career on leased land in Gaines County. The demands of a war in Europe prompted both brothers to enlist in the Marine Corps. They managed to stay together after being shipped overseas and survived the "war to end all wars." Following their service to country, they both returned to Midland and took up their ranching reins again.

Utilizing the combination of hard work and honest words, they prospered. At one time they had under lease most of the land between Midland and Rankin. They owned a sizable herd of cattle and nearly 30,000 head of sheep. In their spare time, they became an unbeatable combination on the regional rodeo circuit, as they both were unmatched horsemen.

Eventually they went their separate ways. Foy became the major cattle buyer and trader in the region. For many years he would consistently ship anywhere from 15,000 to 50,000 head of cattle a year. During one five-day period in the early 1930s, he oversaw the loading of 15,000 head on railroad stock cars from West Texas to Nebraska. The first trainload of 3,000 head had not reached Nebraska before the last train was loaded at Stanton. He remained legendary in range-cattle circles.

During his lifetime Foy Proctor operated the historic Chicago or C Ranch between Midland and Andrews; the Channing Ranch in Hartley County, a former part of the XIT Ranch; the 3-Links Ranch at Wilcox, Arizona; and the Magdalena Ranch in New Mexico.

In 1922 Foy married Hahl Carr Mitchell. She had been raised in Roswell, New Mexico, in a pioneer settler family. She became his constant companion on the rodeo and cutting horse circuits. Hahl had an exceptional voice and was often called upon to sing for local wedding and funerals. She and her woman friends were always on hand to act as the welcoming committee for any and all dignitaries and guests that came to town for the many chamber of commerce–style town promotions.

She served for many years in the First Methodist Church choir, as well as local civic clubs such as the Minuet Club, the Midland Women's Club, the Fine Arts Club, and many other cultural groups. She also became an avid contract bridge player.

Mr. Proctor served on the founding board of the Midland Memorial Hospital, the board of the First National Bank of Midland, the Midland City Council, the school district board, a savings and loan board, the Community Chest Board, and the Midland Fair Co. board, where he and others held world championship rodeos for many years. He was involved in many other civic offering that presented Midland in a positive light.

If you go to the Haley Memorial Library and scan the pages of Hahl Proctor's 1944 diary, you will find a recurring theme: partnership with Foy. She made entries about feed deliveries, letters from cattle customers, snowfall and rainfall amounts, shipping dates, and branding reports. You will see how she read out loud to Foy the best seller of the day in nightly installments. It is evident that they were a true team.

When Mrs. Proctor died in 1972, the year of their fiftieth wedding anniversary, Foy was naturally affected. But not broken. He jumped back on his horse and resumed his role as rancher, banker, businessman, and community builder. These two community role models were always press-shy and behind-the-scenes philanthropists, but were always ready to lend a public hand in the development and progress of a progressive community.

Foy Proctor had his ardent admirers. Rancher Tom Linebery said, "Foy Proctor was the best judge of a man, a cow and a horse that I have ever known." Clarence Scharbauer Jr. said, "Foy Proctor has forgotten more about the cow business than most of us will ever know."

Pat McDaniel is director of the Haley Library and Western Heritage Center in Midland

Part Two: People of Integrity

Judy Rankin

Amid the chaos and havoc left behind in the wake of the biblical flood in Midland on May 9, 1968, there came at least one positive outcome: the deluge gave a young professional golfer the desire to play again.

Judy Rankin had played the LPGA event in Midland several times during the 1960s, including in 1967. In fact it was during the Pro-Am that year when she met Walter "Yippy" Rankin. After a brief courtship the two were married, and a family came soon. Their son Tuey Rankin was still a newborn when the tour stopped again in Midland in 1968. Judy hadn't played at all in 1968, and in fact wasn't so sure she'd ever play professionally again.

"I just wanted to be a married mom. I didn't even know if I had the desire to play anymore," she said.

Judy and Yippy talked and decided she would play in the Midland LPGA tour event in May 1968. The two considered it a kind of experiment to see if perhaps there was still an interest in Judy playing professionally, or if she would instead become a full-time, stay-at-home mother.

Judy wasn't sure what to expect from her game since she hadn't played in so long. The day before the tournament opened, though, it turned out that no one was really sure about their game. A freak storm that flooded Midland dropped torrents of rain on Hogan Park Golf Course and even altered the layout. The No. 17, par-five hole was shortened to a par-three because of the high water. Several other portions of the course were uncomfortably soggy to the assembled professionals.

As inconvenient as it might have been for many LPGA players, the astonishing deluge either directly or indirectly altered Judy Rankin's career path.

Even today she won't speculate whether the course changes had anything to do with her finish in the tournament standings, but Judy's final score for fifty-four holes landed her a fourth-place finish—and brought her and her new husband both surprise and joy. The finish propelled her confidence and gave her what amounted to a second chance at a professional career.

Judy increased the number of tour stops in which she played in 1968 and the years that followed. She even recorded her first tournament victory later in 1968, in Corpus Christi. Her fourth-place finishes improved to third place, and before long she was notching more and more wins on the LPGA. Judy peaked in the mid-1970s: 1973 was a big year, as were 1975 and 1977. She won twenty-six tour events, topping the money list in both 1976 and 1977, and finished on the Top 10 earnings list eleven different years. Judy was a two-time LPGA Player of the Year and was the recipient of the Vare Trophy for lowest scoring average in three different years.

As decorated as Judy is as a player, she is now perhaps equally well known as a commentator. She started on ABC's golf coverage, and is now with ESPN and the Golf Channel. Her second career as a commentator has now spanned some thirty-four years.

Judy Rankin was born and raised in St. Louis, and in April 2013 was awarded a star on the St. Louis Walk of Fame. With an established Midland oilman as a husband and a son who grew up to be on the Midland Lee and Texas Tech football teams, and later a West Texas high school coach, she has made Midland her home, opting to live here instead of a home that most anyone else would have probably chosen over the desert of the Permian Basin.

"We had a place on a golf course in California once when Tuey was in school," Rankin said. "As nice as it was, it was never going to be home for us."

—Jimmy Patterson

PART TWO: PEOPLE OF INTEGRITY

John and Rosalind Redfern
by Rosalind Redfern Grover

Many people from the East Coast came to Midland to seek their fortunes in the oil business. They brought with them a strong work ethic, certain expectations for schools, and a desire for cultural advantages. A few came earlier than the rush of the 1950s, and two such people were John J. Redfern, Jr., who was born on October 4, 1912, in Jersey City, New Jersey, across the Hudson River from Lower Manhattan, and Rosalind Kapps, who was born farther up on the Hudson, in Troy, New York, on April 13, 1913. These were my parents.

My father graduated with a degree in civil engineering from Rensselaer Polytechnic Institute, where he was on the swim team. He enjoyed swimming all of his life and passed on his love of it to his three children and his three grandchildren. My mother graduated with a double major in Latin and French from State University of New York, where she was a college beauty queen. They did not know each other in college, but met at a dance after they graduated, during the Depression. My father was working as a plumbing-supply salesman (the only job he could find at the time), and my mother was teaching school. They married in June 1936.

My father had become interested in what he was reading about the oil business in the periodicals at the time, and after an exploratory trip to West Texas, he persuaded my mother that they could live for five years on a $10,000 inheritance from his grandfather while he tried his hand at the oil business. Their families thought they were more or less crazy, but my parents always considered it a great adventure. Father audited courses in geology and petroleum engineering at the University of Oklahoma and, after studying all the maps, determined that Midland would be the center for the oil business in West Texas. So they packed up their household and their infant son and moved there in the spring of 1939.

They lived on a dirt road on N Street, just south of West Elementary, and had two daughters in the next four years. Across the street was the family of Harvey and Harriet Herd. After the end of World War II, Father and Harvey Herd formed a partnership, Redfern and Herd, which began buying royalties and drilling deals in

Texas and New Mexico. It was a successful partnership, and the families remained close friends all of their lives, but in the early 1960s, the partnership was dissolved so that each partner could pursue his own opportunities. Father went on to found Redfern Oil Company, which was merged with Flag Oil Corporation of Delaware to form Flag-Redfern Oil Company, operating as a large independent oil and gas exploration company until shortly after my father's death in 1986.

Both of my parents were active in the community from the beginning and remained connected to it until the end of their lives. Father made time to work with nonprofits and was instrumental in bringing Little League baseball to Midland. For many years he was the chief fund-raiser for the Junior Baseball Association. He was chairman of the Midland Memorial Foundation and the first chairman of Midland Community Theatre's board of trustees, and he served on many other boards as well. He was one of Midland Memorial Hospital's most successful fund-raisers. He also served for many years as a trustee of Rensselaer Polytechnic Institute. He was inducted into the Permian Basin Petroleum Museum's Hall of Fame in 1986.

My mother ran for the school board and won in the early 1950s. When the decision to desegregate the schools in *Brown v. Board of Education* came down in 1954, she was on the school board and was a strong supporter of civil rights. She told me the board held a meeting in the auditorium of North Elementary and let the community come to speak its mind about what the board ought to do. The meeting lasted from seven in the evening until the wee hours of the following morning. Every citizen had his or her say. The board then went into executive session and voted immediately and unanimously to desegregate the schools, beginning with the first grade.

Mother was instrumental in bringing libraries to the elementary schools in Midland and remained a staunch advocate for libraries her entire life. Periodically over the years, the Commissioner's Court would complain about spending money on the library and threaten to close it. Library supporters would always call Mother and ask her to make an appearance in the court to argue their case. The commissioners were no match for her regal bearing and powerful intellect, and the library escaped the chopping block yet another time.

No one ever said no to my mother. She was a staunch advocate for women's rights and always made up her own mind. (My father said, during the women's liberation movement of the 1960s, that Mother didn't need to be liberated; she was born liberated!) She lived to be almost ninety and never stopped caring about Midland. She was completely bedridden for several months before her death in December 2002, but that November she got out of bed and into her winter overcoat

Part Two: People of Integrity

and wheelchair, and she went to the polling booth in the mall. With a shaky hand, she voted in favor of the controversial school bond because, she said, "Every vote will count. These are our children. They are Midland's future."

I asked my parents once whether they ever regretted coming to Texas, and they both laughed and said no. They did not miss the East. They loved the openness of our land. They loved the sky. They loved being able to see the horizon. They made many contributions to many things in Midland, both through their philanthropy and through their service, and they won many awards for it. But through it all, they remained the people they had always been: down-to-earth, unassuming, and unpretentious, two young people on a great adventure. They were wonderful role models who have provided me with a lifetime of inspiration.

***Rosalind Grover** is a Midland philanthropist, supporter of many causes, and daughter of John L. and Rosalind Redfern.*

Part Two: People of Integrity

The Scharbauer Family
by Linda Cowden

Strength is a theme running through the families who founded Midland. Such characteristics as independence, perseverance, resilience, foresight, a willingness to take risks, a sense of community and family, and a love of God and country were exhibited in the ranching families who came to this area, settled permanently, and left their legacy through multiple generations who still contribute to our community. Midland has produced a preponderance of outstanding citizens who have gone on to national acclaim.

Probably the best example of these characteristics and the legacy of such a family, now passed down through five generations, began with Clarence Scharbauer Sr. The Scharbauer family has had enormous influence on the development of Midland as a center for cattle and banking in the 1800s and a petroleum center in the 1900s. They are best known today for their philanthropy. Clarence Sr. was greatly admired and respected in early Midland. He was instrumental in starting First National Bank, which dominated the Midland banking industry until the early 1980s. I never had the privilege of knowing Clarence Sr., but I have known all the other members of the Scharbauer family, beginning with Ruth Cowden Scharbauer, my great-aunt.

Clarence Sr. and Ruth lived in the penthouse of the Scharbauer hotel, the center of social and business life in Midland. In 1954 I remember attending a Cowden family reunion in the elaborate ballroom of the hotel. Ruth was dressed to the nines and a regal presence in the room. I was quite impressed. The lobby of the hotel was the center of many cattle deals as well as a gathering place for the men to socialize and bemoan the frequent droughts. The implosion of the Scharbauer Hotel in 1973 was attended by every red-blooded West Texan.

The Scharbauer Hotel was the first time the Scharbauer family indelibly changed the skyline of the Permian Basin. The Scharbauer Sports Complex, Ruth Scharbauer Elementary School, and the Dorothy and Clarence Scharbauer Jr. Patient Tower at Midland Memorial Hospital followed through the generosity of the Scharbauer family.

PART TWO: PEOPLE OF INTEGRITY

When Clarence Sr. died in 1942, Clarence Jr. returned from Texas A&M and moved in with his mother. With Foy Proctor as a mentor, he took over his father's ranching and business interests and moved these forward with the same skill, determination, and foresight that his father exhibited.

Today his sons run these businesses. I have had the privilege of working philanthropically with most members of the family: the Museum of the Southwest with Clarence Jr.; cochair with Chris of the 1985 Midland Centennial celebration; and the foundation board of Midland College, and the 2007 Midland College bond campaign, with Clarence III.

Their wives, who all epitomize Southern manners and graciousness, have also contributed their time and resources to the Permian Basin. Now the fourth generation of Scharbauers is ready to step up to the plate.

The Scharbauer generosity and love for all that is West Texas has held my admiration for many years, but what stands out above everything else is the old adage, "Their word is as good as a written contract."

Linda Cowden is a sixth-generation West Texas Cowden and a local philanthropist.

Part Two: People of Integrity

David L. Smith
by Herb Cartwright

James I. Trott was George Abell's petroleum engineer and early guiding hand of the Abell-Hanger Foundation. Mr. Trott often said the smartest thing he ever did was to hire David L. Smith as the foundation's executive director.

One would have to agree with that statement, as through the years David L. Smith's name has become interchangeable with that of the Abell-Hanger Foundation. David has always been quick to focus the attention on Gladys and George Abell and their philanthropy. Without their sense of community building and generosity, the foundation would not exist.

One of the most difficult challenges with a private foundation is remaining true to its donors' intent though times and needs change, never losing sight of what they felt were areas important to support. While performing numerous other functions important in the development of the foundation, David has always remained true to the Abells' intent and continued the leadership they exhibited during their lives.

The best example of this was in 2009, when we as a country experienced the Great Recession, aptly named since the name "Great Depression" was already taken. The Abell-Hanger Foundation's investments suffered huge losses, as did those of all our peers, and the state of Texas was cutting the funding of many nonprofit agencies. This landscape presented the foundation with its greatest challenge in two forms: how do we respond to the community's needs, while acting prudently with the foundation's assets?

David's leadership guided the staff and board through a process of cutting expenditures without detriment to the foundation and reducing our grant giving to only agencies providing essential human services with demonstrated financial need.

During this same period, the foundation was presented the opportunity to support a capital campaign of Midland Memorial Hospital. The Abells had always been supporters of the hospital; without a doubt they would want their foundation to participate. Even though we had not yet recovered financially, with David's

PART TWO: PEOPLE OF INTEGRITY

leadership the board approved a $7 million grant, two and a half times larger than the largest gift to date by the foundation.

I think George and Gladys Abell both would agree that one to the best things Mr. Trott ever did was to hire David L. Smith. They would be pleased with his leadership of their foundation.

Herb Cartwright *is the comptroller of the Abell-Hanger Foundation.*

Part Two: People of Integrity

Charles Spence

The first time I met Charlie Spence, he shook my hand like it had never been shaken before. Many other times I have seen Charlie over the course of the last twenty-five years, he has always given me that familiarly firm grip. In the old days, such a grip was associated with character. My father always told me those kinds of high-integrity shakes always come with a square-in-the-eye look. Charlie has always done that, too.

Charlie Spence was a sort of father figure to me when we moved to Midland, a town my own dad had to convince me would be a good place to call home when we moved here back in 1988. I was fortunate enough to work at the *Midland Reporter-Telegram* for the better part of Charlie's time as publisher there. He always offered a friendly face and a "How are you?" And he would always call you by your first name. Those greetings came whenever he was in the newspaper office, which was most days. Other days, he was firmly planted somewhere in town, doing some type of community service work for the betterment of Midland.

He's a lifetime member of the United Way of Midland. A great amount of Charlie's community efforts were accomplished through the United Way, where he served not only as campaign chair, but also as president of the board. Charlie has always been a hands-on, in-the-trenches volunteer, not simply a check writer. While those are certainly important, too, Charlie gave his time and, with the help of Betty Simmons and Debbie Bounds at the newspaper, always made United Way campaign season fun, with barbeques, contests, games, and the like.

Charlie was also a family-friendly boss. Once when I was fortunate enough to have been honored by the Hearst Corporation, a trip to New York came with that honor. But our infant son was experiencing serious medical concerns. Making the trip to the Hearst offices in New York was not an option, Charlie told me, as long as my attention was needed at home.

The Buffalo Trail Council of the Boy Scouts recognized Charlie with its Distinguished Citizen Award in 2009. He volunteered for the council's advisory board, but his choice as Distinguished Citizen was for more reasons than that. Charlie has

Part Two: People of Integrity

served on more than thirty nonprofit boards in Midland, and was a strong voice for the Midland Chamber of Commerce.

Honoring its former publisher, the *Midland Reporter-Telegram* editorial board wrote of Charlie:

> The employees of the Reporter-Telegram have witnessed the Spence passion for public service and community spirit; he was publisher of the newspaper for 23 years before his retirement in 2007. We, too, have seen Spence at work and can speak firsthand of his dedication, not only to this newspaper, but to our community as well. We can't think of a better person to be added to the growing list of distinguished citizens the Buffalo Trail Council has honored over the years. The impressive list includes all kinds of individuals from just about every level of service, ranging from governors, sports figures, journalists, military leaders, judges, and philanthropists to other movers and shakers of West Texas.[1]

Conrad Coleman, son of Dr. Viola Coleman, told me a story about Charlie once. Several years ago, one of Dr. Coleman's employees was found to have stolen from her. The embezzlement wrecked Dr. Coleman's credit standing. Through the Midland grapevine, Charlie heard that Dr. Coleman's washer and dryer had broken down and she was unable to purchase replacements because her credit had been declined. Charlie went to see Dr. Coleman and gave her his own credit card so that she could purchase the replacement household items. Dr. Coleman thanked Charlie, but politely declined his offer. The two gestures sum up both of them perfectly.

—*Jimmy Patterson*

Part Two: People of Integrity

Dr. John B. Thomas
by Henry E. Meadows Jr.

John Thomas was born January 31, 1878, in Dudley, Texas, and grew up on a farm in Callahan County. He attended college at Simmons University in Abilene and went on to the University of Texas Medical School in Galveston. He graduated in 1902, after having survived the destructive Galveston hurricane of 1900. At the start of his career, Dr. Thomas interned at John Sealy Hospital and practiced briefly in Abilene before accepting an association with Drs. W. K. Curtis and Woods W. Lynch of Midland in 1905.

The offices of the young doctors were located in a frame building at the corner of Wall and Loraine Streets, where they established the first hospital. A few years later, Dr. Thomas, Clarence Scharbauer Sr., and John Scharbauer bought the old Llano Hotel across the street and remodeled the second floor into a hospital complete with an operating room modern for that time.

Dr. Thomas married Read Hurt of Big Spring on May 28, 1908. Read was the daughter of Dr. John Hurt and Lilly M. Read. Dr. Hurt was a physician for the Texas and Pacific Railroad from 1887 until his retirement forty-four years later. Read was a graduate of Potter College in Bowling Green, Kentucky, and from Mary Nash College in Sherman, Texas. The Thomases had four children: Lillian (1910–1915), Lucile (1911–2004), Read (1916–1989), and John Jr. (1919–1945). John Jr. served as a lieutenant in General George S. Patton's Third Army during World War II and was killed in action (two Purple Hearts, Bronze Star) in Germany just three weeks prior to the German surrender. His remains were returned to the United States and interred in Fairmont Cemetery in Midland after the war. The family's primary residence for twenty-nine years was at the corner of Wall and Colorado Streets.

In the early days, medical service to an area such as West Texas often required that Dr. Thomas go to his patients, as they were often not able to come to him. He always went when called, over all of West Texas and New Mexico, usually by horse and buggy, and later by automobile and train. (Sometimes the train would stop and allow Dr. Thomas to disembark and take horse or buggy to complete his trip to

Part Two: People of Integrity

ranch patients.) Some trips took up to six days. The doctor often joked about "watching out for high centers"—as old-timers will appreciate. Bartering with patients over fees was a common practice. Some of the medical procedures introduced to this area, attributed to Dr. Thomas, included complex surgery (including the first kidney operation performed west of Fort Worth), X-ray diagnosis, cancer therapy, and spinal anesthesia. Although surgery was his primary interest, he engaged in the general practice of medicine. His medical skills were updated by terms at New York and Philadelphia Polyclinical Medical Schools.

In 1926 Dr. Thomas built the first multi-story (six floors) office building in Midland. One floor was used as a residence, two floors for medical offices, operating theatre and hospital, and the rest for "newcomers"—the oil companies. In later years, Dr. and Mrs. Thomas resided at 511 North Colorado Street in a house they constructed utilizing some of the old red sandstones reclaimed from the original Midland Courthouse after it was torn down. Dr. Thomas's civic service included terms as school board president, selective service chairman (during World War II), and founding father of Midland Memorial Hospital, in which a plaque memorializing him is enshrined. He also authored a book, published in 1936, entitled *Selected Stories, Quotations and Aphorisms*, brim full of dry wit.

In addition to his many professional and civic accomplishments, Dr. Thomas was a very warm and personable man with innumerable friends. He loved cucumbers, corn bread, buttermilk, and onions, which he would snack on after work with great gusto. He loved cigars, crossword puzzles, and taking care of the family plot in Fairmont Cemetery, which he tended with loving care. He would drive his old Chrysler slowly around town, always wearing gloves. He died November 5, 1966, and was laid to rest, with Masonic services, in his beloved Fairmont plot alongside his family. Mrs. Thomas died January 31, 1976. Dr. Thomas was a true Midland son who was larger than life.

Henry E. Meadows Jr. is a Texas historian, grandson of Dr. John B. Thomas, and brother to John Meadows.

Part Two: People of Integrity

Ed Todd
by Charles Spence

I've known Ed Todd for thirty years, but even so, it is hard to write a story that can truly capture the kind of person he is. To say that he is a character is an understatement. Everyone knows Ed and what a character he is. And not just in Midland, but throughout all of West Texas.

Ed has written thousands of stories and hundreds of obituaries during his years at the *Reporter-Telegram*. Maybe what he's most known for in the newsroom is how he frequently would bust deadlines because he would tinker with his stories until long past the last possible moment.

I used to have lunch years ago with Ed at Luby's. We would finish lunch, and often I would finally have to go out and sit in my car and wait for him because so many people would come up and talk to him on our way out the door.

Dr. Carolyn Rhode once told me that people don't understand the depth of Ed's feelings for other people. He is a saint. He always takes care of people who need help. He's just a different kind of person than most of us are. Animals are like people to him. He loves all of them, and all of us.

A few years ago, Ed had a dog in his backyard, and he also kept chickens. Every once in a while, that dog would start playing with the chickens and chase them down and pick them up with his teeth. Once in a while, Ed's dog would accidentally kill one of them. And it just would move Ed to tears when that happened. If he sees a person step on an ant on the sidewalk, he'll ask, "Now, why did you do that?"

He has become quite a health nut over the years and has run in more than twenty marathons. He wants to do one more when he turns seventy-five. Ed is one of those rare individuals who is the most organized when his desk is the most disorganized. And if that's true, Ed is the most organized person of all time.

He is not a fan of injustice, and every once in a while at the newspaper, a decision would be made that he didn't care for. He wouldn't just sit there and let it by. He'd walk up and down the hallways with a raised voice talking about "confounded this" and "dad-blame that."

Part Two: People of Integrity

Ed once owned a goat named Freckles Rosetta, and the goat would follow Ed around like a dog. Freckles even slept with him. My favorite Freckles Rosetta story had to do with one time when Ed brought Freckles down to the newspaper with him. He would do that on a number of occasions. One time, the goat came to the newspaper when Jim Servatius was the editor, and Jim just happened to be in his office that day. And Jim was the old-fashioned kind of newspaper editor: he didn't suffer fools gladly, and he didn't put up with a lot.

That day he was sitting in his chair, and Ed walked in with that goat. Ed took the goat down the hall to his desk, and then Freckles wandered off back down the hall and stopped right in front of Jim's office and left Jim a great big surprise on the floor outside of his door in the newsroom. What did Jim do? He just started cracking up. Never got mad, never chewed Ed out. Jim never put up with much of anything, but what are you gonna do at that point?

Odd as it is to think about, not everyone knows who he is. One day he and I went to lunch at El Burrito in downtown Midland. Ed had this habit of only paying for things with coins. He never spends greenbacks.

He placed his order and started counting out all this change on the counter, and it was taking him quite a while. Finally, a man who was standing behind us stepped up while he was counting his money and slapped a hundred-dollar bill on the counter.

Ed turned around and looked at him and asked, "What's this for?"

The man looked right back at him and said, "Sir, you need this more than I do."

Charles Spence was the publisher of the Midland Reporter-Telegram *from 1984 to 2007.*

Marvin Ulmer

At 5:30 a.m. on August 30, 1906, Marvin Chesley Ulmer arrived in Midland from Dublin, Texas. He was all of twenty years old. Ulmer arrived a full seventeen years before oil in its grand iteration—known as the Santa Rita No. 1. Although what Ulmer did was perhaps not as grandiose as the black geyser in Reagan County, in retrospect it was quite important.

An hour and a half after Ulmer disembarked the westbound train when it stopped in Midland, he went to work at First National Bank.

His imprint was long lasting, and not just because he was a founding member of the Midland Chamber of Commerce, or the chairman of the campaign that would fund Midland Memorial Hospital in the 1940s, or the mayor of Midland from 1934 to 1943, or a two-term president of the West Texas Chamber of Commerce. Marvin Ulmer's impact was most felt when he, as president of First National, acknowledged that oil loans were a desirable way of doing business for both lender and borrower. Until then, the financial lending world had regarded oil loans as dubious.

"His shrewd liberality," wrote John Howard Griffin in *Land of the High Sky*, "brought oil depositors to the bank, oil men to his board of directors and established oil loans as valid banking."[1]

Ulmer left the bank in 1922 to operate a Ford dealership in Midland but returned to First National in 1925. That was when Ulmer made yet another significant contribution. As mayor, he teamed with Clarence Scharbauer, and the two men, with the help of the Midland Chamber of Commerce, led an effort that would secure the Army Air Force Bombardier Training School at Midand's Sloan Field. Improvements to the facility and a donation by Scharbauer of 450 additional acres helped cement the decision to locate the training school here. In so doing, not only were thousands of bombardiers trained in West Texas, but many stayed behind at the conclusion of the war and made Midland home. Many of those who stayed went on themselves to be significant contributing members of Midland.

Marvin Ulmer died of cardiac arrest in 1952, when he was president of First National Bank. Ulmer was alone at the time of his death because his wife, Helen,

Part Two: People of Integrity

was visiting the couple's daughter in Florida. He had planned to join her there. Ulmer was found by a bank employee at his home after he failed to show up at the bank at his normal time.

He was widely regarded as a "number one civic leader" for all his contributions to Midland.

—Jimmy Patterson

Part Two: People of Integrity

Addison Wadley

Addison Wadley was an early champion of Midland, frequently speaking in the 1930s and 1940s at civic organizations, women's clubs, church gatherings, and civic meetings about the goodness of the town. His family had a major street named after it, and together with the Barron family, one of Midland's first parks. Following are excerpts from Wadley's talks given in and around Midland from the 1940s, printed in a *Midland Reporter-Telegram* article in 1948.[1]

> It was the good old days in Midland when a quarter's worth of steak would feed a family of eight. Haircuts were 35 cents and shaves 15 cents. And the butcher would give you all the liver you wanted.
>
> My father came to Midland in the latter part of 1883 and established the first lumberyard. The family came in 1884. I was four at the time. But I have a very vivid recollection of unloading the household effects at the old two-story section house—there being no station here at the time.
>
> Originally the town was called Midway, it being just halfway between Fort Worth and El Paso. Uncles John Scharbauer, Z. T. Brown, and Herman Garrett were some of the big sheepmen. It was not until 1886 that T. J. Martin, better known as Uncle Tom, started the first cow ranch in this section. It was located about 15 miles southwest of town.
>
> The lack of water had retarded ranching of any consequence. But it was found that water could be had almost any place by digging or drilling wells. With this practice, cattle interests began expanding.
>
> The Texas & Pacific Railroad built through here in 1881. Midland County was organized in 1885, being originally a part of Tom Green County. Midland County's first courthouse did not cost the county a penny. A Mr. Moody owned the section of land adjoining the Townsite Company's land on the east and was making every effort to get the town located on his land.
>
> There was an election to be held to where the town would be located. And

PART TWO: PEOPLE OF INTEGRITY

secretly, both parties were approached with the proposition that if they would put up $5,000 for a courthouse, the election would be thrown to favor their property. This they both agreed to. It was a matter of heads I win tails you lose, as far as the community was concerned. When the results of the election, presided over by R. D. Gage of Pecos, were canvassed, the same twenty-odd votes counted a win for the Townsite Company.

The original frame courthouse served until about 1905. A new three-story one, constructed of red Pecos sandstone, was built at a cost of $26,000....

In its lifetime, Midland has had several newspapers. There was the *Staked Plain* in 1885. It was followed by the *Eye Opener*, the *Midland Gazette*, the *Livestock Reporter*, the *Examiner*, the *Telegram*, and finally, the *Midland Reporter-Telegram*.

Midland used to support two newspapers. And it supported two livery stables too....

Midland's first schoolhouse was a one-room building located on North Baird Street, just east of the present Methodist Church. It had one teacher and about twenty-five pupils, of which I was one....
I believe the growth and progress of the community can be better told by a review of our schools than by almost any other way.

The first church building in Midland was Baptist. It was located on North Marienfeld Street, where now stands the Service Drug. It was soon followed by the establishment of the Methodist, Catholic, Christian, and Presbyterian churches. Other denominations came later.

The first oil well drilled in West Texas was in Midland County, nine miles south of Midland on what was the Bryant Ranch. It was sunk in 1920 to a depth of 4,478 feet. There was a slight show of oil at 4,320 feet. But the well was abandoned and plugged January 11, 1921.

Midland has always been a good town.

Addison Wadley, whose family owned a lumberyard, lived in Midland from 1884 until his death in 1971. One of Midland's busiest thoroughfares was named after the family.

Part Two: People of Integrity

Cyril "Cy" Wagner and Jack E. Brown
by Grant A. Billingsley

Cy Wagner and Jack E. Brown epitomize the self-made Permian Basin independents who built a business from nothing, succeeded in multiple enterprises, and gave back generously to see their community prosper. Starting their partnership on little more than a handshake in 1962, the geologist (Wagner) and the engineer (Brown) blended different personalities and professional backgrounds to make Wagner & Brown, Ltd., a respected industry and community leader that lasted more than five decades.

Different though they were, the two men shared many attributes. Both were driven to succeed, both thrived on exploring new opportunities, and both were interested in making Midland a better place for people and businesses. Both men shunned publicity, and each maintained a low public profile. Their hope was that whatever good things they might be able to do would serve to motivate others also to help the community.

During my twenty-five years at Wagner & Brown, Ltd., I was fortunate to see how they shared their success with others. Both men had a deep appreciation for education and how it could change lives. They supported a broad range of activities designed to bring more and better jobs to the Permian Basin, and they sought to help the less fortunate.

One particular gift by the pair stands out in my mind. In the fall of 1986, the community was in a pronounced bust period with the price of oil having collapsed to about $8 per barrel. Tom Wageman, who had come to Midland to run the successor entity to the failed First National Bank of Midland, urgently requested a meeting with Mr. Wagner and Mr. Brown. He was also the volunteer chairman for the annual campaign of the United Way of Midland. I sat quietly as Mr. Wageman detailed for the pair a dire scenario for that year's campaign. Because of the woeful economy, the United Way's board of directors had taken the unusual step of initiating the campaign with no stated goal, hoping instead simply "to raise every dollar we can." Wageman closed by asking Cy and Jack to do something that had never been done in Midland before—to jointly underwrite the $250,000 annual administrative expenses for the United Way so that every other contribution be dedicated solely to programs that serve people.

In the next moment I witnessed an exchange that would be repeated again and again concerning different opportunities. The two partners immediately looked at one another with one quickly saying to the other, "It sounds like something that could help. What do you think?"

The prompt answer came: "I think so too. Let's do it." And that was it.

That year the United Way raised more than $2.3 million. In 1987, Joe and Beverly Pevehouse made a similar gift to underwrite administrative expenses, and the organization raised a total of $2.4 million. In subsequent years, other donors made generous gifts to reduce annual administrative expenses so that Midlanders could support the United Way knowing that their personal gifts were going to help people.

Grant A. Billingsley served as manager of public affairs for Wagner & Brown, Ltd., from 1986 to 2011.

Part Two: People of Integrity

Clayton Williams Jr.

Clayton Williams Jr. says that Pat McDaniel, director of the Haley Museum and Library, calls him every year and invites him to the museum's annual storytelling event "so you can fill the void with your b.s."

Williams's response to the invitation is always the same: "That I can do," an affirmation that serves more as an acknowledgment of his gift of, well, gab, than as an acceptance of McDaniel's invitation. With that in mind, here are some excerpts from a 2011 conversation:

★ *On Midland politics:* I love Midland. Midland is just Republican, that's what it is. It's been a foundation for many: George W. Bush, George Sr., me to a lesser extent. Ernest Angelo became a statewide leader, and he was a very early bedrock Republican. Some people who came from here and had an Eastern influence when Texas was still a Southern state, some of those guys came down, and this was a pretty Democratic place way back then. But that was when Democrats were conservative. That of course has stayed, the very conservative leaning. Midland has been consistently conservative.

★ *On Midland's families:* The Scharbauer family has been a solid family, and they've contributed a great deal to Midland. Course they ran the bank when the bank and I fought, but that was with C. J. Kelly, not them. I particularly admire them from the standpoint they've kept their ranching heritage in the family, the land in the family. They didn't blow it. So I admire the family. Same thing with the Cowdens. They're basically cow people who made money in oil and gas. You haven't had a rich Cowden going around wasting money. I respect them.

Part Two: People of Integrity

- ★ *On Tom Craddick:* He's a hand. Like any politician, he's been criticized, but certainly he's always held the best interests of Midland in representing us in Austin circles. He's well thought of. He's my friend—I think a lot of him. If he was not in there, a number of highways, the loop, we'd be missing all that. Tom was the first Republican speaker of the house since Reconstruction. He couldn't have done that without living in Midland.

- ★ When "W" was governor, he would always say to me, "I wouldn't have been governor if you hadn't screwed up, Claytie."

Williams has become a full-blooded entrepreneur. Oil, ranching, real estate, and communications made his livelihood, and one of the aspects of his larger-than-life story, aside from his experience in the governor's race against Ann Richards, of course, is his propensity for doing things up big.

In 1984, after he built and opened ClayDesta, Williams once sponsored a Brangus cattle sale in ClayDesta Plaza's atrium, a spot known more for its prom and engagement photo backdrops than for its livestock.

"We'd put a string of pearls on each heifer when they were up for auction," Williams said. "And then we'd take the pearls off and put them on the next heifer that came in."

Most of his livestock auctions at his ranch near Alpine weren't nearly as extravagant. It would usually just be Williams, an auction team, and a few friends.

"To get the buyers to come from all over the state and the country, I'd have big-name bands like Danny Davis and the Nashville Brass, Charley Pride, or George Strait," Williams said. "One time it was just me and [my wife,] Modesta, and eight or nine thousand of our closest friends."

—Compiled by Jimmy Patterson

Michael Williams
by Ernest Angelo

One of Midland's most outstanding former citizens, Michael Williams, was born and grew up in our city. Michael's mom and dad were schoolteachers. He graduated from St. Ann's School and Lee High School. Also at Lee was the future first lady Laura Welch Bush and the future four-star general Tommy Franks. It was pretty amazing for one small group of people to produce three such outstanding citizens.

Michael went to the University of Southern California, where he obtained a law degree. Returning to Midland to start his career, he issued a debate challenge to the sitting mayor over an issue of federal funding that the city council had declined to accept. I was that mayor, and we had an invigorating TV debate. Afterward I told Michael he had great skills and the ability to make a difference. I also told him over time I bet he would come to agree with me on some of the key issues of the day.

Not too long afterward, Michael came to my office to tell me he was going to run for county attorney. I said great. He then said, "You don't understand. I'm running as a Republican." His campaign manager was George W. Bush. While not successful in the primary, Michael went on to be an assistant district attorney.

After President Reagan's election in 1980, Michael began what turned out to be an extraordinarily effective series of jobs in the administrations of Ronald Reagan and George H. W. Bush. He returned to Texas, where Governor George W. Bush appointed him to serve as a member of the Railroad Commission, a position to which he was elected three times by substantial margins. Governor Perry appointed Michael Texas Commissioner of Education on September 1, 2012.

For many years Michael has been known nationally for his successful performance in a number of responsible positions, and for his ability to articulate his philosophical beliefs. This attribute has given him the opportunity to address two Republican National Conventions and every Texas State Republican Convention since his rise to prominence as an elected official. At several of the latter venues, he has announced to the crowd that I was his "political godfather," a title I am proud to hold, justified or not.

Part Two: People of Integrity

Michael has been married for twenty-seven years to Donna Williams, a very successful mechanical engineer. He is creator and cosponsor of Winnovators, a summer camp for eighth through twelfth graders to help inspire them to seek careers in engineering and science. Michael has dedicated his life to public service, where he has made significant contributions across a wide spectrum of society. In the process he has earned the right to be designated a distinguished member of the Midland community.

Ernest Angelo was the mayor of Midland from 1972 to 1980 and was later active in national Republican politics.

Part Two: People of Integrity

Dr. Dorothy Wyvell
by Dr. Debbie Reese

Pediatrician Dr. Dorothy Wyvell was one of the first specialists in Midland and was instrumental in recruiting doctors to the area. She graduated from Duke Medical School before penicillin was introduced. She related stories to me about keeping premature babies warm in her oven, typing blood for transfusions, sharpening and sterilizing intravenous and spinal needles for reuse, and sleeping on the floor overnight to watch over diabetics. For many years she lived in the back of her office along with her dog, Mr. Wallace. She cared for the famous, the rich, and the poor.

Dorothy never had children of her own but helped raise a niece. I laughed when I read her advice to parents: "Strict bed rest for two weeks!" She was gruff, she dressed in men's starched shirts, and she insisted that children behave in her office. But she had a very tender heart. She sat at the bedside of a young boy with polio, counseled grief-stricken parents of a child with leukemia, and saw thousands of patients.

Dr. Wyvell also ran for political office. As a staunch John Bircher, she held somewhat controversial political beliefs. I never subscribed to her conspiracy theories, but she did teach me that involvement in all levels of government was a duty as well as a privilege.

Dorothy was also a poet. E. B. White, of *Stuart Little* and *Charlotte's Web* fame, was her uncle. She wrote this poem toward the end of her life, when her eyesight was failing:

Fading Eyes
by Dorothy Wyvell

I thank Thee, Lord, for all these years
When I have worked among my peers
With eyes directed by Thy light
To always know the wrong from right
And try to do the right.

Part Two: People of Integrity

> I thank Thee, Lord, for eyes to see
> The beauty and tranquility
> Of birth and death and all between,
> Of matters seen and those unseen
> And still remain serene.
>
> I thank you, Lord, for showing me
> That loss of eyes can also be
> A special means for me to see,
> That vision needs not eyes to see
> But only Thee.

Debbie Reese, MD, *is a practicing pediatrician in Midland.*

Part Two: People of Integrity

John and Charlene Younger
by Dr. Charles Younger

After a whirlwind courtship, John and Charlene Younger eloped and married in 1939. A sixty-five-year union of mutual devotion, love, and service to others began.

John, a chemical engineering graduate from Texas A&M, was called to service for our country in World War II. He spent thirty-one months in the port city of Khorramshahr, Iran, rising to the rank of lieutenant colonel in the U.S. Army. He was a decorated executive commander of the facility supplying petroleum products to the Russian front.

Discharged from the military in 1945, he met Eddie Chiles, joined the fledgling Western Company, and moved his family to Midland. While serving as vice president of the Western Company, Mr. Chiles chose to move the headquarters to Fort Worth, and John elected to remain in Midland and continue his career as an independent oil operator and real-estate developer.

John remained a loyal Aggie, and Charlene was an equal supporter. In 1965 he served as president of the Former Students Association of Texas A&M and worked closely with university president General Earl Rudder to promote an unpopular initiative for admission of women to the all-male university. In 1989 John was honored as a Distinguished Alumnus of his alma mater.

John and Charlene gave back generously to their chosen community. Early on, John served two terms as trustee for the Midland Independent School District and was simultaneously president of the Midland Chamber of Commerce. Joining Joan Nobles, the Russell Millers, and others, the Youngers were founding members of High Sky Girls Ranch (now Children's Ranch). They solicited generous Midlanders to keep the doors open during the early lean years of the ranch.

Charlene's true passion, outside of her family, was the Midland Cerebral Palsy Center (now Children's Rehabilitation Center). She volunteered countless hours helping children at the center, "changing their diapers, wiping their noses, and loving every one of them." The Charlene Smith Younger wing at the center honors her service.

Part Two: People of Integrity

She was also known by children in Midland in the mid-1950s and 1960s as the Gingerbread Lady. Each Christmas, she would hand-decorate thousands of cookies and hang them in plastic bags on a tree for children to partake of the tasty treats.

John served many years as a trustee of the Abell-Hanger Foundation. In addition, he worked tirelessly as a founding member of Midland Presbyterian Homes, now known as Manor Park. The Alzheimer's unit of this facility bears his name. John was honored by his peers in 2002 as recipient of the Top Hand Award of the Permian Basin Petroleum Association and the Golden Deeds Award from the Exchange Club of Midland.

An accomplished and humble couple to the end, they left a legacy of honesty, faith, integrity, character, and Christian love.

> **Charles Younger, MD,** *is a noted orthopedic surgeon in Midland and the son of John and Charlene Younger. He and President George W. Bush remain close.*

Part Two: People of Integrity

The People of Midland

If you live in Midland, this book is about you.

Your name may not be on these pages. There wasn't room to include all the Midlanders who have made important contributions to their town, or all the inspiring Midland stories that could have been told. But all the stories in this book are ours. Yours. Because they've affected Midland, they've affected you, too.

When you talk to people today from somewhere other than Midland, or Texas, and they ask you where you live, there's at least a small chance that your answer is, "Midland. It's where George W. Bush is from." Or "It's where the baby fell down the well." Lately, you're even more likely to answer, "Thanks to the oil industry, the economy is quite good right now." Or maybe the other person will say to you, *Friday Night Lights!* And even though that book may be more about Odessa when you get right down to it, it's a lot about us, too.

Midland's history has been made by its movers and shakers: the pioneer families, the oilmen and ranchers who found wealth, the successful politicians, the influential bankers, the generous people who started charitable foundations. But this book clearly shows that many of Midland's movers and shakers didn't necessarily have money or power. By doing whatever they were good at, by speaking up about something they felt was important, by reaching out a friendly hand to help someone else, they wielded a strong influence of their own. The fabric of Midland has been woven by hundreds, thousands, of people like this. Midland welcomes everyone to become involved in making it a better place. It's an easy place to get to know people, and an easy place to lend a hand.

Joan Baskin is not a native Midlander, but she's been championing Midland every day since she moved here. She likes to talk about what she calls our intellectual infrastructure. Many ideas, she says, become realities in Midland simply because people had the courage to express an idea.

Just ask the Jaycees. Back in the 1950s, they wanted to bring the Soap Box Derby to Midland but couldn't because there was no hill. They didn't walk away lamenting, "Oh well, at least we tried." They built a hill, and then proceeded to have

Part Two: People of Integrity

Soap Box Derbies for years. The people who brought the dirt to build that hill didn't have an abundance of money. They had an idea, and they followed through.

A more recent example is the story of a woman who lives in Midland, works in Odessa, and has a child in the Midland public schools. When Midland suffered through a rash of teenage suicides in 2011, she felt something needed to be done to help. But she didn't want to wait for someone else to take action. She had heard of a program called Challenge Day, based in California. She picked up the phone, expressed her concerns, and eventually brought Challenge Day to Midland's high schools, where students can spend a day sharing and talking about their lives, opening up to one another, and growing in their confidence. The program is aimed at cutting down on bullying and other behaviors that can ultimately be detrimental to a youth's life.

The woman who brought Challenge Day to Midland is an office worker for a physician. The point is that one person without a lot of money can indeed make something important and needed happen here.

Midland has always been a mom-and-pop kind of town, as former mayor Wes Perry likes to call it. With its recent rampant growth, Perry and others hope that while we enjoy the prosperity that the energy economy has afforded us, we never forget the small-town atmosphere that made Midland what it has been for so very long. And we can all help accomplish that, too.

So start with a viable idea, something you care about. Or join a friend or neighbor or existing organization whose cause you support. Then, as Joan Baskin puts it, "pick up the ball and run with it."

That's how Midlanders get things done. And that's how history is made—and character is built—by all of us.

—Jimmy Patterson

afterword

That Is Midland: City's Character Shines After Tragedy

by Wes Perry, former mayor of Midland

Every year since 2004, the Hunt for Heroes Weekend has officially started with lunch under the wings of the only flying B-52 bomber in the world as it sits at the Commemorative Air Force Hangar at Midland International Airport. These heroes—veterans of foreign wars—and their wives look like many young couples. They are quiet and humble and not comfortable with attention. Most have served in Iraq and Afghanistan and have seen atrocities that you and I will never experience. It is truly our hope in Midland to show them how much we honor them and their wives and families.

When I became mayor, one of our native citizens, Terry Johnson, expressed a desire to honor these veterans with a special recognition from Midland. I later came up with the idea of giving them a key to the city. (By the way, they are the only ones who received a key to the city during my tenure.) Think about who has a key to your home. They are the people in your life you trust the most, people who can come and go as they please. These veterans and their families will always be welcome in Midland.

As I handed out the key to each soldier over the years, something happened and we connected. They knew how much Midland cares for them.

People always ask if the veterans are from Midland. But Terry picks them from all over the country, about fifty veterans per year, for a reason. He often says, "We want the guy from Ohio to go back and say, 'You're not going to believe what they're doing in Midland.' At some point while they are here, a lot of them will say, 'Man, I want to move here. You guys are the best people, the friendliest people I've ever met.

Afterword

Where I'm from, when I came home from the war, it's like I never left. But I come here and you don't even know me, but you love me.'"

Thursday, November 15, 2012

The Hunt for Heroes event in November 2012 began as all the other celebrations had. We were honored that these brave men and women were in our midst. And they were moved because we felt honored.

Noon
After lunch our guests loaded back up in their limousines, escorted by the sheriff's and police officers' cars plus dozens of motorcycles from the Patriot Guard Riders.

3 p.m.
The big parade through Midland was about to start. It began at the soldiers' hotel downtown. Thousands of Midlanders lined the streets, waving their hands and flags to honor the heroes. As the lead cars lined up, the veterans and their wives climbed onto flatbed trailers. They were on the way to the Hunt for Heroes main event that evening, a banquet in their honor, which hundreds of supporters and volunteers had been preparing for a year.

4:45 p.m.
I received a phone call saying that there had been a terrible accident, something about the soldiers and a train—it made no sense. I immediately drove to the accident site.

I've never seen so many first responders. It was total pandemonium. After the collision, the freight train was stopped in the tracks, so from my vantage point on the north side, I could see nothing of the actual accident. All I knew was that the train had hit a trailer, and it looked like the war zones they had all been in overseas. My role was to stay out of the way and allow the experts to do their job. Later I would learn that the driver of the truck had pulled onto the tracks, thinking he could get across, but was stopped by a traffic jam ahead. He could not move forward and he could not back up. He could do nothing. Go nowhere.

I was in shock, as everyone was. Now, looking back, I describe the feeling as the same way I felt when I watched the second plane fly into the Twin Towers on 9/11:

Afterword

pure helplessness, sadness, disbelief. I remember thinking there was just no way this could happen in Midland, Texas, to friends we all wanted to honor.

9 p.m.
I wasn't prepared to handle this situation. Midland had been through emergencies before, but never anything quite like this. Mayors of many bigger cities have crisis-preparation training, but I hadn't. I did know that someone needed to speak to the media and citizens.

The first event was a press conference with the fire and police chiefs. I don't remember anything except that the first responders and hospital personnel had done an amazing job and were doing all they possibly could. We needed to pray for them and the families of the soldiers. What had started out as one of my best days ended up as the worst day of my entire career in public service.

Friday, November 16

There was no organization, no plan. Of course the police, firefighters, nurses, and doctors knew what to do, but as a community we had no idea.

Morning
It occurred to me that when bad things happen, families just want to get together, so that's what we did in the form of a community gathering later that morning. The idea was for us just to be together as a family.

The turnout was overwhelming. Pastors from different churches led us in prayer. Songs were sung. The international and national media was there, so the whole world could see.

Probably the most poignant moment I had was with Terry Johnson, the organizer and founder of Hunt for Heroes. I have never seen a man so distraught, so sad. We just hugged for a long time; there was nothing to say.

Afternoon
The rest of that day and the next were spent answering media questions. The deceased soldiers had given their lives saving others. It was overwhelming to think that these young men I had met only a day earlier were now gone. They had traveled to the most dangerous parts of the world protecting our freedom, and they had lost

Afterword

their lives here. It was beyond our comprehension.

The many women who volunteered to host the soldiers' wives over the weekend went into high gear. They took charge and did more to care for those families than anyone. I am convinced they were the ones who truly made the difference.

Saturday evening, November 17

The facts came to light that four soldiers had been killed, and sixteen passengers from the flatbed trailer were injured, five seriously.

Again we felt that a community gathering was the thing to do. This time some of the soldiers and their wives were with us. It was heartbreaking to watch one of the wives come up in a wheelchair. I was awestruck by her courage and willingness to be there. Not only were the soldiers heroes, their wives were too. This proved it.

Sunday morning, November 18

My wife, Roni, and I stopped by the hotel after church to tell a soldier and his wife good-bye. The Hunt for Heroes volunteers were attending to every need for this young couple. As I was standing there, a woman started coming at me and was a bit intimidating. I could tell she was part of their family, and I was expecting to be yelled at. Instead, she gave me a hug and said she was the mother of the lady in the wheelchair. Then she told me, "I have never been treated this way in my life. The love, the care, the concern and the outreach from Midland—it's overwhelming." She added, "If I could, I would live here."

All I could say to her was, "That is Midland."

One fact that I had known in all my years of living here was proved even more that morning. After the woman thanked us, Roni and I walked away from the hotel. As the Patriot Guard Riders revved up their motorcycles, and the sirens from the police and sheriff's cars started—all of whom served as a convoy to take that family to the airport so they could return home—I knew just what a special place Midland is.

I am glad to say that Hunt for Heroes has continued. In November 2013 it held its tenth-anniversary event.

appendix

Key Events That Shaped Midland's Character

September 1849: Marcy crosses Mustang Draw. Captain Randolph Marcy mapped a route through West Texas on his way from Santa Fe, New Mexico, to Fort Smith, Arkansas. Had he not been instructed by his commanding officer to take a southern return route, Midland might not have received the start it did.

Feb. 28, 1885: Midland County organized from Tom Green County. Tom Green County originally comprised 60,000 square miles. When it was split up by the state legislature, twelve new counties were created, including Midland County. Some of the settlers who put down roots in Midland, or Midway as it was called in its earliest days, pushed for their new town to be the county seat and Midland its own county.

June 15, 1885: First County officials elected.
Aug. 10, 1885: First County Commissioners meeting held. No geographically defined group of people can survive without leadership. Midland's first governmental structure began in the summer months of 1885.

Aug. 23, 1885: First Methodist church organized (later First United Methodist).
Dec. 22, 1885: First Presbyterian Church organized.
January 10, 1886: First Baptist Church organized. The Christian faith began to take root in Midland in the last half of 1885 and into early 1886, when three of the largest denominations in Midland today first swung open their doors. Although the number fluctuates, Midland now has well over 100 churches.

September 9, 1885: First Midland County Courthouse completed. Hunter and Weller Construction was awarded the bid to build Midland's first courthouse, a three-story wood frame

APPENDIX

structure, at a cost of $2,934.65. Also included were a bandstand, a town windmill, and a watering pond. That first courthouse served the people of Midland for nineteen years.

1886–1887: Drought, blizzards bring the "Great Die-Off." Early citizens had to learn quickly to deal with a lack of moisture. During the devastating "Great Die-Off" of the 1880s, cattle and other livestock perished in greater numbers than in other droughts in the late nineteenth century. The devastating droughts were accompanied by white-out blizzards in 1887.

1887: John Scharbauer settles in Midland. When John Scharbauer brought his sheep here, he set in motion a gift to the people of Midland that has been giving for 130 years: that of the Scharbauer family's generous philanthropic efforts, handed down for four generations. John's decision to settle in Midland was indeed one of the most important individual decisions made by any pioneer who came through the Staked Plains. In 1889, John encouraged his brother, Christian, to leave his New York home and come to Midland. Chris did so, and he brought his family, including his ten-year-old son, Clarence.

1887: Midlanders place windmills in their yards. Always with a knack for finding ways to survive, Midlanders beat the water shortage problems of the late nineteenth century by building windmills in their front yards, so much that Midland earned the moniker "The Windmill Town." Prior to personal windmills, Midlanders had retrieved their water from downtown water wells. Before that, they had to wait for water to be hauled in from Monahans Well, fifty miles to the southwest.

June 16, 1890: First National Bank chartered. For almost a century the most reliable and civic-minded institution in West Texas was First National Bank. It was not just a bank, but a community gathering place, supporter of dreams, and ultimately, a bank that met an early death, even though it was in its nineties when its doors were shut by the FDIC. The bank's story began when John Scharbauer cofounded the bank with the Connell brothers in 1888, and was chartered two years later.

November 27, 1891: Lorenzo Porez executed by hanging on courthouse lawn. Lorenzo Porez's execution tells an important story, not just because he was put to death, but in the years after that execution, Midland county juries have rarely opted for capital punishment. Porez's death was the only execution ever carried out in Midland County, and since the day he was hanged, only three other convicted criminals have been put to death in almost 130 years. A fifth offender sentenced by a Midland County jury remains on death row in 2014.

Appendix

1893: North Ward Elementary becomes first school building. Midland's formal education process began with the creation of the school district more than ten years later, but children first began meeting in school buildings as early as the 1890s. North Ward Elementary was the first large school building in the county and also served as a Boy Scout hall and clubhouse. It was demolished in 1946.

1903: Odessa National Bank charters, moves to Midland, becomes Midland National Bank. An institution that proved to be the competition of First National, Midland National Bank built its own reputation for community-minded leaders and examples of generosity. When it opened its doors, it was located directly across the street from First National Bank.

April 15, 1907: Midland Independent School District organized. Afterwards, the district hired its first 12 teachers at a rate of $50 a month. Five years later there were 14 schools in the district. A professor from the University of Texas, Dr. J. L. Henderson, called Midland High School "one of the best in West Texas."

December 1, 1908: Clarence Scharbauer marries Ruth Cowden. The wedding that brought together two of Midland's most prominent families was called the social event of the decade.

January 9, 1909: Midland Christian College charters. It would have a short life, closing its doors in 1921, but Midland Christian College was the town's first successful attempt at providing higher education for its residents. More than 100 students enrolled in classes the first semester, September 1910. Ultimately the town's small population, and the fact that many wealthy ranchers chose to send their children elsewhere for an education, prompted the school's closure.

1905 through 1910: Four major fires fought downtown. A 1909 blaze destroyed the Llano Hotel, First National Bank, and many other downtown establishments, prompting Mayor J. A. Haley and other town officials to install a town water system. A December 1910 blaze was huge, but the water system was much more adequate to fight it than the previous bucket brigades had been.

July 4, 1912: John Pliska builds, flies plane. In 1912 John Pliska, a local blacksmith from Austria, built his own airplane and then flew it over Midland. He was able to fly the machine for intervals of up to fifteen minutes. Aided by local auto mechanic Gray Coggin, Pliska completed construction and test-flew his plane after first witnessing the stopover of the Wright Brothers' Model B aircraft in Midland in 1911.

Appendix

1919: Dr. John B. Thomas sees need for hospital care. Dr. Thomas remains one of the most significant yet perhaps under-appreciated Midlanders of the early days. He was largely responsible for the progress of medical care in Midland. Not only did he perform the first kidney surgery in West Texas, he constructed the first medical facility on the second floor of the rebuilt Llano Hotel, and then opened a hospital floor in his own Thomas Building, a six-story structure still standing in downtown. Later, Thomas led the town's effort to build Midland Memorial Hospital.

1919: First oil well in West Texas drilled nine miles south of town; dry hole. Significant in that it was the first drilling effort, it also prompted the earliest of oilmen to never give up even in the face of repeated dry holes. Such occurrences would become commonplace through the years.

1921: Broadway of America built through Midland. Like the railroad, this throughway put Midland on the map, giving business to the Scharbauer Hotel and other establishments. The roadway was also called the Bankhead Highway, named after Alabama senator John Bankhead, grandfather of Tallulah Bankhead, a famous Hollywood actress at the time.

May 28, 1923: Santa Rita gusher begins, Texon. Significant not just to West Texas and Midland, but to the entirety of domestic oil production. Its importance cannot be overstressed almost a century later.

1925: McCamey Field discovered, moving oil headquarters from San Angelo to Midland. Oil headquarters would begin falling toward Midland like dominoes, especially later when it was learned Midland had the business infrastructure and was the natural center of the oil business in the Permian Basin.

Oct. 15, 1926: Gulf Oil Corporation moves its offices to Midland. Petroleum historians have recorded that the beginning of Midand's reputation as an oil city can be traced to this date.

January 1, 1928: Thomas Building opens.
Mid-1928: Scharbauer Hotel opens.
The Thomas Building was the first major downtown structure built, and opened on January 1, 1928. It was followed a few months later by the Scharbauer Hotel. Both structures, along with the still-to-come Hogan Building, helped give Midland its reputation for being the oil capital of West Texas.

Appendix

1928: Eighteen-foot stretch of Wall Street paved. Progress sometimes comes in baby steps. Some residential half-bathrooms in Midland mansions today are probably longer. But it was progress.

July 3–4, 1929: Grand opening of the Hogan Building. Before it became the landmark historical treasure it is, it would be known as Hogan's Folly as oil companies mostly ignored it during the Great Depression.

1935: Humble Oil moves seventy houses and families to Midland, single largest population increase in Midland in one day. Thanks in part to Humble's move and the establishment of Midland as an oil center, the town's population exploded, from 5,484 in 1930 to 9,352 at the dawn of 1940, an increase of 70 percent in just one decade.

October 2, 1942: Clarence Scharbauer dies. The passing of the man who arguably did more for Midland than anyone in its history was felt both by the entire town, and by his young son, Clarence Jr., who would continue on the family's philanthropic tradition into the twenty-first century.

February 6, 1942: First class of bombardier cadets arrive. Midland Army Flying School, also known as the Bombardier College, receives its first class of cadets from Ellington, Texas. Before the end of training in 1946, the peak population reached 4,000 and graduated a total of 6,627 officers.

September 26, 1942: Midland Army Airfield designated. Another facility whose worth is immeasurable to Midland history. Aside from the valiant Greatest Generation airmen the school turned out, many of them chose to return to the states and call Midland home. Their relocation here, which affected Midland for generations, is still felt.

Summer 1945: Ohio native Art Cole returns to Midland following World War II, proposes community theatre. There was no one as important to the development of the cultural scene in Midland as Art Cole, who moved here from Ohio after he had been stationed at the Army Air Forces Bombardier Training School and returned to West Texas after the war. In 1946, he and his own army of volunteers created Midland Community Theatre.

November 1945: Oil first struck in Midland County. According to Samuel Myres's book *The Permian Basin: Era of Advancement*, the first commercial oil in the county was struck in

Appendix

November 1945 in what became known as the Midland Field. The discovery well was the Humble Oil and Refining Company's No. 1 Mrs. O. P. Buchanan. The well yielded 4,540 barrels in 1945 and another 11,700 barrels before dropping off substantially.

December 1, 1947: Petroleum Club of Midland chartered. The Petroleum Club grew out of a group of men who met regularly at the Scharbauer Hotel for lunch. It met in the Wolcott Home on 219 N. Big Spring Street until 1980, then moved to its current location on Marienfeld and Wall Streets.

April 1950: George H. W. Bush moves to Midland, becomes cofounder of two oil companies. Both George H. W. Bush and George W. Bush would later tout the values they learned in Midland. On November 7, 1961, the family purchased what is now the landmark designated the George W. Bush Childhood Home on Ohio Avenue.

July 11, 1950: Midland Memorial Hospital opens. Midland Memorial Hospital became the first state-of-the-art medical facility in West Texas.

October 29, 1963: Juliette Turner murder. There has been no crime more infamous in Midland than the murder at the Turner mansion. Twenty-two-year-old James Lee Marion beat Mrs. Turner to death in the couple's lavish home while Fred Turner was away on his annual hunting trip. Turner would never again set foot in the mansion and died four months later. Dorothy Turner Scharbauer was severely beaten in the attack and suffered a serious head wound. Marion was sentenced to die, a ruling later overturned. He has since been released.

December 18, 1953: KMID goes on air, becoming the first TV station in Midland. At first KMID was an NBC affiliate but became an ABC affiliate in 1981. For years it was known simply as Big 2.

1964: Barbara Culver becomes first woman elected County Judge. Barbara Culver, now Barbara Culver-Clack, became a groundbreaking legal figure by being named the first female judge in West Texas. She would also become a key part in the Republican Party's growth in Midland. In 1988 she was appointed to the Texas Supreme Court.

May 9, 1968: 4.75 inches of rain received in two-hour period; one man killed. The deluge happened during business hours, when Midlanders were at work and their children at school. Massive flooding resulted and a visiting salesman from Lubbock drowned when his car was swept off Business 20.

November 5, 1968: Tom Craddick elected Speaker of the Texas House of Representatives. Craddick made history when he became the first Republican to hold this position since Reconstruction. His voice in Austin for West Texas has been significant to the residents of the Permian Basin.

June 19, 1968: MISD votes 6–1 to implement controversial secondary integration plan.
September 3, 1968: Busing of Midland secondary students begins. Carver School closes. As Midland struggled to comply with federal integration laws, compliance was time-consuming and controversial. Carver Junior-Senior High School fell victim to the public school changes as the board announced it would close the beloved school that had educated many in the African American community.

October 23, 1973: Construction begins on Midland College. Born out of the controversy and politics surrounding the establishment of the University of Texas of the Permian Basin, Midland College established itself as a first-class, nationally renowned community college. Forty years later, its enrollment rates topped 6,000 students, and it remains the jewel of the community.

September 10, 1976: MISD trustees approve controversial cluster system. The plan called for the busing of elementary school students in the fourth, fifth, and sixth grades, and proved to be the ultimate answer that met Department of Justice desegregation requirements. While not everyone liked it, both sides agreed it was an equal inconvenience for all parties.

Summer 1986: First Legacy Scholarships awarded. Three of Midland's longtime philanthropic families—Helen and Barney Greathouse, Harriet and Harvey Herd, and Dorothy and Clarence Scharbauer Jr. joined George and Gladys Abell to make the Legacy Scholarships possible. Established in 1986 by the Abell-Hanger Foundation, the Legacy Scholarship pays tuition at Midland College for all graduating seniors in Midland County who wish to apply. Over the years, thousands of students have taken advantage of the generous offer to further their education.

January 1999: New airport terminal opens. As important to the town as Midland's airport was in the early twentieth century, the construction of the new Midland International Airport terminal in the 1990s was also vital to the city's progress. A state-of-the-art facility designed in the tradition of John Wayne Airport in Orange County, California, the new building provides travelers to and from Midland with a clean, efficient terminal.

Appendix

August 30, 1999: Loop 250 dedicated. Before the construction of Loop 250, north Midland was a series of frontage roads for a future loop loosely pulled together by a business here and a residential apartment building there. The loop changed all that, as north Midland has become an important retail and dining center in the city.

January 20, 2001–January 20, 2009: George W. Bush serves two terms as U.S. president. Midland's favorite son, a product of the city's schools, churches, baseball fields, and later its oil companies and nonprofit organizations, serves as forty-third president of the United States. "George W.," as he is still commonly and affectionately known by West Texans, made Midland his last stop before flying to Washington. When his eight years were over, he returned with his wife, Laura, and parents, President George H. W. Bush and Barbara Bush, to a triumphant Midland homecoming, flying in Air Force One at a low altitude over downtown Midland on his way to a rally in Centennial Plaza, where more than ten thousand greeted him.

2002: Scharbauer Sports Complex opens. Because Christensen Stadium was no longer meeting the needs of baseball fans, and historic Memorial Stadium was insufficient for high school football fans and teams, the city responded by building the Scharbauer Sports Complex. Built on land donated by its namesake family, the complex represents another diamond in the desert. With the city bearing the brunt of the cost of the football stadium, Midland Independent School District had itself a shiny new facility at no cost.

Spring, Summer 2011: Drought and wildfires rake Midland. The temperature soared to 107 on May 28, 2011, a sign of a brutal summer ahead that saw an outbreak of devastating wildfires throughout the entire region, not to mention an ominously growing shortage of water.

December 18, 2012: Midland Memorial Hospital's historic expansion. Midland voters approved a $115 million bond package for a historic renovation of the city's hospital, which included an eight-story patient tower that rivals anything in larger cities. More than half of the total cost of the improvements was funded by philanthropic families in West Texas, including a $25 million donation by the Scharbauer family. As a result, the new patient facility was named the Dorothy and Clarence Scharbauer Jr. Patient Tower.

May 13, 2013: T-Bar pipeline opens. Midland officials worked feverishly for several years to establish the T-Bar Ranch water supply. Water levels fell to dangerously low levels, and some area lakes, including O. C. Fisher in San Angelo and Lake Meredith in the Texas

Panhandle, evaporated completely. Lake Ivie, Midland's primary surface water source, fell to 15 percent of capacity in May 2012 before a significant rainfall came in September 2012, a deluge that gave Ivie enough moisture to keep the supply plentiful enough until the T-Bar supply could be turned on.

endnotes

Preface
1. Stephen Ives and Ken Burns, *The West* (Boston: Little, Brown and Company, 1996), p. xvii.
2. Smith Ray, "A History of Midland," Midland Centennial files.

Prologue: "The Response of This Community Was Remarkable"
1. All direct quotations from David and Carole Wayland in the prologue are from the author's interview with them, February 2012.
2. *Midland Reporter-Telegram*, August 10, 2011.
3. Col. Joe Richards, "A Colonel Says Thank You to Midland," *Midland Reporter-Telegram*, August 10, 2011.
4. All remaining direct quotations from Col. Joe Richards are from the author's interview with him, March 2012.

Part One: A Place with Character . . . and Colorful Characters

Chapter 1: What the First White Settlers Found
1. Judge John Hyde interviews, November 2009–November 2011.
2. Thomas W. Cutrer, "Marcy, Randolph Barnes," *Handbook of Texas Online* (Denton, TX: Texas State Historical Association), http://www.tshaonline.org/handbook/online/articles/fma43
3. Judge John Hyde interviews.
4. Thomas W. Cutrer, "McClellan, George Brinton," *Handbook of Texas Online* (Denton, TX: Texas State Historical Association), http://www.tshaonline.org/handbook/online/articles/fmc09
5. Judge John Hyde interviews, November 2009–November 2011.
6. Cutrer, "Marcy, Randolph Barnes."
7. The Report of Capt. R. B. Marcy's Route from Fort Smith to Santa Fe, p. 208. Presented to the 31st Congress, July 1850.
8. John Howard Griffin, *Land of the High Sky* (Midland, TX: First National Bank of Midland, 1959), p. 9.
9. Cutrer, "Marcy, Randolph Barnes."
10. Paul H. Carlson and Bruce A. Glasrud, *West Texas: A History of the Giant Side of the State* (Norman: University of Oklahoma Press, 2014), p. 10.
11. Judge John Hyde interviews, November 2009–November 2011.
12. John Leffler, "Midland, TX," *Handbook of Texas Online* (Denton, TX: Texas State Historical Association), http://www.tshaonline.org/handbook/online/articles/hdm03

Endnotes

13. Gus Clemens, *Legacy* (San Antonio, TX: Mulberry Avenue Books, 1983), p. 108.
14. Officer Down Memorial Page, "Anglin, Private William B.," http://www.odmp.org/officer/18653-private-william-b-anglin
15. Griffin, *Land of the High Sky*.
16. Judge John Hyde interviews, November 2009–November 2011.
17. Addison Wadley, "Addison Wadley, Retired Merchant, Says Opportunities Are Unlimited," *Midland Reporter-Telegram*, February 29, 1948.
18. Griffin, *Land of the High Sky*, Chapter 3, "Frontiersmen Move West."
19. Leffler, "Midland, TX," *Handbook of Texas Online*.
20. Nancy McKinley, ed., *The Pioneer History of Midland County, Texas 1880–1926*, Limited Centennial Edition, p. 83.
21. Leffler, "Midland, TX," *Handbook of Texas Online*.
22. Judge Hyde interviews, November 2009–November 2011.
23. Scharbauer family video.
24. J. Evetts Haley interviews O. B. Holt, January 3, 1927, Haley Memorial Library and History Center archives.
25. Ibid.
26. Ibid.
27. Ibid.
28. Ibid.
29. Pat McDaniel interviews, August 2011, May 2013.
30. Ibid.
31. Ibid.
32. Linda and June Cowden interviews; *Cowden: the Cowden Family History*; Pat McDaniel interviews, August 2011, May 2013.
33. Ibid.
34. Ibid.
35. Cowden, *Cowden, the Cowden Family History*.
36. Pat McDaniel interviews, August 2011, May 2013.
37. McKinley, ed., *Pioneer History of Midland County, Texas, 1880–1926*, p. 96.
38. Ibid., p. 97.
39. Ibid.
40. Ibid., p. 86.
41. Pat McDaniel interviews, August 2011, May 2013.
42. Robert H. Ryan, "Midland: The Economic Future of a Texas Oil Center," Bureau of Business Research, University of Texas, 1959.

Chapter 2: A Young Town Pulls On Its Cowboy Boots

1. Gus Clemens, *Legacy* (San Antonio, TX: Mulberry Avenue Books, 1983); "The Baylor-Sibley Invasion of New Mexico," p. 87.
2. John Leffler, "Midland, TX," *Handbook of Texas Online* (Denton, TX: Texas State Historical Association), http://www.tshaonline.org/handbook/online/articles/hdm03
3. John Howard Griffin, *Land of the High Sky* (Midland, TX: First National Bank of Midland, 1959), pp. 69–70.
4. Ibid., p. 70.
5. Bert Rawlins, *Midland Gazette*.
6. Griffin, *Land of the High Sky*, p. 70.
7. Ibid.
8. Ibid., p. 63.
9. Ibid., p. 128.

Endnotes

10. Clemens, *Legacy*, p. 123.
11. Hallye Jordan, "Droughts, Floods, Dot West Texas Weather Pattern," *Midland Reporter-Telegram*, July 4, 1985.
12. Griffin, *Land of the High Sky*, p. 82.
13. Clarence Scharbauer Jr. interviews, May 2012, January 2013, March 2013, April 2013.
14. Griffin, *Land of the High Sky*, p. 127
15. Judge John Hyde interviews, November 2009–November 2011.
16. Ibid.
17. Ibid.
18. Fairview Cemetery records.
19. Nancy McKinley, ed. *The Pioneer History of Midland County, Texas, 1880–1926*, limited centennial edition (Dallas: Taylor Publishing Co., 1984), p. 55.
20. Ibid.
21. Edna Brown Hibbits, "Citizens Join Forces to Solve Health Problems," *Midland Reporter-Telegram*, July 4, 1985.
22. Ibid.
23. Clemens, *Legacy*, p. 138.
24. Henry E. Meadows and John Meadows interview, November 2012.
25. Ibid.
26. Ibid.
27. Ibid.
28. John Paul Pitts, "Scharbauer Hotel: Oil Fortunes Were Made and Lost in Lobby of Famous Midland Hotel," *Midland Reporter-Telegram*, July 4, 1985.
29. Clarence Scharbauer Jr. interviews, May 2012, January 2013, March 2013, April 2013.

Chapter 3: A Town of Faith and Morals

1. Janine Green, "Methodists First Church to Organize"; "First Baptist Has Lots to Remember in Its 100th Year," both in *Midland Reporter-Telegram*, July 4, 1985.
2. *St. Ann's Church: The First 100 Years* (St. Ann's Church, Midland, Texas, 1997).
3. Janine Green, "Methodists First Church to Organize."
4. Janine Green, "First Baptist Has Lots to Remember in Its 100th Year."
5. Janine Green, "Methodists First Church to Organize."
6. Janine Green, "First Presbyterian Church Ministers to 'Heart of the City,'" *Midland Reporter-Telegram*, July 4, 1985.
7. Ibid.
8. Ibid.
9. Ibid.
10. Ibid.
11. Ibid.
12. Janine Green, "First Baptist Has Lots to Remember in Its 100th Year."
13. Judge John Hyde interviews, November 2009–November 2011.
14. Janine Green, "First Baptist Has Lots to Remember in Its 100th Year."
15. *St. Ann's Church: The First 100 Years*.
16. Ibid.
17. *St. Ann's Church: The First 100 Years*.
18. Ibid.
19. First Christian Church, *Dedicated to the Glory of God*, June 21–24, 1959.
20. Ibid.
21. John Howard Griffin, *Land of the High Sky* (Midland, TX: First National Bank of Midland, 1959), p. 76.

22. Ibid., p. 77.
23. Ibid., p. 76.
24. *Midland Reporter-Telegram Centennial edition*, July 4, 1985.
25. Midland County archives; Judge John Hyde files.
26. Midland County Courthouse records.
27. Judge John Hyde interviews.

Chapter 4: Land of Droughts and Sandstorms, Blizzards and Floods
1. Hallye Jordan, "Droughts, Floods, Dot West Texas Weather Pattern," *Midland Reporter-Telegram*, July 4, 1985.
2. Ibid.
3. Judge John Hyde interviews, November 2009–November 2011.
4. Jordan, "Droughts, Floods, Dot West Texas Weather Pattern."
5. John Howard Griffin, *Land of the High Sky* (Midland, TX: First National Bank of Midland, 1959), p. 77.
6. Ibid., p. 78.
7. Ibid., p. 75.
8. J. Evetts Haley. Interview with O. B. Holt, January 3, 1927, Haley Memorial Library and History Center archives.
9. Ibid.
10. Ibid.
11. Scharbauer family archives.
12. National Public Radio, July 7, 2012, "How One Drought Changed Texas Agriculture Forever."
13. Rosalind Grover interview, September 2011.
14. Judge John Hyde interviews, November 2009–November 2011.
15. Jordan, "Droughts, Floods, Dot West Texas Weather Pattern," *Midland Reporter-Telegram*, July 4, 1985.
16. Clarence Scharbauer Jr. interviews, May 2012, January 2013, March 2013, April 2013.
17. Joan Nobles interview, October 2011.
18. Ibid.
19. Jordan, "Droughts, Floods, Dot West Texas Weather Pattern."
20. T. O. Midkiff interview, March 2011.
21. *Midland Reporter-Telegram*, and Associated Press, "Midland Mops Up after Storm," May 10, 1968.
22. *Midland Reporter-Telegram*, "One Killed, Losses Run to Millions," May 10, 1968.
23. Ibid.
24. Jack Swallow interview, June 2012.
25. Craig Hubbard interview, June 2012.
26. Lloyd McDonald interview, April 2011.
27. Ibid.
28. Judge John Hyde interviews.

Chapter 5: How Midland Became the Oil Capital of West Texas
1. Woodeene Koenig-Bricker, *365 Saints* (San Francisco: HarperCollins, 1995).
2. Rotelle, John, *Book of Augustinian Saints* (Villanova, PA: Augustinian Press, 2000).
3. Ibid.
4. Martin W. Schwettmann, *Santa Rita: The University of Texas Oil Discovery* (Austin: Texas State Historical Association, 1943), p. 11.
5. Ibid., p. 37.

Endnotes

6. Judge John Hyde interviews, November 2009–November 2011.
7. Roger M. Olien and Diana Davids Hinton, *Wildcatters: Texas Independent Oilmen* (College Station: Texas A&M University Press, 2007), p. 19.
8. Ellen Hopkins, "The Grand Old Hotels, *Midland Reporter-Telegram*, October 2, 1989.
9. Pitts, John Paul, "Scharbauer Hotel: Oil Fortunes Were Made and Lost in Lobby of Famous Midland Hotel," *Midland Reporter-Telegram*, July 4, 1985.
10. Ibid.
11. Hopkins, "The Grand Old Hotels."
12. Judge John Hyde interviews.
13. Schwettman, *Santa Rita: The University of Texas Oil Discovery*, p. 34.
14. John Russell Bartlett, *Personal Narrative of Explorations and Incidents in Texas, New Mexico, California, Sonora, and Chihuahua, Connected with the United States and Mexican Boundary Commission During the Years 1850, '51, '52, and '53*. New York: Appleton, 1856. Digitized by the Internet Archive in 2012 with funding from the University of North Carolina at Chapel Hill. http://archive.org/details/personalnarrativ01bart
15. Judge John Hyde interviews, November 2009–November 2011.
16. Clarence Scharbauer Jr. interviews, May 2012, January 2013, March 2013, April 2013.
17. Permian Basin Petroleum Museum Hall of Fame biography, Thomas S. Hogan.
18. Gus Clemens, *Legacy* (San Antonio, TX: Mulberry Avenue Books, 1983), p. 139.
19. Judge John Hyde interviews, November 2009–November 2011.
20. Clemens, *Legacy*, p. 139.
21. Samuel D. Myres, *The Permian Basin: Petroleum Empire of the Southwest: Era of Discovery from the Beginning to the Depression* (El Paso, TX: Permian Press, 1973), p. 366.
22. Ellen Hopkins, *Midland Reporter-Telegram Permorama Edition*, February 19, 1995.
23. James Mims interviews, June 2010; April 2012.
24. Hopkins, *Midland Reporter-Telegram Permorama Edition*.
25. Ibid.
26. Ibid.
27. Ibid.
28. Samuel D. Myres, *The Permian Basin: Petroleum Empire of the Southwest: Era of Advancement from the Depression to the Present* (El Paso, TX: Permian Press, 1977), pp. 339–340.
29. Ibid.
30. Paul Vickers, 1930 Midland City Directory.
31. Myres, *The Permian Basin: Era of Advancement*, pp. 339–340.
32. Ibid.
33. Hopkins, *Midland Reporter-Telegram Permorama Edition*.
34. Gus Clemens, *Legacy*, p. 144.
35. John Howard Griffin, *Land of the High Sky* (Midland, TX: First National Bank of Midland, 1959), p. 159.
36. United States Census Department.
37. Olien and Hinton, *Wildcatters*, p. 78.
38. Benjamin Franklin Haag Biography, Haag family archives; Merle Haag interview, April 2011.
39. Ibid.; Ibid.
40. Bruce Partain, letter to Permian Basin Petroleum Museum's Hall of Fame nominating committee, nominating B. Frank Haag, Haag family archives.
41. Benjamin Franklin Haag Biography, Haag family archives.
42. "Haag at Point of Death in Angelo," *Midland-Reporter-Telegram*, July 12, 1933.
43. "Representative Haag is Dead," *Midland Reporter-Telegram*, July 13, 1933.
44. Ibid.
45. Frank Stubbeman, *Texas Bar Journal*, November 23, 1933.

46. Susan Lindsay, "Petroleum Club Promotes Fellowship within Oil Industry," *Midland Reporter-Telegram*, July 4, 1985.
47. Midland County Historical Museum archives.
48. *Midland Reporter-Telegram*, November 1, 1973.
49. Ibid.
50. Ibid.

Chapter 6: The Scharbauer Legacy

1. Clarence Scharbauer III interview, February 2013.
2. John Howard Griffin, *Land of the High Sky* (Midland, TX: First National Bank of Midland, 1959), p. 121.
3. Ibid.
4. Ibid., p. 84.
5. *Midland Reporter-Telegram*, "Funeral Services for Clarence Scharbauer to Be Sunday at First Baptist Church," October 3, 1942.
6. Ibid.
7. Ibid.
8. Clarence Scharbauer Jr. interviews, August 2011, April–May 2013
9. James L. Colwell, "Midland Army Air Field," *Handbook of Texas Online* (Denton, TX: Texas State Historical Association), http://www.tshaonline.org/handbook/online/articles/qbm02
10. *Midland Reporter-Telegram*, "Funeral Services for Clarence Scharbauer to Be Sunday at First Baptist Church," October 3, 1942.
11. Clarence Scharbauer Jr. interviews, May 2012, January 2013, March 2013, April 2013.
12. *Midland Reporter-Telegram*, "Funeral Services for Clarence Scharbauer to Be Sunday at First Baptist Church."
13. Ibid.
14. Ibid.
15. Ibid.
16. Clarence Scharbauer Jr. interviews, May 2012, January 2013, March 2013, April 2013.
17. Ibid.
18. Ibid.
19. Texas Thoroughbred Association, "Texas Stakes Renamed for Scharbauer," www.texasthoroughbred.com
20. Rosalind Grover interview, September 2011.
21. Clarence Scharbauer Jr. interviews, May 2012, January 2013, March 2013, April 2013.
22. Obituary of Clarence Scharbauer Jr., *Midland Reporter-Telegram*, February 22, 2014
23. Ken Carson interview, February 21, 2014.
24. Clarence Scharbauer III interviews, February 2013, April 2011.
25. Clarence Scharbauer Jr. interviews, May 2012, January 2013, March 2013, April 2013.
26. Ibid.
27. Edward Bowen, "Aly to the Roses," *The Blood Horse*, May 9, 1987.
28. Clarence Scharbauer Jr. interviews, May 2012, January 2013, March 2013, April 2013.
29. Jack Van Berg interview, July 2013.
30. Clarence Scharbauer Jr. interviews, May 2012, January 2013, March 2013, April 2013.
31. Bowen, "Aly to the Roses."
32. *Louisville Courier-Journal*, "Alysheba, '87 Derby winner, Euthanized," May 28, 2009.
33. Clarence Scharbauer III interviews, February 2013, April 2011.
34. Ibid.

Endnotes

Chapter 7: Wassail, Gingerbread, and Generosity
1. Mike Bradford interview, May 2012.
2. Clarence Scharbauer Jr. interviews, May 2012, January 2013, March 2013, April 2013.
3. John Howard Griffin, *Land of the High Sky* (Midland, TX: First National Bank of Midland, 1959), pp. 167–168.
4. Ike Fitzgerald interview, February 2011.
5. Dean Rucker interview, August 2013.
6. Ernest Angelo interviews, November 2010, February 2013.
7. *Midland Reporter-Telegram*, October 20, 1997.
8. Jane McAbee interviews, May 2011, March 2013.
9. Ibid.
10. Permian Basin Petroleum Hall of Fame records.
11. *Midland Reporter-Telegram*, October 20, 1997.
12. David Mims interview, September 2011.
13. Katie Spriggs interview, May 2013.
14. David L. Smith interview, April 2011.
15. Ibid.
16. Judge John Hyde interviews, November 2009–November 2011.
17. Ibid.
18. Judge John Hyde, History of Midland presentations.
19. Mike Bradford interview.
20. David L. Smith interview.
21. David Lindemood interview, April 2011.
22. Katie Spriggs interview, May 2013
23. David L. Smith interview.
24. Jane McAbee interviews.
25. Mike Bradford interview.
26. Guy McCrary interview, September 2010.
27. Ibid.
28. Clarence Scharbauer III interview, April 2011.
29. Jane McAbee interviews, May 2011, March 2013.
30. Ibid.
31. Ibid.
32. *Midland Reporter-Telegram*, October 20, 1997.
33. Full-page advertisement published in the *Midland Reporter-Telegram*, October 24, 1997.

Chapter 8: Aviation in the Land of the High Sky
1. Richard Hardin, "Pliska Was Planning Aeroplane as Early as 1908," *Midland Reporter-Telegram*, July 4, 1985.
2. Pliska Aeroplane: A Blacksmith's Aeroplane, City of Midland exhibit, Midland International Airport.
3. Julia Cauble Smith, "Pliska, John Valentine," *Handbook of Texas Online* (Denton, TX: Texas State Historical Association), http://www.tshaonline.org/handbook/online/articles/fpl05
4. Hardin, "Pliska Was Planning Aeroplane as Early as 1908."
5. George E. Alexander: *The Stars Were Big and Bright: The United States Armed Forces and Texas During World War II* (Vol. 2), Austin: Eakin, 2000, p. 101.
6. Mary Dargenio, "Science of War Taught," *Midland Reporter-Telegram*, July 4, 1985.
7. Judge John Hyde, "Midland Airfield Plays Crucial Role in Developing U.S. Airpower During WWII," *Midland Reporter-Telegram*, November 6, 2011
8. Mary Dargenio, "Science of War Taught," *Midland Reporter-Telegram*, July 4, 1985.

9. Ibid.
10. Midland Army Airbase Museum archives
11. Judge John Hyde, "Midland Airfield Plays Crucial Role in Developing U.S. Airpower During WWII," *Midland Reporter-Telegram*, November 6, 2011.
12. Midland Army Airfield Museum.
13. Midland International Airport History, http://www.flymaf.com/army_airfield.aspx
14. *Midland Reporter-Telegram*, October 7, 1942.
15. Midland Army Airbase Museum.
16. David Lindemood interview, April 2011.
17. Rosalind Grover interview, September 2011.
18. Cope Routh, "Five Civilians, Two Webb Pilots Killed, *Midland Reporter-Telegram*, October 25, 1956.
19. *Midland Reporter-Telegram*, "Mayor Expresses Sympathy, Commendation in Disaster," October 25, 1956.
20. Routh, "Five Civilians, Two Webb Pilots Killed," October 25, 1956.
21. Carroll Thomas interview, September 2011.
22. Bobby Burns interview, October 2010.
23. Carroll Thomas interview, September 2011.
24. Ibid.
25. Ibid.
26. Ibid.
27. Bobby Burns interview, October 2010.
28. Ibid.
29. Ibid.

Chapter 9: "This Sprawling, New, Oil-Rich Town"
1. Arlen Edgar interview, January 2012.
2. Ibid.
3. Ibid.
4. Samuel D. Myres, *The Permian Basin: Petroleum Empire of the Southwest: Era of Advancement from the Depression to the Present* (El Paso, TX: Permian Press, 1977), p. 34.
5. Dr. Diana Davids Hinton interview, April 2011.
6. Ibid.
7. Roger M. Olien and Diana Davids Hinton, *Wildcatters: Texas Independent Oilmen* (College Station: Texas A&M University Press, 2007), p. 99.
8. Dr. Diana Davids Hinton interview.
9. Buddy Sipes interview, March 2011.
10. Ibid.
11. Ibid.
12. Olien and Hinton, *Wildcatters*, p. 101.
13. Ibid., p. 103.
14. Olien and Olien, *Oil Booms*, p. 177.
15. Myres, *The Permian Basin: Era of Advancement*, pp. 340–341.
16. Olien and Olien, *Oil Booms*, p. 82.
17. Dr. Diana Davids Hinton interview, April 2011.
18. Ibid.
19. Buddy Sipes interview, March 2011.
20. Jim Henry interviews, March 11, August 2012.
21. Gus Clemens, *Legacy* (San Antonio, TX: Mulberry Avenue Books, 1983), p. 149.
22. Midland Centennial archives.

ENDNOTES

23. Myres, *The Permian Basin: Era of Advancement*, p. 341.
24. Olien and Olien, *Oil Booms* p. 82.
25. Olien and Hinton, *Wildcatters*, p. 99.
26. Ibid., p. 101.
27. Rosalind Grover interview
28. Joe O'Neill interview, October 2010
29. Dr. Charles Younger interview, September 2011
30. George W. Bush interview
31. Sid Trevino interview
32. Rosalind Grover interview, September 2011.
33. Edna Brown Hibbits, "Citizens Join Forces to Solve Health Problems," *Midland Reporter-Telegram*, July 4, 1985.
34. Ibid.
35. Ibid.
36. Ibid.
37. Ibid.
38. Ibid.
39. *Midland Reporter-Telegram*. "Civic Leaders Laud Hospital," July 9, 1950.
40. Hibbitts, "Citizens Join Forces to Solve Health Problems."
41. Ibid.
42. Midland Memorial Hospital, "History of Midland Memorial Hospital," marketing information and brochure obtained in December 2012.
43. President Gerald Ford, presentation at opening of Permian Basin Petroleum Museum and Hall of Fame, Midland, Texas, September 13, 1975.
44. Olien and Hinton, *Wildcatters*, p. 78.
45. Abell-Hanger Foundation archives.
46. Ibid.
47. David L. Smith interview, April 2011, May 2012.
48. Joe Mabee interview, May 2012.
49. *50 Years: Abell-Hanger Community Celebration*, video of tribute to George and Gladys Abell, Midland Center, September 16, 2004.
50. Rebecca Bell, Public Information Office, Midland College, February 5, 2014.
51. David L. Smith interview.
52. Ibid.
53. David L. Smith interviews, July 2014.
54. June Cowden interviews, August 2011, May 2013.

Chapter 10: Theatre, Music, and a Mickey Mouse Rumor

1. Texas State Historical Commission marker, 208 N. Colorado, Midland, Texas.
2. Ibid.
3. Ibid.
4. Tim Jebsen, conversation with author, May 2014.
5. Judge John Hyde interviews, November 2009–November 2011.
6. Art Cole interview, July 2011.
7. Ibid.
8. Ibid.
9. Ibid.
10. Jim Salners interview, July 2011.
11. Ibid.
12. Bill and Katie Heck interview, November 2010.

13. Rosalind Grover interview, September 2011.
14. Art Cole interview, July 2011.
15. Jimmy Patterson, "Roy Orbison: West Texan's First Huge Hit, 'Only the Lonely,' Written in East Midland Duplex," *Midland Reporter-Telegram*, February 15, 2009.
16. W. W. Bear Mills, "Midland Concert Helped Orbison 'Cash' In on Music Career," *Midland Reporter-Telegram*, April 22, 2007.
17. Ibid.
18. Ibid.
19. Bobby Burns interview, October 2010.
20. Ibid.
21. Ibid.
22. Ibid.
23. Ibid.
24. Ibid.

Chapter 11: Race Relations in Midland
1. *Texas Almanac, 2014–2015*, p. 350.
2. *Midland Reporter-Telegram*, June 22, 1952.
3. Harold Whittington, "Charge Midland Is 'Boiling Cauldron of Hate' Stirs Prompt Protests, Denials," *Midland Reporter-Telegram*, June 24, 1952.
4. Ibid.
5. Conrad Coleman interview, March 2008.
6. Ibid.
7. Coleman family archives .
8. Ibid.
9. Dr. Laurie Green interview, April 2008.
10. Letter from Daniel Byrd to Viola Johnson, Coleman family archives.
11. Dr. James Fuller interview, April 2008.
12. Dr. Viola Coleman section up to this point is based largely on two sources: interview with Conrad Coleman, March 2008; and Jimmy Patterson, "Letters Found in South Midland Home Tell Story of Viola Coleman's Significant Role in Civil Rights," *Midland Reporter-Telegram*, May 4, 2008.
13. Margaret Williams interview, February 2013.
14. Dr. James Fuller interview, April 2008.
15. Joe Chavez interview, April 2010.
16. 519 F.2d 60.
17. *The Hornette*, November 1958.
18. *Midland Reporter-Telegram*, "Events listed in Midland Independent School District Desegregation," July 4, 1985.
19. Joe Chavez interview, April 2010.
20. Sid Trevino interview, May 2010.
21. Barbara Yarbrough interview, April 2010.
22. Ibid.
23. Jose Cuevas interview, May 2011.
24. Pastor George Bell interview, April 2012.
25. Ibid.
26. Pastor George Bell interview, April 2012.
27. Ibid.
28. Michael Williams interview, April 2012.
29. Ibid.

Endnotes

Chapter 12: Midland Debates Key Issues in the High Courts
1. 397 S.W.2d 919.
2. *Avery v. Midland County*, 390 U.S. 474 (1968).
3. Bill and Katie Heck interview, November 2010.
4. Ibid.
5. *Avery v. Midland County*, 390 U.S. 474 (1968).
6. Bill and Katie Heck interview, November 2010.
7. *Avery v. Midland County*, 390 U.S. 474 (1968).
8. Anntoinette Moore, "Events listed in Midland Independent School District Desegregation," *Midland Reporter-Telegram*, July 4, 1985.
9. Ibid.
10. Ibid.
11. Ibid.
12. Ibid.
13. Antoinette Moore, "MISD Not Fully Integrated Until 1976," *Midland Reporter-Telegram*, July 4, 1985.
14. Joe Dominey interview, November 2013.
15. Ibid.
16. Ibid.
17. 519 F.2d 60.
18. 5 Cir. 1971, 443 F.2d 1180.
19. 519 F.2d 60.
20. 96 S.Ct. 1106.
21. Joe Dominey interview, November 2013.
22. Ibid.
23. Ibid.
24. Ruth Campbell, "Attorneys: School System Provides Equitable Education for All," *Midland Reporter-Telegram*, August 24, 2008.
25. Joan Baskin interview, April 2010.
26. *The Hornette*, November 1958.
27. Moore, "Events listed in Midland Independent School District Desegregation."
28. Joan Love-Davis interview, March 2013.
29. *Carver School Newspaper*, "The History of Carver Junior-Senior High School," November 1958.
30. Moore, "Events listed in Midland Independent School District Desegregation."
31. Ibid.
32. Conrad Coleman interview, January 2014.
33. Ibid.
34. Moore, "Events listed in Midland Independent School District Desegregation."
35. Ibid.
36. Joan Love-Davis interview, March 2013.
37. Ibid.
38. Campbell, "Attorneys: School System Provides Equitable Education for All."
39. *Green v. County School Board of New Kent County*, 391 U.S. 430 (1968), cited in http://educational-law.org/261-dual-and-unitary-systems.html
40. Campbell, "Attorneys: School System Provides Equitable Education for All."
41. Ibid.
42. Ibid.
43. Joe Dominey interview, November 2013.

Endnotes

Chapter 13: An Infamous Murder
1. Clarence Scharbauer Jr. interviews, August 2011, May 2012, June 2012, February 2013.
2. Ibid.
3. Ibid.
4. Ibid.
5. Ibid.
6. Ibid.
7. Clarence Scharbauer Jr. interview, January 2013.
8. Ibid.
9. Tom Craddick interviews, September 2013
10. Ibid.
11. Ibid.
12. "Negro relates murder details," Cope Routh, *Midland Reporter-Telegram*, October 30, 1963.
13. Ibid.
14. Ibid.
15. Ibid.
16. Ibid.
17. Ibid.
18. Ibid.
19. Ibid.
20. Ibid.
21. *Midland Reporter-Telegram*, "Experts Say Young Negro Slayer Sane," October 31, 1963.
22. Ibid.
23. Cope Routh, "State to Ask Death Penalty For Marion," *Midland Reporter-Telegram*, March 16, 1964.
24. David Lindemood interview, September 2011.
25. Cope Routh, "Nine Seated as Marion Case Jurors," *Midland Reporter-Telegram*, March 18, 1964.
26. Ibid.
27. *Midland Reporter-Telegram*, "Marion Juror Accepted," March 19, 1964.
28. Ibid.
29. *Midland Reporter-Telegram*, "Testimony Starts in Lubbock Trial," March 20, 1964.
30. Ibid.
31. *Midland Reporter-Telegram*, "State Draws Net Tighter at Lubbock," March 21, 1964.
32. Cope Routh, "Marion Condemned to Die," *Midland Reporter-Telegram*, March 23, 1964.
33. Clarence Scharbauer Jr. interview, January 2013.
34. Ibid.
35. Ibid.
36. Ibid.
37. Clarence Scharbauer Jr. interview, January 2013.
38. *Midland Reporter-Telegram*, "Seizure Claims Fred Turner Jr.," February 5, 1964.
39. Ibid.
40. Clarence Scharbauer Jr. interviews, August 2011, May 2012, June 2012, February 2013.
41. Ibid.

Chapter 14: Midland's Shift from Democratic to Republican
1. Ernest Angelo interview, November 2010.
2. Educational Broadcasting Corporation, "Jim Crow Stories," *The Rise and Fall of Jim Crow*, 2002, http://www.pbs.org/wnet/jimcrow/stories_org_democratric.html
3. Liberal Arts Instructional Technology Services, "History and Politics: Political Parties and

ENDNOTES

Party Systems," *Texas Politics*, University of Texas at Austin, 2009, http://texaspolitics.laits.utexas.edu/4_3_0.html
4. Midland County Election Office
5. Ernest Angelo interviews, November 2010, February 2013.
6. Ernest Angelo, correspondence with author, June 2014.
7. Ernest Angelo interviews, November 2010, February 2013.
8. Ernest Angelo, correspondence with author, June 2014.
9. Ernest Angelo interview, November 2010.
10. Ibid.
11. Ibid.
12. Ibid. Ernest Angelo interviews, November 2010, February 2013.
13. Bill and Katie Heck interview, November 2010.
14. Ernest Angelo interviews, November 2010, February 2013.
15. Ernest Angelo interview, November 2010.
16. Ernest Angelo interviews, November 2010, February 2013.
17. Ibid.
18. Ernest Angelo interview, November 2010.
19. Ibid.   Ernest Angelo interviews, November 2010, February 2013.
20. Ernest Angelo interview, November 2010.
21. Ibid.
22. Ibid.
23. Ibid.
24. Ibid.
25. Ernest Angelo interviews, November 2010, February 2013.
26. *Midland Reporter-Telegram*.
27. http://en.wikipedia.org/wiki/Ernest_Angelo.
28. Barbara Culver-Clack interview, August 2010.
29. Ibid.
30. Tom Craddick interviews, November 2010, September 2013.
31. Ibid.
32. Ibid.
33. Nadine Craddick interview, May 2011.
34. Ibid.
35. Ibid.
36. Ibid.
37. Tom Craddick interviews, November 2010, September 2013.
38. St. Ann's School Records, "Distinguished Alumni of St. Ann's School."
39. Tom Craddick interviews, June 2012, September 2013.
40. Texas House of Representatives Online: http://www.house.state.tx.us/members/member-page/?district=82
41. S. C. Gwynne, "Tom Craddick: How Did Tom Craddick Become the Most Powerful Speaker Ever—and the Most Powerful Texan Today? Let Us Count the Ways." *Texas Monthly*, February 2005.
42. Ibid.
43. Ibid.
44. Lou Brown interview, November 2013.
45. Ibid.
46. Juandelle Lacy interview, October 2013.
47. Ibid.
48. Ibid.

Endnotes

Chapter 15: The Longest Love Affair in the History of Midland
1. Melissa Handley, "Midland Christian College," *Handbook of Texas Online* (Denton, TX: Texas State Historical Association), http://www.tshaonline.org/handbook/online/articles/kbm23
2. Ibid.
3. Ibid.
4. First Christian Church, *Dedicated to the Glory of God*, June 21–24, 1959.
5. Melissa Handley, "Midland Christian College," *Handbook of Texas Online* (Denton, TX: Texas State Historical Association), http://www.tshaonline.org/handbook/online/articles/kbm23
6. Ibid.
7. Ibid.
8. Scharbauer Jr. interviews, May 2012, January 2013, March 2013, April 2013.
9. Ibid.
10. *Midland Reporter-Telegram*, obituary of Richard Slack, March 6, 2013.
11. Clarence Scharbauer Jr. interviews, May 2012, January 2013, March 2013, April 2013.
12. Ibid.
13. Ernest Angelo interviews, November 2010, February 2013.
14. Ibid.
15. Ibid.
16. Doug Henson interview, February 2011.
17. Ibid.
18. Dr. Jess Parrish interview, August 2010.
19. "Permian Junior College System," *Handbook of Texas Online* (Denton, TX: Texas State Historical Association), http://www.tshaonline.org/handbook/online/articles/kcp04
20. Ralph Way interview, Dec. 2011.
21. Eileen Piwetz interviews, November 2012.
22. Dr. David Daniel, Introduction to *Midland College: The First Twenty-Five Years*, by Karen Lanier and H.A. Tuck (Baltimore: Gateway Books, 1996), p. 2.
23. Ibid., p. 1
24. Ralph Way interview, December 2011.
25. Eileen Piwetz interview, November 2012.
26. Ibid.
27. Ibid.
28. Meredith Moriak, "Midland College Unveils Facilities Master Plan," *Midland Reporter-Telegram*, October 20, 2013.
29. Rebecca Bell, Midland College Public Relations Department records.
30. Eileen Piwetz interview, November 2012.
31. Ibid.

Chapter 16: "We'll Never See a Bank Like That Again"
1. Terry Williamson, "Permian Loses Mojo Magic," *Midland Reporter-Telegram*, October 15, 1983.
2. Lana Cunningham, "Waiting Game Ends," *Midland Reporter-Telegram*, October 17, 1983.
3. Ibid.
4. Ibid.
5. *Midland Reporter-Telegram*, "RepublicBank Takes Over First National Bank," October 17, 1983.
6. Ibid.
7. Ibid.
8. Ibid.
9. Ibid.

ENDNOTES

10. Lana Cunningham, "Waiting Game Ends."
11. Ibid.
12. Jim Presnall, "Odessa Bank Insolvent, Closed," *Midland Reporter-Telegram*, October 8, 1983.
13. *Midland Reporter-Telegram*, "RepublicBank Takes Over First National Bank."
14. David L. Smith interview, April 2011.
15. Ibid.
16. Ibid.
17. Ibid.
18. Judge John Hyde, "A Look Back at 10 Events That Define Our Community," *Midland Reporter-Telegram*, June 5, 2011.
19. David L. Smith interview, April 2011.
20. Joe Mabee interview, June 2012.
21. Guy McCrary interview, September 2010.
22. Ibid.
23. Ibid.
24. *Midland Reporter-Telegram*, "New Accounts Have Been Pledged to FNB," October 19, 1983.
25. *Midland Reporter-Telegram*, "Our Finest Hour; Perhaps Odessa's." October 19, 1983.
26. Ibid.
27. Ibid.
28. Mary Lou Cassidy interview, August 2011.
29. Jane McAbee interview, May 2011.
30. Ibid.
31. Katie Spriggs interview, May 2013.
32. Ibid.

Chapter 17: Toddler's Rescue Brings Much-Needed Optimism
1. Patrick Crimmins, "Rescuers Struggle Toward Toddler," *Midland Reporter-Telegram*, October 15, 1987.
2. Patrick Crimmins, "Rescue Workers Drill Shaft Beside Well in Rescue Try," *Midland Reporter-Telegram* October 14, 1987.
3. Patrick Crimmins, "Rescue Matter of Time," *Midland Reporter-Telegram*, October 29, 1987.
4. Crimmins, "Rescuers Struggle Toward Toddler."
5. Ibid.
6. Ibid.
7. Ibid.
8. Ibid.
9. James Roberts interview, November 2011.
10. Crimmins, "Rescuers Struggle Toward Toddler."
11. Carroll Thomas interview, September 2011.
12. Dr. Debbie Reese interview, May 2012.
13. Ramona Nye, "Jessica Free, under Doctor's Care," *Midland Reporter-Telegram*, October 17, 1987.
14. Ibid.
15. Ibid.
16. Dr. Debbie Reese interview, May 2012.
17. Lisa Belkin, "Death on the CNN Curve," *The New York Times*, July 23, 1995.
18. Tom Barnett interview, May 2013.
19. Ibid.
20. Ibid.
21. Patrick Crimmins, "Vice President Also Will Honor Community," *Midland Reporter-Telegram*, by October 17, 1987.

22. Jane Marlar Dees, "Plush Zoo Opens World's Wishes for Jessica," *Midland Reporter-Telegram*, October 17, 1987.
23. Rick Brown, "Playful Jessica Meets the Press," *Midland Reporter-Telegram*, October 29, 1987.
24. Bob Greene, "Rescue Reminds Us of Real Heroes," Chicago Tribune Media Services/*Midland Reporter-Telegram*, October 29, 1987.
25. Dr. Debbie Reese interview, May 2012.
26. Carroll Thomas interview, September 2011.
27. Carroll Thomas, "An Open Letter to the Community," *Midland Reporter-Telegram*, October 18, 1987.
28. James Roberts interview, November 2011.
29. Bob Campbell, "Officer's Life Fell Apart after Baby Jessica's Well Rescue," *Midland Reporter-Telegram*, July 31, 2005.
30. *People* magazine, May 15, 1995.
31. Dr. Debbie Reese interview, May 2012.
32. Ibid.
33. James Roberts interview, November 2011.

Chapter 18: Midlanders on the National Political Scene

1. Sid Trevino interview, May 2010.
2. Ibid.
3. Mike Cochran, *Claytie* (College Station: Texas A&M University Press), pp. 108–109.
4. Ibid.
5. Ibid.
6. Ibid.
7. Clayton Williams Jr. interview, September 2012.
8. Ibid.
9. Cochran, *Claytie*, p. 269.
10. Ibid., p. 296.
11. Clayton Williams Jr. interview, September 2012.
12. Ibid.
13. Ibid.
14. Permian Basin Petroleum Museum.
15. Clayton Williams Jr. interviews, September 2012
16. Ibid.
17. Brett Clanton, "One of the Last Wildcatters Is Upbeat About the Oil Business," *Houston Chronicle*, June 13, 2011.
18. George W. Bush, speech during appearance in Midland, Texas, January 19, 2001.
19. George W. Bush interview, February 2012.
20. Ibid.
21. Ibid.
22. Ibid.
23. Joe O'Neill interview, October 2010.
24. Charles Younger interview, September 2011.
25. Ibid.
26. Ibid.
27. K. Michael Conaway interview, August 2011.
28. Ibid.
29. Ibid.
30. Ibid.

Endnotes

Chapter 19: City's Bold Progress Continues
1. Russell Meyers, "Wednesday Will Bring a New Day for Health Care in Midland," *Midland Reporter-Telegram*, December 16, 2012.
2. Rosalind Grover interviews, September 2011.
3. Ibid.
4. Ibid.
5. Ibid.
6. Ibid.
7. Ibid.
8. Ibid.
9. Ibid.
10. Ibid.
11. Ibid.
12. Bobby Burns interview, October 2010.
13. Ibid.
14. Ibid.
15. Ibid.
16. Ibid.
17. Ibid.
18. Ibid.
19. Ibid.
20. Ibid.
21. Ibid.
22. Ibid.
23. Ibid.
24. Bobby Burns interview, October 2010.
25. Ibid.
26. Ibid.
27. Ibid.
28. Ibid.
29. Ibid.

Chapter 20: How the Wolfberry Changed Midland
1. Jim Henry interviews, March 2011, August 2012.
2. Ibid.
3. Ibid.
4. *Midland Reporter-Telegram*, "Damn Lizard!" December 25, 2011.
5. *The Economist*, "The Father of Fracking," August 3, 2013.
6. Ibid.
7. Jim Henry, presentations to Permian Basin Petroleum Association, September 2011, and Society of Professional Engineers, April 2012.
8. Jim Henry, speech to Permian Basin Petroleum Association and the Society of Petroleum Engineers, Midland Country Club, Midland, Texas, April 8, 2010.
9. Jim Henry, speech to Society of International Petroleum Earth Scientists, Midland Country Club, January 19, 2012.
10. Jim Henry, presentations to Permian Basin Petroleum Association, September 2011, and Society of Professional Engineers, April 2012.
11. Dr. Diana Davids Hinton interviews, May 2010.
12. Ibid.
13. Jim Henry presentations to Permian Basin Petroleum Association, September 2011, and Society of Professional Engineers, April 2012.

14. *Midland Reporter-Telegram*, "*Forbes* Magazine Lists Odessa, Midland as Best Cities for Jobs," May 10, 2012.
15. *Midland Reporter-Telegram*, "Housing Just Can't Keep Up with the Boom," April 29, 2012.
16. *Midland Reporter-Telegram*, "Man Hitchhikes from Georgia to Midland Looking for Job, Finds More," March 30, 2013.
17. U.S. Census: Race, Hispanic or Latino, Age, and Occupancy: 2010.
18. Jerry Morales interview, June 2013.
19. Jerry Morales interview, July 2014.
20. Permian Basin Board of Realtors.
21. *Midland Reporter-Telegram*, "For Some, Camping Is Home Sweet Home," April 29, 2012.
22. Jerry Morales interview, July 2014.
23. James Beauchamp interview, March 2013.
24. Kathleen Petty, "Population Increase Strains Roads," *Midland Reporter-Telegram*, September 30, 2012.
25. James Beauchamp, interview, March 2013.
26. Jerry Morales interview, July 2014.
27. Sara Higgins, "Area Could Become Traffic Nightmare," *Midland Reporter-Telegram*, October 24, 2012.
28. Ibid.
29. Ibid.
30. Wes Perry interviews, September 2012, March 2013.
31. Ibid.
32. Ibid.

Chapter 21: Water Precious as Oil

1. Judge John Hyde interviews, November 2009–November 2011.
2. Colorado River Municipal Water District historical statistics.
3. Mike McGregor interviews, July 2012, January 2013.
4. Ed Magruder interview, June 2013.
5. Kathleen Thurber, "Council Enacts Drought Contingency Plan," *Midland Reporter-Telegram*, June 15, 2011.
6. Ibid.
7. Berry Simpson interview, September 2013.
8. Audrie Palmer, "A Very Trying Season," *Midland Reporter-Telegram*, May 29, 2011.
9. Ibid.
10. Jimmy Patterson, "West Texas Burning," *West Texas Angelus*, May 2011.
11. Ibid.
12. National Weather Service.
13. http://blog.chron.com/sportsupdate/2011/06/memories-of-drought-past-and-present/
14. Colorado River Municipal Water District.
15. Judge John Hyde interviews, November 2009–November 2011.
16. Audrie Palmer, "Weekend Rains Replenish Lake Ivie," *Midland Reporter-Telegram*, October 2, 2012.
17. *Midland Reporter-Telegram*, "Tall City Gets Soaked," September 29, 2012.
18. Mike McGregor interview, July 2012
19. Palmer, "Weekend Rains Replenish Lake Ivie."
20. Ibid.
21. Wes Perry interviews, September 2012, March 2013.
22. Mike McGregor interviews, July 2012, January 2013.
23. Ibid.
24. Joseph Basco, "T-Bar Ranch Pipeline 50 Years in the Making," *Midland Reporter-Telegram*, May 26, 2013.

Endnotes

25. Ed Magruder interview, June 2013.
26. *Midland Reporter-Telegram*, "Let the Water Flow," by Joseph Basco, June 1, 2013
27. Wes Perry interview, January 2014.

Chapter 22: Midland: A City of Character
1. Judge John Hyde interviews, November 2009–November 2011.
2. Roger Robles interview, March 2011.
3. George W. Bush, correspondence with author, February 2012.
4. Gary Painter interview, October 2010.
5. Joan Baskin interview, April 2010.
6. Grant Billingsley interview, November 2010.
7. Barbara Yarbrough interview, April 2010.
8. Wes Perry interviews, September 2012, March 2013.
9. David Mims interview, September 2011.
10. Felipe Morales interview, February 2013.
11. Fred Poe interview, February 2011.

Part Two: People of Integrity, Past and Present

George Bell
1. Jimmy Patterson, "George Bell Has Gone From His Grandfather's Knee to Community Leader," *Midland Reporter-Telegram*, December 21, 2008.

Laura Bush
1. Laura Bush's letter to middle and high school students, widely distributed in American and European news outlets, September 17, 2001.

Frank Cahoon
1. Tom Craddick interviews, June 2012, September 2013, October 2013.
2. Ed Todd, "Former State Rep. Cahoon Leaves Legacy of Service," *Midland Reporter-Telegram*, February 1, 2013.

Bill Collyns
1. *Midland Reporter-Telegram* editorial, May 16, 1996.
2. Ibid.
3. Ellen Hopkins, "Midlanders Attribute Much of City's Success to One Man's Vision," *Midland Reporter-Telegram*, May 16, 1996.

The Cowden family
1. Rosalind Grover interviews.
2. Ibid.

Ed Darnell
1. Gary Painter interview.

Newnie Ellis
1. Nancy McKinley, ed. *The Pioneer History of Midland County, Texas, 1880–1926*, limited centennial ed. (Dallas: Taylor Publishing Co., 1984), p. 78.
2. Ed Todd, "Midland Loses Newnie Ellis, a Friend to Family and Community," *Midland Reporter-Telegram*, October 26, 2011.

Endnotes

Herman Garrett
1. Nancy McKinley, *The Pioneer History of Midland County, Texas, 1880–1926*, limited centennial ed. (Dallas: Taylor Publishing Co., 1984), p. 83.
2. Gus Clemens, *Legacy* (San Antonio: Mulberry Avenue Books, 1983), p. 130.

Frank Haag
1. Letter from John Howe in Rotarians' newsletter, Midland Rotary Club records.

Henry Halff
1. Nancy McKinley, ed., *The Pioneer History of Midland County, Texas, 1880–1926*, limited centennial ed. (Dallas: Taylor Publishing Co., 1984), p. 86.
2. Ibid., p. 16.

T. S. Hogan
1. John Hyde, "A Look Back at 10 Events That Define Our Community," *Midland Reporter-Telegram*, June 4, 2011.
2. John Howard Griffin, *Land of the High Sky* (Midland, TX: First National Bank of Midland, 1959), page 151.
3. Gus Clemens, *Legacy* (San Antonio: Mulberry Avenue Books, 1983), p. 139.

W. W. Lackey
1. Nancy McKinley, ed. *The Pioneer History of Midland County, Texas, 1880–1926*, limited centennial ed. (Dallas: Taylor Publishing Co., 1984), p. 93.
2. Mabel Glass, untitled history of Midland, Texas, Haley Memorial Library and History Center collection, 1950
3. Nancy McKinley, *The Pioneer History of Midland County*, p. 93

Dr. Al G. Langford
1. Karen S. Lanier and H. A. Tuck, *Midland College: The First Twenty-Five Years* (Baltimore: Gateway Books, 1996), p. 19.
2. Ibid., pp. 17 and 24.
3. Ibid., p. 55.
4. Ibid., p. 11.

The Mabee family
1. Joe Mabee interview, May 2012.
2. Ibid.
3. Ibid.
4. Ibid.

Ed Magruder
1. Ed Magruder interview, June 2013.
2. Ibid.
3. Ibid.
4. Ibid.

Randolph Marcy
1. Max A. Clampitt, *Images of America: Hobbs and Lea County, NM* (Mount Pleasant, SC: Arcadia Publishing, 2008), p. 7.

Endnotes

Len "Tuffy" McCormick
1. Lloyd McDonald interview, April 2011.
2. Len "Tuffy" McCormick interview, November 2010.
3. Ibid.
4. Ibid.
5. Ibid.
6. Ibid.

Nancy McKinley
1. Nancy McKinley, ed. *The Pioneer History of Midland County, Texas, 1880–1926*, limited centennial ed. (Dallas: Taylor Publishing Co., 1984)
2. Modisett, Bill, and Nancy Rankin McKinley, eds., *Historic Midland, An Illustrated History of Midland County* (Midland County Historical Society, 1998).
3. *The First Christian Church (Disciples of Christ)*.

Gary Painter
1. Gary Painter interview, October 2010.
2. bid.
3. Ibid.

Frank Pickrell
1. Martin W. Schwettmann, *Santa Rita: The University of Texas Oil Discovery* (Austin: Texas State Historical Association, 1943), p. 5.
2. Ibid.

Charles Spence
1. Editorial in the *Midland Reporter-Telegram*, July 12, 2007.

Marvin Ulmer
1. John Howard Griffin, *Land of the High Sky* (Midland, TX: First National Bank of Midland, 1959), p. 168.

Addison Wadley
1. Addison Wadley, "Addison Wadley, Retired Merchant, Says Opportunities Are Unlimited," *Midland Reporter-Telegram*, February 29, 1948.

bibliography

Print and Internet Sources

Abell-Hanger Foundation archives, Midland, Texas.

Avery v. Midland County, 390 U.S. 474 (1968).

Bartlett, John Russell. *Personal Narrative of Explorations and Incidents in Texas, New Mexico, California, Sonora, and Chihuahua, Connected with the United States and Mexican Boundary Commission During the Years 1850, '51, '52, and '53*. New York: Appleton, 1856. Digitized by the Internet Archive in 2012 with funding from the University of North Carolina at Chapel Hill. http://archive.org/details/personalnarrativ01bart

Basco, Joseph. "T-Bar Ranch Pipeline 50 Years in the Making." *Midland Reporter-Telegram*, May 26, 2013.

———. "Let the Water Flow." *Midland Reporter-Telegram*, June 1, 2013.

———. "Mayor: Courthouse to Be Demolished." *Midland Reporter-Telegram*, March 14, 2013.

———. "Midlanders Have Their Say." *Midland Reporter-Telegram*, August 21, 2013.

Battles, Ted. "Affair with Baseball Long-Running Romance." *Midland Reporter-Telegram*, July 4, 1985.

Belkin, Lisa. "Death on the CNN Curve." *The New York Times*, July 23, 1995.

Bell, Rebecca. Midland College Public Relations Department records.

Benjamin Franklin Haag Biography. Haag family archives, Midland, Texas.

Bowen, Edward L. "Aly to the Roses." *The Blood Horse*, May 9, 1987.

Brown, Rick. "Playful Jessica Meets the Press." *Midland Reporter-Telegram*, October 29, 1987.

Burns, Ken, and Stephen Ives. *The West*. Boston: Little, Brown and Company, 1996.

Bush, President George W. Speech at appearance in Midland, Texas, January 19, 2001.

Campbell, Bob. "Officer's Life Fell Apart after Baby Jessica's Well Rescue." *Midland Reporter-Telegram*, July 31, 2005.

Campbell, Ruth. "Attorneys: School System Provides Equitable Education for All." *Midland Reporter-Telegram*, August 24, 2008.

Carlson, Paul H., and Bruce A. Glasrud. *West Texas: A History of the Giant Side of the State*. Norman: University of Oklahoma Press, 2014.

Carver School Newspaper. "The History of Carver Junior-Senior High School," November 1958.

Clanton, Brett. "One of the Last Wildcatters Is Upbeat about the Oil Business." *Houston Chronicle*, June 13, 2011.

Clemens, Gus. *Legacy*. San Antonio, TX: Mulberry Avenue Books, 1983.

Cochran, Mike. *Claytie*. College Station: Texas A&M University Press, 2007.

Coleman family archives, Midland, Texas.

Colorado River Municipal Water District historical statistics.

Cowden, Margaret. *Cowden: The Cowden Family History*. Unpublished manuscript.

Crimmins, Patrick. "Rescue Workers Drill Shaft Beside Well in Rescue Try." *Midland Reporter-Telegram*, October 14, 1987.

Bibliography

_____. "Rescue Matter of Time." *Midland Reporter-Telegram*, October 29, 1987.

_____. "Rescuers Struggle Toward Toddler." *Midland Reporter-Telegram*, October 15, 1987.

_____. "Vice President Also Will Honor Community." *Midland Reporter-Telegram*, October 17, 1987.

Cunningham, Lana, "Waiting Game Ends." *Midland Reporter-Telegram*, October 5, 1983.

Cutrer, Thomas. "Marcy, Randolph Barnes." *Handbook of Texas Online*. Denton, TX: Texas State Historical Association. http://www.tshaonline.org/handbook/online/articles/fma43.

_____. "McClellan, George Brinton." *Handbook of Texas Online*. Denton, TX: Texas State Historical Association. http://www.tshaonline.org/handbook/online/articles/fmc09.

Daniel, David. Introduction to *Midland College: The First Twenty-Five Years*, by Karen Lanier and H. A. Tuck. Baltimore: Gateway Books, 1997.

Dargenio, Mary. "Science of War Taught." *Midland Reporter-Telegram*, July 4, 1985.

Dedicated to the Glory of God, First Christian Church, June 1959.

Dees, Jane Marler. "Plush Zoo Opens World's Wishes for Jessica." *Midland Reporter-Telegram*, October 17, 1987.

Dunn, Roy Sylvan. "Droughts." *Handbook of Texas Online*. Denton, TX: Texas State Historical Association. http://www.tshaonline.org/handbook/online/articles/ybd01

Economist, The. "The Father of Fracking." August 3, 2012.

Green, Janine. "Methodists First Church to Organize." *Midland Reporter-Telegram*, July 4, 1885.

_____. "First Baptist Has Lots to Remember in its 100th Year." *Midland Reporter-Telegram*, July 4, 1885.

_____. "First Presbyterian Church Ministers to 'Heart of the City'" *Midland Reporter-Telegram*, July 4, 1885.

Greene, Bob. "Rescue Reminds Us of Real Heroes. *Midland Reporter-Telegram*/Chicago Tribune Media Services, October 29, 1987.

Griffin, John Howard. *Land of the High Sky*. Midland, TX: First National Bank of Midland, 1959.

Gwynne, S. C. "Tom Craddick: How Did Tom Craddick Become the Most Powerful Speaker Ever—and the Most Powerful Texan Today? Let Us Count the Ways." *Texas Monthly*, February 2005.

Haley, J. Evetts. Interview with O. B. Holt, January 3, 1927. Haley Memorial Library and History Center archives.

Handley, Melissa. "Midland Christian College." *Handbook of Texas Online*. Denton, TX: Texas State Historical Association. http://www.tshaonline.org/handbook/online/articles/kbm23

Hardin, Richard. "Pliska Was Planning Aeroplane as Early as 1908."
Midland Reporter-Telegram, July 4, 1985.

Henry, Jim. Presentations to Permian Basin Petroleum Association, September 2011, and Society of Professional Engineers, April 2012.

Hibbitts, Edna Brown. "Citizens Join Forces to Solve Health Problems," *Midland Reporter-Telegram*, July 4, 1985.

Higgins, Sara. "Area Could Become Traffic Nightmare," *Midland Reporter-Telegram*, October 24, 2012.

Hopkins, Ellen. *Midland Reporter-Telegram Permorama Edition*, February 19, 1995.

Hyde, John. "Several Events Have Helped Shape Unique Nature of Midland." *Midland Reporter-Telegram*, June 4, 2011.

_____. "A Look Back at 10 Events That Define Our Community." *Midland Reporter-Telegram*, June 5, 2011.

Bibliography

———. History of Midland presentations

Jordan, Hallye. "Droughts, Floods, Dot West Texas Weather Pattern." *Midland Reporter-Telegram*, July 4, 1985.

Koenig-Bricker, Woodeene. *365 Saints*. San Francisco: HarperCollins, 1995.

Leffler, John. "Midland, TX." *Handbook of Texas Online*. Denton, TX: Texas State Historical Association. http://www.tshaonline.org/handbook/online/articles/hdm03.

Louisville Courier-Journal, "Alysheba, '87 Derby Winner, Euthanized," May 28, 2009.

Mashhood, Farzad. "Current Drought Pales in Comparison with 1950s 'Drought of Record.'" *Austin American Statesman*, August 4, 2011.

McKinley, Nancy, ed. *The Pioneer History of Midland County, Texas, 1880–1926*, limited centennial ed. Dallas: Taylor Publishing Co., 1984.

Midland Army Airbase Museum archives.

Midland Chamber of Commerce archives.

Midland County Election Office.

Midland County Historical Museum archives.

Midland International Airport History, www.flymaf.com/army_airfield.aspx

Midland Police Department statistics, Traffic Division.

Midland Reporter-Telegram. "Charge Midland a 'Boiling Cauldron of Racial Hatred' Stirs Prompt Protests, Divides," June 23, 1952.

———. "Damn Lizard!" December 25, 2011.

———. "Deaths on County Roads Hit 20, How Do We Move Forward?" May 12, 2013.

———. "Droughts, floods dot West Texas weather pattern." July 4, 1985.

———. "Events Listed in Midland Independent School District desegregation." July 4, 1985.

———. "Experts Say Young Negro Slayer Sane." October 31, 1963.

———. "For Some, Camping Is Home Sweet Home." April 29, 2012.

———. "*Forbes* Magazine Lists Odessa, Midland as Best Cities for Jobs." May 10, 2012.

———. "Funeral Services for Clarence Scharbauer to be held Sunday at First Baptist Church," October 3, 1942.

———. "Housing Just Can't Keep Up with the Boom." April 29, 2012.

———. Editorial, "Our Finest Hour; Perhaps Odessa's," October 19, 1983.

———. "Man hitchhikes from Georgia to Midland looking for job, finds more." March 30, 2013

———. "New Accounts Have Been Pledged to FNB," October 19, 1983.

———. "RepublicBank Takes Over First National Bank, October 15, 1983."

———. Richard Slack obituary, March 6, 2013.

———. "Seizure claims Fred Turner, Jr." February 5, 1964.

———. "State draw net tighter at Lubbock," March 21, 1964.

———. "Tall City Gets Soaked, September 29, 2012.

———. "Testimony starts in Lubbock trial," March 20, 1964.

———. "Wednesday Will Bring a New Day for Health Care in Midland." December 16, 2012.

Mills, Bear. "Midland 1955: When Orbison Met Elvis." http://www.elvisinfonet.com/spotlight_bigOmeetselvis.html Story also appeared in *Midland Reporter-Telegram*, 2005.

Moore, Antoinette, "MISD not fully integrated until 1976." *Midland Reporter-Telegram*, July 4, 1985.

Moriak, Meredith, "Midland College unveils facilities master plan." *Midland Reporter-Telegram*, October 20, 2013.

Myres, Samuel D. *The Permian Basin: Petroleum Empire of the Southwest: Era of Discovery from the Beginning to the Depression*. El Paso, TX: Permian Press, 1973.

Bibliography

———. *The Permian Basin: Petroleum Empire of the Southwest: Era of Advancement from the Depression to the Present.* El Paso, TX: Permian Press, (1977).

National Public Radio, "How One Drought Changed Texas Agriculture Forever." July 7, 2012.

Nye, Ramona. "Jessica Free, under Doctor's Care." *Midland Reporter-Telegram,* October 17, 1987.

Officer Down Memorial Page, "Anglin, Private William B.," http://www.odmp.org/officer/18653-private-william-b-anglin.

Olien, Roger, and Diana Davids Olien. *Oil Booms: Social Change in Five Texas Towns,* University of Nebraska Press, Lincoln & London, 1982.

Olien, Roger M., and Diana Davids Hinton. *Wildcatters: Texas Independent Oilmen.* College Station: Texas A&M University Press, 2007.

Palmer, Audrie. "Weekend Rains Replenish Lake Ivie." *Midland Reporter-Telegram,* October 2, 2012.

People Magazine, May 15, 1995.

Permian Basin Board of Realtors statistics, February 2013.

Permian Basin Petroleum Museum Hall of Fame biography, Thomas S. Hogan.

Petty, Kathleen. "Population increase strains roads." *Midland Reporter-Telegram,* September 30, 2012.

Pitts, John Paul. "Scharbauer Hotel: Oil fortunes Were Made and Lost in Lobby of Famous Midland Hotel." *Midland Reporter-Telegram,* July 4, 1985.

"Pliska Aeroplane: A Blacksmith's Aeroplane." City of Midland exhibit, Midland International Airport.

Presnall, Jim. "Odessa Bank Insolvent, Closed." *Midland Reporter-Telegram,* October 8, 1983.

Ray, Smith. "A History of Midland." Midland Centennial files.

Rotelle, John. *Book of Augustinian Saints.* Villanova, PA: Augustinian Press, 2000.

Routh, Cope. *Midland Reporter-Telegram,* October 30, 1963.

———. "Nine Seated as Marion Case Jurors." *Midland Reporter-Telegram,* March 18, 1964.

———. "Marion juror accepted." *Midland Reporter-Telegram,* March 19, 1964.

———. "Marion condemned to die." *Midland Reporter-Telegram,* March 23, 1964.

Ryan, Robert H. "Midland: The Economic Future of a Texas Oil Center." Bureau of Business Research, University of Texas, 1959.

Smith, Julia Cauble. "Pliska, John Valentine." *Handbook of Texas Online.* Denton, TX: Texas State Historical Association. (http://www.tshaonline.org/handbook/online/articles/fpl05).

Scharbauer family video, 1995. Scharbauer family archives.

Schwettmann, Martin W. *Santa Rita: The University of Texas Oil Discovery.* Austin: Texas State Historical Association, 1943.

St. Ann's Church First 100 Years. St. Ann's Church, Midland, Texas, 1997.

St. Ann's School Records, "Distinguished Alumni of St. Ann's School."

Stubbeman, Frank. Texas Bar Journal, November 23, 1933.

Texas House of Representatives Online: http://www.house.state.tx.us/members/member-page/?district=82]

Texas State Historical Commission marker, 209 N. Colorado, Midland, Texas.

Thomas, Carroll. "An Open Letter to the Community." *Midland Reporter-Telegram,* October 18, 1987.

Thurber, Kathleen. "Council Enacts Drought Contingency Plan. *Midland Reporter-Telegram,* June 15, 2011.

"Tribute to George and Gladys Abell, A." The Midland Center, Midland, Texas.

United States Census Department records.

United States Census: Race, Hispanic or Latino, Age, and Occupancy: 2010.

Bibliography

Vickers, Paul. Midland City Directory, 1930.
Wadley, Addison. "Retired Merchant Says Opportunities Are Unlimited." *Midland Reporter-Telegram*, February 29, 1948.
Williamson, Terry. "Permian Loses Mojo Magic." *Midland Reporter-Telegram*, October 15, 1983.

Interviews

Angelo, Ernest, November 2010, February 2013
Barnett, Tom, May 2013
Baskin, Joan, April 2010
Beauchamp, James, March 2013
Bell, Pastor George, April 2012
Billingsley, Grant, November 2010
Bradford, Mike, May 2012
Brown, Lou, November 2013
Burns, Bobby, October 2010
Bush, President George W., February 2012
Cassidy, Mary Lou, August 2011
Chavez, Joe, April 2010
Cole, Art, July 2011
Coleman, Conrad, March 2008
Conaway, K. Michael, August 2011
Cowden, Linda and June, August 2011, May 2013
Craddick, Nadine, May 2011
Craddick, Tom, June 2012, September 2013, October 2013
Cuevas, Jose, May 2011
Culver-Clack, Barbara, August 2010
Dominey, Joe, November 2013
Edgar, Arlen, January 2012
Fitzgerald, Ike, February 2011
Fuller, Dr. James, April 2008
Green, Dr. Laurie, April 2008
Grover, Rosalind, September 2011
Haag, Merle, April 2011
Heck, Bill and Katie, November 2010
Henry, Jim, March 11, August 2012
Henson, Doug, February 2011
Hinton, Dr. Diana Davids, April 2011
Hubbard, Craig, June 2012
Hyde, Judge John, November 2009–November 2011
Lindemood, David, April 2011
Love-Davis, Joan, March 2013
Mabee, Joe, May 2012
Magruder, Ed, June 2013
McAbee, Jane, May 2011, March 2013
McCormick, Len "Tuffy," November 2010
McCrary, Guy, September 2010

Bibliography

McDaniel, Pat, August 2011, May 2013
McDonald, Lloyd, April 2011
McGregor, Mike, July 2012, January 2013
Meadows, Henry E. and John, November 2012
Mims, David, September 2011
Mims, James, June 2010; April 2012
Morales, Felipe, February 2013
Morales, Jerry, June 2013
O'Neill, Joe, October 2010
Painter, Gary, October 2010
Parrish, Dr. Jess, August 2010
Perry, Wes, September 2012, March 2013
Piwetz, Eileen, November 2012
Reese, Dr. Debbie, May 2012
Richards, Colonel. Joe, March 2012
Roberts, Chief James, November 2011
Roberts, Juandelle Lacy, October 2013
Robles, Roger, March 2011
Rucker, Judge Dean, August 2013
Salners, Jim, July 2011
Scharbauer, Clarence III, February 2013, April 2011
Scharbauer, Clarence Jr., May 2012, January 2013, March 2013, April 2013
Simpson, Berry, September 2013
Sipes, Buddy, March 2011
Smith, David L., April 2011, May 2012
Spriggs, Katie, May 2013
Swallow, Jack, June 2012
Thomas, Mayor Carroll, September 2011
Trevino, Sid, May 2010
Van Berg, Jack, July 2013
Way, Ralph, December 2011
Wayland, David and Carole, February 2012
Williams, Clayton Jr., September 2012
Williams, Margaret, February 2013
Williams, Michael, April 2012
Yarbrough, Barbara, April 2010
Younger, Dr. Charles, September 2011

index

Abell, George Thomas, 102, 104–8, 326–27
Abell, Gladys Hanger, 105–6, 108
Abell-Hanger Foundation
    directors, leadership, 361–62, 382
    establishment, 106, 256
    programs, community-building activities, 104, 106–8, 265
Adam, Bill, 160
Advanced Technology Center (Midland College), 181, 292, 351
African American community
    Carver Junior-Senior High School, 128, 136–39, 142–45
    experience of racial prejudice, 120, 129–130, 133–34
    See also Bell, Dr. George; Coleman, Conrad; Coleman, Dr. Viola Johnson; public schools, Midland
Ahders, Judge Bill, 343
Air Force One, 208–9
airplane crash, 1956, 87–88
Alexander, George E., 84
Al G. Langford Chaparral Center (Midland College), 179, 324
Allday, Martin, 244
Allison, James N., 102
Allison, Sheriff W. D., 37
Allison Fine Arts Center (Midland College), 324
Alpine, Williams's ranch near, 376
Alysheba (racehorse), 68–70
Ambrose, Kenneth, 338
Angelo, Ernest ("Mr. Republican")
    background, education, 160
    commitment to the Republican Party, 158–160, 162, 165, 258
    on election night, 1972, 164–65
    friendship with Baskin, 165
    honors and awards, 259
    on Kelly, 74
    and the locating of UTPB, 176
    move to Odessa, 160
    as petroleum engineer, 259
    political activities, election as mayor, 162–64, 258–59

    portrait of Craddick, 288–89
    portrait of Williams, 377–78
    and the Young Republicans, 161
Angelo, Penny, 164–65
Anglin, W. B., 13
Apache Corporation, 250
Arbusto Energy, 212
Army Air Corps, 111, 296, 315, 338
Army Air Force Bombardier Training School, 65, 84–86, 111, 369
Army Corps of Engineers drainage plan, 328
Asher, Jack, 70
Austin Junior High School, 143
Avery, Hank, 241
Avery v. Midland County, 136–38

Bain, Bill, portrait of Conaway, 284–85
Ballet Association, 315
Baltimore Sun, on boom conditions in Midland, 96
Bankhead Highway ("Broadway of America"), 12
Baptist congregation and churches, 32, 64, 122, 154, 284, 337, 372. *See also* Bell, Dr. George
Baptist Corner area, 32
Barbara Yarbrough Parenting Center, 129
Barnett, F. W., 50
Barnett, Tom, 197–98
Barron, Annie Aycock, 31
Barron, J. H., 31
Barron, Judge Elliott H., 59
Barron, Ralph M., 66, 102
Barron family, 15, 20
Bartlett, John, 52
baseball
    Little League, 97–98, 357
    Midland Cubs minor league team, 221
    and Reyes-Nelms-Mashburn Park, 131
Baskin, Joan
    altruism, 261
    arrival in Midland, 247
    community-building activities, 260–61
    education, marriage, 247.261, 261
    honors and awards, 261
    on Midland's intellectual infrastructure, 383–84
    portrait of Piwetz, 351

Index

response to the cluster system, 142
   on vision and the Midland character, 248
Baskin, Judge Pat
   and the cluster system, 141
   election as judge, 165
   friendship with Angelo, 165
   Hyde's comments about, 244
   marriage, 261
   on community commitment to Midland College, 351
   run for mayor, 163–65
   switch to Republican Party, 165
Beauchamp, James, 229–230, 231
Bedford, H. G., 102
Bell, Dr. George
   community-building activities, 132
   early career, 262
   experience of racism, 133–34
   on his grandfather, Ellis, 133
   ordination and ministries, 262–63
   philosophy, 263
Bell, Rebecca, 180
Bellingham, Thomas, 84
Benedum Field, Reagan County, 92
Benson, Cedric, 220–21
Berry, James D., 185
Berry, Weldon, 139
Billingsley, Grant A., 248–49, 373–74
Black & Veatch Contractors, 240
Bloys Camp Meeting, Fort Davis, 341–42
"Blue Angel" (Orbison and Melson), 116
Board of Nursing Examiners (BNE), 179–180
Boniface, H. A., 33
Bounds, Debbie, 363
Bradford, Judge Mike, 72–73, 75, 78–80, 334
Branson, Ray W., 103
Brown, Doug, 304
Brown, Jack E., 373–74
Brown, James, 134
Brown, Lou, 158, 171
Brown v. Board of Education of Topeka, 138, 357
Bryant, Alvey, 137
Bryant Ranch, 372
Bueno, Irma, portrait, 264–65
Bullock, Maurice, 107
Burney, F. H., 31
Burns, Arvy, 217
Burns, Bobby
   airport renovation, 89–90
   background, education, 217
   and the Disney theme park, 118
   on the importance of the oil and gas industry, 91
   Loop 250, 218–19, 222–23
   on Midland's success as a city, 213
   on Thomas Carroll, 89
   vision/achievements as mayor, 83, 217–220, 266–67

Burton-Lingo Lumber Company, 14
Bush, A. J., 33
Bush, Barbara Pierce (Mrs. George H. W.), 270
Bush, Governor Jeb, 208
Bush, Jenna and Barbara, 196
Bush, Laura Welch (Mrs. George W.), 208, 210, 268–70, 273
Bush, President George H. W.
   arrival in Midland, 207, 272
   character, 270–71
   inauguration, 305
   McCormick's relationship with, 332
   oil company, 209
   visit to the McClure family, 198
Bush, President George W., 207
   ambition to become Major League Baseball Commissioner, 212
   Arbusto Energy, 209, 212
   arrival in Midland, 99
   character, 270–71
   childhood and education, 98, 208, 272
   enduring attachment to Midland, 99–100, 209, 273
   Evans's role in campaigns of, 298
   first meeting with Laura, 210
   as governor of Texas, 208
   importance of friends from Midland, 203, 209–10
   marriage, 273
   Men's Community Bible Study, 209, 273
   as M. Williams's campaign manager, 377
   O'Neill on, 210
   return to Midland, 208, 272–73
   on risk-taking as part of the Midland character, 246–47
Butler, Alva Wallace, 74, 274, 323
Butler, Hardin Richard, 74
Butler, Jno. P.
   as charter member of hospital board, 102
   childhood, arrival in Midland, 74–75, 274
   commitment to First National Bank, 72–75, 184, 190–91, 274–75
   community-building activities, 75, 79, 80–81
   death, tributes, 81–82
   employment by the RepublicBank, 191
   enjoyment of Westerns and baseball, 81
   friendliness and likeability, 72, 76–79
   friendship with Dr. John Thomas, 28
   honors and awards, 75
   on Lackey, 323
   loan policy, 75, 247
   Mabee on, 327
   military service, 76
   during negotiations to establish UTPB, 175
   parenting approach, 81
   respect shown, 74
   trustworthiness, 76–77
Butler, Sophronia Jane, 74

Index

Byrd, Daniel, 123–154

Cactus Drilling Company, 321
Cahoon, Frank
    civic activities, 277
    and Craddick, 167–68, 276–77
    political activities, political elections, 159, 164, 276, 288
Caldwell, J. M., 24
Callaway, Rev. S. B., 32
Campaign for Tomorrow (Midland Memorial Hospital), 308–9
Campbell, John, 262
Canyon Reef development, Scurry County, 91–93
Captain, Margaret, 189
Carlson, Paul H., 12–13
Carson, Ken, 68
Cartwright, Herb, 360–61
Carver Junior-Senior High School, 128, 136–39, 142–45
Casa de Amigos, 265
Casebier, Garland, 153–54
Cassidy, Mary Lou
    portrait of Cole, 278–79
    on rally to save the First National Bank, 190
Catholic congregation, 32–33
cattle ranching business; ranchers
    and drift fences, 24
    Halff family, 19–20, 312
    Holt, 16
    impact of the 1950s drought, 41–42
    Martin, 371
    Proctor brothers, 352
    role of the railroad, 14
    Scharbauer family, 15, 16, 41–42, 50, 64
    and socializing among rancher families, 341–42
    Williams, 376
CEED Fire, acres burned, 236–37
Centers for Children and Families, 315
Challenge Day program, 384
Chamber of Commerce. *See* Midland Chamber of Commerce
Chancellor, Mr. and Mrs. C. W., 148
Chaparral Center (Midland College), 179, 324
Chaparral Circle Endowment Fund, 292
Chappel, Clovis, 335
Chavez, Honorable Sylvia, 128
Chavez, Joe, 127
Children's Ranch. *See* High Sky Children's ranch (formerly Girls Ranch)
Children's Rehabilitation Center, 381
Childs, Frank, 68
Chiles, Eddie, 93, 381
Christensen, Doug, 270
churches. *See specific churches and congregations*
Cisco Christian College (Randolph Junior College), 174

City Council, Midland, 218–19
Civil War veterans, in Fairview Cemetery, 26
Clajon Gas Company, 206–7
Clark, Jerry, 160
ClayDesta Plaza, 204, 213, 376
Claytie (Cochran), 205
Clayton Williams Energy, 207
Clearwater Ranch water supply, 240, 242
Clemens, Gus, 302
Clements, Governor Bill, 166, 180
Cleveland, Reese, 60
Cline Shale Play, 50, 92
Cloverdale Farms purchase, 58
Club Granada, 204
cluster system, 141–44
CNN coverage of McClure rescue, 197–98
Cochran, Mike, 205
Cogdell Learning Center (Midland College), 181
Coggin, Gray, 83–84
Cole, Art
    arrival in Midland, 111
    charisma and legacy, 114–15
    death, 115
    establishment of the Midland Community Theatre, 112, 278
    on fund raising in Midland, 114
    on Midland's cultural environment, 109
    military service, 111
    public relations skills, 112
    as teacher, 278–79
    as theater director, 278
    See also Midland Community Theatre
Cole, Mary and Buster, 341
Cole, Ruth, 112, 115, 278–79
Coleman, Conrad
    on community response to closing of Carver School, 144
    on discovery of mother's suit against LSU, 123
    on plans for integrating Midland's schools, 143–44
    portrait of Coleman, 280–81
    story about Spence, 364
Coleman, Dr. Viola Johnson ("Dr. Vi")
    arrival and settlement in Midland, 125, 280
    commitment to her patients, 280
    early efforts to establish a practice, 125
    emphasis on spiritual and psychological wellbeing, 281
    family dinners and discussions, 280–81
    on the impact of closing Carver School, 144
    lawsuit to speed pace of integration, 139
    loan to set up practice, 126, 300
    love for baseball, 126
    as pioneer for racial equality, 122–24
Coleman, Raymond, 125
Coleman, Reginald, 123
Collyns, Bill
    arrival in Midland, 282

427

INDEX

on Butler, 74–75, 79
humility, 283
and the Midland International Airport, 282–83
on Scharbauer, 64
support for Midland and West Texas, 282
Colorado River Municipal Water District (CRMWD), 236
Comanche, the, 11–13
Commemorative Air Force, 277, 385
commissioner system and voting, 137–38
community colleges
    Daniel's advocacy for, 292
    enrollment patterns, 180
    Langford's support for, 325
    Permian Basin Junior College System, 178
    See also Midland College
Conaway, Congressman K. Michael ("Mike")
    and building of a new sports stadium, 221
    childhood in Odessa, 284
    core values, 285
    as deacon, 284
    on George W. Bush, 212–13
    on Laura Bush, 268
    long-lasting friendships, 284
    as representative of West Texas in Congress, 284–85
    spiritual commitment, 284
Conaway, Julie, 284
Conaway, Suzanne, 284
Connell, W. E., 72
Considine, Corby, 270
Constitution Party, 160
Continental Airlines, Midland service, 282–83
county commissioner system, 137–38, 162
Cowan Performing Arts Series (Midland College), 351
Cowden, Caroline Mary Liddon (Mrs. William), 18
Cowden, Elizabeth Whiteside (Mrs. George), 17
Cowden, E. P., 102
Cowden, Frank Jr., 17, 102, 341
Cowden, Frank Sr., 18, 286–87
Cowden, George Franklin, 16–17
Cowden, June Wilkinson (Mrs. Frank), 17, 108, 341–42
Cowden, Linda
    on father, Frank, 17
    portrait of the Scharbauer family, 359–360
Cowden, Martha Courtney (Mrs. Fred), 17–18, 142
Cowden, William Frederick ("Fred"), 17–18
Cowden, William Hamby, 16–18, 20, 72
Cowden family, 14, 244, 375
Craddick, Christi, 289
Craddick, Nadine Nayfa, 168–69, 289
Craddick, Russ, 150, 167
Craddick, Thomas Jr., 289
Craddick, Tom
    arrival in Midland, 167
    on Cahoon, 276–77

conservative philosophy, 289
and the discovery and arrest of Marion, 150
efforts at tort reform, 169
interest in politics, 167
marriage, wedding, 168
political background, 167
support for Angelo, 163–64
support for energy industry, 288–89
in the Texas House of Representatives, 163, 167–68, 170, 288
Williams on, 376
Craddick Drug Store (Tull's Drug Store, Service Drug Store), 167
Crisman, John, 250–51
Crowden, Emma Long (Mrs. Fred), 17
Crowe, Mrs. Billy, 88
Cuevas, Jose, 131–32, 241
Culver, John, 290
Culver-Clark, Barbara
    early activities with the Midland County Republicans, 166
    integrity, 290
    judgeship, 167, 290–91
    move to Midland, 290
    work with juvenile offenders, 290
    and the Young Republicans, 161
    youth as conservative Democrat, 166
Cunningham, Lana, 183–85, 282–83
Czech, Richard, 194

Daniel, Dr. David
    on community support for Midland College, 173, 179
    on the establishment of Midland College, 178–79
    as president of Midland College, 181, 292
    programs instituted by, 292–93
    skill as fundraiser, 292, 351
    tribute to the Abells, 108
Darnell, Sheriff Ed, 35–36, 148–49, 294
Davidson Distinguished Lecture Series (Midland College), 181, 292–93, 351
Davis, Bill, 159–160, 166–67, 276, 288
Davis, Paul, 42–43, 175
Davis, Rev. A. L., 154
Dawson County oil deposits, 92
Dawson Geophysical, 304
Day, Ken, 89
Dearen, Patrick, 312
Debuck, Dean, 184
Democratic Party, 158–160
DeZavala Elementary school, 139
"Dirty Thirty," 288
Discovery Exploration, 259
Disney theme park, 117–19
Dominey, Joe, 139–140, 142, 146
Dorothy and Clarence Scharbauer Jr. Patient Tower (Midland Memorial Hospital), 71, 104, 214–16, 359

428

Index

Downing, Delberty, 103
droughts, 39–42, 233–36
Dunagan, Clint, 102
Dunaway Associates traffic congestion study, 230–31
Durham, Fredda Turner, 155
Durham, Lynn Jr., 156, 185, 301

Early College High School, 180
Ector County, 177, 233–34
Edgar, Arlen
  portrait of Kelly, 321–22
  on the Spraberry Trend, 91–92
Edison Junior High School, 143
Edwards, Kirk, 230
Eisenhower, President Dwight David, 159
Eldorado, Texas, 332
Elkin, Frank, 174
Ellis, Angela, 297
Ellis, Charlotte Jane Posey, 297
Ellis, David M. ("Doc"), 153
Ellis, George, 133, 262
Ellis, Newman W. Jr., 152–53, 296–97
Ellis, Newman W. Sr. ("Newnie W."), 296
Ellis, Newnan H. ("Newnie H.," "Dr. Ellis"), 296
Ellis, Priscilla, 297
Ellis and Sons Plumbing, 132–33, 262
Ellis Funeral Home, 296
El Nopal (Tejano record shop), 339
Energy Future Holdings, 299
Enterprise (newspaper), on creation of Midland County, 23
EOG Resources, 347
Evans, Donald L. ("Donnie"), 210, 298–99
Evans, Susan Marinis ("Susie"), 298
Everybody's Baby: The Rescue of Jessica McClure (movie), 198
expo center. *See* Midland Horseshoe Expo Center

"Fading Eyes" (Wyvell), 379–380
Fahrenkamp, Mrs. W. F., 40
Faircloth, J. D., 89, 131
Fairview Cemetery, 25–26, 38
Family Counseling Services (Centers for Children and Families), 315
Farish, Webb, 259
Fasken, Murray, Fasken Foundation, 126, 300–301
Faudree, Harriet, 341
Feavel, Dave, 226
Federal Deposit Insurance Corporation (FDIC), 183–84
"fellowshipping," 34–35
Ferguson, Kuby, 34
Fiftyshadesofgold (racehorse), 68
Finley, Joy, 304
First Baptist Church, 18, 32, 122, 64, 337
First Christian Church: Disciples of Christ, 33–34, 174, 334

"First in Family to Attend College" program (Midland College), 351
First Methodist Church, 353
First National Bank
  Bradford's experience working at, 79–80
  building, 28, 204–5, 213
  Christmastime celebrations, 77
  collapse, impacts, 187–89, 200, 286–87
  Collyns work at, 282
  during the Depression, Scharbauer's handling of, 65
  economic development division, 80
  efforts to save, 7, 189–190
  failure and sale, 183–85, 275, 327
  founding, 24–25, 64, 303, 353, 359
  hospitality offered by, 77–78
  loan policies, 73–77, 369
  Mabee's contribution, 327
  McCrary's experience working at, 80, 188
  opening and chartering, 72
  presidents, 16, 73–74, 103, 186, 369
  See also Butler, Jno. P.; Kelly, C. J.
First Presbyterian Church of Midland, 2–3, 31, 209, 261, 335
First United Methodist Church, Midland, 31, 332
Fitzgerald, Ike, 46, 73–74
Five Wells Ranch, 67
Flag-Redfern Oil Company, 101, 315, 357
"Flats, The," 263
flooding, 1968, 43–46, 354
Forbes, on employment opportunities in Midland and Odessa, 228
Forbes, Steve, 202
Ford, President Gerald, 104–5
Fort Smith, Arkansas, 12, 330
fracking, hydraulic, 225–26
Frame, Mrs. J. H., 38
Francis, Nadine, 163
Franks, General Tommy, 203, 268
Frazier, Charles, 186
Fuller, C. P., 31
Fuller, James, 125, 127
Fuller, Robbyne Hocker, 142
Fullinwider, Jerry, 185
Furman v. Georgia, 155–56
Furr's Cafeteria, 18

Gage, R. D., 371
Garett, Henry, 174
Garner, James, 332
Garney Construction, 240
Garrett, Elizabeth ("Lizzie"), 303
Garrett, Herman, 13–14, 302–3
Garrett, Jim, 302–3
Garrett, Lucy Ann Bohannon, 303
Garrett, Sam and Malinda, 302
Gataga No. 2 well, 206–7

Index

George W. Bush Foundation/Presidential Center, 299
Gerardo's Casita (restaurant), 251, 339
Gideon, Wayne, 151
Gillespie, Charlie, 160, 162
Girls Ranch. *See* High Sky Children's Ranch
Glasrud, Bruce A., 12–13
Glass, George W., 102
Glass, Mabel, 323
Glasscock, Andy, 201
Goddard Junior High School, 304
Goldwater, Barry, 159
Grace Lutheran Church, 321
Graham, Betty, 304
Graham, Bobby, 154
Graham, Pete, 304
Graham, Susan ("Suzy"), 203, 304–5
Gramm, Senator Phil, 206
Grant, John, 240
Grant, Joseph M., 188
Grant, Lester, 102
Great Depression, 55–56
Great Die-Off, 1886-87, 25, 40
Greater Ideal Baptist Church, 132, 263
Greathouse, Barney R., 106, 265, 306
Greathouse, Helen Maddox, 106, 265, 306–7, 396
Greathouse Charitable Trust, 277
Great Texas Banking Crash, The (Grant), 188
Green, Laurie, 124
Green, Tom, 22–23
Greene, Bob, 199
Greenwood Volunteer Fire Department, 250
Griffin, John Howard
 on early arrests and criminal offenses, 36
 on the Great Die-Off of 1886, 40
 on Hogan, 317
 on Humble's move to Midland, 57
 on the importance of church to Midland social life, 34–35
 on the naming of Midland as the county seat, 23
 on role of religion in West Texas, 30
 on Scharbauer, 64
 on Ulmer, 369
Griffin, Ruth Ann, 304
Grover, Arden, 87
Grover, Hank, 164–65
Grover, Rosalind Redfern ("Roz")
 commitment to quality, 309
 on Cowden Sr.'s response to bank collapse, 286
 on the drought of the 1950s, 41
 on first meeting Scharbauer Jr., 67
 fundraising skills, 214–16, 308–9
 kidnapping plot, 101
 memories of Little League games, 97–98
 memories of McCormick, 332
 portrait of the Redferns, 356–58
 on the Scharbauer family legacy, 63
 support for the Midland Community Theatre, 114

Guinn, Judge Ernest, 140
Guiterrez, A. V., 121
Gulf Building (Hogan Building), 204–5
Guly, Josephine, 27, 102

Haag, Benjamin Franklin ("Frank"), 57–60, 310
Haag, Merwyn, 57–58
Hackler, Glenn, 219
Haley, J. Alva, 20
Haley, J. Evetts, 20
Haley Memorial Library and History Center
 annual storytelling event, 375
 McDaniel's leadership, 15, 334, 353
 naming, 20
Halff, Adolph, 19
Halff, Henry, 19–20, 312
Halff, Mayer, 19
Halff, Rosa Wechsler, 312
Harper, O. C., 102
Hardeman, Dorsey, 162–63, 176–77
Hardeman's Regiment, Texas Cavalry, 18
Hardie, Ibby, 315
Harris, Barbara Oliver, 142–43
Heck, Bill, 137, 160, 162
Heck, Katie, 114, 160
Hedrick, Wyatt C., 110
Hejl, Goodrich, 183, 189
Helen Greathouse Charitable Trust, 306–7
Hendrickson, A. N., 102
Henry, Jim
 community-building activities, 314
 drilling technologies, 92
 on Midland's pioneering spirit, 95
 partnership with Johnson, 313
 partnership with Landenberger, 313
 on the Wolfberry discovery and production, 224–25
 work ethic, education, 313
Henry, Paula, 314
Henry Petroleum, Henry Companies, 95, 225, 313–14
Henson, Doug, 80, 177
Herd, Harriet Daniel, 106, 265, 315, 356
Herd, J. Harvey, 106, 265, 315–16, 356
Herd, Tevis
 fund raising for the Scharbauer Tower, 215
 portrait of the Herds, 315–16
Herd Family Endowment Fund, 316
Hibbitts, Edna Brown, 102
Hickman Fire, acres burned, 236
High Sky Children's ranch (formerly Girls Ranch), 336, 341, 381
Hillard, A. W., 72
Hilton Hotel, 62
Hinton, Dr. Diana Davids, 50, 92–95, 227
Hispanic community
 discrimination against, 121, 127–28, 139
 Hispanic Chamber of Commerce, 245

430

Index

and improving race relations, 245–46, 252
and Midland College performing arts programs, 182
size, 120
Historic Midland, An Illustrated History of Midland County (McKinley and Modisett), 334
Hitt, Harold, 139, 143
Hodge, Mrs. J. Howard, 102
Hodge Carillon Tower (Midland College), 325
Hogan, Fred, 53
Hogan, Thomas S. ("T. S.")
    arrival in Midland, 317
    building of the Yucca Theatre, 109–10
    honors and awards, 53
    physical appearance, 53
    promotion of Midland, 59, 317–18
    vision for Midland, 52–53
Hogan Building (Shell Building/Petroleum Building)
    building and opening, 28–29, 53–55
    importance to Midland's development, 50, 53, 117, 213
    revival after 1935, 57
Hogan Park, 341, 354
Hogg, James, 36–37
Holifield, Cecil Jr., 117
Holifield, Ted, 31
Holly, Buddy, 115
Hollywood Theaters, 222–23
Holt, Mrs. O. B., 26
Holt, O. B., 16, 40, 323
Honest John Table (Petroleum Club of Midland), 60
Honolulu Oil, 54
Hopkins, Ellen, 313–14
Horse Feathers (Midland Community Theatre production), 113
Horseshoe, the (expo center), 219–220, 261
"Hospital of the Plains." *See* Midland Memorial Hospital
House, John W., 102
Houston Chronicle, photos of dry Lake Meredith, 237
Howbert, Doris and Van, 160
Howe, John, 311
Humble Oil and Refining Company
    Collyns's employment with, 282
    Henry's employment with, 313
    Humble Building, 335–36
    Meadows's employment with, 335
    move to Midland, 57
    the No. 1 Mrs. O. P. Buchanan well, 91
Humes, Parker, 141
Humphries, Colonel, 349
Hunt for Heroes Weekend, 385–88
Hurt, Dr. John, 365
Hurt, Lilly M. Read, 365
Hutchinson, B., 36
Hyde, Judge John
    on Baskin, 244
    on buffalo skinning, 14
    childhood and education, 243
    on Civil War veteran burials, 26
    on the flood of 1968, 46
    on Hogan, 317
    on hospitality offered by the First National Bank, 77
    on impact of current drought, 233–34
    on impact of discovery of Permian Basin oil deposits, 49
    on impact of Humble's move to Midland, 85
    on impact of the First National Bank collapse, 187
    on the importance of the Midland Army Flying School, 84–86
    judicial wisdom, 317
    on Marcy's arrival in area, 52
    on McClure's rescue, 244
    on McCormick, 331–32
    on Midland's attorneys, 244
    on McKinley, 333–34
    role in saving of the Yucca Theatre building, 110–11
    on the Scharbauers and the Cowdens, 51, 244
    selflessness, 317–18
    story about a sandstorm, 39
    on trust as part of the Midland character, 243
    on water supply needs, 41
Hyde, Sharon, 243

Inman, Curtis, 241
International Amateur Theater Festival, Monte Carlo, 278
Isaacks, S. J., 24

Jacobs, Stan, portrait of Langford, 324–25
Jal Ranch, 20
James, John, 236
Jane Long Elementary School, 88
Jastrow, Kenny, 87, 244
Jennings, Waylon, 115
John Ben Shepperd Leadership Series (Odessa), 266–67
John Birch Society, 379
Johnson, Dennis, 224–25, 226, 313
Johnson, President Lyndon Baines, 158, 276
Johnson, Terry, 385
John T. McElroy Ranch, 53
John Wayne Airport, Anaheim, CA, 89
Joiner, Dad, 349
Jones, Bob, 300–301
Jones, Franklin G., 174
Jones, Tommy Lee, 203, 268
Jones, Tugboat, 99–100
Jowell, Spencer, 20
Jumburrito restaurant, 131
Junior Chamber of Commerce (Jaycees), 383–84
Junior League, 114

431

Index

KCRS radio, 64, 141
Kelley, Father Thomas, 132
Kelly, C. J.
  community-building activities, 80–81, 244
  confrontation with Williams, 204–5
  loan to Grace Lutheran Church, 321–22
  as president of the First National Bank, 73–74
Kennedy, Judge William, 36–37
Kennedy, President John, 160
Kennedy, Ted, 305
Kentucky Derby winners associated with Midland, 68–69
Kentucky Horse Park Hall of Champions, 70
To Kill a Mockingbird (Midland Community Theatre production), 113
King, Larry, 196
Kirk, Pastor Luther, 122
Kirwan, John, 160
Kleine, Bill, 97, 98
KMID television, 116–17
Krupp, Hayman, 348

Lackey, Superintendent W. W., 323, 337
Lacy, Rhonda, 171
Ladies Cemetery Association (LCA), 26
Ladies Professional Golf Association (LPGA), 354
Lake Ivie, 238, 241
Lake Meredith, 237
L'Amour, Louis, 81
Lancaster, E. B., 24
Lancaster, Naomi, 112
Landenberger, Bob, 313
Land of the High Sky (Griffin), 30, 34–35, 317, 369
Landrum, Will, 36–37
Langford, Dr. Al G., 178–181, 324–25
Late, Steve, 189
Laurel, Oscar M., 120–21
Layman, H. B., 110
L Bar ranch, 341
Lea, Preston, 241
League of United Latin American Citizens, 120–21
Lee High School, 143, 268, 304
Lee Street (southeast side, Midland), 132–33
Legacy (Clemens), 302
Legacy Scholarship, 106–8, 264
Legg, Reagan, 324
Leggett, Dr. Lloyd W., 102
Liddon, Catherine, 18
Life magazine, article on the Midland oil industry, 50–51
Lindemood, David, 78, 87, 153
Lindsey, Judge Victor, 153
Linebery, Tom, 353
Little, Dale, 236–37, 250
Little League. *See* baseball
Llano Estacado (Staked Plains area), 13

Llano Hotel, 25, 27, 64
Lonesome Dove (television series), 203
Loop 250, 219–220, 222, 229–230, 266
Lough, Ken, 189
Love-Davis, Joan, 144–45
Lowe, Ralph, 102
Lucas, A. F., 349
Lynn, Dr. Matthew, 335
Lyster, Alec, 238

Mabee, Guy, 326
Mabee, Joe E.
  on Abell, 106
  as charter member of hospital board, 102
  on the First National Bank collapse, 187–88
  on the flood of 1968, 45
  as rancher, 326
Mabee, Ruby, 326
Mabee Foundation, 326
Mace, Robert, 43
Maes, Cynthia ("Cindy"), 339, 340
Magruder, Edwin ("Ed")
  arrival in Midland, 328
  community-building activities, 328
  on the current drought, 235
  on infrastructure improvements following 1968 flood, 328–29
  as mayor of Midland, 328
  military service, 328
  and the T-Bar pipeline, 241–42
Magruder, Ed, portrait of George H. W. Bush, 270–71
Major League Baseball Commissioner, 212
Manor Park (Midland Presbyterian Homes), 306, 382
Manuel (Marcy's Comanche guide), 12
Manulik, Martha Mims, 338
Marcy, Captain Randolph (Marcy Trail), 11–12, 52, 303, 330
Marion, James Lee
  account of robbery and murder, 151–52
  assault on Dorothy Scharbauer, 149
  break in at Turner home, 148–150
  conviction and sentence, 155–56
  murder of Juliette Turner, 148–49
  pretrial actions, 153
  search for, discovery and arrest, 150–51
  trial, 153–55
Marquis, Robert L., 174
Marshall, Thurgood, 123–24
Martin, T. J., 371
Max Christensen Stadium, 221
May and Williams oil and gas company, 206
M Bar ranch, 341
McAbee, Jane Butler
  on Butler as a father, 81
  on closing of the First National Bank closed, 190
  on father's early banking experience, 75
  on father's likeability, 79

Index

on Lackey, 323
McCarron, Chris, 70
McCaskill, Scott, 19
McCleskey, Robert, 210
McClure, Chip, 194
McClure, Jessica ("Baby Jessica"), rescue
    aftermath, 196, 200–201
    celebrations following, 198–99
    as community effort, 7, 178–79, 192–93, 200
    Hyde's perspective on, 244
    initial fall, 192–93
    media coverage, 196–98
    as metaphor for strength and endurance, 199–200
    rescue plan and execution, 192–95
McClure, Reba Gayle ("Cissy"), 192, 194, 199
McCormick, Len ("Tuffy"), 331–32
McCrary, Guy, 80, 188–89
McCullough, Hugh, 241
McCurdy, Malcolm, 87
McDaniel, Pat
    annual storytelling event, 375
    on the courage and fortitude of early pioneers, 20–21
    on the Crowden family, 17–18
    on Holt, 16
    on McKinley, 334
    on the Midkiff family, 18–19
    on Midland's early economy and history, 14–15
    portrait of Proctor, 352–53
    on reasons for Midland's success, 22
    on rivalry between Odessa and Midland, 35–36
McDonald, Lloyd, 45–46, 81, 331–32
McGregor, Mike
    on the Lake Ivie water supply, 241
    on possibility of running out of water, 239–240
    on precipitation in Midland, 234, 238
    work on CRMWD contract with Poe, 241
McKinley, Nancy Elizabeth Rankin
    books authored by, 334
    on buried treasure at Fairview Cemetery, 26
    childhood in Midland, 334
    devotion to preserving Midland's history, 11, 333–34
    on the Ellis family, 296
    on Garrett, 302
    on Halff, 312
    on Lackey, 323
    personality, 333
McLemore, James, 123–24
McNight, Euell, 177–78
Meadows, Henry, 27, 335–36
Meadows, Henry E. Jr., 365–66
Meadows, John, 27, 335–36
Meadows, Read Thomas, 335
medical services, Coleman's contributions and vision, 126
Medlin, Lum, 13–14, 302

Melson, Joe, 115–16
Melson, Linda, 115–16
Menchaca, Rick, 347
Men's Community Bible Study (First Presbyterian Church), 209, 273
Mercantile National Bank of Baltimore, 55
Merritt, Wayne, 187
Messer, Bill, 170
Methodist church/congregation, 31
Metro Bank of Midland, 185–86
Mexia, oil development at, 349
Mexican Americans. *See* Hispanic community
Meyers, Russell, 214, 308–9
Midkiff, John Rufus, 18
Midkiff, Lillie Davenport, 19
Midkiff, Thomas Oscar ("T. O."), 19, 43
Midland, City of
    bond financing, 90, 96, 103, 178–80, 182, 214, 216–17, 292, 309, 324, 329, 358
    courthouse construction, 25, 366, 371–72
    churches, number of, 30–31, 249
    districting lawsuit, 136
    as dry town, 294
    early history, 13–14, 25, 30–31, 330, 333
    expansion and growth, 26–29, 49–50, 85, 92, 94–97, 101–3, 228–230, 313, 384
    "Flats, The," 263
    incorporation, 24
    independent community college district, 178
    mayors, 20, 24, 58, 164–65, 258, 266, 267, 271, 328, 347–48, 369
    newspapers, number of, 372
    population, 1910, 24
    population, 1930, 54
    population, 1940, 57
    population, 1950 and 1960, 94
    population, 2014, 228
    selection as county seat, 23
    skyscrapers, 213, 304
    southeast side, 132
    Texas Historical Commission landmarks in, 333
    unemployment rates, 2014, 227–28
    Vision 2000 and Beyond, 261
    water supplies, drought planning, 58, 236
Midland and Lee High School, 336
Midland Army Airfield, 84–86, 111
Midland Army Flying School, 86–87
Midland Centennial Celebration, 1985, 96, 360
Midland Center, failure of, 220
Midland Cerebral Palsy Center (Children's Rehabilitation Center), 381
Midland Chamber of Commerce, 56, 59, 310. *See also individual Midland residents*
Midland Christian College, 173–74, 352
Midland City Council, 236, 276, 353
Midland College
    Advanced Technology Center, 181, 292, 351

433

INDEX

Allison Fine Arts Center, 324
athletic program, 181, 324, 345
Bueno's attendance at, 264
Chaparral Center, 324
Cogdell Learning Center, 181
community support for, 173, 179–80, 324, 351
Cowan Performing Arts Series, 181–82, 292–93, 351
Davidson Distinguished Lecture Series, 181, 292–93, 351
development of an endowment for, 292
enrollment, 180
expansion plans, 2013, 180
fight to establish, 178–79
"First in Family to Attend College" program, 351
groundbreaking, 324
growth and expansion, 179, 324
Hodge Carillon Tower, 325
landscaping fund, 325
Legacy Scholarship program, 106–7
National Young Artists' Competition, 315
nursing program, 346
Occupational-Technical building, 324
opportunities associated with attending, 265
Petroleum Professional Development Center, 180
presidents, Piwetz on, 180–81
Scharbauer family contributions to, 360
Scharbauer Student Center, 180
See also Daniel, Dr. David; Langford, Dr. Al G.; Parrish, Dr. Jess; Piwetz, Eileen; Thomas, Dr. Steve
Midland College: The First Twenty-Five Years (Lanier and Tuck), 178–79
Midland Community Theatre
first production, 112
founding, 278
Redfern's role at, 357
restoration of the Yucca Theatre, 111
Summer Mummers event, 113–14, 162
volunteer spirit, 112–13
See also Cole, Art
Midland Country Club, 75, 270, 335–36
Midland County
attraction of ranchers to, 14
Collyns support for, 282
drought, 233–34
establishment of, 22
first elections, 24
first oil recovery, 91
Jal Ranch, 20
Midkiff business interests in, 18
naming of county seat for, 23
Painter's election as Sheriff, 344
population, 1910, 24
Quien Sabe Ranch, 19
race/ethnicity diversity in, 120
and the Republican party, 159

wildfires, 2011, 236–37
See also oil and gas industry; Permian Basin; West Texas
Midland County Courthouse, 371–72
Midland County Historical Commission, 333, 336
Midland County Historical Society and Museum, 61–62, 333–34
Midland County Library Board, 260
Midland County Public Library, 333
Midland County Republicans, 290
Midland County Republican Women, 171
Midland Cubs, 221
Midland Development Corporation, 80
Midland Fair and Rodeo Association, 328, 353
Midland Festival Ballet, 279
Midland Gazette, marketing of Midland by, 23
Midland High School
baseball games, 220
Cash and Presley concert, 1955, 116
Haag's role in establishing, 59
relocation of Carver students to, 143
tribute to Wayland, 4
Midland Horseshoe Expo Center, 219–220, 261
Midland Independent School District (MISD)
Abell's service to, 256
achievement of unitary status, process and challenges, 145–46
cluster system, 141
formation, 24
integration plans and process, 138–39
rain day, 239
United States v. Midland Independent School District, 139–140
Younger's service to, 381
Midland International Airport
Commemorative Air Force, 277, 385
infrastructure problems, 88
renovation/rebuilding of, 89–90, 266
terminal building, 219
See also Sloan Field
Midland Junior College District, 177–79
Midland Memorial Foundation, 102
Midland Memorial Hospital
Abell-Hanger Foundation's contributions to, 361–62
Abell's contributions to, 256
building, opening, 102
Campaign for Tomorrow, 308–9
charter board members, 102
Dorothy and Clarence Scharbauer Jr. Patient Tower, 71, 214, 359
founding, 353
growth and expansion, 103–4, 316
Herd's contributions to, 315
McClure's treatment at, 195
Redfern as fund raiser for, 357
Thomas's contributions to, 366

434

Index

Ulmer's contributions to, 369
volunteers, community support, 277
See also Coleman, Dr. Viola Johnson; Thomas, Dr. John B.
Midland National Bank, 20, 25, 34–35, 300
Midland-Odessa Symphony & Chorale, 279
Midland-Odessa Transportation Alliance, 229
Midland Opera Theater, 279
Midland Park Mall, Disney Store, 118
Midland Presbyterian Homes (Manor Park), 256, 306, 382
Midland Regional Airport, 86
Midland Reporter-Telegram
   on airplane crash over Midland, 1956, 88
   on the Army Air Force Bombardier Training School, 65, 84
   on assertions about Midland's racism, 120–22
   on Bell's philosophy, 263
   on building the Scharbauer Tower, 214
   on building the T-Bar pipeline, 241
   on the cloudburst of 1968, 43–46
   Collyns's role as editor, 64, 74, 282–83
   on community efforts to save the First National Bank, 189–190
   Craddick's comments following Cahoon's death, 276–77
   coverage of the Ted Holifield controversy, 31–32
   on the demolition of the Scharbauer Hotel, 61–62
   on early arrests and criminal offenses, 36
   on fatality associated with 1968 flood, 44
   on fire at First Christian Church, 34
   on the First National Bank closing, 185
   football headline, 1983, 183
   on growth rate and traffic congestion, 230
   on Hyde's background and importance to Midland, 243–44
   on the importance of Midland Memorial Hospital to Dr. Thomas, 102–3
   on Marion's arrest and trial, 151–55
   on the mayoral election, 1972, 163–64
   on McClure's rescue, 193–94, 199
   on meeting between Cash, Presley and Orbison, 116–17
   Myrick's article on Lackey, 323
   obituary for Clarence Scharbauer Sr., 65–66
   obituary for Patrick Wayland, 3–4
   on the Permian Basin Petroleum Museum, 104
   on the Petroleum Club, 60–61
   Pitts's comments on Midland's early development, 28–29
   on the Pliska Plane, 84
   on rain event, 2012, 238
   on RepublicBank's introduction to Midland, 185
   on response to cluster system, 141–42
   Richard's tribute to Midland's citizens, 3–5
   Spence's role as publisher of, 363
   tribute to Ellis, Jr. in, 297
   tributes to Butler in, 81–82
   on Hogan, 317
   on Wadley's talks, excerpts, 371–72
   on wildfires, 2011, 236–37
Midland Republican Party, 276. *See also* Republican party
Midland Rotary Club, 310–11, 337
Midland Lions Club, 75
Midland Woman's Club, 341
Midland YMCA, 270
Midway Station (Texas and Pacific Railroad), 13, 302
Millar, Dr. Felix P., 26–27
Miller, Russell L., 102, 381
Millican, Rev. Leander, 32
Mills, Bear, 116–17
Mims, David, 251
Mims, James
   on Butler, 76
   character, personality, 338
   community-building activities, 338
   education, early ambitions, 337
   faith, Christian practice, 338
   forebears, 337
   on use of Hogan Building to store hay, 54
   military service, 338
   nostalgia for "small-town" Midland, 338
   at opening of the Hogan Building, 54
   return to Midland after World War II, 338
   as storyteller, 338
Mims, Joseph, 337
Mims, Mary Bell (Mrs. James), 338
Mims, Maureen Littlejohn (Mrs. Percy), 337
Mims, Percy, 66, 337
Minnie (Fasken family housekeeper), 301
Miracle on Tyler Street, 263
Mitchell, George, 225–26
Modisett, Bill, 334
Monaghan, Bob, 164–65
Moore, J. A., 31–32
Morales, Celia, 339
Morales, Felipe, 251, 339–340
Morales, Jerry
   community-building activities, 340
   as mayor of Midland, 228, 252, 339
   on Midland's population growth, 228
Morales, Novert, 251–52, 340
Morales and Maes Insurance and Financial Services, 251
Moreland, Clark, 137
Muirhead, Mrs., 32
Muñoz, Paula, 339
Murray, Sam, 36
Museum of the Southwest, 256, 360
Mustang Draw, 303
Myres, Samuel D., 55–56, 92, 104
Myrick, Mrs. Clinton, 323

Index

National Association for the Advancement of Colored People (NAACP), 123–24
National Bank of Odessa, 185–86
National Junior College Athletic Association (NJCAA), 345
Neal, Martin, 163
Neighbors, H. D., 44
Neilson-Gammon, John, 235–36
Nelson, Gaylord, 257
New Jack Ministry, 262–63
New Jerusalem Baptist Church, 262
New Orleans Times-Picayune, article about Coleman's lawsuit, 124
New York Times, on CNN's coverage of McClure's rescue, 197
Nixon, President Richard, 160, 163
Nobles, Gerald, 42
Nobles, Joan Stocks, 42, 341–42, 381
Noland, J. S., 102
Northeast Volunteer Fire Department, 250
North Gail Field, Borden County, 92
Nuessle, Joe, 164–65
Nye, Ramona, 196

Occupational-Technical building (Midland College), 324
O. C. Fisher Reservoir, San Angelo, 237
Odessa, City of
    Conaway's childhood in, 284
    contributions to save the First National Bank, 189–190
    and the fight over the location of UTPB, 162–63, 174–76
    low unemployment rate, 228
    opposition to Midland's efforts to set up its own taxing district, 178
    reputation for sinfulness, 35–36
    rivalry with Midland, 35, 177
Odessa National Bank, 25, 35
O'Donnell, Robert, 200–201
    Glasscock on, 201
O'Donoghue, David, 349
oil and gas industry
    attraction of Easterners to, 356
    Depression-era impacts, 55–56
    duration of production (well life), 92
    field development, 313–14
    fracking, 225
    and growing U. S. consumption, 57, 94, 227
    Henry's drilling techniques, 92
    Hogan's role in promoting, 53–54
    impact of Arab Oil Embargo, 186, 258
    impact of droughts, 39
    independent operators, appeal of Midland to, 28–29, 49–50, 54, 73, 91, 95–96, 317, 369
    mandated slowdown in production, 1953, 97
    natural gas flares, 97
    post-World War II field development and production, 93, 227
    price fluctuations, 186–87, 225
    Redfern enterprises, 356–57
    and Santa Rita #1, 49, 348–49
    the Spraberry Trend, 91–92
    in West Texas, Midland as center for, 49–50
    See also Spraberry Trend; transportation infrastructure; Wolfberry Play *and specific individuals and families*
Oil Boom (Olien and Olien), 97
Old Red Brick Church, 34
Olien, Roger M., 50
O'Neill, Joe, 98, 210
Orbison, Roy, 115–16
Osborne, Lewis, 137
Our Lady of San Juan Church (San Miguel Arcángel), 132

Painter, Sheriff Gary, 243, 245–47, 294, 343–44
Palmer Drug Abuse Program, 256–57
Parent Teacher Association, 337
Parkhill, Smith and Cooper, 240
Parks, Harriet and Roy, 341
Parrish, Dr. Jess, 177–78, 345–46
Parrish, Norma, 345
Partain, Bruce, 58
Patterson, Jimmy
    portrait of Bell, 262–63
    portrait of Cahoon, 276–77
    portrait of Collyns, 282
    portrait of the Cowden family, 286–87
    portrait of Culver-Clark, 290–91
    portrait of Darnell, 294–95
    portrait of Ellis, 296–97
    portrait of Garrett, 302–3
    portrait of Haag, 310–11
    portrait of Halff, 312
    portrait of Hogan, 317
    portrait of Lackey, 323
    portrait of Laura Bush, 268–69
    portrait of the Mabee family, 326–27
    portrait of Magruder, 328–29
    portrait of Marcy, 330
    portrait of McCormick, 331–32
    portrait of the Morales family, 339–340
    portrait of Painter, 343–44
    portrait of Perry, 347–48
    portrait of Pickrell, 348–49
    portrait of Rankin, 354–55
    portrait of Spence, 363–64
    portrait of Ulmer, 369–370
    portrait of Williams, 375–76
Paul Davis Field, 42–43, 96
paving projects, 137
Paxton, Bob, 160
Peeler, Ken, 324

Index

Permian Basin, 47–49, 51–52, 92. *See also* oil and gas industry; West Texas
Permian Basin, The: Era of Advancement (Myres), 92, 104
Permian Basin Area Foundation, 187–88
Permian Basin Junior College System, 178
Permian Basin Petroleum Museum
    Abell's contributions, 256
    Butler's contributions, 75
    Chaparral Gallery, 277
    community funding for, 104
    establishment, 104
    Hall of Fame, 53, 104–5, 349, 357
    Meadows's contributions, 336
    Top Pioneer Award, 271
Permian building, 95–96
Permian Estates area, airplane crash over, 87–88
Permian Junior College System, 324
Permian Sea, 47–48
Perry, Governor Rick, 131, 377
Perry, Roni, 348
Perry, Wes
    charitable activities, faith, 348
    on high rate of traffic accidents, 231–32
    on "Hunt for Heroes Weekend," 385
    leadership shown by, 347
    on Midland's entrepreneurial/caring spirit, 232, 250–51, 384
    on Midland's growth potential, 230
    portrait of Bobby Burns, 266–67
    service as mayor and city manager, 230, 267, 347
    and the T-Bar water supply, 240–42
Perryman, Ray, 228
Petroleum Building. *See* Hogan Building
Petroleum Club of Midland, 60–61
Petroleum Museum. *See* Permian Basin Petroleum Museum
Petroleum Pioneers Association, 315
Petroleum Professional Development Center, 292
Pevehouse, Joe and Beverly, 80, 374
Phelps, Dennis, 226
Pickett, Judge Perry, 121, 153
Pickrell, Frank T., 48–49, 348–49
Pioneer History of Midland County, Texas, The (McKinley), 26, 296, 302, 323, 334
Pitts, John Paul, 27–29
Piwetz, Eileen
    portrait of Daniel, 292–93
    on rivalry between Odessa and Midland, 178
    skills and personality, 351
Pliska, John, 83–84
Pliska Plane, 83–84
Poe, Fred, 43, 241, 252
Porez, Lorenzo, 36–38
Poss, Delnor, 345–46
Prado, Judge Edward C., 145
Prendergast, Sam, 325

Prentice, Miles, 221
Presbyterian church/congregation, 31–32
Presley, Elvis, 116
Preston, Rabe, 312
Proctor, Foy
    admiration for, 353
    as charter member of hospital board, 102
    childhood and education, 352
    community-building activities, 353
    marriage, partnership with wife, 353
    Matador Ranch, 42
    as mentor, 360
    military service, 352
    ranching career, 352
Proctor, Hahl Carr Mitchell, 352–53
Proctor, L. C., 352
Proctor, Leonard, 36, 352
Proctor, Mike, 210
Proctor, Rieta, 352
public schools, Midland
    Baskin's support for, 260–61
    busing program, 144
    cluster system, 141–44
    first schoolhouse, 372
    and growth in the student population, 94
    integration process, 122, 126–27, 138–142
    quality of, Lackey's role, 323
    unitary status, efforts to obtain, 144–45
Purvis, Stuart, 236

Quien Sabe Ranch (Halff family), 19–20, 312

Ranchland Hills Country Club, 86
Rankin, Judy, 354–55
Rankin, Porter and Julia Estes, 334
Rankin, Walter "Yippy," 354
Rathbun, Charles, 22–23
Rawlins, Burt, 23
Ray, Theo, 24
Reagan, President Ronald
    Angelo's role in Texas campaigns of, 159, 165–66, 258
    phone call to the McClures, 198
Reagan County, oil discoveries in, 49, 92
Redfern, John, 308, 315
Redfern, John J. Jr.
    childhood and education, 356
    community-building activities, 357
    and the establishment of Little League in Midland, 97–98
    fears about kidnapping plot, 101
    honors and awards, 357
    interest in oil business/move to Midland, 356
    love for Midland and West Texas, 358
    low profile kept by, 101
    marriage, 356
Redfern, Rosalind Kapps, 356–58

Index

Redfern and Herd, 356–57
Redfern Oil Company, 357
Reese, Dr. Debbie
   care for Bush daughters by, 196
   and the McClure rescue, 192, 195–96, 200–201
   portrait of Wyvell, 379–380
Reiger, W. D. Dunn, 41–42
Reigle, E. E., 94
Republican National Committee, 166, 258
Republican Party
   Angelo's work to build in the Midland area, 160, 165
   candidates for State Representative, 159
   Craddick's commitment to, 288
   Culver-Cark's commitment to, 290
   dominance in Midland, 375
   growing strength in Midland, 163
   Midland County Republican Women, 171
   post Civil War, 158
   Texas Federation of Republican Women, 171–72
   Williams's commitment to, 377
RepublicBank
   Butler's employment with, 191
   failure, 188
   purchase of the First National Bank, 184–85
Reyes-Nelms-Mashburn Park, 131
Rhode, Dr. Carolyn, 196
Richards, Ann, 205–6, 376
Richards, Colonel Joseph, 1, 4–5
Ricker, Rupert P., 348
Rio Rita (Yucca Theatre grand opening event), 110
Rita, Saint (Santa Rita), 48
Ritz Theater, purchase by Novert Morales, 251
Roberts, James
   on CNN's coverage of McClure's rescue, 198
   on O'Donnell's depression following McClure's rescue, 200–201
   on rescue plan for McClure, 193
Roberts, Juandelle Lacy
   Midland County Republican Women, 171–72
   portrait of Ernest Angelo, 258–59
Robles, Roger, 245–46
Rockhounds team, 220, 221
rodeos, 20, 341–42, 352
Rogers, Doss, 270
Rountree, A. B., 24
Routh, Cope, 151
Rucker, Judge Dean, 74, 317–18
Rudder, Earl, 381
Rutherford, John, portrait of Susan Graham, 304
Ruth Scharbauer Elementary School, 359
Ryan, Dr. W. E., 101–2

SACROC oil development, 94
Safe Place, 6, 265
Saint, Clarence, 34
Salners, Jim, 112–13

San Angelo Standard/Standard-Times, 23, 325
sandstorms, dust storms, 39, 41
San Jacinto Junior High School, 18
San Miguel Arcángel, 132
Santa Rita (Schwettman), 51–52, 348–49
Santa Rita No. 1 (oil well), 47–49, 348
Saunders, R. A., damage to home of following airplane crash, 88
Scharbauer, Chris, 67
Scharbauer, Christian, 15
Scharbauer, Clarence
   auto accident, 59
   cattle ranching business, 15, 64
   character, 51
   as community-builder, 359
   and the creation of the Army Air Force Bombardier Training School, 65, 86, 369
   death, obituary, funeral, 65–66
   early life, 63
   education, 63–64
   family background, 15
   final illness and death, 65
   and the hospital wing at the Llano Hotel, 27
   Legacy Scholarship, 265
   marriage and children, 24, 64
   role at the First National Bank, 73
   Sloan Field renovations, 85–86
   tribute to Haag, 60
   See also Scharbauer Hotel
Scharbauer, Clarence Jr.
   on Alysheba, 70
   birth, 64
   childhood, 52
   on father's character, 51
   on founding and running of the First National Bank, 25, 65
   on Foy Proctor, 353
   generosity, graciousness, 67
   Grover's first meeting with, 67
   honors and awards, 67
   illness and death, 68
   on the impacts of mother-in-law's murder, 156
   inheritance, 360
   during Marion's trial, 147–49, 155
   marriage and children, 67
   military service, 66
   praise for the Morales family, 252
   purchase of the Matador Ranch, 42
   as ranchman and horse breeder, 67
   response to father's illness and death, 66
   role in founding of Midland College, 175–76
   seed money for the Scharbauer Tower, 215–16
   Young's call for help to, 148
Scharbauer, Clarence III
   on Alysheba, 70
   on the demolition of the Scharbauer Hotel, 62
   on father's love for Midland, 68

Index

on impacts of grandmother's murder, 157
inheritance and sense of responsibility, 70–71
on Kelly's and Butler's contributions to Midland, 80–81
Scharbauer, Dorothy Turner (Mrs. Clarence Jr.)
   love for Thoroughbred racing, 68–69
   Marion's assault on, 149
   marriage and children, 67, 147
   testimony during Marion's trial, 155
   Young's call for help to, 148
Scharbauer, Douglas, 67
Scharbauer, Ferdinand, 15
Scharbauer, Jennie McCarty, 15
Scharbauer, John, 12, 14–15
Scharbauer, John Christian ("J. C."), 64, 67–68
Scharbauer, Kate Tompkins, 15
Scharbauer, Pam, 67, 68–69
Scharbauer, Rosa, 15
Scharbauer, Ruth Cowden (Mrs. Clarence Sr.), 24, 64, 102, 332, 359
Scharbauer Cattle Company, 16, 41–42, 50, 64
Scharbauer family
   community-building activities, 286
   historical video about, 71
   Hyde's comments about, 244
   Legacy Scholarship program support, 106
   Scharbauer Foundation, 71, 248
   Williams's comments about, 375
Scharbauer Hotel
   building of, 28–29, 50
   closing and demolition, 61–62, 359
   contribution to Midland's development, 50
   deal-making in lobby of, 50–51
   importance, 29
   as Midland's meeting place, 324
   penthouse apartment, 52, 65, 359
   Petroleum Club at, 60
Scharbauer Sports Complex, 71, 219–222, 261, 266, 359
Schorr, Steve, 2
Scurry County, Canyon Reef oil discovery, 92–93
Seaboard Oil Company, 93
Sealy, Tom, 60, 175
Selected Stories, Quotations and Aphorisms (Thomas), 366
Selig, Bud, 212
September 11, 2001 terrorist attack, Laura Bush letter following, 268–69
Servatius, Jim, 368
Shaner, Bill, 160, 343–44
Shaner, Douthea, 160
Sharp, Courtney, 236, 347
sheep ranching
   by Garrett family, 302–3
   importance of railroad to, 14
   and the original settlement of Midland, 13–14
   Scharbauer Sr.'s childhood experience in, 63–64

Shelby, H. Joe, 184
Sidwell, Ernest, 88
Simmons, Betty, 363
Simpson, Berry, 236, 242
Sipes, Buddy, 93, 94–95
Skelly Oil, 313
skyscrapers, 213
"The Sky's the Limit" slogan, 304
Slack, Dick, 175–76
Slaughter, C. C., 41
Sloan, Samuel and Harvey, 338
Sloan, Stewart, 85
Sloan Field, 85, 338, 369
Smith, Dallas, 343, 344
Smith, David L.
   on Abell, 105
   and the Abell-Hanger Foundation, 106, 361
   on Butler, 76–78
   on Kelly, 73
   on the First National Bank collapse, 186–87
   on the Legacy Scholarship program, 106–7
   portrait of the Abells, 256–57
   portrait of the Greathouses, 306–7
Smith, Governor Preston, 156, 179
Smith, Monroe, 77
Snelson, Pete, 162–63, 176–77
Soap Box Derbies (Jaycees), 383–84
Sohio Petroleum, 259
South Plains Bankers Association, 75
Sparks, Don, 259
Spence, Charles ("Charlie"), 363–64, 367–68
Spindletop, oil development at, 349
Spoken from the Heart (L. Bush), 268
sports complex. *See* Scharbauer Sports Complex
Sports Illustrated, on the Chaparral Center, 324
Spraberry, Abner, 94
Spraberry Trend
   costs of drilling a well in 1943, 326
   development and production levels, 50, 93–94, 313
   discovery, 91, 290
Spriggs, Katie
   on Butler's commitment to the First National Bank, 76
   on Butler's compassion, 78–79
   on impact of First National Bank closing, 190–91
   portrait of Butler, 274–75
Spring Valley Baptist Church, Dallas, 284
St. Ann's Church, 32–33
St. Ann's School, 86
Stars Were Big and Bright, The: The United States Armed Forces and Texas During World War II (Alexander), 84
State Republican Executive Committee, 171
Stegall, Red, 71
Stevenson, Adlai, 159
Stocks, Banky, 341
Stotz, Carl, 98

439

INDEX

Strange, Judge Rick, 145
Streator, Virginia, 172
Strickling, Ben and Roxanne, 2
Strickling, Kelly, 2
Stubbeman, Frank, 60, 102
Summer Mummers fundraising events, 113–14, 279
Summit Petroleum, 224–25
Superconducting Super Collider (SSC) project, 248
Swallow, Jack, 45, 97, 260–61
Swann v. Charlotte-Mecklenburg Board of Education, 140
Swayze, Patrick, 156
Sweatt, Hemon, 125
Sweeney, Dr. James B., 33–34
Szczesny, Don, 230

T-Bar pipeline, 240–42
T-Bar Ranch, 240
Teen Kings (Orbison band), 116
Texas Alcoholic Beverage Commission, 131
Texas American Bank failure, 188
Texas and Pacific Railroad
 Hurt's role as physician to, 365
 importance to Midland's development, 23, 303, 330
 importance to the ranching industry, 14
 and the Marcy Trail, 12
 Midway Station, 13
Texas Christian University (TCU), 173–74
Texas Constitution Revision Commission, 291
Texas Cowboys, 298
Texas Family Law Code revisions, 290
Texas Federation of Republican Women (TFRW), 171–72
Texas Good Roads Association, 75
Texas Highway Patrol, 44
Texas House of Representatives, 276
Texas Monthly
 cover featuring Williams, 206
 on the Midland Country Republican Women organization, 171
 on Tom Craddick, 170
Texas National Republican Committee, 159
Texas Parks and Wildlife Commission, 258
Texas Public Safety Commission, 258–59
Texas Railroad Commission
 limits to commingling production zones, 226
 slowdown of oil production in 1963, 97
 Williams's service on, 134, 377
Texas Rangers Baseball Club, 208
Texas Restaurant Association, 131
Texas Society of Professional Engineers, 259
Texas Stallion Stakes, 68
Texas State Guard, 44
Texas State Historical Association, 312
Texas State Historical Commission, 47, 173–74, 333
Texas Tech Health Sciences Center, 175–76

Texas Tech University, 289, 290
Tex-Harvey Field, Midland County, 92
Texon, Texas, 49
Texon Oil & Land Company, 49, 348
Thomas, Carroll, 88–89, 195, 200
Thomas, Dr. John B.
 as charter member of hospital board, 102
 childhood and education, 365
 community-building activities, 26–27, 366
 as country doctor, 365–66
 daughter, introduction to Meadows, 335
 death and burial, 366
 friendship with Butler, 28
 oil business, 28
 personality, 27, 366
 residence in Midland, 366
 support for the Midland Memorial Hospital, 27, 101–3
 See also Thomas Building, the
Thomas, Dr. Steve, 180–81, 264–65
Thomas, John Jr., 365
Thomas, Lillian, 365
Thomas, Lucile, 365
Thomas, Read (daughter), 365
Thomas, Read Hurt, 365–66
Thomas Building, the
 building of, 26–27, 50, 366
 hospital floor, 27, 101–2
Thomason, Congressman R. E., 85
Tighe, Charles, 136, 141, 146
Todd, Ed
 character, love for people and animals, 367–68
 concern with health, justice, 367
 Freckles Rosetta, 368
 portrait of McKinley, 333–34
 portrait of Mims, 337–38
 work for the *Reporter-Telegram*, 367
Tom Brown, Inc. (TBI), 298
Tom Green County, 22–23
Tomy Lee (racehorse), 68
Tower, Senator John
 appearance with the Summer Mummers, 109, 114, 162
 election, in 1964, 276
 visit to Midland, 1961, 161
Townsite Company, 371
Tradewinds Corridor, congestion, 230–31
transportation infrastructure
 Haag's vision, 57–58, 310
 Loop 250, 218
 paving projects, 137
 Scharbauer's contributions to, 64
 and traffic accidents, 231, 347
 traffic congestion, 229–231
Trevino, Sid
 on discrimination against Hispanics, 128–29
 fears of kidnapping plots, 100–101

Index

as Midland's first Hispanic police detective, 204
on Williams, 204
Trevino, Vidal, 121
Trinity Episcopal Church, 75
Trobaugh, Alan "Moose," 80, 187
Trott, James I., 361
T. S. Hogan Building (Shell Building), 317, 333
Tubb, Dr. Terry, 195
Tuck, H. A., 178–79
Tucker, Darla, 198
Turner, Fred Jr., 102, 147, 156–57
Turner, Juliette, 147–49, 152–53
Turner, Kathleen ("Kathy"), 113
Turner, Ted, 197
Tyson, Paul, 335

Ulmer, Marvin Chesley
  arrival in Midland, 369
  as charter member of hospital board, 102
  community-building activities, 73
  death, 369–370
  as mayor of Midland, 369
  as president of the First National Bank, 73, 369
  renovations at Sloan Field, 85–86
Uncle Russ's Toy Shop (Peyton's Toys and Bikes), 167
United States v. Midland Independent School District, 139–140
United Way of Midland
  G. W. Bush's contributions, 209
  Henry's contributions, 314
  Parrish's contributions, 346
  private support for, 373–74
  Spence's contributions, 363
University Lands system, 348–49
University of Texas of the Permian Basin (UTPB)
  Bueno's attendance at, 265
  Craddick's contributions, 289
  siting in Odessa, controversy over, 174–79
Upper Colorado Municipal Water District, 238
U. S. Department of Commerce, 298
U. S. National Bank of San Diego, failure, 184

V&J Tower, 95–96
Valor Farms, Pilot Point, Texas, 68
Van Berg, Jack, 69
Verlarde, Randy, 220
veterans. *See* Hunt for Heroes Weekend
Vickers, Paul, 56, 59, 83
Vision 2000 and Beyond, Midland, 261

Wade, Reverend Hubert, 237
Wadley, Addison, 371–72
Wadley, T. B., 24
Wadley-Barron Park, 45–46, 328, 371
Wadley family, 14
Wageman, Tom, 373
Wagner, Cyril ("Cy"), 373–74

Wagner-Noel Performing Arts Center, 219–220, 307
Walgreen, 306
Walker, J. T., 86
Walker, Robert L. ("Bobby"), 86
Ward, Joe H. E., 241
water supplies
  during the 1930s, 56
  and the building of windmills, 24–25
  contingency plans, 242
  and current drought, 233–34, 236
  in early Midland, 14, 371
  Haag's efforts to secure, 58, 310
  Holt family well, 16
  impact of September 28, 2012 rainfall, 238
  from Lake Ivie, 238, 241
  maintaining, as constant challenge, 41, 239–240
  the Paul Davis Field, 42–43
  and population boom of the 1960s, 96
  T-Bar water supply, 240–42
Watts, W. D., 31
Way, Ralph, 178
Wayland, Carole, 2–4, 6–7
Wayland, David, 1–3, 6, 6–7
Wayland, Marine Second Lieutenant Patrick Trevor, 2–4, 6
Wayland, Meagan, 6
Webb, Walter Prescott, 233
Wemple, Fred, 102
Western Clinic-Hospital, 102
Western Company, 381
West Texas
  bank failures, 1983, 185–86
  blizzards, 40
  and the building of character, 245, 305
  the Comanche, 11–13
  core values, 6, 268, 285
  droughts, 39–40
  exodus from during the Depression, 55–56
  Hispanic community, 338
  musicians from, 115
  racial prejudice, 120
  wildfires, 236–37
  See also oil and gas industry; Permian Basin
West Texas (Carlson and Glasrud), 12–13
West Texas Chamber of Commerce, 369
West Texas Heritage Hall of Fame, 296–97
Whalen, Jim and Barney, 16
Wheeler Dealers (movie), 332
White, E. B., 379
White, Jim, 193
White, Mark, 189
Whittington, Harold, 121
Wicker, Jack, 103
Wilco Building, 95–96, 213
Wildcatters: Texas Independent Oilmen (Olien and Hinton), 50, 92–93, 97
wildfires, 2011, 236–37, 250

441

Index

Wilkinson, Jack, 95–96, 168, 213
Wilkinson-Foster building, 95
Williams, Bill, 131
Williams, Clayton ("Claytie") Jr.
   on Craddick, 376
   entrepreneurial activities, 204, 207, 376
   gubernatorial race, 1990, 205–7, 301
   as independent oil and gas operator, 206–7
   on Midland politics, 375
   purchase of the Gulf Building, 204–5
   on the Scharbauer and Cowden families, 375
   singing voice, 204
   as storyteller, 375
Williams, Donna, 378
Williams, Johnny, 144
Williams, Margaret, 126
Williams, Michael
   on African Americans in Midland, 134
   appointment as Commissioner of Education, 377
   bid for county attorney, 377
   education and accomplishments, 134–35, 377
   impact of segregation on, 134
   on impacts of the closing of Lee Street, 134
   public service, 378
   service on the Texas Railroad Commission, 377
   Winnovators program, 378
Williams, Modesta, 207
Williamson, Terry, 183
Williams Regional Technical Training Center, Fort Stockton, 292
Wills, Bob, 115
Winfrey, Oprah, 198
Wink Westerners (Orbison band), 116
Winnovators program, 378
Wisdom, Judge John Minor, 140–41
Wolcott, George, 61
Wolcott Home, 60, 61
Wolfberry oil field
   anticipated production volume, 224
   application of hydraulic fracking to, 226
   discovery/development of, 50, 92, 225
   location and geology, 224–25
   yields from, 226–28
   See also oil and gas industry; Spraberry Trend
Wolfcamp oil field (Henry Petroleum), 50, 92, 224, 313–14

Wolffork oil field, 92
Wood, Robert L. ("Bob"), 93, 103
Wright, Fred S., 102
Wyche family, 341
Wyvell, Dr. Dorothy
   and the Constitution Party, 160
   kindness and compassion, 379
   as pediatrician in Midland, 379
   poetry by, 379–380
   political views, 379

Yarborough, Barbara
   arrival in West Texas, 249
   on impacts of desegregation, 130
   on Midland's commitment to young people, 249–250
   on racial prejudice in Midland, 120, 129–130
Yearby, Rev. Vernon, 122
YMCA, 315, 336
Young, Juanita, 142, 148–49
Younger, Charlene, 381, 382
Younger, Dr. Charles W. ("Charlie")
   on friendship with George W. Bush, 210–11
   honors and awards, 382
   memories of Midland childhood, 98–100
   military service, 381
   portrait of Evans, 298–99
   portrait of George W. Bush, 272–73
   portrait of the Youngers, 381–82
   support for Texas A&M, 381
   visit to George W. in the White House, 211
Younger, John, 106, 381
Young Republican organization, 160–61
Yucca Theatre
   building and design, 53, 109–10
   closing, 110
   designation as Texas landmark, 333
   discriminatory seating, 128–29
   grand opening, 110
   Summer Mummers melodramas, 113–14
   uses for, 110

Zonne, Bob, 99

about the author

JIMMY PATTERSON came to Midland in 1988, planning to stay for just a couple of years, but he fell in love with the town. He and his wife, Karen, raised three children in Midland. During his twenty years as a journalist at the *Midland Reporter-Telegram*, Jimmy came to know hundreds of Midlanders from diverse backgrounds and became fascinated by the history of his adopted hometown.

Jimmy has frequently been honored by the Associated Press, the Hearst Corporation, and the Texas Association of Broadcasters for his writing. In 2007 the Knights of Columbus recognized him with the Father Michael J. McGivney Award for Distinguished Journalism for his series on the international relief effort to assist the poor in the village of Boquillas, Mexico. He received national awards from the Catholic Press Association both in 2009 as a family columnist and in 2013 for investigative reporting and news writing from the Middle East on the Syrian refugee crisis in Jordan.

Jimmy has written three novels with Midland attorney Tom S. Morgan and is currently writing a series of books with renowned Midland oilman Jim Henry.

To learn more, visit **historyofcharacter.com**